Robert He

The Many Faces of a Th

Robert Helpmann
The Many Faces of a Theatrical Dynamo

Edited by Richard Allen Cave
and
Anna Meadmore

DANCE BOOKS

First published in 2018
by Dance Books Ltd.,
Southwold House,
Isington Road,
Binsted,
Hampshire
GU34 4PH

ISBN: 978-1-85273-179-3

A CIP catalogue record for this book is available from the British Library

Printed and bound in Great Britain by Latimer Trend & Co Ltd., Plymouth

Cover: Robert Helpmann c. 1947-1956. Angus McBean Photograph ©
Houghton Library, Harvard University. Source: Victoria and Albert Museum,
London (Kathrine Sorley Walker Collection). Insets: see plates 17, 14, 5, 52, 9.

Dedication

Dedicated to the memory of David Drew (1938 – 2015) with affection and gratitude.

A member of The Royal Ballet for almost fifty years, he was a great actor-dancer, and a true champion of the work of Robert Helpmann and fellow artists from the founding generation of British ballet. He will be much missed.

Contents

Appendices

List of Illustrations

wartime home of the Sadler's Wells Ballet Company from January 1941. Photo: J. W. Debenham © Victoria and Albert Museum, London. Source: The Royal Ballet School Special Collections

13 Robert Helpmann and Margot Fonteyn in Frederick Ashton's *Dante Sonata* (Vic-Wells Ballet, January 1940). Photo: Gordon Anthony © Victoria and Albert Museum, London. Source: The Royal Ballet School Special Collections

14 Robert Helpmann impersonating the actress, Margaret Rutherford, in a revue entitled *'Swinging the Gate'* at the Ambasssadors Theatre, London, May 1940. Photo: Gordon Anthony © Victoria and Albert Museum, London

15 Robert Helpmann impersonating the actress, Margaret Rawlings, in the same revue. Photo: Gordon Anthony © Victoria and Albert Museum, London

16-17-18 Robert Helpmann as the inebriated Mr O'Reilly in Ninette de Valois' ballet *The Prospect Before Us* (1940). Photos: Gordon Anthony © Victoria and Albert Museum, London

19 Robert Helpmann as Mr O'Reilly, twirling 'en pointe'. Photo: Gordon Anthony © Victoria and Albert Museum, London. Source: The Royal Ballet School Special Collections

20 Robert Helpmann as Dr Coppélius in the popular wartime revival of *Coppélia* (Vic-Wells Ballet, 1940). Verso inscribed by Gordon Anthony: 'RH has both danced in *Coppélia* as Franz and played it as Dr. Coppélius [from 1941] – with equal success. What other actor dancer could claim such a unique position?' Photo: Gordon Anthony © Victoria and Albert Museum, London. Source: The Royal Ballet School Special Collections

21 Robert Helpmann as Comus, attempting to seduce The Lady (Margot Fonteyn) in his ballet *Comus* (1942). Designed by Oliver Messel. Scenario by Helpmann and Michael Benthall, based on Milton's masque. Photographed by Tunbridge-Sedgwick. Credit: Royal Opera House /ArenaPAL

22 Depiction of the set design by Leslie Hurry for Robert Helpmann's one-act ballet *Hamlet* (1942). This painting by Martin Sutherland was made for an exhibition celebrating Hurry's career (1987). © The Royal Ballet School (Monica Mason Collection)

23 Tableau seen at the beginning and the end of Robert Helpmann's ballet *Hamlet* (Sadler's Wells Ballet, 1942). Photographed by Tunbridge-Sedgwick. Credit: Royal Opera House/ArenaPAL

24 'Our sometime sister, now our Queen': David Paltenghi as Claudius and Celia Franca as Gertrude in Robert Helpmann's ballet *Hamlet* (Sadler's Wells Ballet, 1942). Photographed by Tunbridge-Sedgwick. Credit: Royal Opera House / ArenaPAL

25 'A Freudian Triangle': Robert Helpmann as Hamlet with David Paltenghi as Claudius and Celia Franca as Gertrude in Helpmann's ballet *Hamlet* (Sadler's Wells Ballet, 1942). Photographed by Tunbridge-Sedgwick. Credit: Royal Opera House/ArenaPAL

Williamson, *Contemporary Ballet* (London: Salisbury Square, 1946), plate 29. Photo: Baron

37 Robert Helpmann as Shakespeare's Hamlet, musing over Yorick's skull. Directed by Michael Benthall (Shakespeare Memorial Theatre, Stratford-upon-Avon, 1948). Angus McBean Photograph © Houghton Library, Harvard University. Source: Victoria and Albert Museum, London

38 Robert Helpmann in the title role of Shakespeare's *Hamlet*, during the "O what a rogue and peasant slave am I" soliloquy that culminates in his decision to kill Claudius. Directed by Tyrone Guthrie (Old Vic Company, New Theatre, 1944). Photo: Edward Mandinian © Victoria and Albert Museum, London

39 Robert Helpmann as Hamlet in the same soliloquy in a later production, directed by Michael Benthall (Shakespeare Memorial Theatre, Stratford-upon-Avon, 1948). Photo: Angus McBean. Credit: University of Bristol. Source: Victoria and Albert Museum, London

40 Robert Helpmann as Shylock in Shakespeare's *The Merchant of Venice*, directed by Michael Benthall (Shakespeare Memorial Theatre, Stratford-upon-Avon, 1948). Angus McBean Photograph © Houghton Library, Harvard University. Source: Victoria and Albert Museum, London

41 Robert Helpmann as Prince Florimund, in Act II of the Royal Opera House production of *The Sleeping Beauty* (Sadler's Wells Ballet, Feb.1946). Photo: Gordon Anthony © Victoria and Albert Museum, London

42 Robert Helpmann as the Fairy Carabosse, in the Prologue of the Royal Opera House production of *The Sleeping Beauty* (Sadler's Wells Ballet, Feb.1946). Photo: Gordon Anthony © Victoria and Albert Museum, London

43 Robert Helpmann making up for the role of the Fairy Carabosse in *The Sleeping Beauty* (Sadler's Wells Ballet, ROH, 1946). The drawing above his dressing table (see left-hand image) shows Carabosse's make-up, and may have been provided for reference by the production's designer, Oliver Messel. Photographer unknown. Source: Victoria and Albert Museum, London

44 Robert Helpmann as the elderly Adam Zero/Principal Dancer in his ballet *Adam Zero* (Sadler's Wells Ballet, ROH, April 1946). The multi-layered work referenced Shakespeare's 'Seven Ages of Man'. Photo: Baron. Source: The Philip Richardson Library, Royal Academy of Dance

45 Robert Helpmann as the young Adam in his ballet *Adam Zero*, in a 'classical' *pas de deux* with June Brae as the Choreographer-Ballerina/First Love-Wife-Mistress/Death (Sadler's Wells Ballet, ROH, April 1946). Photo: Baron. Source: The Royal Ballet School Special Collections

46 and 47 Portrait of Robert Helpmann as Wycroft in the film *Caravan*, and in a scene from the same film with the actor Brooks Turner (dir. Arthur Crabtree, UK, April 1946). Photos: Rank Films © ITV/REX/Shutterstock

48 Robert Helpmann in his created role of Adelino Canberra in *Les Sirènes*, a humorous ballet by Frederick Ashton (Sadler's Wells Ballet, ROH, Nov.1946).

Helpmann's pose echoes the neo-classicism of Ashton's *Symphonic Variations*, which had premièred earlier that year. Photo: Gordon Anthony © Victoria and Albert Museum, London

49 Robert Helpmann as Flamineo with Margaret Rawlings as Vittoria Corombona, in John Webster's play, *The White Devil*. Costumes designed by Audrey Cruddas; directed by Michael Benthall (Duchess Theatre, 1947). Angus McBean Photograph © Houghton Library, Harvard University. Source: Victoria and Albert Museum, London

50 and 51 Robert Helpmann with Margot Fonteyn in her dressing room, and (below) in rehearsal with Fonteyn and Moira Shearer (Edinburgh, September 1948). Photographers unknown. Credit: *Evening Dispatch*. Source: The Royal Ballet School Special Collections

52 and 53 Film stills of Robert Helpmann as the malign Coppélius, seen in close-up, and in action with Moira Shearer as the hapless doll, Olympia. From *The Tales of Hoffmann* (dir. Powell and Pressburger, UK, 1951). Photographers unknown. Credit: Ronald Grant/ArenaPAL

Between pages 194-195

54 Michael Benthall, Katharine Hepburn and Robert Helpmann stride along a beach – all wearing trousers. Publicity shot for the Old Vic Company's Australian Tour, May-November 1955. Photo: Australian Consolidated Press. Source: Victoria and Albert Museum, London

55 Katharine Hepburn as Epifania and Robert Helpmann as the Egyptian Doctor in George Bernard Shaw's *The Millionairess,* directed by Michael Benthall (New Theatre, London). *Theatre World*, August 1952, p. 6. Angus McBean Photographs © Houghton Library, Harvard University. Source: The Royal Ballet School Special Collections

56 and 57 Robert Helpmann as Petruchio and Katharine Hepburn as Kate, rehearsing and performing scenes of 'comic violence' in Shakespeare's *The Taming of the Shrew* (Old Vic Company, Tivoli Theatre, Sydney; Australian Tour, May-November 1955). Photo: Australian Consolidated Press. Credit: University of Bristol/ArenaPAL

58 Robert Helpmann as Petruchio in Shakespeare's *The Taming of the Shrew* (Old Vic Company, Australian Tour, May-November 1955). Photo: G.R. Flack, Australian Consolidated Press. Source: Victoria and Albert Museum, London

59 Robert Helpmann exuding an 'exaggerated masculinity' as Petruchio, in the same production. Photo: Australian Consolidated Press. Credit: University of Bristol/ArenaPAL

60 Robert Helpmann and Katharine Hepburn during a break in rehearsals for the Old Vic Company's Australian Tour, 1955. Photo: Australian Consolidated

Press. Credit: University of Bristol/ArenaPAL

61 Robert Helpmann making up for the role of Shylock in Shakespeare's *The Merchant of Venice* (Old Vic Company, Australian Tour, May-November 1955). Photo: Australian Consolidated Press. Source: Victoria and Albert Museum, London

62 Robert Helpmann as Shylock in Shakespeare's *The Merchant of Venice* (Old Vic Company, Australian Tour, May-November 1955). The image demonstrates how Helpmann brought to his acting the 'sustained carriage' of a trained dancer. Photographed by Doug Kerrigan and Noel Rubie. Credit: University of Bristol/ArenaPAL

63 Robert Helpmann as Angelo in Shakespeare's *Measure For Measure* (Old Vic Company, Australian Tour, May-November 1955). Photographed by Allan Studios. Credit: University of Bristol/ArenaPAL

64 Robert Helpmann in the title role of Shakespeare's *Richard III*, directed by Douglas Searle, with designs by Leslie Hurry (Old Vic Theatre, 1957). As Richard, Duke of Gloucester, Helpmann spoke the opening soliloquy before the backdrop of a spider's web. Angus McBean Photograph © Houghton Library, Harvard University. Source: Victoria and Albert Museum, London

65 Robert Helpmann as Doctor Pinch, a schoolmaster and 'conjuror', in Shakespeare's *The Comedy of Errors* (Old Vic Theatre, 1957). With Pinch's great book of spells open on the floor, Helpmann's interpretation appears to reference the ballet-mime of Dr Coppélius. Angus McBean Photograph © Houghton Library, Harvard University. Source: Victoria and Albert Museum, London

66 Robert Helpmann, 'nude with violin', at the time of his appearance in Noël Coward's comedy of that title (Globe Theatre, London, 1957, and on tour in Australia and New Zealand, 1958). Angus McBean Photograph © Houghton Library, Harvard University. Source: Victoria and Albert Museum, London

67 Robert Helpmann at an informal event in Melbourne, undated. Photo: Australian Consolidated Press. Source: The Royal Ballet School Special Collections

68 Robert Helpmann and Michael Benthall in a domestic setting, probably their home in Eaton Square c.1960. Photographer unknown. Source: Victoria and Albert Museum, London (Kathrine Sorley Walker Collection).

69 Robert Helpmann's expanded revival of his ballet *Elektra* (Australian Ballet, 1966), designed by the Australian artist Arthur Boyd. The image captures one of the acrobatic 'throws' where the Erinyes (the Furies) attack Elektra (Kathleen Geldard). Photo: Australian News and Information Bureau. Source: The National Archives of Australia

70 Joseph Janusaitis as a Fury in Helpmann's *Elektra* (Australian Ballet, 1966). The cast all wore individually designed make-up referencing the face and body-painting traditions of the Australian indigenous peoples. Photo: Walter Stringer. Source: The National Library of Australia

71 Janet Karin as Klytemnestra [Helpmann's preferred spelling of the name], and Warren de Maria as Aegisthus in *Elektra* (Australian Ballet, Melbourne 1966). Photo: Walter Stringer. Source: The National Library of Australia

72 Action shot of the scene in which Elektra (here, Kathleen Gorham, prone on the floor) persuades Orestes (Brian Lawrence, leaping) to murder their mother Klytemnestra (Janet Karin), seen here with a cloak (Australian Ballet, 1966). Photo: Australian News and Information Bureau. Source: The National Archives of Australia

73 Robert Helpmann and Frederick Ashton reprising their created roles of the Stepsisters in the 1965 revival of Frederick Ashton's *Cinderella* (1948). This major revival by The Royal Ballet featured new costumes and scenery by David Walker and Henry Bardon. Photo: Donald Southern © Royal Opera House. By kind permission Royal Opera House Collections

74 and 75 Robert Helpmann as the Child Catcher in *Chitty Chitty Bang Bang* (dir. Ken Hughes, UK, 1968). These film stills reveal Helpmann's distinctive use of his body on camera; while creating the illusion of a 'speeding frenzy' (above), or 'leading the movement' with his eyes (below). Credits: Christophel/ArenaPAL (above) and Ronald Grant/ArenaPAL (below)

76 A portrait of Robert Helpmann (1909–1986) in later life (signed print, undated). Photo: Anthony Crickmay © Victoria and Albert Museum, London

Contents of the DVD

Track 1. Filmed recollections of Robert Helpmann as a colleague, performer and choreographer with Dame Beryl Grey and Maina Gielgud AO in interview.

Track 2. Excerpts from Lynne Wake's film made for the ROH Collections, *Dancing in the Dark – The Royal Ballet during the Second World War.*

Track 3. *Miracle in the Gorbals* reconstruction workshops (2011). A documentary film made by David Drew, Michael Byrne and Nigel Hodgson; edited by Michael Byrne. With contributions from Pauline Clayden, Gillian Lynne, Julia Farron, Henry Danton, Jean Bedells and Henry Roche.

Track 4. An interview with Gillian Lynne, recorded by Víctor Durà-Vilà.

Track 5. *Adam Zero*: a rehearsal demonstration with students of The Royal Ballet School in new choreography by Andrew McNicol (2013), filmed by Michael Byrne and Nigel Hodgson; edited by Michael Byrne.

Track 6. Recollections of Robert Helpmann and the Australian Ballet: Maina Gielgud interviewed by Rupert Christiansen.

Foreword

It was in March 1958 when Robert Helpmann returned to ballet, after almost ten years spent as an actor in Britain and abroad. To celebrate his return to The Royal Ballet there followed something of a 'Helpmann Season' at the Royal Opera House, Covent Garden. He appeared as The Rake in Ninette de Valois' *The Rake's Progress*, as Dr Coppélius in *Coppélia*, and in two of his own creations, *Miracle in the Gorbals* and *Hamlet*. To my delight, I read on the Company noticeboard that I was cast as Ophelia to Helpmann's Hamlet, and further, I realised that he himself was going to coach me in the role.

As a dancer I had always enjoyed roles with a dramatic element and often regretted that The Royal Ballet School, at the time, had never included drama classes in their curriculum. Here was a wonderful chance to work with a superb actor to coach me in this complex role. Concentrating on the 'mad scene', Helpmann explained how Ophelia's thoughts and confusions, as expressed in Shakespeare's words, related to the steps, gestures and movements he'd choreographed. I remember one particular moment when he explained why Ophelia kneels down to stroke and feel the ground with her hands, 'as if her father is lying "i' the cold ground" beneath her.' Once I'd learnt the role, Helpmann urged me (and made me promise) that from then on, starting with an open rehearsal in front of my fellow dancers, I must shed any of my English reticence and 'get inside that role and live it every time'. Good advice! Thank you, Bobby!

Anya Linden, Lady Sainsbury

Acknowledgements

This book and the symposium on which it is loosely based would not have happened but for the terrific enthusiasm of the late David Drew, who ardently wished to see Helpmann's ballets re-staged and his theatrical genius re-discovered by a younger generation. Without David's input – his calling on many friends from The Royal Ballet School and Companies, past and present; his generosity with his time, his advice and expertise – neither symposium nor book would have been possible. Everyone involved in this project recognises the profound debt they owe him, and it is a source of great delight that David himself appears as a contributor in parts of the accompanying DVD.

All students of Helpmann's artistry inevitably start their work with a close study of his three biographies, each with its distinct perspective on the multifaceted nature of his personality and career. That is true for all contributors to this volume, who wish to record their debt to the three authors: Elizabeth Salter (1978); Anna Bemrose (2008); and Kathrine Sorley Walker (2009). This book, like the symposium that preceded it, appears under the aegis of The Royal Ballet School and we are especially grateful for the support and advice of Jay Jolley, Mark Annear, and the late Gailene Stock; also to Christopher Powney, Artistic Director of The Royal Ballet School, and Kevin O'Hare, Director of The Royal Ballet, who have allowed us to include filmed material featuring dancers of the School and Company. Further thanks go to the Royal Opera House for kindly allowing Jennifer Jackson access to archival recordings of revivals of Helpmann's *Hamlet*; also for permission to include on the DVD an excerpt from Lynne Wake's film documentary, *Dancing in the Dark* (2007), made for The Royal Ballet in association with the Imperial War Museum. Great thanks, too, must go to Lynne Wake herself, who freely gave us access to her extraordinary work. We would also wish to thank the many individuals who contributed with such energy and commitment to the workshops on *Miracle in the Gorbals* and on *Adam Zero* (full acknowledgements are made in this book's introductions to the related DVD material).

Enterprises of this kind rely heavily on the input of numerous individuals; and for such help we wish to record our thanks especially to Elizabeth Marshall for sourcing articles over several days in the Arnold Haskell Dance Library at White Lodge, which provided the editors with vital background information; Eleanor Fitzpatrick for giving us access to photographs held by the Philip Richardson Library at the Royal Academy of Dance, and for information on Helpmann's RAD exam; Julia Creed for her kind efficiency at the Royal Opera

House Collections; Biddy Hayward at ArenaPAL; Dale Stinchcomb at the Houghton Library, Harvard University; Rupert Christiansen, who generously gave of his time to conduct meticulously researched interviews and to chair panels of experts; Nicola Katrak for transcribing the deliberations of one such panel; Marius Arnold-Clark, Emily Dixon, Bennett Gartside, Dr Víctor Durà-Vilà, Michael Byrne, and Nigel Hodgson who were all in various ways responsible for filming and editing of materials for the DVD that is included with the book; Patrick Marshall, who shared his memories of Helpmann's performances throughout the five-year Folio Seasons at the Old Vic in the 1950s; Colin Jones, who recalled in remarkable detail his experiences of the initial performances of *Elektra* at Covent Garden in 1963 and Amanda Selby for recommending that we contact him – a vital link.

The original symposium was shaped by a committee of advisers and we have been considerably influenced by their work in the organisation of this volume: Jay Jolley, Jane Pritchard, Dr Libby Worth, Olwen Terriss, Dr Víctor Durà-Vilà, and Francesca Franchi, to all of whom we extend heartfelt thanks. To the many contributors to this volume either in print or recorded on the DVD, we owe more than an expression of gratitude for their patience while waiting for their work finally to appear in print and for their (often wittily expressed) forbearance throughout the editorial process. If *Robert Helpmann: the Many Faces of a Theatrical Dynamo* has breadth of scope, it is entirely a reflection of their scholarship and ardour for the study of dance and the vital part it plays in the theatre, and on screen.

Numerous institutions have provided invaluable assistance with the sourcing of images and other materials: the British Library; the London Library; the Westminster Reference Library; the Theatre and Performance Collections at the Victoria and Albert Museum, London; the University of Bristol Theatre Collection; the Library of the Shakespeare Centre, Stratford upon Avon; the Royal Opera House Collections; The Royal Ballet School Special Collections; the National Gallery of Australia; the National Archives of Australia; and the National Library of Australia. The courtesy, insight, attention to detail and genuine support of the staff in these organisations greatly facilitated the researches of our contributors and ourselves.

We have endeavoured in a variety of ways to make this volume as much a visual archival resource as a textual exploration of Helpmann's career, but such ambitions are expensive to implement, and we are indebted to a number of organisations and individuals for their extremely generous sponsorship and contributions: the Consortium for Drama and Media in Higher Education for extensive help with the costs of reproducing and copyrighting photographs and music (their last funding project before closing their books); the Vic-Wells Association, which funded the production of the DVD, as well as several members of the Vic-Wells Association who responded magnificently to our appeal with personal donations – often made in gratitude for their treasured theatrical memories of seeing Helpmann perform.

Liz Morrell, our editor, and David Leonard, our publisher, were immensely encouraging through the enthusiasm they showed for the venture from the start, while their tactful exactitude in preparing the book for printing has been deeply appreciated by us at every stage of the process. Our sincere thanks to them both.

A.M. and R.A.C.

Introduction

Anna Meadmore and Richard Cave

"I am intensely interested in all aspects of the theatre."[1]

"It would be difficult to say who was the luckier one that memorable day when Helpmann walked into Sadler's Wells and was given his first job in the *corps de ballet* – Miss de Valois in backing her hunch that 'something might be done with that face',[2] or Helpmann in receiving the opportunity which was to lead him to a permanent place among the Great Ones of Ballet." This assessment of Robert Helpmann's significance in the annals of ballet history might now seem rather lofty, but the critic P.W. Manchester was writing soon after the end of World War II; and it is telling that she went on to insist: "English audiences owe them both [de Valois and Helpmann] a tremendous debt of gratitude for the chances so magnificently given and taken."[3]

This volume sets out to examine this and other such claims, expanding upon the existing body of knowledge about Helpmann's unique career, which began in his native Australia in 1917,[4] flourished in Britain and abroad from 1933, and resumed in his native Australia in 1955, where he was largely based from 1965. Robert Helpmann (b. 9 April 1909 – d. 28 September 1986) has been described as a 'chameleon' of the theatre;[5] both during and after his lifetime his multi-faceted career was alternately the subject of enthusiasm, hyperbole, neglect, and even a degree of derision. This book takes the form of a compilation of essays, interviews, and video recordings of performance reconstructions; it represents a body of recent research prompted by a symposium held by The Royal Ballet School in October 2013, entitled *The Many Faces of Robert Helpmann*.

Context is all in enabling us, at a distance of some eight decades, to assess the full impact of Robert Helpmann's career on the development of a national ballet in Britain. Practically fresh off the boat from his native Australia,[6] he had joined the Vic-Wells Ballet in 1933, shortly before his twenty-fourth birthday. At the time, male dancers in England were so scarce that even the "less than mediocre" could be certain of regular employment.[7] But as P. W. Manchester continues: "With the arrival of Robert Helpmann the Vic-Wells male *corps de ballet* showed almost its first signs of life. He was spotted immediately by an audience not used to so much liveliness and gay intelligence [...]. His air of vast enjoyment and enthusiasm over everything he undertook could hardly have been overlooked."[8]

Helpmann made as much of an impact on his colleagues. In his autobiography, aptly titled *In Good Company, Sixty Years With The Royal Ballet*, Leslie Edwards recalled the way in which Helpmann was perceived by his fellow dancers:

> No one escaped those great, searchlight eyes, no one's cherished foible was lost on him. He became the leader of the pack while also cultivating the lifestyle of a star performer. Not for him the journeys back and forth to Rosebery Avenue on the number nineteen bus, but a taxi to and from the theatre; and one felt that there was already a table earmarked for him at the Ivy restaurant, the West End bastion of the theatrical hoi ristoi. All that seemed natural to him; and indeed, as he was the son of a wealthy Australian, it was. [...] In keeping with this image Helpmann would never buy one of anything, but always a quantity: half a dozen pairs of shoes, a whole rack of ties. And oh, how he could make us laugh.[9]

Much has been said about the limitations of Helpmann's slight physique and uneven Classical ballet technique – probably the result of his rather intermittent training before he joined the Vic-Wells Company. This anecdote is typical: "balletomanes [...] used to joke: 'Bobby's such an artist . . . (pause) . . . With his technique he had to be'."[10] Manchester would concur with this view: "His most ardent admirer could hardly say that he was a great or even a very good dancer, but his other qualities so outweigh his technical deficiencies that [...] this fact is hardly noticed." She continued with the intriguing observation that "these qualities of Helpmann have, at the Wells, inclined to alter the primary conception of what makes a male dancer".[11] In the light of this, we should consider Helpmann's own approach to ballet technique:

> Learning to dance is like learning the violin. You must first master the technique. Only when the technique has ceased to be creaky can you think beyond it. On the whole I feel acting is more mentally creative than dancing, less rigid if more emotionally exacting.[12]

Clearly, this suggests that Helpmann felt he *did* have sufficient mastery to allow him to 'think beyond' technique, and to engage creatively with his roles, a view with which Audrey Williamson would agree, as her study of Helpmann as a performer (included in this volume as Chapter 3) demonstrates. Would Ashton, one wonders, have choreographed a piece as technically demanding as the *pas de trois* in *Les Rendezvous* (1933), which Helpmann danced with de Valois and Stanley Judson, had Helpmann's technique so early in his career been severely wanting? Intricate steps and continual changes of direction must be realised with great speed of execution, all precisely synchronised to the rhythms of Auber's deft score: the very sharpness of attack required is no easy feat to realise, and a poor rendition would immediately expose the perpetrator of a slack performance.

Almost from the moment he joined the Vic-Wells ballet, Helpmann had also wanted to appear as an actor in plays at the Old Vic Theatre. In early 1938 he told readers of the *Old Vic and Sadler's Wells Magazine*, he was sure that "ballet training will help me with my acting. For I realise that my past experiences as an actor have helped me with regard to certain aspects of the ballet".[13] Sorley Walker has related how Helpmann set out to achieve this key ambition, convincing the Old Vic's singular manager, Lilian Baylis, that instead of a pay rise she should give him the chance to audition for Tyrone Guthrie, and try for the part of Oberon in his new production of Shakespeare's *A Midsummer Night's Dream*. A consummate theatre professional, Helpmann was "well aware that there might be some resentment over the use of a ballet dancer as an actor", so he wisely "sought Margaret Rawlings's advice about a coach and benefited from working with Beatrice Wilson, who eradicated the last traces of an Australian accent". More remarkably, in his audition Helpmann deliberately avoided "all balletic movements or gestures".[14] Helpmann's plan to achieve his aim had been meticulously devised and carried out. The whole episode serves to illustrate the almost relentless approach to work which was a key feature of his life. His first appearance with the drama company of the Old Vic was an unqualified triumph, and Guthrie recorded that *A Midsummer Night's Dream* was the most successful production of the year 1937/38:

> ...with the full Mendelssohn score and beautiful décor in early Victorian style by Oliver Messel. Ralph Richardson, as Bottom, led a team of mechanicals [...] Helpmann was Oberon, Vivien Leigh Titania; we had a splendid quartet of lovers; Ninette de Valois lent fairies from the Ballet and directed the dances. We even had fairies flying on wires. The production played to capacity business.[15]

There is no denying that Helpmann captured the public imagination as a versatile man of the theatre: although he was very much a company player, he became a hugely popular star in his own right – a veritable one-man synthesis of the arts, producing "energy as a dynamo produces electricity".[16] Because of his Australian citizenship, he was exempt from national service; during the course of the 1939-45 World War and in the years immediately following, his presence in the denuded cultural landscape became intensified, and even more vivid than before. As the leading man of the Sadler's Wells Ballet (performing contrasting classical and character roles); a bold and theatrical choreographer (for ballet, theatre and film); a remarkable actor (of stage and screen); and even as an impersonator in revue, Helpmann became an omnipresent figure in various media.

Most notably, perhaps, Helpmann appeared in several major wartime productions: he was the wily Bishop of Ely in Olivier's film of *Henry V* (1944); he inhabited the mantle of Hamlet first as a dancer in his own choreography (1942), and then as an actor (1944). Such milestones were crowned by a remarkable feat, in which Helpmann appeared in the same performance as both the wicked fairy Carabosse and an elegant Prince Florimund to Margot Fonteyn's Aurora, in a landmark revival of *The Sleeping Beauty*.[17] This magnificent Tchaikovsky/Petipa ballet of 1890 was mounted by the Sadler's Wells Ballet in February 1946, and marked the re-opening of the Royal Opera House after the war. Three years later, the same production brought the Company great acclaim in America, and made international stars of Fonteyn and Helpmann.

Of course, there were dissenting voices: it did not help that among Helpmann's many fans, some indulged in what Sorley Walker identified as "unwise adulation", which drove others into "an equally unbalanced state of animosity toward him and his undoubted versatility".[18] An article written for *Ballet Carnaval* in 1947 was headed, 'Where do we go from here?'

> If versatility is a virtue, in the theatrical sense, then Robert Helpmann's halo should be visible even on a dull day. Recently, however, I have been wondering whether it is not a limitation [...]. Maybe the business of combining so many careers at once leads to neglect of consistent work. Maybe a little [...] less variety appearances and absolutely no impersonations, would bring us a Helpmann whom we could place among the immortals [...] at least we could place him [...] too much versatility can be a dangerous thing.[19]

It is possible that Helpmann may have overreached himself in certain instances: weaving in and out of his crowded work schedule was a complex social existence, also lived at full throttle, which partly shaped the unpredictable trajectory of Helpmann's career. His social networks were as varied, demanding and unconventional as those of his professional life, and often overlapped with them. While many of Helpmann's friendships were marked by fruitful collaborations, which were central to his work (as is clear from many of the essays included in this volume), during the mid-1930s he became a leading light of a social milieu "known as 'High Bohemia', with its cosmopolitan, artistic aesthetic and irreverent exuberance".[20] This world of the rich, titled and *louche* was dismissed by some – de Valois among them – as altogether too frivolous, and generally a corrupting influence. Julie Kavanagh suggests that "Helpmann was as committed a performer socially as he was on stage", and she has written extensively about the complex dynamics of the Frederick Ashton, Constant Lambert and William Chappell 'set' in her seminal biography of Ashton.[21] Sorley Walker has summed up the general picture:

> Ashton, by temperament and upbringing, passionately desired to be accepted as part of [these socialites' gatherings] [...] Helpmann, with his inborn Australian independence [...] was delighted to test them out as an audience on which to sharpen his perceptions and flex his inventive muscle. [...] [H]e was frequently tempted to challenge them with flamboyant and provocative behaviour. [...] The saving grace, however, for all the young dancers who were lured into the parties...of the powerful rich was that they were sincerely dedicated to their demanding careers. [...] [T]hey were primarily bound to the disciplines of dance theatre, to classes and teachers, rehearsal and performances, and the steady enlarging of their artistic horizons.[22]

No other dancer's horizons extended further than Helpmann's; as he reached one, he invariably spied another stretching away before him. By the Fifties, those busy work-schedules traversing Britain between Stratford or Edinburgh and London were replaced with international jet-setting as Helpmann began moving between England, America and Australia.[23] However acid-tongued at times his social persona might be, as a director he was much sought after for his sensitivity not only to the given medium of theatre he was working in but to the performers he was working with. He may have delighted in and to some degree exploited Nadia Nerina's utter fearlessness in *Elektra* (1963), but he was wholly sympathetic in releasing Gailene Stock from the central role in *Perisynthyon* (1974) during rehearsals, when the management of Australian Ballet refused her request for additional insurance, since his choreography for this embodiment of the moon required her to engage in circus-style acrobatics suspended from a rope high above the stage.[24] The great operatic soprano, Elizabeth Schwarzkopf, recalled Helpmann's remarkable understanding of, and feeling for the music when directing her in *Madam Butterfly* at the Royal Opera House in 1950 and his willingness to redesign his groupings of chorus and principals to allow everyone a good view of the conductor.[25] Whether directing Shakespeare's *The Tempest* at the Old Vic or Rimsky-Korsakov's *Le Coq d'or* for the Royal Opera House (1954), Cole Porter's *Aladdin* at the Coliseum (1959), Giraudoux's *Duel of Angels* with Vivien Leigh at the Helen Hayes Theatre, New York (1960), Lerner and Loewe's *Camelot* at Drury Lane Theatre (1964), revivals of *The Sleeping Beauty* for Australian Ballet and for American Ballet Theatre (1976), Handel's *Alcina* for Australian Opera (1981) or Lehár's *The Merry Widow* for San Diego Opera (1985), his casts, talking in interview of rehearsals, recalled the originality of his vision, his fastidious attention to detail, his humour, his endless patience and, as Vivien Leigh observed, his "great facility for helping actors".[26] That generosity extended beyond the ranks of dancers and actors: Helpmann gave opportunities to numerous fledgling designers (Leslie Hurry, Chiang Yee, Loudon Sainthill, Arthur Boyd, John Truscott); he pursued and sustained close creative collaborations with composers in the shaping of his choreographies (Constant Lambert, Arthur Bliss, Malcolm Arnold, Malcolm Williamson); and it stands repeatedly on record how sensitively supportive a partner he was to the ballerinas with whom he was paired. For his enduring mentor, Ninette de Valois, "[t]o work with Robert Helpmann was always an inspiration".[27]

To expect any one author to write in detail and at length about all the many fields in which Helpmann's genius was manifest would be asking for the impossible. Three excellent biographers, Sorley Walker, Bemrose and Salter, have provided the facts of Helpmann's astonishing life history, their different points of emphasis defining how each personally chose to interpret the material they expertly handled. It is indicative of the challenge that life history poses that three such eminent writers have evoked quite different persona under the name of Robert Helpmann. Clearly the enigmas, the complexities, the continual shape-changing, the games with role-play that masked a profound, whole-hearted and life-long commitment to all that we understand by the term, 'theatre', were bound to elude precise definition, however searching and exhaustive the scholarship that underpinned that endeavour. Hence this anthology of essays, which has grown out of a symposium, where one-time colleagues and performers, historians, scholars, and young creators came together to share their knowledge of and responses to the range of Helpmann's artistry. The wealth of specialisms required to cover Helpmann's achievements indicates in itself the magnitude of that range.

The essays that follow address aspects of Helpmann's choreography; his art as an actor onstage and in film; his dance invention and his acting and movement skills on the cinematic screen; his gifted deployment of make-up to finesse his characterisations in dance and drama; his collaborations with four of his designers, with his partner, Michael Benthall, and with the American actress, Katharine Hepburn; his return to Australia, his placing of himself in the Australian cultural landscape and his work with Australian Ballet. (Notes and cross-references indicate other themes worth following, which are not directly addressed by a specific essay.)

Two items not written by contemporary authors perhaps need some justification for their inclusion. It seemed appropriate to us as editors that that we find some place in this volume for Robert Helpmann's own words and ideas. Consequently we have gathered together some seven short items published at key moments during his career that are not easily accessed today. Helpmann never contemplated writing an autobiography, but these short pieces, written often on the spur of the moment, do communicate a lively sense of the man himself, his theatrical vision and his principles in performance, his ability as writer or speaker to adapt to differing readers and listeners, his sharp wit and precise, no-nonsense style, and, above all, the shrewd intelligence, underpinning all his work, which even adverse critics unfailingly honour. The subject of Helpmann as a performer is difficult to negotiate at this point in time. While thankfully there are many spectators who can still recall his performances in *Checkmate* and *Cinderella* in his later years, there are few individuals alive today who saw Helpmann as Albrecht in *Giselle*, as the Prince in *The Sleeping Beauty*, as the Poet in *Les Sylphides*, or as Siegfried in *Swan Lake*. We decided therefore to include an essay by an informed critic, Audrey Williamson, originally published in 1950, which addresses these roles in particular, his status in de Valois' Company as it moved from the Vic-Wells theatres to the Royal Opera House, his technique in the classics, and his artistry in partnering.[28]

The printed chapters are supplemented with materials recorded for a DVD, which investigate attempts to recreate two of his major choreographic works (*Miracle in the Gorbals* and *Adam Zero*) from extant documentation but starting from very different standpoints regarding how those traces of the originals might be developed. These attempts are then discussed and evaluated by a panel that includes dancers and a practising choreographer together with dance, music and theatre historians. Also to be found here on page and on DVD are recorded or transcribed interviews with former colleagues: Dame Beryl Grey, Dame Monica Mason, Maina Gielgud, David Drew, Jean Bedells, Pauline Clayden, Henry Danton, Julia Farron and Dame Gillian Lynne. There is finally a detailed Filmography, outlining the extent of Helpmann's engagement with cinema and television, and a bibliography that brings together all works cited in the various chapters.

Here then is a different kind of biography, where the attempt is to come at some sense of the artist and the man through critiques, verbal and visual, of the challenges Helpmann relentlessly set himself and, with few exceptions, invariably accomplished. It is now some thirty years since Helpmann died; he was at the height of his creative and interpretative powers many decades ago, and so for our many contributors this has often meant working with traces, memories, monochrome images, anecdotes, badly focused filmed recordings, and published critical opinions that were informed by different aesthetic, ideological and social values from those obtaining today. Despite these seeming drawbacks, Helpmann's creative exuberance shines through. The *Oxford English Dictionary* defines *traces* as "vestiges or marks remaining and indicating the former presence, existence or action of something" or (one may add) of someone. To summon that presence has been the objective of everyone engaged in the creation of this study, sensing to what degree we may follow the track made by the passage of Helpmann himself through time.[29] We have used the sources that are still available to us in the hope that, by bringing them together and offering a fresh interpretation of their significance, we may create a new resource that will place Robert Helpmann securely in the histories of ballet, cinema and theatre, both national and international. To that end, this publication offers both a critique and a homage.

Endnotes

1   Robert Helpmann, "The public has the final say; to become a cultural power Australia must train its own dancers and actors – and they'll have to be good", article for [the Australian journal] *Woman*, June 20, 1955, p. 155.

2   A widely quoted anecdote, which de Valois herself recorded in her first volume of autobiography. Sorley Walker wrote: "Telling it later, Helpmann suggested that it was not said in any flattering tone but meant that something would *have* to be done about it." See Kathrine Sorley Walker, *Robert Helpmann, A Rare Sense of the Theatre* (Alton: Dance Books, 2009), p. 13.

3   P. W. Manchester, *Vic-Wells: a Ballet Progress* (London: Victor Gollancz, 1947), pp. 93-94.

4   See *Robert Helpmann, A Rare Sense of the Theatre*, Appendix 3 – Chronology, pp. 184, which lists Helpmann's first stage role as a child extra in Allan Wilkie Shakespeare Company's production of Shakespeare's *A Midsummer Night's Dream* in Adelaide (1917).

5   Anon, "Robert Helpmann: A Portrait", *Dancing Times*, June 1953, p. 539. See also Tatlock Miller, "Helpmann, Chameleon of the Theatre", *Dance and Dancers*, Vol. 1, No. 5, May 1950, p.16.

6   Robert Helpmann, *A Rare Sense of the Theatre*, p. 12. Sorley Walker notes: "After arriving in Europe in January 1933, he stayed for ten days in Paris, going to classes with the famous expatriate Russian ballet teachers and, unforgettably, seeing Josephine Baker on stage."

7   *Vic-Wells: a Ballet Progress*, p. 73.

8   Ibid, p. 90.

9   Leslie Edwards, *In Good Company, Sixty Years with The Royal Ballet* (Alton: Dance Books, 2003), p. 24. Edwards joined the Vic-Wells Ballet in January 1933, two months earlier than Helpmann; he officially retired from the Company in 1993.

10   Colin Jones, email to Richard Cave, October 2013.

11   *Vic-Wells: a Ballet Progress*, pp. 74-75

12   "The public has the final say...", p. 155.

13   Robert Helpmann, "Shakespeare and the Ballet", *Old Vic and Sadler's Wells Magazine*, January 1938, pp. 4-5. For the full text, see Chapter 1 of this volume, p. 2.

14   *Robert Helpmann, A Rare Sense of the Theatre*, pp. 32-33.

15   Tyrone Guthrie, *A Life in the Theatre* (London: Hamish Hamilton, 1960), pp. 172-173.

16   George Bartram "Robert Helpmann – Human Dynamo" (an interview with RH), *Picturegoer*, 3 July 1948, p. 5.

17   The production was by Nicholas Sergeyev, Ninette de Valois and Frederick Ashton, after the original choreography by Marius Petipa. Scenery and costumes were by Oliver Messel. Under the direction of Monica Mason this iconic production was lovingly restored (with some small but contested adjustments) to mark the 75th anniversary of The Royal Ballet in 2006.

18   *Robert Helpmann, A Rare Sense of the Theatre*, p. 59.

19   Dail Ambler, 'Where do we go from here?' An analysis of a career", *Ballet Carnaval*, No 6, June-July 1947, pp. 142-144.

20   Sofka Zinovieff, *The Mad Boy, Lord Berners, My Grandmother and Me* (London: Jonathan Cape, 2014), p. 67. Zinovieff relates (on p. 150) an account of a house-party at Faringdon, the home of Lord Berners: "Helpmann recalled entering the drawing room at teatime and having to wait while a horse was fed buttered scones before being introduced to his fellow guests." These included Gertrude Stein and Alice B. Toklas. An extended version of the story also appears in Helpmann's 'official' biography by Elizabeth Salter (Brighton: Angus and Robertson, 1978), pp.77-78.

21   Julie Kavanagh, *Secret Muses, the Life of Frederick Ashton* (London: Faber and Faber, 1996), p. 160. Kavanagh remarks: "Recognising, in Lambert, Ashton and Chappell, kindred spirits with a similar sense of humour, Helpmann attached himself to them from the start, becoming so inseparable from the two dancers in particular, that Lambert used to call them the Three Bears. They never stopped entertaining each other and everyone else..." *Secret Muses* examines in detail the ways in which Ashton was, variously, Helpmann's friend, colleague, and professional rival.

22   *Robert Helpmann, A Rare Sense of the Theatre*, pp. 28-29.

23   The sheer stamina required to sustain these demanding schedules may well explain an incident from later in Helpmann's life that occurred on the occasion when the dancers of the Australian Ballet resigned through what they considered overwork and an unreasonable demand from management that at the close of a three-month international tour they go immediately into rehearsals for a gala and an unexpected season in Melbourne without being allowed a break. Peggy van Praagh, Helpmann's co-director, sided with the dancers, arguing that there is a limit to how much such performers can take. Helpmann shocked her by asking what the fuss was all about: "The trouble is dancers today don't know what hard work is...". From anyone else the observation might appear insensitive, but not from any member of the Sadler's Wells Company who had experienced the gruelling years through the Thirties and Forties and especially not from a man whose working week regularly found him shifting between different genres of theatre, and on occasion moving between ballet and revue in one night. (The incident is recorded in Christopher Sexton, *Peggy van Praagh: A Life of Dance* (Melbourne: Macmillan, 1985), p.171.)

24   Gailene Stock in conversation with the editors during preparations for the symposium on Helpmann at The Royal Ballet School in 2013.

25   Elizabeth Schwarzkopf in interview for *The Stage*, 3 March 1950.

26   Vivien Leigh during an interview for BBC radio, October 1960. Observations of cast members were culled from *Robert Helpmann, A Rare Sense of the Theatre*, passim.

27   Ninette de Valois, "Helpmann: a rare sense of the theatre", *The Daily Telegraph*, 29 September, 1986.

28   This seemed to us an appropriate choice, since Helpmann had a high

regard for Williamson as a critic and historian of the dance, as is evidenced by his comments about her in his essay "British Choreography and Its Critics", which is included in the chapter "Helpmann In His Own Words", see pp. 6-12 and especially p. 11.

29   A further definition of the noun, 'trace', reads: "The track made by the passage of any person or thing, whether beaten by feet or indicated in any other way."

In His Own Words[1]

a selection of published articles and talks
by Robert Helpmann

Learning to be a good dancer

[*Old Vic and Sadler's Wells Magazine*, April 1934, p 4][2]

My father did not really want me to be a dancer; but when I persisted in hankering after training, he said that if he gave in I must determine to become a very good one. This was in Australia, where opportunities for learning the sophisticated art of ballet are not as many as they are in Europe. (My father is Austrian, my mother English, and I was born in Australia, so my nationality is a little involved)[3]. But, when I was fifteen, Anna Pavlova[4] and her company came to us after their tour in the East; and my father went to Novikoff[5], her partner and a former ballet master at the Chicago Opera House, and asked him to take me as a pupil.

So I went with Pavlova's tremendous organisation all over Australia and New Zealand [...] having my lessons, watching rehearsals and performances, and sometimes dancing a little myself in the bigger ensembles [...]. But she and her company went back to Europe at the end of 1927[6] and then there was rather a hitch in my endeavour to learn to be a good dancer; and for a true fairy-tale period of seven years I served my apprenticeship in musical comedy – two of them I spent very happily playing opposite Maisie Gay in *This Year of Grace*[7] – and towards the end of that period, in "straight" plays.

Then I came to England with Margaret Rawlings[8] and her husband in *The Barretts of Wimpole Street*.[9] Gabriel Toyne[10] suggested I should go to Ninette de Valois for a few lessons, and take up my old ambition. My only idea at the time was to learn; but the Vic-Wells ballet happened to be wanting men dancers at the time, and Miss Baylis[11] offered me an engagement with the company. So I returned to my old love; and with the help and advice and inspiration that Miss de Valois has given me, it will be entirely my own fault if at some distant date I do not fulfill my father's injunction.

It would be out of place for me to say what I think of my tireless, brilliant, original teacher, and besides, I know that most people in the [Vic-Wells] audience feel very much the same about her. I will only say what many others far better qualified to judge than I have already said – and that is that *Job* above all else, was an epoch-making creation in the history of ballet.[12] It was a tremendous honour for me to follow Dolin in the part of Satan[13];

quite the most marvelous experience I have ever had, and in April I am to have a new and wonderful responsibility – that of creating a part in a new ballet [*The Haunted Ballroom*].[14] [The role of the Master of Treginnis] is a part after my own heart, for it is splendidly dramatic (and I admit that I prefer dramatic to purely classical dancing) [...]. From a dancer's point of view, I suppose there is no task in the world so absorbing as working out the choreography of an entirely new ballet [...] and I can only devote all my energies to grasp with both hands the chance she [de Valois] has given me!

Shakespeare and the ballet

[*Old Vic and Sadler's Wells Magazine*, January 1938, pp 4-5]

My first professional appearance, at the age of six was made in *A Midsummer Night's Dream*, in Australia, as one of the children engaged to appear in the wood scene.[15] Now I am to play Oberon.[16] It is difficult for me to say anything about it, but I regard it as one of the very important things in my life.

Ever since I joined the Vic-Wells ballet almost five years ago, it has been one of my ambitions to play at the Old Vic [...]. I have no desire to leave the Ballet which I love but I believe my ballet training will help me with my acting. For I realise that my past experiences as an actor have helped me with regard to certain aspects of the ballet. I consider that there is a close relationship between ballet and the Shakespearean plays, inasmuch as many of Shakespeare's works would make admirable subjects for ballet production. I believe that in the production of Shakespeare the collaboration of a producer and a choreographer would have very interesting results. I do not mean that the verse in any way should be sacrificed, but if the movements, groupings and climaxes are produced on some of the principles generally thought applicable only to choreography, the dramatic value of such movements should only enhance the verse.[17]

I consider it a great honour to be given the opportunity to play such a wonderful role as Oberon [...] I will do everything in my power to justify this wonderful belief. Further, I know that I will meet with the [...] help that it has been my good fortune to have had since I joined the personnel of these two great theatres.

The function of ballet:
a reply to some critics

[*Dancing Times*, September 1942, pp. 584-586.][18]

At the beginning of my talk I would like to make one point. Before I came to England and joined the Ballet, I was for quite a number of years in the theatre in Australia. I wish to make this point very clear, as all my formative years in the theatre were completely uninfluenced by any traditions of the Ballet proper. I have now been on the stage since I was fifteen, and although I am not going to say how long that is, it is quite long enough for me to have formed one opinion – that, in all the branches of the theatre with which I have been connected (Revue, Drama, Shakespeare, Musical Comedy and Ballet) by far my happiest years have been with the ballet, and it is the side of the theatre I care for most deeply. But equally as much, it is the side of the theatre about which more nonsense is talked than any other, and usually by the people most closely connected with it, and most anxious to help Ballet.

The Ballet world, to me, seems like an anxious parent who will never place any belief in the abilities of the new generation. Each dancer or choreographer has found this, I am quite sure, and so my talk to you will be an answer to many criticisms I have heard applied not only to myself but to all modern choreographers. I make this point because, as some of you perhaps know, I have recently become, or tried to become a Choreographer. When I was invited by Miss de Valois to do choreography for Sadler's Wells, my first problem was to find for myself a definite line, and my natural tendency was directed towards the more dramatic, and because of my interest in drama I was influenced a great deal to take my themes from some of the great English dramatists. A Ballet, like a play, is an elastic medium which must be used by each creator in an individual way. Naturally my themes, being based first on a Masque by Milton and secondly on a Play by Shakespeare, involved a great deal of Mime.

Mime is as legitimate an element in the medium of ballet as dancing; in fact, what distinguishes choreography from an arrangement of dance steps is its concentration on the composition as a whole – not merely the dance movements but also the mime. To have attempted to treat either of my dramatic subjects, *Comus* or *Hamlet*, in terms of *fouettés* and *entrechats*, would have been completely wrong, both dramatically and musically; but to exclude a choreographic dramatic rendering of such subjects because they demand a larger element of mime than pure dancing, seems to me to be dangerously limiting the scope of the ballet as a whole. I therefore tried to adjust the conventional mime of the classical school and combine it with the movement thereby evolving a type of mimetic-movement which should be more understandable to a modern audience.

As an Australian, brought up with no traditional knowledge of the Ballet, I have always felt that the Ballet audience was limited by the lack of technical knowledge on the part of the man-in-the-street. And so I have thought for many years that the appeal of the Ballet, as well as being technical, must also be theatrical. The man-in-the-street may not understand a beautifully executed set of *brisés*, but he does understand and will react to a dramatic situation and I see no reason why Ballet should not be able to draw on these dramatic situations as much as any other form of the theatre. All this does not mean that I do not appreciate and love the classical ballets, but one must remember that in their time they were accused of containing too much mime and too little dancing.

I speak now not only for myself but for all modern Choreographers. For many years I have watched the critic of modern Ballet always ready to say, "Very nice, very dramatic, very beautifully presented, but no dancing". What do they mean, "no dancing"? No fifth positions perhaps, no *pirouettes* perhaps, no *entrechats* perhaps – but Dancing. Every movement made on the stage by a dancer must be Dancing. Even to walk across the stage is, I find, to the average dancer often more difficult than a set of *brisés* and impossible for the average actor. I am quite sure that, if the dancer during training were taught not only to execute the technical steps but to move and to dance, the difference between Mime and Dance would not be so noticeable.

I have been asked why, if I believe so deeply in the power of Mime, did I think it necessary to introduce into *Comus* the two speeches[19] – why did I not mime them? Or did I want to show that I could be an actor when I was too old to dance? The only answer I can give is that Mime, as such, has its limitations just as classical technique, as such, is limited, or modern technique; and there are moments when mime cannot say all that is necessary. And I felt justified in introducing speech, not because I wished to show people that I could act, but on the grounds that it was well within the traditions of the English Masque, which is the nearest foundation England has to a tradition of Ballet. I am sure that, if the modern Ballet Critic could attend more rehearsals of Ballets and learn to understand the real reason for modern Ballet, there would be less mistaken criticism of ballet today. I have in ten years at Sadler's Wells danced in most of the Classical ballets – *Sleeping Princess*, *Coppélia*, *Le Lac des Cygnes*, and *Giselle* – and, with the possible exception of *Giselle*, there is less dancing in any of these Classical ballets from the male dancer's point of view than in most of the shortest of modern ballets.

I hope I do not appear to have what may be called a "down" on the

Classical school. Nobody appreciates more than I do how essential it is that the classical ballets should be retained in the repertoire; without them, the whole basic technique of the Ballet, Classical or Modern, would disintegrate. But it is impossible to imagine that the English Ballet could have a form and tradition of its own if it relied on revivals of *Le Lac des Cygnes* and *Giselle*, etc., for its repertoire. Therefore, if a tradition is to be built up in this country, it must necessarily be based upon such things as the Masque and the Pantomime – fundamentals of the English theatre.

A problem which faces the modern Choreographer continually is the music. Petipa and Coralli[20] had composers to sit with them during their rehearsals, who wrote music, suitable to the steps, even to the exact number of bars required. But the modern Choreographer often has to work to music already written as a composition complete in itself. This adds greatly to the difficulties of production, and the quite justifiable approach on the part of the critics – namely, "Does the choreography add anything to the music?"

Finally there is one other point I would very much like to make. It is that Ballet is essentially a theatrical art; its function is in the theatre, so that its appeal must be theatrical, and therefore to me, and I am quite sure to many other choreographers, the first and foremost thing is to appeal to the theatre-going public and not to a specialised few. No artist likes to imagine that his art appeals only to a specialised few. And I feel quite convinced that, if the ballet is to take its place in the Public's heart beside the cinema and the other forms of theatre in this modern age of action, its appeal must be theatrical as well as purely technical.

In conclusion, the reason why I speak today on this subject is because I know that The Royal Academy has a great influence on the teachers and the future dancers of England. Therefore it is important that it should, as an organisation, sympathise with and understand and help the modern dancers to be equipped, not only physically but in mental outlook as well, to fulfil the demands that will be made upon them by the Choreographers of this generation. Just to encourage The Royal Academy of Dancing to help us, I will tell you about a letter that I received just after the production of *Hamlet*:

> Dear Mr. Helpmann,
> I want you to know how very much I enjoyed your new ballet.
> As I have many times said to my husband, "Hamlet always has been ruined by the words..."

British choreography and its critics[21]

[Peter Noble (ed.), *British Ballet* (London: Skelton Robinson, 1949), pp.27-36.][22]

British choreography is a relatively new development in ballet history. Beginning on an important scale with Ninette de Valois' masterpiece *Job* in 1931, it has in the course of seventeen years become a creative form with a number of distinctive national features.[23] For, like all arts, ballet is many-sided and capable of developing in new directions from period to period, according to the conditions under which it is produced and the nation that produces it.

Speaking as a choreographer, I should say that the development of this original style of ballet in England, with the distinctive national features mentioned above, has been its strength; and the failure of some older writers on ballet in this country to appreciate the extremely individualist course it has taken, and the influences that have guided it, has caused the present weaknesses in much British ballet criticism.

The art flourishes both at home and abroad, as the enormous artistic success of the Sadler's Wells ballet on its visits to Paris, Brussels and Russian-occupied Vienna, as well as in its London seasons, has shown.[24] But there is an obvious gap between the spirit of the new ballets and new audiences on the one hand and the spirit of much English ballet criticism on the other. The first belongs to the present, the second is still buried hopelessly in the past. "Where are the snows of yesteryear?" would seem to be its inevitable theme.[25] It is as if dramatic critics were to refuse to consider seriously any English plays not written in the style of Molière or Racine![26]

I have deliberately chosen a foreign example here, since it particularly applies. The yardstick by which these critics judge British ballet is the Russian ballet of Diaghilev, or even earlier. If they admit anything good in the present at all, it must have a foreign label attached, or follow a foreign model so closely as to become drained of any vitality or individuality. We all know Gilbert's derision in *The Mikado* of this typically British form of pseudo-cultural snobbery, his "Idiot who praises with enthusiastic tone/ Every century but this and every country but his own!" I suspect W. S. had a prophetic vision of a certain type of modern balletomane.[27]

Every new development in the arts, of course, is opposed by a certain class of conservative. Wagner[28] was attacked for creating his music-dramas just as Fokine,[29] had he stayed in Russia, would have been attacked for creating his one-act dance-dramas (ballet in Russia today remains largely pre-Fokine in its influences). No one in his senses would deny that Fokine's influence through his ideals of the dance-drama is felt today in all responsible ballet companies in England and America.[30] But just as Fokine's work was coloured by his own Russian nature and materials it was inevitable that the ballet of other nations would produce strong characteristics of their own, and omit many which belonged strictly to the Russian temperament.

In England there have been many influences apart from Fokine's, and some quite outside the ballet sphere. It is a national characteristic to "dramatise" the arts – perhaps our greatest painter is Hogarth[31] – and the influence of the drama and painting on British ballet have in particular been very strong.[32] To take the example of *Job*: the main influence, the guiding force of the whole work, was Blake's engravings,[33] but Miss de Valois' work on play production in the legitimate theatre,[34] her interest in Dalcroze eurhythmics,[35] her training as a classical dancer[36] and experience in the Diaghilev Company,[37] all contributed to the style of ballet she finally evolved.

I should say that Ninette de Valois' greatness was as a "choreographic producer", a form of blended talent that has enormously influenced the trend of British choreography. I myself was more influenced by her, both as creator and dancer, than by any other choreographer. Both of us think in terms of drama, character and the handling of groups in the mass as much as in terms of dance. Frederick Ashton is a great choreographer in its original sense of "dance-composer"; he thinks primarily in terms of the sheer beauty of dance movement, and always prefers to work on an abstract theme rather than a dramatic story and to deal with symbolic rather than realistic characters.[38] Yet he also can give a dramatic effect to the dance – *Nocturne*[39] and *Dante Sonata*[40] are both in this sense "dramatic" ballets – and is often influenced by painting. His choreography in *The Wise Virgins* was influenced by Italian Renaissance painting[41] and that in *Dante Sonata* by a study of Flaxman and Doré.[42] Doré in particular inspired many of the actual poses and movements in *Dante Sonata,* just as El Greco inspired my movements as the Stranger in my own ballet *Miracle in the Gorbals.*[43]

One sometimes hears the view expressed that British choreography has been greatly influenced by the Ballets Jooss.[44] This is absolutely untrue. The Ballets Jooss are not a classical ballet company at all and no British choreographers have made any study of Jooss' system of training and form of dance. He has taken some technique from classical ballet, and some from Rudolph Laban and the Central European School.[45] All the movement in our ballets, however, derives from the classic in "line", and it could generally only be performed by classically trained dancers. Jooss' dancing is devoid of this form of "line". I think Jooss dancers might perform *Miracle in the Gorbals,* nevertheless, but certainly not *Dante Sonata*, in spite of its plastic movement and bare feet. The lines of the whole ballet are infused with Ashton's classical training and instinct (as I well know, since I have danced in it).

I myself have only seen one performance by the Ballets Jooss – their first in England many years ago[46] – and, although my ballets *Hamlet* and *Miracle in the Gorbals* could be said to derive in style from *Job* and *The Rake's Progress*, they could never be said to derive from any dance source outside classical ballet (excepting, of course, the Scots reel and jitterbug introduced into *Miracle* for reasons of local colour). *Job*, of course, was produced before the work of Jooss was ever seen in England, and the direct inspiration of *The Rake's Progress* was Hogarth.[47] (Hogarth, you will remember, used his art as a means of social criticism a century or more before Kurt Jooss was born.)

This is not, of course, to belittle Jooss, whose *The Green Table* is a great work produced strictly according to his own methods;[48] I am merely pointing out that these methods have never been studied or employed by British classical ballet choreographers.

There seems a prevalent idea that only dancing "on the toes" is classical and that anything off them is copied from the Ballets Jooss or modern dance! But the Russian classical ballets all contain plastic folk dances and character dances, and Fokine always discarded "pointe work", whenever he thought it unsuited to the theme or style of the ballet. Yet no one thinks of accusing Fokine of copying Jooss – it would be too obvious an anachronism.

It is, indeed, from Fokine and the Russian classical tradition that British choreography derives, even though it has given the form added freedom on occasion and concentrated more on drama and character. I should say that we actually keep closer to the roots of pure Russian classicism than – for instance – the work of the modern Russian, Massine, whose works are far more of a "*demi-caractère*" or "character" nature in actual movement.[49] Classical dancers often find them difficult to perform at first for this reason (which does not, of course, detract from their brilliance and originality – on the contrary in some respects).

The London-born choreographer Antony Tudor[50] – now working with Ballet Theatre in America – is sometimes referred to by his admirers as the most "classical" British choreographer because he uses "full pointe" a great deal in all his ballets. Perhaps his earlier ballets were classical – *Jardin aux Lilas*,[51] when I saw it some years ago, seemed not dissimilar in style to Ashton's *Nocturne* – but his *Romeo and Juliet* and *Undertow*, danced by the Ballet Theatre of New York at Covent Garden in 1946,[52] employed a quite different style of movement, which seemed to myself and other dancers to be totally unclassic, in spite of the numerous "pirouettes" and "pointe work". The "lines" were distorted and broken – quite intentionally I imagine – and I should certainly place the dance farther away from pure classicism than that of Massine. A ballet such as *The Rake's Progress* is far more "classical", though not less dramatic. *On Stage!*, on the other hand, by the young American choreographer Michael Kidd[53], contained a most beautiful *pas de deux* (danced by Nora Kaye and John Kriza[54]) which I should describe as perfectly classical in style. The difference I am discussing is one of style, and not of quality.

Tudor has been called the "inventor" of the "psychological ballet" but it is of course not new for ballet to suggest psychological processes in its characters. "Drama" in ballet goes back to Noverre[55], nearly two centuries ago, and the dividing line between "dramatic" and "psychological" ballet is very thin. In a sense *Giselle* is a psychological study,[56] and so is *The Rake's Progress.* Tudor in *Pillar of Fire*[57] and *Undertow* is now showing the direct influence of Freud and modern psycho-analysis, but the emphasis on psychology and drama is a *trait* of British ballet generally.

Of course the work of every choreographer reflects his personality to an extent. Miss de Valois, Mr Ashton and myself all show different characteristics of our own in our ballets, as well as certain racial similarities. I tried myself, when I began to compose ballets, to strike a style particularly suited to British dancers and to get away from some previous conventions just as Fokine did when he created *Petrouchka.*[58]

I had never seen the Diaghilev ballet as I lived in Australia until after Diaghilev's death, so its modernistic productions of the 'twenties did not influence me. In fact I took the "dramatic" ballet further along the lines suggested by the choreography of Ninette de Valois. I tried to translate a Shakespearean theme in *Hamlet*, and to bring British ballet in touch with modern slum life in *Miracle in the Gorbals.*[59] *Adam Zero* was an exercise in various dance styles and expressionistic stage production, with a symbolic contemporary background implied in some scenes.[60] *Corroboree* is a choreographic reproduction of the tribal dances of Australian aboriginals,[61] and I hope will help to widen the British repertoire to include certain purely national and non-classical dance forms from the Empire. Russian ballet has always made great use of the folk dances of the various races that live within its national territory, and I think British ballet might be enriched if it did the same.

A more practical, mundane and immediate influence on my work has been the company of dancers at my disposal. Many people fail to realise the effect the company must have on the ultimate "shape" of a ballet. They often accuse the choreographer of not composing a certain type of ballet; had they known the difficulties, they would have realised how impossible this was under the circumstances. At the time my first ballet, *Comus,* was created,[62] the Wells were running short of male dancers owing to the call-up and we were uncertain how long we would retain even those we had left.

The choreography for the *corps de ballet*, therefore, was composed so that the male parts could, if necessary, be taken over by girls, and the masks and costumes were also designed with this possibility in view. There were no "lifts" in the choreography for this reason, and I added my own "lifted" entrance as Comus much later when it became certain that we could continue with male dancers. The "Furies" in Ninette de Valois' ballet *Orpheus and Eurydice*[63] were created under the same conditions (and Laertes in my *Hamlet* was a static role simply because John Hart,[64] its creator, was expected to be called into the Forces before the ballet was completed and an inexperienced boy student substituted!).

In the main the dancers were then very young and obviously high technical demands could not be made on them; but British dancers do possess a natural instinct for dramatic and character work, as they have shown again and again in *The Rake's Progress*, and this material I determined to use to the full.

These difficulties are obviously no excuse for poor choreography, for it is the artist's business to turn even his liabilities into assets and to use his imagination to create an effective new form if for practical reasons he cannot compose in the old. This is what I tried to do and I would not now change a movement in *Hamlet*, as its style seems to me the one most dramatic and suitable for its theme and atmosphere.

Many of the confusions in ballet criticism as to dance styles and choreographic forms spring from an unfortunate lack of real knowledge on the part of many people who write on ballet, and sometimes the wildest assumptions as to a choreographer's "influences" are made in print. For example I was recently accused of "lifting" my *Adam Zero* birth scene from that in Tudor's *Undertow* – although at the time *Undertow* had not been seen in England. Unfortunately for this theory the scenario of *Adam Zero* was written by Michael Benthall in Holland in 1944 – months before *Undertow* was produced in America.[65]

I mention the above instance of a certain form of "criticism" because it shows the fantastic lengths to which balletomanes may go when they wish to support a personal prejudice in print. It does not make the artist's work easier in this country that inaccuracies and distortions in the writing even of critics of reputation are frequent. American visitors to our ballet during the war – some of them former dancers then in the Forces – often came round to see me and remarked with pleasure and some surprise on the high standard of our choreography and dancers. One can understand their surprise; they had previously read about them only in the books of a British writer on ballet whose prejudice against Sadler's Wells ballets and dancers is notorious over here.

The odd tendency to belittle the work of their own national ballet is something not to be found among writers in any other country. Foreign critics in the countries where we have travelled all show tremendous pride in their own ballet, mixed with a sound critical judgement, and the great success we have had on the Continent has been won on our merits in spite of this national pride and critical attitude towards the new "rival". In the end the praise has been generously accorded and the critics have shown an open-minded appreciation of our particular style, with nothing of the narrow conservatism met with so frequently in ballet magazines and books in our own country.

There is often a great gap in England between the written judgements of the professional critic of the national and literary papers and those of the balletomane writer who likes (with, alas, very often a limited technical knowledge) to consider himself a ballet "specialist". The first recognises far more frequently the true quality of a work, since he criticises it from the angle of the artistic and theatrical effect which was intended, and his judgement is usually supported by artists in ballet circles and the public generally, while over and over again in England the "balletomane" writer proves himself to be wrong (and often spiteful) about a new choreographic work.

Mr Arnold Haskell[66] and Miss Joan Lawson[67] are among the critics who have been helpful to British ballet because they have been free from general prejudice against it and have tried, on the whole, to judge it by the new individual qualities it has produced. One of the few recent books which has seemed of value to artists and teachers within the theatre is Miss Audrey Williamson's *Contemporary Ballet*,[68] partly because this critic writes with factual knowledge and with understanding of the choreographer's intentions. It is particularly important to the artist that writers should have this good judgement and knowledge because too many people, unfortunately, base their judgements on the written word instead of the actual work.

Miss Williamson, significantly, is also a dramatic critic. One of the most serious defects in English ballet criticism generally is the lack of any understanding of dramatic values in dancers or choreography. Some critics seem unable to distinguish between good mime and bad. (Even Margot Fonteyn's Giselle – by any acting standards the finest now to be seen – has been under-rated by certain writers who have praised much inferior performances.)

If ballet is to remain the great expressive and dramatic art Noverre and Fokine wished it to be, ballet critics should try to use their knowledge of dramatic standards, and throw off the personal prejudices and "theorising" that make so much of their criticism valueless from the artist's point of view. For British ballet will continue to develop on lines of the dance-drama, and its greatest strength, as I have said, has been in its creation of this national style.[69] It has become a part of English theatrical tradition and has never quite lost sight of its ancestor, the dramatic Masque.[70]

How to Become a Ballet Dancer

[*The Listener*, 14 April 1949, p.611][71]

'"Work" is the keyword in describing the life of a dancer', said Robert Helpmann, broadcasting in *The Musician's World*. 'Even when one has reached a 'star' position in a company, one never stops, and that life of work begins on the first day one enters a ballet class. It cannot be too much emphasised that ballet dancing is physically an exhausting profession; it requires the utmost of the artist in health and physical stamina. The average person couldn't get through a ballet class of an hour. The necessary stamina is, of course, acquired by the dancer through a long process of training. For the actual technique of ballet – what we in the ballet call "the classical technique" – a good average age for a girl to begin is nine or ten, and for a boy twelve.[72] In most cases – though there are exceptions – after fifteen is too late, if you want a first-rate technique.

'I began classical dancing myself at fourteen, and this is a little on the late side; but I was helped by the fact that I had learned acrobatic dancing from a very early age, and this meant my limbs were already thoroughly loosened and supple. It is, in fact, a very good thing for a child to be taught dancing from the age of six or even earlier: it is specially helpful in developing the child's musical sense and natural grace. But it should be a free and spontaneous form of dance. The classical technique should be left till later, and it can do great physical harm for a girl to be forced to dance on the tips of her toes in blocked shoes – what we in ballet call 'point work' – before the age of nine or ten.[73]

'Ballet classes always follow the same form. The child at her first lesson, and the famous ballerina, both take a daily class along the same lines: that is, they begin with exercises at the *barre* and follow this with practice in the centre of the room. The *barre* is the handrail that runs all round a classroom at elbow height; throughout the *barre* work the dancer holds on to this rail for support. It helps her to turn out the leg and thigh (which is essential for balance in technical feats), and it helps to strengthen her jumps, to gain poise and balance, to hold her head, shoulders and hips correctly. *Barre* work consists of what we call "limbering" – exercises to loosen the limbs – and it also includes a great deal of intricate footwork that goes to form the classical technique. In the centre practice which follows, the teacher weaves the steps learnt at the *barre* into sequences – what we call *enchaînements*; these are, in fact, tiny dances, in which the student learns to apply the placings of the body learnt at the *barre* to the actual technique of dancing. Still there is a daily class, usually from 10 to 11 in the morning.[74] From 11.30 to 12.45, in the Sadler's Wells Company, to which I belong, there will be rehearsals of ballets in the repertoire, and after lunch, from 2 to 4, more rehearsals. At night there will usually be a performance.

'On joining a company the young dancer will have to learn the *corps de ballet* dances in all the ballets in the repertoire, as well as in new ballets as they occur. She will watch the dancers of small parts in readiness if necessary to understudy or take them over, and later she will watch and learn the leading roles in the same way. The ballerina has to work no less than the members of the *corps de ballet*. She too will take daily classes and rehearsal, and not only the company classes but also private lessons with individual teachers. All dancers find teachers whose methods are specially helpful to their own needs, teachers who excel in one particular branch of teaching. You may go to one to acquire strong and fast *pirouettes* or turns, and to another to acquire elevation or jump. The great teacher will teach all branches well, but still some dancers will find they can learn something further from another teacher. No dancer, however famous, ceases to learn.

'Dancers, on entering a company, are classified according to their physical style,[75] just as singers are classified as soprano, contralto, tenor or bass. In the *corps de ballet* they will have to dance all types of dancing; but when it comes to big parts they will usually be cast according to their natural style – that is classical or character. The classical dancer must belong to a certain physical type: a good average height for a ballerina is 5ft. 3ins., for the male dancer who partners her 5ft. 10ins. Character dancers, and certain classical dancers of strong technique who confine themselves to solo work, can be shorter.'

Formula for Midsummer Magic

(The Choreographer-principal of the new, America-bound Old Vic production of *A Midsummer Night's Dream* describes the problems involved in reaching that goal)[76]

[*Theatre Arts Monthly*, September 1954, pp.76-77 and 95]

A production of *A Midsummer Night's Dream* presents to the director and choreographer an amazing number of problems, which are so conflicting that each time I have been associated with this play, they have involved endless rejections of ideas, plans and methods.

The main problem is to wed the classical Greek (the play is set in Athens) with the association of the Elizabethan theatre, since there is no doubt that *A Midsummer Night's Dream* is an English play; and although Shakespeare set it in Athens and a wood near Athens, the real essence is England and Warwickshire in particular. His genius surmounts all frontiers, but the essential quality is a wood in Warwickshire; even the flowers mentioned – musk rose, honeysuckle, eglantine, mustard seed – are all English flowers. The humour of Bottom and his companions is essentially that of English rustics. So much for the first problem.

Add to this the classical Victorianism of the Mendelssohn score and you have a second.[77] Some people, I know, consider it quite possible to do *A Midsummer Night's Dream* without the Mendelssohn music. Personally, and I repeat personally, I find the two cannot be separated. In some curious way in the first few magic bars of the overture, Mendelssohn, a German, caught the same wonderful magic that Shakespeare did in his supreme verse, and so these very problems offer to the director and choreographer endless, endless ideas about which line to follow.

In 1937 I first played Oberon for the Old Vic, with Vivien Leigh as Titania.[78] This was the first time I had left the Sadler's Wells Ballet to appear in a straight speaking role with the Old Vic. Tyrone Guthrie, who directed the production, took the line of the Mendelssohn music.[79] He followed it in all its Victorian romanticism with all this involved – Victorian classical fairies, Greece seen through Victorian eyes – and there evolved an enchanting production which made a great impression on me, as indeed it did on the whole British public. It is still talked about.

When I was invited to appear in this present production of *A Midsummer Night's Dream* and also to do the choreography, I had many discussions with Michael Benthall, director of the Old Vic and also director of the present production, about the line he wished to take.[80] He too had seen the Victorian production at the Old Vic and also had done a most enchanting production of his own at Stratford-upon-Avon in 1948,[81] which he had based on classical Renaissance at the time of Shakespeare. After many discussions Benthall said he had decided to base this present production on classical Greece seen through Elizabethan eyes and leave the Mendelssohn score and the choreography to underline, with its own particular flavour, the other elements of the play.

For me this immediately raised other problems – the length of the ballet skirt, for instance. Anything that looked like *Sylphide*[82] or *Giselle*[83] immediately became romantic Victorian; and the use of point shoes at first appeared to be an anachronism. What was I to do? Completely Greek classical fairies argued with the rustic and English quality in the play; completely rustic and English fairies argued with the Mendelssohn score. As always with any Shakespearean production, one has to clear one's mind and sit and try to think out what Shakespeare wanted; and I am sure that he wanted to convey through Oberon and Titania the complete opposite of the reality of Bottom, the lovers and the court of Theseus, to convey, in fact, the magic of moonlight. It is unbelievable how stupidly one can get involved in theories when the author makes it so clear by calling his play *A Midsummer Night's Dream*.

And so in this production I have tried through the choreography to convey the moonlight of a midsummer night and the use of the point[84] as an indication of flight. When the point shoe was originally introduced in the classical ballet, this was its real intention. When the ballerina was *sur le point* as in *La Sylphide*,[85] this signified that she was flying. Using this as logic, I have reserved the use of the point shoes for Titania and her train as opposed to the other dancing. I have tried to follow the classical form of the Mendelssohn music in the use of the basic classical steps, combined with the freedom of the imagination of the verse. It is particularly lucky that both Moira Shearer[86] and I have been trained as dancers; therefore Oberon and Titania, for what is probably the first time, are being played by people who can also dance in the full classical tradition. This makes the problem of separating their qualities of unreality and otherworldliness much easier than would otherwise have been the case.

Feeling that I cannot see my own effects when I am dancing myself, we invited Frederick Ashton[87] to conceive the nocturne as a climax to the reconciliation of Titania and Oberon.[88] Ashton, a superb example of a modern choreographer who completely understands and uses the classical ballet to its great advantage, has in his beautiful arrangement completely clarified all that I felt, furthering the hope that the combination of our choreography, Benthall's direction and Robin and Christopher Ironside's decor and costumes[89] will bring about a resolution of the problems of which I have spoken at the beginning. While I said that *A Midsummer Night's Dream* is essentially an English play, the magic of it is essentially worldwide.

The public has the final say

(To become a cultural power Australia must train its own dancers and actors – and they'll have to be good)[90]

[*Woman*, June 20 1955]

The person who hasn't a large slice of make-believe in his character would never go on the stage. Now don't misunderstand me. There's no room for make-believe in being a ballet dancer – it's sheer hard work. I'm speaking of acting, of make-believe in its most subtle and creative form. An imaginative child can project himself into fantasy and become its central character. A good actor does fundamentally the same thing as the child, the important difference being that his make-believe is subtle, controlled and backed by talent. This element of make-believe is essential to actors because for them there is no set technique. Everyone has different ways of reaching the particular emotional pitch he feels he needs. If he lacks the capacity to shed his own personality in favour of the character he's playing, he'll have a thin time of it. In ballet this isn't nearly so important. A dancer has to fulfil certain technical requirements before he is given a role. Learning to dance is like learning the violin.

You must first master the technique. Only when the technique has ceased to be creaky can you think beyond it. On the whole I feel acting is more mentally creative than dancing, less rigid if more emotionally exacting.

I am intensely interested in all aspects of the theatre. *Being an Australian, I'd like to see a strong national theatre here on the lines of England's Old Vic.* When I left here it was difficult for an Australian to work in the ballet or the classical drama. There was no permanent place to practise these particular forms of the theatre and one had to rely on visiting companies. Coming home after 25 years I find the Borovansky Ballet Company already formed and the beginnings of an Elizabethan Trust to promote theatre in Australia.[91] If these organisations are to achieve anything of lasting importance they must build their own stars, not depend on importations from overseas.

I feel very strongly on that point. When Ninette de Valois started the Sadler's Wells Ballet Company in London nearly 30 years ago, she said: "I may have it rough for 10 years but I'll build my own stars." At that time the company, small and unknown, was giving only one performance a month to not very full houses. Everyone thought de Valois was mad. They said she'd never make a success of it without famous Russian dancers in the leading roles. She proved how wrong they were. Within 20 years she had made stars of Margot Fonteyn and me – stars with our own public – and Sadler's Wells had become world famous.

The Australian theatre would do well to follow her lead by training its own promising actors and dancers. Ballet and the drama are today in much the same position in this country as Sadler's Wells and the Old Vic were in England 25 years ago. They are at their beginning, and it's only through the hard work and enthusiasm of everyone concerned that they will be able to develop into first-class organisations. *The public can help by supporting the movement – for it's the public that has the final say.*

Australia today is culturally a wasteland to most of the English. They know gumtrees grow here and sheep graze steadily beneath them, but at that point their minds stop dead. It never occurs to them that here books are being written, pictures painted, ballets and plays performed. When the film, *The Overlanders*, was shown in London, some friends of mine were astounded when they saw scenes of Brisbane. "Cities!" they exclaimed incredulously. This, I think, is mainly the result of bad publicity.

When you pass Australia House in London, you see nothing but pictures of men on horseback, sheep, gumtrees and an occasional koala. Very pretty but unenlightening. Though they don't exactly think of us as savages over there, they hardly think of us as they do of the Europeans. They know people like Joan Hammond, Eileen Joyce, Leo McKern, Melba and Sylvia Fisher came from Australia – and Peter Finch, who, after all, they're quick to tell you, was born in England.[92]

And the Australian accent is not favoured by English producers or audiences. You have to lose it fast, as people from Cornwall or Scotland or Birmingham have to lose theirs, if they want stage work. You must cultivate a neutral accent. I had trouble with mine when I first played in drama. I didn't think I had any trace of it left but I was told I had – a slight one, just on certain words. If Australia ever reached the point where she could send a company overseas, it would be most unwise to use the native accent.[93]

I have often been asked to advise young people whether or not they should go on the stage. My answer is, you can never advise anyone about going on the stage. The person who'd listen meekly to my telling him not to go on the stage and then say, "Thank you, Mr. Helpmann" and go away and get a job as a clerk would never have stayed on the stage anyway. No one can say who will succeed and who won't. Many times I've seen those who fail miserably in tests end up as successes. *I failed in my elementary exam at the London Royal Academy of Dancing.*[94] It's often just chance when a talented person makes good, and those of you who want to go on the stage will do it whatever I say to you. Only time will tell how long you'll stay there.

On the practical side I can give you two hints. Dancers should begin to train early – girls at about nine years of age, boys at ten to twelve. And for acting you must be dedicated: you must love it for its own sake, because the monetary rewards are small. Top salaries don't compare even with those of the lesser known film actors. Kate Hepburn is one of the dedicated actresses. On stage she is the most concentrated player I've ever met. Working with her is rather like working with a dancer. Physically and emotionally she's like a tightly wound spring, tensed, ready to leap forward into her role. She has that faculty of projecting herself forward into her parts, which I have called the most subtle and fascinating form of make-believe. In a word, she is an artist.

There must be many in Australia today who, given the chance, could develop into fine actors and actresses. Next time I come home I hope to see them in their own theatre, with their own public applauding them from the gallery, the circle and the stalls.

Endnotes

1   Helpmann was not given to writing manifestos in de Valois' manner, but at various points in his life he gave broadcast talks or lectures that were subsequently printed or he contributed salient articles to programmes or theatre journals. These six items have been chosen and arranged chronologically to record his personal reactions to key moments in his career: his joining the Vic-Wells Ballet, playing his first major role as an actor on the London stage, his response to critics of his first works as choreographer, his concern to stress that the life of a dancer is determined by unrelenting hard work, his bringing an English production by Michael Benthall and the Old Vic to America when there was a perceived need to explain the ideas it promulgated about the relation of Shakespeare to the dance, and his return to Australia and voicing a clarion call for the development of an all-Australian ballet scene (one in which he was later to play a prominent part).

2   Lilian Baylis regularly encouraged members of her Company (actors, singers, dancers, directors, designers and choreographers) to write short essays for the *Old Vic and Sadler's Wells Magazine*. It was her means of building up a good rapport between performers and spectators, along with her celebrated parties to mark the opening and closing of a season, Twelfth Night and Shakespeare's birthday where audience members were invited to invade the stage and meet her casts. The Vic-Wells Association still exists and the parties are maintained in honour of Baylis's memory.

3   Kathrine Sorley Walker, *Robert Helpmann, A Rare Sense of the Theatre* (Alton: Dance Books, 2009, p 4-6). Sorley Walker's family research concluded that Helpmann, who only added the final 'n' to his surname after he joined the Vic-Wells Ballet, had "no German or Austrian origins", as his name suggested, but that his ancestry was British. "On his mother's side, Robert's forebears were all Scottish" while his father was "descended from a Devonshire family of Helpmans with strong Royal Navy and British Army connections".

4   Anna Pavlova (1881-1931) had danced with the Imperial Russian Ballet and briefly with Diaghilev's Ballets Russes; she settled in London after 1912 and in her later years toured world-wide with her Company as well as extensively in England. She had considerable influence on the next generation of dancers, including Frederick Ashton and Alicia Markova. Helpmann toured with the Company in Australia from April to August 1926, when it visited Melbourne, Sydney, Brisbane, Adelaide and New Zealand.

5   Laurent Novikoff (1888-1956) trained at the Bolshoi Ballet School and danced with Diaghilev's Company in 1909 and from 1919 to 1921. He joined Pavlova's Company as her principal partner from 1911 to 1914 and again from 1921 to 1928. He subsequently settled in America, was Ballet Master for the Chicago Opera (1929-1933), and danced at the New York Metropolitan Opera (1941-1945), before forming his own ballet school in Michigan in the decade before his death.

6   Actually in 1926.

7   Noël Coward's revue, *This Year of Grace,* had a successful run for over nine months in London before transferring to Broadway where it ran for a further 157 performances. Maisie Gay had starred in the London staging, along with Sonnie Hale, Jessie Matthews and Tilly Losch, but was replaced by Beatrice Lillie when the production moved to New York. Gay opened a staging in Melbourne in March 1929 in which Helpmann performed various roles till the end of August.

8   Margaret Rawlings (1906-1996) who possessed a rich contralto-pitched voice and a fine ear for verse rhythms (her earliest appearances were with John Masefield's Company in Oxford), performed regularly both in the West End and numerous experimental and alternative theatres from 1927 to 1979. She was co-founder of Equity. She played Vittoria Corombona to Helpmann's Flamineo in Michael Benthall's production of Webster's *The White Devil* in 1947.

9   This romantic drama by Rudolf Besier, first staged by Barry Jackson at the Malvern Festival in 1930, tells of the poet Robert Browning's courtship of Elizabeth Barrett and, given her father's opposition to their marriage, their eventual elopement. Helpmann played the very minor role of Septimus, one of Elizabeth Barrett's brothers.

10   Gabriel Toyne (1905-1963) was Margaret Rawlings' husband. He directed her and played supporting roles but eventually after their separation became a valued fight director, working with Komisarjevski and Tyrone Guthrie. During the season of Besier's play, the Toynes produced *Business à la Russe,* a short ballet choreographed by Helpmann, in which he created the part of The Young Man. It was Rawlings who actually gave him a letter of introduction to Ninette de Valois. The two women had known each other since de Valois choreographed Salome's dance when Rawlings was playing the titular role in Wilde's tragedy for Peter Godfrey at the Gate Theatre Studio in 1931.

11   Lilian Baylis (1874-1937) became the lessee and manager of the Old Vic Theatre after the death of her aunt, Emma Cons, in 1912. She rapidly transformed it into a house that staged opera and drama (chiefly Shakespeare) and in the later 1920s began to introduce performances of ballet by de Valois' School. As the dance grew in popularity and a company was formed, Baylis took over and developed the dilapidated Sadler's Wells Theatre, installing a rehearsal room for de Valois' dancers, which is where Helpmann first presented himself to her.

12   *Job,* a masque for dancing, was choreographed by de Valois to music by Ralph Vaughan Williams in 1931, to a scenario by Geoffrey Keynes based on William Blake's illustrations, which inspired both her composition and the designs by Gwen Raverat. It was originally performed for the Camargo Society at the Cambridge Theatre, London. It was later revived with new scenery by John Piper and lighting by Michael Benthall at the Royal Opera House in May 1948.

13   Satan, the most spectacular, wholly danced role in Job, was created on Anton Dolin (1904-1983), who at the time was the *premier danseur* with the Vic Wells Company, regularly partnering Alicia Markova with whom he was soon to form the Markova-Dolin Ballet. Their leaving de Valois' Company was to offer Helpmann remarkable opportunities within a remarkably short time after

joining her dancers. The first indication of what was shortly to follow was de Valois' casting of Helpmann as Satan at the start of the 1933-1934 season (he had previously danced one of Job's sons and one of the trio, War, Pestilence and Famine, in the production from April 1933).

14   De Valois choreographed *The Haunted Ballroom* for the Vic-Wells Ballet to music and a scenario by Geoffrey Toye and with designs by Motley in 1934. It is a romantic and melodramatic piece about the Master of a great house being haunted by the ghosts of women who have featured in his and his ancestors' lives, who eventually bring about his death and then turn their malevolent attentions to his young son. The Master of Treginnis was the first role to be created on Helpmann.

15   This was as a child extra with the Allan Wilkie Shakespeare Company in Adelaide in 1917.

16   Helpmann auditioned for and was cast as Oberon in Tyrone Guthrie's production of *A Midsummer Night's Dream*, which opened at the Old Vic on Boxing Day, 1937. The cast also included Vivien Leigh as Titania; the designs were by Oliver Messel. For further material on this production see "Formula for Midsummer Magic" later in this chapter and also Richard Allen Cave's essay in this volume, "The actor, Robert Helpmann: voice, text and theatrical intelligence", pp. 66-67.

17   This idea was shared with Michael Benthall and they both devised Shakespearean productions that experimented with this practice at the Memorial Theatre at Stratford-upon-Avon and at the Old Vic, after Benthall became the Artistic Director there in 1953.

18   This is the text of "an address given to Members of The Royal Academy of Dancing at Claridge's Hotel, London, on July 17th". It comprises the closest Helpmann came to a manifesto about his principles as a choreographer. The article was illustrated with a monochrome image of Helpmann in the role of Hamlet, photographed by Tunbridge-Sedgwick. (Typographical errors in the printing of the essay have been silently corrected; some adjustments have been made both to the punctuation of the article the better to clarify Helpmann's ideas and to the format of paragraphs to avoid too many short sections of prose. Throughout, Helpmann uses the terms, "choregraphy" and "Choregrapher", as de Valois did in her writings at this time, but these spellings have been modernised to "choreography" and "Choreographer" to accord with current usage.)

19   These were Comus's invocation to Night (from "The star that bids the shepherd fold / Now the top of heaven doth hold..." to his command to his attendant rout of followers, "Come, knit hands and beat the ground / In a light fantastic round"); and his temptation of the chaste Lady to "be wise and taste" the cup of wine that he proffers which, if she succumbs, will transform her into one of his creatures. The speeches, heavily edited, deployed lines 93-144, and a distillation of selected lines from Comus's three speeches, lines 683-831. Michael Benthall, who had been instrumental in Helpmann's choice of Milton's masque, doubtless assisted with the editing.

20   Marius Ivanovich Petipa (1818-1910), a French dancer, teacher and

choreographer, who became Ballet Master of the St Petersburg Imperial Theatres, created over fifty ballets, most notably those choreographed to the three scores by Tchaikovsky (his version of *Le Lac des cygnes* was a revival which with Ivanov he completely transformed). Jean Coralli (1779-1854) was from 1831 the Ballet Master of the Paris Opéra; his finest work was his collaboration in 1841 with Théophile Gautier (scenario) and Adolphe Adam (music) at the instigation of Jules Perrot to create *Giselle* as a vehicle for Carlotta Grisi.

21   This article, commissioned by Peter Noble, is of particular interest in that Helpmann uses it as a means to assess how to situate himself in relation to his choreographic contemporaries: de Valois, Ashton, Massine, Jooss and Tudor. The nature of Noble's book, which offers a survey of all that is best on the current British ballet scene, doubtless encouraged Helpmann to adopt this wider perspective. While the essay is in many ways a personal defence, it also allows Helpmann to define what he most values in ballet as an art-form.

22   Noble preceded Helpmann's article with a paragraph-length summary of his author's career as dancer, choreographer and actor, concluding with comment on his contributions to the film of *The Red Shoes*. He ends: "Robert Helpmann takes his place as one of the most distinguished dancers and choreographers in the history of British ballet" (p.27).

23   See notes 12 and 13 above. This was de Valois' first major choreographic creation, though she had composed some seventy works previously over a range of subjects and styles for herself and her companies at the Cambridge Festival Theatre and the Abbey Theatre, Dublin, as well as for Sadler's Wells Ballet.

24   In January and February 1945 ENSA and the British Council arranged for the Company to perform in Brussels at the Théâtre des Variétés and the Théâtre de la Monnaie and in Paris at the Marigny Theatre and the Théâtre des Champs-Elysées. Later in November of that same year, the Company gave seasons in Hamburg and Berlin and in September 1946, they appeared in Vienna at the Volksoper. In 1947 the Company toured to Prague, Warsaw, Poznan, Oslo and Malmo. Throughout the later years of the War the Company's home had been the New Theatre till June 1944, when they joined the Sadler's Wells Opera Company at the Prince's Theatre (now the Shaftesbury Theatre).

25   "Mais où sont les neiges d'antan?" is the refrain of a poem, "Ballade des dames du Temps-jadis" (Ballad of the Ladies of Times Past), by François Villon, included in his collection, *Le Testament*, first published in 1533.

26   These were the celebrated seventeenth-century French masters of (respectively) comedy and tragedy.

27   The reference is to the comic opera, *The Mikado or the Town of Titipu*, by W[illiam] S[chwenck] Gilbert and Arthur Sullivan, which was first staged at the Savoy Theatre in 1885. Ko-Ko, the Lord High Executioner, boasts that he has "got a little list /Of society offenders who might well be underground /And who never would be missed", including the said "Idiot". Unfortunately, Helpmann has somewhat misremembered the lines, since the original runs: "all centuries but this...".

28   Richard Wagner (1813-1883) revolutionised the traditions of opera by

devising the form he called *gesamtkunstwerk* (opera as a total work of art) in which the constituent elements of music, song, design, and movement were all conceived as a synthesised and unified entity.

29   Michael Fokine (1880-1942) was the foremost choreographer of the earliest years of Diaghilev's Company, popularising the self-contained one-act ballet with such works as *Les Sylphides* (1909), *The Firebird* (1910), *Schéhérazade* (also 1910) and *Petrushka* (1911). Traditional Russian ballet was focused primarily on the three-act narrative ballets of choreographers such as Marius Petipa.

30   Helpmann is here subtly linking the choreographic practices of Fokine, de Valois and (by implication) his own: though they shaped their various works differently and in relation to different principles, those works nonetheless fall within the over-riding category of dance-drama.

31   William Hogarth (1697-1764), a political and moral satirist, favoured painting that promoted a powerful narrative which dramatised his unique vision of social corruption.

32   De Valois had turned the narrative elements of one of Hogarth's series of paintings entitled *The Rake's Progress* into a narrative ballet. First staged in 1935, it has sustained a continuing place in the repertory of The Royal Ballet, proving Helpmann's point.

33   Blake's illustrations to the Book of Job comprise two sets of watercolours (1806 and 1821) and twenty-two engraved prints (1826).

34   De Valois had worked as choreographer and as what today would be called a movement director for Terence Gray at the Cambridge Festival Theatre (1926-1933), W.B. Yeats at the Abbey Theatre (1928-1934) and for Lilian Baylis at the Old Vic on operas and plays (1926-1937).

35   Émile Jacques-Dalcroze (1865-1950) promoted a method of learning and experiencing music through movement, which he termed Eurythmics. The comment is interesting: while Marie Rambert had famously trained in the Method under Dalcroze himself in Geneva (it helped her assist Nijinsky in choreographing the original staging of *The Rite of Spring* in 1913), it is less well known that de Valois had studied Eurhythmics for two years as a girl in England, and often opined that the Method was the best start possible for a child's training in dance.

36   De Valois' classical training was particularly rich: she studied with numerous teachers, foremost among them were Édouard Espinosa, a teacher of the venerated French School; Enrico Cecchetti, the acknowledged 'maestro' of brilliant Italian technique; and Nicolai Legat, a legendary teacher of the great Imperial Russian School.

37   De Valois performed with Diaghilev's Company from 1923 to the summer of 1925, returning for short periods as a guest artist in 1926 and 1928.

38   Ashton's finest works in the "abstract" style, created prior to the writing of this essay, were *Symphonic Variations* (1946) and *Scènes de ballet* (1948).

39   This narrative ballet (1936) about an impoverished flower girl (danced by Fonteyn), who is rejected by a caddish young man (Helpmann) in favour of a

rich girl (June Brae) was danced to Delius's symphonic poem, *Paris*. The flower girl suffers a breakdown and dies.

40   *Dante Sonata*, composed during 1940 to Liszt's *D'Après une lecture de Dante*, is a full-scale company work, depicting the sufferings of fallen angels (the Children of Darkness) who attack penitential souls reaching after salvation (the Children of Light). The inspiration is the first two parts (*Hell* and *Purgatory*) of Dante's *Divine Comedy*. The writhing, battling forms are lit such that they appear to be surrounded by menacing shadows that advance and recede about the dancers. That the ballet was a commentary on the early years of World War II is starkly conveyed.

41   Danced to the music of J.S. Bach, this work of 1940 was inspired by the parable told in St. Matthew's Gospel. In Ashton's hands it becomes a morality play about the rewards of purity and patience, focusing on the role of the Bride (originally danced by Fonteyn) as, guided by her parents, she prepares for matrimony. The costumes by Rex Whistler suggest the influence of Botticelli and Veronese.

42   The costumes, designed by Sophie Fedorovich were described in the programme as "after Flaxman". The influence of Gustave Doré (1832-1883) on Ashton's creative imagination was possibly made evident to Helpmann and the cast during the rehearsal process. The artist completed sets of illustrations to *Hell* (1866) and to *Purgatory* and *Paradise* (1867), which may have been referred to by the choreographer, or shown by him to his cast.

43   See the observation of Henry Danton, one of Helpmann's original cast, on this point in Chapter 10, p. 141 and also plate 31.

44   Kurt Jooss (1901-1979) founded his own School and Company with Sigurd Leeder, after working with Rudolf von Laban. Disliking abstract dance, he devised works that foregrounded moral and political issues; he deployed movement patterns from a range of sources, including classical ballet and German *Ausdruckstanz*, naturalistic gesture and unison work: the power lay in the stylistic fragmentation and juxtapositions. Fleeing Nazi Germany in 1933, Jooss and Leeder moved to the Netherlands before finally settling at Dartington College, Devon, until 1949 when he returned to Essen with his Company, where one of his notable students and performers was Pina Bausch.

45   Rudolf von Laban (1879-1958), one of the pioneers of modern dance and of movement analysis and notation, was a choreographer who developed the art of the movement choir, privileging always the group over the individual in accord with his political beliefs. In 1936 Goebbels banned Laban's *Vom Tauwind und der Neuen Freude* (Of the Spring Wind and the New Joy) as not sufficiently Nazi in its inspiration. After travelling first to Paris in 1937, Laban settled at Dartington with the Jooss Company, where he became a highly innovative theorist, exploring movement skills for actors, dancers and for the general workforce. Unlike his friends, Mary Wigman and Kurt Jooss, he is not survived by an important body of choreography but by over fifteen volumes of his writings exploring numerous perspectives on the mastery of movement. He was a seminal influence on countless German choreographers in the 1920s and

1930s, who styled themselves as practitioners of *Ausdruckstanz*, which is meant here by Helpmann's reference to the "Central European School".

46   The Company's first major season in London, which included performances of *The Green Table* and the later masterpiece, *Pandora*, was at the Haymarket Theatre in 1944 (they had performed at minor venues in London and at the Arts Theatre, Cambridge, from the time of their arrival in England in 1933).

47   De Valois was generally critical of the German School, especially of Wigman, but she wrote appreciatively of Kurt Jooss in *Invitation to the Ballet* (London: John Lane at the Bodley Head, 1937, pp. 178-180). Sir Peter Wright informed Richard Cave in August 2002 that de Valois had once confided in him that she had been considerably influenced in her composition of group movement in the Gambling and Brothel sequences in *The Rake's Progress* (1935) by the Boardroom Scenes from *The Green Table* (1932).

48   *The Green Table* is Jooss's masterpiece: composed in 1932 to music by Fritz Cohen and designs by Hein Heckroth; it is a frightening indictment of war and the impact of business interests in furthering such violence. It has been consistently revived world-wide, since Jooss's Company was disbanded in 1953.

49   Helpmann is referring here less to the symphonic ballets created by Léonide Massine (1896-1979) such as *Les Présages* (1933) or *Choreartium* (1933) than to his more popular works, *The Good-Humoured Ladies* (1917), *The Three-Cornered Hat*, (1919) and *La Boutique Fantasque* (1919).

50   Antony Tudor (1908-1987) was more associated with Marie Rambert's Company than with Sadler's Wells Ballet, and it was for them that he created his earliest dance works, the most enduring of which are *Jardin aux Lilas* (1936) and *Dark Elegies* (1937). In 1940 he emigrated to America where he joined Richard Pleasant and Lucia Chase's Ballet Theater, which later became American Ballet Theater, for whom he most notably created *Pillar of Fire* (1942). He was invited to The Royal Ballet in 1967 to choreograph, *Shadowplay*, as a showcase for the young Anthony Dowell.

51   *Jardin aux Lilas* (1936) does bear narrative resemblances to Ashton's *Nocturne*, composed the same year, since it is also concerned with disrupted attempts at intimacy, hints of sexual or emotional infidelity, and the loss of innocence at the hands of more worldly elders. The focus throughout is on the psychology of the four main characters trapped in a tragic vortex.

52   Tudor's version of *Romeo and Juliet* had first been staged in 1943, set to music by Delius. At the time of its performance at Covent Garden, de Valois' Company did not as yet own a production of what is a highly popular subject for ballet: MacMillan's version was not created for the Company till 1965, though Ashton had created a ballet based on Shakespeare's tragedy in 1955 for the Royal Danish Ballet. *Undertow* (1945), set to a commissioned score by William Schumann, anticipates the themes of many of MacMillan's ballets in being focused on the life-history of a figure called by Tudor, the Transgressor, who is caught in the sexual underworld of a big city and eventually commits murder in sheer desperation.

53   Michael Kidd (1915-2007) began his career in ballet, dancing with Lincoln

Kirstein's Ballet Caravan and Eugene Loring's Dance Players before joining American Ballet Theater, where his roles included one of the sailors in Jerome Robbins's *Fancy Free* (1944). Though *On Stage!* (1945) was much admired, Kidd abandoned ballet for Broadway and achieved further fame choreographing for filmed musicals, most notably *The Band Wagon* (1953) with Astaire and Charisse, *Seven Brides for Seven Brothers* (1954), *Hello Dolly!* (1969) with Streisand and Matthau, and *The Goodbye Girl* (1993) with Bernadette Peters.

54   Nora Kaye (1920-1987) excelled in dancing dramatic roles with American Ballet Theatre, which she joined in 1940. She created roles in a number of Tudor's works, including his Juliet and the repressed Hagar in *Pillar of Fire*; she also excelled as the haughty Russian Ballerina in his witty *Gala Performance* (1938) in which, when Tudor recreated it for ABT, she satirised her own impassioned stage persona. John Kriza (1919-1975) danced with American Ballet Theater from 1940 to 1966, originating roles by Balanchine, Massine, de Mille, Robbins and Tudor. He won success with the title role in a revival of Loring's *Billy the Kid*, the Pastor in de Mille's *Fall River Legend* (1948) and as the Champion roper in de Mille's earlier *Rodeo* (1942).

55   Jean-Georges Noverre (1727-1810) initiated the French *ballet d'action*, which privileged emotional truth in the characters being performed rather than scenic spectacle, as in the *ballets de cour* of the seventeenth century. His *Lettres sur la danse et les ballets* (1760) considerably influenced the evolution of the narrative ballets of the next century and revolutionised dance training, the proper education of the choreographer, and established the expressive priorities of a good dance performance.

56   In the sense that through narrative and movement, *Giselle* (1841) explores emotional betrayal, loss of innocence, madness, suicide and a journey to forgiveness and atonement.

57   *Pillar of Fire*, Tudor's stark one-act ballet of 1942 set to Schoenberg's *Transfigured Night*, examines the plight of Hagar, a woman surrounded by a judgemental rural community, who tries to find emotional and sexual fulfillment but becomes a victim of the sexist and macho men in the town.

58   *Petrushka* or *Petrouchka* was first performed by Diaghilev's Company in Paris in 1911. The cast included Nijinsky, Karsavina and Cecchetti. For further discussion of this ballet, see Chapter 3, p. 62 n. 14.

59   *Hamlet* opened at the New Theatre in 1942; *Miracle in the Gorbals* at the Prince's Theatre in 1944.

60   *Adam Zero* was first staged at Covent Garden in 1946.

61   At the time of writing this essay, this ballet – to be set to the music of John Anthill with designs by William Constable – was clearly for Helpmann a major project, but a six-month long period of illness and recovery meant that his plans had to be abandoned. Helpmann had responded to the indigenous native rhythms of Anthill's score and vividly recalled the dance gatherings (corroborees) he had seen in his childhood. He intended to study aboriginal dance forms recorded on film at Australia House in a pursuit of authenticity, much as he was later to do with Japanese music and dance in preparing his choreography for *Yugen*

(1965), which he created for Australian Ballet. Interestingly it was to Australian indigenous dance that Kenneth MacMillan turned when shaping his version of *The Rite of Spring* (1962), and his chosen designer was the Australian painter, Sidney Nolan.

62   First staged at the New Theatre in January 1942.

63   This ballet to Gluck's music and with designs by Sophie Fedorovich was first staged at the New Theatre in 1941. Helpmann and Pamela May danced the lovers; Margot Fonteyn appeared as Love and Mary Honer as the Leader of the Furies. De Valois' notebooks in which particularly she designed the groupings of the Furies as they assail Orpheus are to be found in The Royal Ballet School Collections.

64   Francis John Hart (1921-2015), a pupil of Judith Espinosa, joined the Vic-Wells Ballet in 1938 and rapidly graduated to dancing major roles, including (before he was called up in 1942) one of the young swells in "Popular Song" in Ashton's *Façade* (1940), Monsieur Vestris in de Valois' *The Prospect Before Us* (1940), one of the Brothers in Helpmann's *Comus* (1941) and, for the initial run of performances, Laertes (1942). After 1946 he returned to the Company as a Principal (until 1955), Ballet Master (until 1962) and then Assistant Director of The Royal Ballet (1962-1970). Subsequently he was Director of several American companies and of PACT Ballet, Johannesburg, before becoming Artistic Director of Ballet-West, Utah (1985-1997).

65   The only factor that the two ballets have in common is the decision to shape the narrative around the life and death of an Everyman figure. Helpmann is right to ridicule attempts to draw influences where clearly none exist.

66   Arnold Lionel Haskell (1903-1980), was one of the foremost dance critics of his day, co-founder of the Camargo Society (1930), and a strong supporter of de Valois' ambitions for dance in England, eventually becoming the first appointed Director of the Royal Ballet School (1947-1965). He published over twenty books about ballet, focusing chiefly on the Diaghilev and de Basil companies, the Vic-Wells Ballet, and his own reflections as a ballet theorist and historian.

67   Joan Lawson (1907-2002) studied with Margaret Morris and Serafina Astafieva and danced with a range of companies before teaching at The Royal Ballet School (1963-1971). Her publications address a range of fields: folk dance, theory and technique in classical ballet, the history of ballet, and the importance of a knowledge of anatomy in achieving good technique, which clearly drew on her practice as a teacher.

68   Audrey Williamson (1913-1986) possessed a prodigious range of critical and scholarly interests and her published output was prolific, but always she wrote with precision as well as passion, being gifted with a remarkable memory for what she had seen in the theatre and the ability to evoke it for readers succinctly. While she wrote on Wagner, Shaw and Gilbert and Sullivan in performance, her principal theme was the state of contemporary theatre, which included dance and opera. She was a respected historian of the Old Vic Theatre and its companies and of the Vic-Wells Ballet, and was always in demand for

articles and reviews about their achievements, which she placed firmly in the cultural contexts of the decades (1920s to 1950s) when she was most active. *Contemporary Ballet* was published by Rockliff in 1946.

69   This is an accurate prediction, as the works of John Cranko, Kenneth MacMillan, David Bintley and latterly Christopher Wheeldon and Liam Scarlett have shown.

70   The form of the court masque was perfected as a type of theatrical entertainment during the reigns of James I and Charles I. The style followed Italian and French models in giving importance to scenic spectacle (usually created by Inigo Jones). Writers like Ben Jonson sought to shape the proceedings to give moral and political depth to the extravagant display of sumptuous costumes, scenery and special lighting effects and to synthesise the contributing elements of song, poetry, narrative and dancing. The climax of a masque generally featured extended choreographic performances, designed by such dancing teachers to the aristocracy as Robert Johnson, Thomas Giles, Nicholas Confesse or Jeremy Herne. Many masques followed a narrative journey or quest, which led to new understanding or some form of enlightenment, invariably reflecting on the beneficence of the presiding monarch. Many features of the masque were in time incorporated into pantomime, which also made space for extensive danced contributions within the development of the plot.

71   This talk was printed in *The Listener* within the section entitled, "Did You Hear That?" which was a means of including in the magazine a number of shortened versions of recently broadcast lectures. Helpmann had originally given the talk for the BBC Forces Educational Programme on 19 June 1948, but it was repeated on BBC Radio Home Service on 1 April 1949. It might seem an odd choice to reprint in this collection of Helpmann's essays and articles, since to any trained dancer the content (the structure of ballet classes, a typical day in the life of a ballet company, the progress from member of the *corps* to Principal, the relentless call on one's energies and stamina) is all too familiar. But it is a good example of Helpmann's ability to talk in a straightforward manner about specialised experience to an audience unfamiliar with the behind-the-scene routines of theatre life. The style is neither elitist nor patronising, while still being frank and personal. In the same vein Helpmann contributed the narration to accompany the film, *Steps of the Ballet* (1948), designed to explain how a ballet is choreographed. It is good too (and typical of the man) that he stresses the sheer grit and tenacity that lie behind the seductively illusory world that dancers create onstage. That Helpmann's initial audience of listeners were members of the Armed Forces is culturally significant: de Valois had agreed to the Company performing for ENSA in the aftermath of the War and had won enthusiastic new audiences for ballet as a consequence, so discussion of issues concerning ballet had a rightful place in the Forces Educational Programme. The whole tenor of the piece is indicative of the man who had created *Miracle in the Gorbals* (1944) and *Adam Zero* (1946), directly out of his own and Michael Benthall's experience of the war years and the bombed landscapes of post-war Europe.

72   It still remains possible for boys to begin their classical ballet training slightly later than girls, although this difference is continually being eroded, as the demands of extreme flexibility (and even the ability to work on pointe) are increasingly being made of both genders, requiring systematic training to begin for boys and girls at nine or ten, the age which Helpmann identifies. Interestingly, his comment about encouraging 'free and spontaneous' movement from the age of 'six or even earlier' still resonates with current thinking.

73   It is worth noting that best teaching practice continued the trend identified in Helpmann's article, eventually delaying the normal introduction of dancing on pointe to around twelve years of age. 'Pointe work' is now the usual spelling.

74   Daily class in a professional company is now usually up to 90 minutes long, and many dancers will have completed an aerobic workout, Pilates session, or other targeted fitness programme, before class begins.

75   While this remains the case in some instances, generally the lines separating physical and stylistic types of dancer have become less marked: body shapes have become more uniform across both genders, and the height of a dancer is no obstacle to the repertoire they might be expected to perform. It is possible to argue that this has led to a loss of stylistic contrast, which greatly enriched the ballet at the time Helpmann was writing. Ironically, Helpmann himself was notable for breaking the boundaries between the 'classical and the character' that he describes in his article, excelling as both a *danseur noble* and character performer.

76   The article was accompanied by three photographs. Valerie Adams is seen with the two designers, the brothers Robin and Christopher Ironside; she is in costume as the chief dancing fairy and holds a sketch of their costume design for her. The second shows a page of designs for Theseus's courtiers. The third is a group shot of Helpmann with Moira Shearer, who played Titania, and Michael Benthall, the director. Helpmann both played Oberon and devised most of the choreography. A month after Helpmann's article appeared, a second two-page spread featuring four photographs was published in *Theatre Arts Monthly* (November 1954, pp.14-15) showing Shearer as Titania; Helpmann and Shearer with the corps de ballet; Helpmann in close-up as Oberon, revealing his make-up and headdress; and a group shot of Philip Locke (Flute), Philip Guard (Puck), and Norman Rossington (Snout). An accompanying caption tells the history of the production: how it premièred at the Edinburgh Festival (31 August to 11 September) before a season at the Metropolitan Opera House in New York and a tour to eleven cities, ending in Montreal on 19 December. The tour is described as "presented by Sol Hurok" in collaboration with the trustees of the Old Vic, London.

77   Felix Mendelssohn Bartholdy (1809-1847) composed his music for *A Midsummer Night's Dream* over two separate periods: the concert overture was completed in 1826, while his incidental music, commissioned by King Frederick William IV of Prussia for a production of the play, staged at Potsdam, followed in 1842. The complex score, into which the existing overture was incorporated, includes songs and choral passages, intermezzi, melodramas and extended

instrumental movements (a scherzo, nocturne and the famous wedding march).

78   For a detailed account of this production, see Richard Allen Cave's essay in this volume, "The actor, Robert Helpmann: voice, text and theatrical intelligence", pp. 66-86 and plates 10 and 11.

79   Tyrone Guthrie (1900-1971) had directed for a year at the Festival Theatre Cambridge under the aegis of Anmer Hall and Ninette de Valois' cousin, Terence Gray, before joining Lilian Baylis's Old Vic from 1933 to 1939, staging a particularly impressive *Hamlet* with Laurence Olivier in the title role that was subsequently mounted at Elsinore. He with Michael Benthall mentored Helpmann's career as an actor in its earliest years (he directed him as both Oberon and Hamlet) and he offered pithy advice over the shaping of Helpmann's balletic version of *Hamlet* (1942). In his later years Guthrie found time to maintain a hectic directorial schedule while also promoting the cause of thrust stages, inspiring the creation of auditoria at Stratford Ontario, the Chichester Festival Theatre, Sheffield Crucible, and the Guthrie Theatre at Minneapolis.

80   For a detailed discussion of the private and working partnership of Helpmann with Michael Benthall, see Jann Parry's essay in this volume, "The creative partnership of Michael Benthall and Robert Helpmann", pp. 102-112.

81   Helpmann has misremembered the date: 1948 was the year he acted at the Shakespeare Memorial Theatre; Benthall's production of *A Midsummer Night's Dream*, which "presented its fairies as a corps de ballet", was staged in 1949 (RSC website: "Productions 1920-2008: a selection of our productions of *A Midsummer Night's Dream* listed by year and director").

82   *La Sylphide*, a two-act romantic ballet, was created first by Filippo Taglioni in 1832 and subsequently by August Bournonville in 1836, using the same scenario but different music; it tells of a sylph's passion for a Scottish farmer and its tragic consequences. Famously Marie Taglioni, who created the role of the Sylph in her father's version, shortened her skirt to three-quarter length to show off her exquisite pointe work. Made of diaphanous material, it gave the illusion of her floating. Is Helpmann by omitting the article deliberately eliding this ballet with Fokine's *Les Sylphides* (1909), a homage to *les ballets blancs*, set to Chopin's music, that depicts a group of sylphs dancing in a woodland glade by moonlight with a poet whom they inspire as muses? Neither version of *La Sylphide* was as well known in England or America at this date as Fokine's work for Diaghilev's Company. Helpmann himself had regularly performed the role of the Poet with the Vic-Wells Ballet after 1934.

83   *Giselle* is the epitome of Romanticism: its narrative explores the plight of a betrayed girl, who after her death is assimilated into a world of vengeful female ghosts pledged to dance men to their deaths, but who saves her repentant lover from that fate. The librettists, St Georges and Gautier, took their inspiration for the scenario in part from poems by Heine and Hugo. The choreography was by Jules Perrot and Jean Coralli to music by Adolphe Adam. The entire second act, which takes place in a moonlit woodland in the vicinity of Giselle's grave, was conceived as a *ballet blanc*. Helpmann first danced the role of Hilarion with the Vic-Wells Ballet in January 1934, but within ten months had assumed the

male lead, Albrecht, which he danced with most of the Company's Principals, including Fonteyn.

84   "Point" is how Helpmann spells the word throughout this and the previous essay; more conventionally nowadays the preferred spelling is "pointe", which has been observed in the annotations.

85   The use of the article here confines the reference explicitly to the Taglioni/ Bournonville ballet (see note 82 above).

86   Moira Shearer (1926-2006), after dancing with Mona Inglesby's Company, had joined Sadler's Wells Ballet in 1941, becoming a Principal in 1944. She took leave of absence from de Valois' Company in 1948 to star with Helpmann in the films, *The Red Shoes* and *The Tales of Hoffmann*. Though she had largely retired from ballet in 1953, she was persuaded to head the cast of *A Midsummer Night's Dream*, because it offered her the chance to develop her potential as an actress.

87   It is a pity that no vestige of Frederick Ashton's choreography for this production has survived, since it would be valuable to detect how much of this *pas de deux* stayed in his memory and influenced what he subsequently composed in 1964 for the Nocturne in his ballet, *The Dream*, which with his designers, Henry Bardon and David Walker, he notably chose to set in the 1840s, as had Benthall in his production.

88   Too often modern productions of Shakespeare's comedy tend to move on rapidly away from Oberon's calling for a dance, once he has removed the illusion that has clouded Titania's perceptions and she has registered with horror the sleeping figure of Bottom nearby. But the dance is the means Oberon deploys to entice Titania to renew their emotional amity and their marriage. Though a piece of stage business unaccompanied by dialogue, it marks the climax of their part in the play's action. Benthall, Helpmann and Ashton were right to give the sequence due weight with the creation of this extended duet.

89   Robin Ironside (1912-1965) and his brother, Christopher (1913-1992) led independent careers in fine and applied art but collaborated in designing this production for Benthall and later Ashton's second full-length ballet, *Sylvia* (1952) for Sadler's Wells Ballet, which they described as in the style of Arcadian rococo.

90   This essay was "specially written" by Helpmann, rather than being an article developed from an interview; it was published during his tour of Australia with Katharine Hepburn and the Old Vic Drama Company in 1955. The tour marked Helpmann's first visit to Australia since he left his native country in December, 1932. (Spelling and some punctuation have been regularised; paragraphing has been altered to avoid the journalistic format of breaking up extended prose into numerous short sections; passages in italics in the original have been reproduced.)

91   The Borovansky Ballet had been initially founded by Edouard Borovansky (1902-1959) in the early 1940s, financially backed after 1942 by J.C. Williamson Theatres Ltd.; the Company disbanded in 1948 but reformed in 1951, when their repertoire came steadily to include classics such as a complete *Sleeping Princess* and works by Fokine, Massine, and Cranko together with Lichine's staging of

The Nutcracker. After Borovansky's death, the Company, under their newly appointed Artistic Director, Peggy van Praagh (1910-1990), formed the basis in 1962 of the Australian Ballet. The Australian Elizabethan Theatre Trust was established in 1954 with the aim of establishing orchestras, theatre, opera and ballet companies nationally. One of its most enduring ventures was the founding with J.C. Williamson Theatres Ltd. (a company that Elizabeth Schafer describes as "ruling Australian theatre for decades") of Australian Ballet in 1962, which van Praagh directed (1962-74) and co-directed with Robert Helpmann (1965-74). Helpmann then became sole director till 1976.

92   Joan Hammond (1912-1996) was a renowned opera singer with an immense repertoire and a gift for popularising operatic song; after her retirement, she became a gifted teacher. Eileen Joyce (1908-1991) was a brilliant concert pianist, famed for her remarkable stamina, playing over fifty concerts a year in London at the height of her career and what were popularly known as her "marathon concerts", when with great bravura she would play as many as four concertos in a single evening. Leo McKern (1920-2002) was an accomplished actor who appeared at the Old Vic and the Shakespeare Memorial Theatre, Stratford-upon-Avon before moving chiefly to televised drama for his later years, when he achieved particular fame in *Rumpole of the Old Bailey*. Nelly Melba (1861-1931) was the first Australian to achieve international recognition as an operatic soprano: her lyrical range covered Italian and French grand opera, works by Verdi and Gounod being particular favourites. Sylvia Fisher (1910-1996) was another powerful operatic soprano, specialising in Wagner (she was a notable Isolde at Covent Garden in 1952) and Strauss (her Marschallin in *Der Rosenkavalier* was considered exemplary); one of her last roles at the Royal Opera House was as Miss Wingrave in Britten's *Owen Wingrave* (1971). Peter Finch (1916-1977) was an English-born Australian actor, mentored initially for the theatre by Laurence Olivier, who eventually achieved his greatest successes as the romantic lead in numerous films but graduated effortlessly into playing middle-aged men who were amorous failures such as Boldwood in *Far from the Madding Crowd* (1967) and the ageing gay lover, Daniel Hirsh, in *Sunday Bloody Sunday* (1971), both directed by John Schlesinger.

93   This was not the case when Ray Lawler's *Summer of the Seventeenth Doll* toured to England in 1957 with many of the original Australian cast and featuring Lawler in the central role of Barney (Ibbot); the play had opened at the Union Theatre, Melbourne in 1955.

94   The italics are Helpmann's own. Eleanor Fitzpatrick, Archives and Records Manager at the Royal Academy of Dance, has been unable to confirm if Helpmann took an RAD examination because only successful results were published. She also points out that the first RAD examinations in Australia were in 1935, when Helpmann had already left.

The Many Faces of Robert Helpmann: theatrical make-up and 'make-believe'

Anna Meadmore

> Helpmann has an unusual and sensitive face, with the play of nerves, as in so many fine actors, perceptibly near the surface, and his command of make-up and acting (for the first is useless unless animated by feeling from *within*) ranges from the romantic to the farcical and daemonic.[1]

Robert Helpmann's dexterity, application and attention to detail were evident in every aspect of his stagecraft: during a career spanning six decades[2] he attempted, and usually mastered, an astonishing range of theatrical genres and techniques. A constant factor was his skilled and deliberate use of stage make-up, a tool of his trade that had fascinated him since childhood. His mother, Mary Helpman, recalled that during their frequent excursions to the theatre in Adelaide, young Robert "seized any opportunity of getting to know stage people and of talking to them about make-up. Many [...] let him come into their dressing-rooms and liking his youthful eagerness good naturedly explained the technique." The result, she asserted, was that from the outset of his professional career, he was "ready to make-up for any part", and that he "went on experimenting until he had few rivals in the art".[3]

Numerous accounts remark upon Helpmann's distinctive physiognomy, and describe his apparent ability to manipulate his features, using both make-up and facial expression, to create a veritable gallery of highly contrasting and wholly convincing characterisations. In an essay written in 1946, entitled 'Make-up and Character in Ballet', Audrey Williamson observed:

> In his early ballet appearances [Helpmann's] small and curiously medieval face, with its expressive but unnaturally round eyes and parted lips, gave all his stage characters an individual and Puckish quality, charming but immature. Later he learned to lengthen the eyes, to give a firmer and graver contour to the mouth, with the result that in romantic parts the whole face has taken on a character and dignity. This is of course due in some part to increased maturity, and like everything else where an actor's work is concerned make-up is only half the battle [...]. "The only real secret," in Helpmann's own words, "is *sincerity*."[4]

In thus concluding her essay, and allowing Helpmann those vital last words, Williamson was careful to dispel any suggestion that he *relied* on make-up to define a role. Similarly, Kathrine Sorley Walker[5] would insist that Helpmann's portrayals of key character roles within the ballet repertoire "contributed real people with depth and background behind the surface portrait, and added to their memorability by apt and effective make-up. It was easy to fill in the daily life [...of such characters], and discover a person conceived in the round."[6]

Significantly, Helpmann implied that he sought to shed his own personality in performance:

> The person who hasn't a large slice of make-believe in his character would never go on the stage. Now don't misunderstand me. There's no room for make-believe in being a ballet dancer – it's sheer hard work. I'm speaking of acting, of make-believe in its most subtle and creative form. [...] This element of make-believe is essential to actors because for them there is no set technique. Everyone has different ways of reaching the particular emotional pitch he feels he needs. If he lacks the capacity to shed his own personality in favour of the character he's playing, he'll have a thin time of it.[7]

One can only draw the conclusion that Helpmann regarded the ability to make-believe – his imagination – as a profound source of his own theatrical creativity. This may provide the most direct clue to understanding the unprecedented variety of the many faces he created at different times and in various contexts: quite simply, he inhabited his roles, and he employed both technical skills and theatrical imagination to bring about these transformations. Arnold Haskell observed that, because Helpmann was so "perfectly disciplined", his strong personality remained contained within "the framework of [a] ballet as a whole", adding further: "His range is enormous: classical, romantic, broad farce or subtle comedy. [...] The essence of Helpmann's work is his extraordinary intelligence and the fact that he is a born 'theatre man'."[8] Sorley Walker believed that Helpmann's endless creativity and invention were key: "He always came to a performance with a fresh approach. However bored he might be at the thought of yet another *Coppélia* or *Façade*, when he stepped on stage in costume and make-up (and he was a supreme make-up artist) histrionic impulses began to circulate in his veins, and audiences responded with keen enjoyment."[9]

In the Foreword to his book of photographs, *Studies of Robert Helpmann* (1946), Gordon Anthony admitted: "It is frankly almost impossible to do justice to his 'genre' by use of the camera alone, particularly as balletic 'make-up' bears a certain similarity whatever the role depicted. However

[...] Helpmann's own force of characterisation counteracts that to a very great extent." Anthony pointed to his photographs of Helpmann's wartime appearances in West End revue,[10] which captured his impersonations of two *grandes dames* of the theatre, Margaret Rawlings and Margaret Rutherford, "where the very minimum of make-up is used, yet an uncanny likeness is attained in both cases".[11] (See plates 14 and 15) Sorley Walker tells us more about these performances: "He wore a neat lounge suit and used only a hat, a wig or a boa to support his characterisation."[12] The wig for 'Miss Rutherford' was particularly voluminous, forming a dominant part of Helpmann's make-up ensemble; less obviously, the tousled fringe emerging from the hat of 'Miss Rawlings' was a fine example of a little detail going a very long way. It is worth noting that Helpmann often had to rush over and join the revue after a ballet performance at Sadler's Wells, so in this case, his minimal approach to make-up may well have been determined by practical necessity.

In other instances, according to the dance critic Mary Clarke, Helpmann sometimes "wore enough make-up to sink a battleship!"[13] She recalled with affection and pleasure his memorable cameo as the Bishop of Ely in Laurence Olivier's film *Henry V* (1944), on which *Picturegoer* magazine reported: "He [...] was so well made up that many filmgoers did not recognise the young face of Robert Helpmann."[14] In similar vein, the actor, Paul Scofield, with whom Helpmann shared a dressing room at the Shakespeare Memorial Theatre, Stratford-upon-Avon in 1948, remarked on Helpmann's unusually vivid make-up. They appeared together in Shakespeare's *King John*, with Scofield playing the King of France, and Helpmann in the title role: Scofield remembered his co-star as "a 'baleful' King John 'in full chrome make-up'".[15] However, one reviewer described Helpmann's King John as a "pale, evil-purposed, red-haired fox with minatory hands",[16] which indicates it may have been the colour of the wig which so impressed itself on Scofield's memory; or simply, that the make-up appeared heavy off-stage, but paled considerably under stage lighting. That season, Helpmann and Scofield also alternated in the title role of Hamlet. According to Williamson, "Helpmann's make-up in *Hamlet* the play, [was] a purely realistic conception in which eyes, lips and skin were only very lightly touched up."[17] (See plates 37-39)

What Scofield distinctly recalled of Helpmann's Hamlet was his physical deftness, relating that "on the couplet, 'The play's the thing/Wherein I'll catch the conscience of the king,' Helpmann, with a perfect throw, unerringly pierced the stage floor with his dagger where it stuck quivering in the wood. Scofield, following suit, could never get it right. It slithered, bounced, skidded, but never went in clean".[18] Helpmann's attributes as an actor went more than skin deep, and Scofield was among many who recognised and admired the highly practised physical articulation and control that lay at the core of his performances.

Other important facets of Helpmann's characterisations remain less tangible, because they sprang from his irrepressible personality and wit. His "monkey tricks" gave rise to innumerable anecdotes, much relished at the time.[19] Scofield described "Bobby" as "one of the funniest men I have known, and our preparations of these plays were enlivened by his caustic observations, his imitations of actors, and his infectious ribaldry".[20] It is interesting that Julie Kavanagh, when pointing out how "the characters of the dancers helped to define their roles" in the ballets of Frederick Ashton, cites Helpmann's created role of the Bridegroom in *A Wedding Bouquet* (1937).[21] This, she says, gave Helpmann his first real "opportunity to be funny on stage. Those who remember his performance insist that he really was outrageously amusing, delighting the audience, and making the dancers 'corpse' helplessly with his antics and hissed verbal asides, while maintaining an illusion of deadpan decorum."[22]

There had been an earlier, less successful, role created for Helpmann in Ashton's *Façade*, originally made for the Camargo Society in 1931, and taken into the Vic-Wells repertoire in 1935.[23] For this revival, Ashton inserted a new Country Dance featuring Helpmann as "the wicked Squire who exercises his *droit de seigneur* and lures the Maiden [Pearl Argyle] away from the Yokel [Richard Ellis]". According to David Vaughan, the role of the Squire "was intended to exploit Helpmann's talent for comedy, but in spite of some droll by-play with a shooting-stick, the number was only mildly funny".[24] Mary Clarke thought Helpmann "hilarious" in his deerstalker hat, worn with matching plus fours,[25] but the number was eventually dropped, and only when he took on Ashton's own created role of the Tango-dancing "Dago" in 1939, did Helpmann fully come into his own in *Façade*. Photographs and written accounts reveal that, while Ashton's Dago was a smooth character, sporting a finely painted moustache and sideburns, Helpmann's man somehow appeared altogether sleazier, although his make-up hardly differed from Ashton's. Sorley Walker associated Helpmann's enormous success in the part with his "inventive and perfectly timed comedy," which gave "delight to countless audiences over the years".[26] She quoted Clement Crisp's review of a Royal Opera House "Tribute to Margot Fonteyn", marking the great ballerina's sixtieth birthday in 1979, at which she and Helpmann – then aged seventy – closed the show with a reprisal of their former roles: "*Façade* – with the bonus of Sir Robert Helpmann back in the black velvet, hair-oil and curlicues of the Dago. [...] Dame Margot was as zany and faintly amazed by it all as ever; Sir Robert even more luxuriant in [diamond] rings and rolling eyes."[27]

Both as the roué Bridegroom and the disreputable Dago, Helpmann's hair was slickly brilliantined in what immediately became his trademark fashion at the Vic-Wells Ballet. Helpmann loved to tell the story of Lilian Baylis pointing out to Ninette de Valois that she could not take her eyes off him in the *corps de ballet* because he had "too much grease on his hair", to which de Valois had replied, "I think that that is his idea."[28] De Valois' own account of the conversation attributes a less than flattering comment to Baylis, which is noteworthy in the context of this essay: "I like the boy, dear, who puts too much brilliantine on his hair; do stop him, his head's rather large anyway, and it makes one keep looking at him."[29] It was not just Helpmann's face, but his whole eye-catching head, which in de Valois' words, "collected his public from stalls to gallery".[30] Mary Helpman related that Robert had gone to great lengths as a small boy to train his hair into the style he wanted: "He cut off the top of one of my stockings, tied the cut end, and after plastering his hair with water, pulled on the tight stocking. [...] [H]e wore it after school, and all night for weeks, till he was satisfied with his smooth shining head, which he plastered well every day with brilliantine."[31] Hair and wigs are fundamental to full stage make-up, and it is no surprise to learn that Helpmann had been mindful of his hairstyle all his life; although it does seem remarkable that he set out to 'construct' his appearance from such an early age.

It is important to consider the way in which Helpmann's exuberant humour was expressed through his use of make-up. The comic characters devised by Robert Helpmann are among his most legendary creations. Caryl Brahms wrote that the role of Doctor Coppélius was "foremost among them", claiming that: "Helpmann has taken the fustian doll-maker and touched him to veritable life [...] impish at its ebb, vitalised by spite, warmed by rage – a cranky, creviced, spell-spun life, which has been lying in the old work waiting for Helpmann to discover it. [...] And incidentally this is one of Helpmann's masterpieces of make-up."[32] With his narrow face elongated by a thin, down-turned mouth and bulging eyes, exaggerated by bushy tufts of hair on either side of his balding head, Helpmann as Coppélius set a new benchmark for the role; indeed, Sorley Walker stated that his endless invention in the part over many years meant that "dancers are [still] reproducing ideas of his in the belief that they are part of that role's choreography".[33] (See plate 20)

If the most enduring of his early comic roles was that of Dr Coppélius, the most endearing was surely his Mr O'Reilly.[34] (See plates 16-19) Clearly a dipsomaniac, with dark circles beneath his eyes, a tell-tale ruddy nose, a bedraggled fringe and unruly tuft of hair which refused to lie flat, Helpmann made him up like a traditional clown, investing him with a clown's pathos and sweetness. Brahms asserted that: "Once again his virtuosity in make-up plays a major part in his realisation [and] Helpmann has created a characterisation that ranks with Massine's [best known roles]".[35] De Valois acknowledged: "In *The Prospect Before Us* I created in Mr O'Reilly a role that was deliberately inspired by Helpmann. He has made of this fantastic Rowlandson figure an endearing and entrancing character study of a balletic clown – culminating in the now famous inebriated dance that will have to be buried with its first and only performer."[36] (See plate 18) Williamson had watched Helpmann applying his make-up for these and other parts at first hand, and her observations are worth quoting at length:

> Helpmann as Mr O'Reilly and Dr Coppélius [...] favours the clown touch [...] its partial derivative being the Harlequinade make-up of the Grimaldi tradition.[37] The green half-moons under the eyes combine with the red nose and thin slit of mouth, curving upwards or downwards at will, to give Mr O'Reilly a watery drunken cheerfulness or glumness, and in Dr Coppélius one senses throughout, in the gait and pucker of the mouth, a real old man beneath the caricature. The basic make-up before the caricature is added is, indeed, that of a realistic ancient, shrivelled and yellow of skin, and the transformation from nonagenarian to clown is fascinating to watch.

> Helpmann's face is naturally plastic and transformable and falls easily into the lines of Dr Coppélius, which make-up, though it looks so much more elaborate, is in fact much quicker to complete than that of Hamlet,[38] where the eyelashes have to be painstakingly applied with "hot-black," the skin given a cream-like smoothness and the curve of lips and eyebrows drawn with extreme care. Out of the theatre lights this make-up, with its buff-coloured basis, violet eyelids and vermilion mouth, has a fantastic beauty.[39]

There are two points here which remind us of the particular skills required to apply stage make-up at the time: the first is Helpmann's use of lurid colour, which appeared so strange outside the powerful stage 'up-lighting' of the period, but was designed to give his eyes and mouth clear definition once he was under those lights. The second mentions "hot-black", usually heated over a candle before being used to build up the eyelashes one by one. Williamson also observed that Helpmann found the make-up for Coppélius easier to achieve than that for the classical role of Hamlet, hinting that his features and personality lent themselves more naturally to humour. His face was delicate, with a high forehead and finely-shaped chin; his most outstanding features being his large, slightly protruding eyes, while his nose and mouth were well-defined, but unremarkable – the perfect blank canvas.

Another element of Helpmann's outstanding success in comic roles can be found in what de Valois called his "complete lack of theatrical snobbery".

She explained: "I have seen him on tour rush from the last act of a full-length classical ballet to get to the second house of the local music-hall. For what? To worship at the shrine of some skilful music-hall comedian." Helpmann's professionalism, she notes, is his "by studied application".[40] De Valois had good reason to recognise the true source of Helpmann's talent as sheer hard work and a studied attention to detail. His first created role was in her ballet, *The Haunted Ballroom* (1934), made a year after Helpmann joined the Vic-Wells Ballet in March 1933. Sorley Walker offers the telling note that: "Even before *The Haunted Ballroom*, he knew the great American actors Alfred Lunt and Lynn Fontanne, and Lunt had advised him on make-up for the Master of Treginnis."[41] From his earliest days in England, therefore, Helpmann had continued his long-established practice of self-improvement, actively seeking advice in all areas of his craft from talented friends and fellow professionals.

Helpmann certainly set out to make the most of the opportunity given him by de Valois, describing his new role as, "a part after my own heart, for it is splendidly dramatic".[42] *The Haunted Ballroom* was a popular addition to the Vic-Wells repertoire, a gothic horror ballet, with Helpmann's portrait of a haunted man driven to his death at the centre of the piece. Cyril Beaumont recorded that "Robert Helpmann as the Master of Tregennis (sic) dominates the ballet throughout [...] he is possessed of a real dramatic sense and appreciation of character [...] which lives in the memory."[43] Photographs of Helpmann in the role[44] reveal that the make-up for his eyes and lips was minimal, but that he used a very pale foundation, giving his face a drawn look by vertical shading, and deep circles beneath his eyes. His hair was made to seem both wild and distinguished, mirroring the state of his distraught character; it was swept back from his face, with white streaks echoing the pallor of his skin. Intriguingly, the photographs show that Helpmann's nails were rather long, and filed to a finely rounded point, a level of detail that – if deliberate – seems extraordinary, and may conceivably have been inspired by contemporary horror films.[45]

In the more "stylised and restrained drama"[46] of an earlier de Valois ballet, *Job* (1931),[47] Helpmann had taken over Anton Dolin's created role of Satan, just six months after joining the Vic-Wells Ballet in 1933. It was to become his most familiar daemonic incarnation onstage,[48] prompting de Valois herself to write: "Other dancers may make good in this role, but Helpmann's study is to me the completely intelligent and sincere rendering."[49] Williamson noted how the "muscles of the limbs and body, to give the superhuman effect of Blake's biblical illustrations, are emphasised with greasepaint".[50] Because we can consult the works of Blake, we can deduce the colours – oranges, greens and greys – of the greasepaint used. The body make-up was integral to the design of the work and was equally a feature of Dolin's Satan,[51] but Williamson claims that Helpmann superseded its surface effect, achieving "a sense of evil [...] which seems actually to add to his physical stature: much as the great little actor [Edmund] Kean [...] gave the impression of a far bigger man by sheer power of suggestion".[52] (See plate 2)

Another major role in a de Valois ballet, which became identified with Helpmann in the minds of both the choreographer and the public, was that of the title role in *The Rake's Progress* (1935),[53] based on the series of paintings by William Hogarth. (See plate 3) Once again, Williamson wrote about the process behind Helpmann's make-up for the role, highlighting it as being fundamental to his concept for the part:

> Helpmann has said that before attempting his characterisation of the Rake he studied the faces in Hogarth's original pictures with a magnifying glass, which may explain why his skin in the Lunatic scene has the effect of the pigmentation, that faint iridescent blend of amethyst and green, in a portrait in oils. His whole make-up scheme in *The Rake's Progress* combines with his acting to reveal the gradual degeneration of the character. Already in the Orgy scene the lines of the face are beginning to sag in dissipation, and there are ugly bags under the eyes. [By the final scene] the eyes have become raw-rimmed and lashless and the face [...] seems the more poignant for the sinister, bleeding gash in the cheek.[54]

Williamson's highly descriptive accounts are unusual because they consider the specific use of make-up; most of our knowledge of the make-ups for Helpmann's many theatrical guises relies on contemporary photographic studies. A prolific generation of theatre and society photographers have left us with a rich record to consult: J. W. Debenham, Edward Mandinian, Angus McBean, Baron, Merlyn Severn, Russell Sedgwick and Gordon Anthony[55] dominate the list of those whose stunning work enables us to see the ways in which Helpmann created a strikingly individual aesthetic for each of his roles. The obvious caveat is that nearly all the photographic prints from the 1930s and '40s are black and white, and in spite of their tonal subtlety, a huge amount of critical information about Helpmann's use of colour in make-up is simply not available.

There are a few tantalising exceptions, including one of Helpmann's most celebrated forays into the dramatic theatre, when he appeared as Oberon in Shakespeare's *A Midsummer Night's Dream* at the Old Vic in 1937. This hugely successful production was directed by Tyrone Guthrie, and designed by Oliver Messel (who later made a colourful painting of the beautiful *mis-en-scène*, based on a photograph by Gordon Anthony). It is evident that make-up was fundamental to the creation of Helpmann's Oberon: almost as exquisite as his Titania – played by Vivien Leigh – Oberon's cheeks were highlighted in shades of green, with lines resembling fronds of unfurling bracken picked out in glittering colour. (See plate 10) Mary Helpman told the story of the famous occasion when the young Princesses, Elizabeth and Margaret, were taken to see a matinée of the production: "During the interval Vivien and Bob were taken to the Royal Box to be presented to Her Majesty [Queen Elizabeth, the Queen Mother]. As they talked Princess Margaret whispered to her mother and the Queen told him she had asked about green sequins he had stuck on his eye lids. He explained that they were kept in place with glue."[56]

Five years later, in 1942, Helpmann was to work again with the designer, Oliver Messel, on *Comus*, his first major choreography for the re-named Sadler's Wells Ballet, which took the unusual form of a Masque. Not only was this a patriotic celebration of English literature and theatre history made in the depths of World War II,[57] but it also affirmed Helpmann's personal interest in the broad theatrical tradition of his adopted (and ancestral) country. We have seen how this interest manifested itself in the Grimaldi-inspired make-up for his comic characters; indeed, Margot Fonteyn was even to suggest: "One can imagine Grimaldi's spirit in the wings of his beloved Sadler's Wells Theatre observing Helpmann with a paternally approving smile."[58] In an essay on choreography, which Helpmann wrote in 1949, he asserted that: "British Ballet will continue to develop on lines of the dance-drama [...]. It has become a part of English theatrical tradition and has never quite lost sight of its ancestor, the dramatic Masque."[59] Helpmann's first work for the Company impressed the critic Caryl Brahms, who noted: "Comus speaks. [...] He speaks Milton's lines upon the stage. And speaks them beautifully." Brahms continued that the ballet "achieves an effective statement in movement [...those words] that are spoken add to the intensity with which the Masque is enacted".[60]

That "intensity" was brought about by multiple layers of content – something de Valois identified as "Helpmann's remarkable capacity for producing unity of purpose".[61] In *Comus*, he brought together music and voice, movement and poetry: "Both speeches are spoken by Helpmann with authentic fire and music and his superb insolence, like an evil flame, holds the stage."[62] Strong characterisation and drama were heightened by Messel's designs, to which Helpmann's elaborate make-up for the central role made a highly distinctive contribution. His Comus was described by the *Dancing Times* as "diabolical and wanton",[63] his face framed by a Bacchanalian headdress made up of vine leaves and grapes – the colours probably greens and purples. The make-up lines of his eyebrows curled like tendrils,[64] then swept upwards with a flourish, while his lips were shaped to appear decadently overripe – one imagines a wine-stained colour. There is also a glossy finish to the lips evident in some photographs, creating a lascivious effect.[65] (See plate 21) Writing in 1947, P.W. Manchester declared that Helpmann's gifts as a "character mime" were "truly great by the highest standards, and his range seems to be infinite". She noted, as did many of her contemporaries, comparisons with Léonide Massine: "by far the finer dancer, though one cannot see him at all in classical ballet, which Helpmann, in spite of his limitations, can carry off by reason of his strong sense of the stage, and his magnificent partnering."[66] Manchester seems to suggest that it was Helpmann's extraordinary "sense of the stage" (perhaps another way of describing the "theatrical imagination" discussed earlier), just as much as his attentiveness in the grand *pas de deux*, which enabled him to assume the elegant mantle of the *danseur noble* in the Classical repertoire. "Perfectly musical, he is a perfect partner," wrote Arnold Haskell, "for partnering is a question of ear as well as of strength and good manners. [...] Without an extraordinary [ballet] technique he is incapable of making an ungraceful movement."[67]

It may be useful here to consider Gordon Anthony's observation, cited earlier, that ballet make-up is essentially similar "whatever the role depicted". His reference was to Helpmann's leading man roles, particularly in the nineteenth century repertoire, which the Camargo Society[68] and Vic-Wells Ballet imported to England during the 1930s, employing Nicholas Sergeyev to reconstruct the masterpieces of French Romanticism and Russian Classicism. Thus, in Bland's neat summary: "the Maryinsky style had been transferred from Imperial Russia to a modest theatre in Islington".[69] Within a year of joining de Valois' Company, Helpmann made his first attempts at these most demanding, and exposing, of roles, inheriting them from their earliest British exponents, Anton Dolin and Stanley Judson. It was his acting ability, suggested Williamson, that gave Helpmann's Classical roles "a moving, flesh and blood quality they never possessed before".[70] Anthony's camera captured two of the most purely Romantic of Helpmann's faces during this early period,[71] that of Count Albrecht in *Giselle* (1934) and Prince Charming in the 1939 Vic-Wells production of *The Sleeping Princess*.[72] (See plates 8 and 9)

Initially, Helpmann had performed the mimed role of Hilarion in the Vic-Wells Ballet's first performances of *Giselle* (January 1934), an iconic ballet created at the Paris Opera in 1841. The London production was led by two British dancers, both former stars of the Diaghilev Ballets Russes: Alicia Markova danced Giselle, with Anton Dolin as Albrecht. Just ten months later, Helpmann – a comparative ballet novice – was entrusted with Dolin's former role, and with partnering the supreme Markova. He set out to convince – if his dancing was not his strongest point, he was certainly going to *look* the part: photographs show Helpmann beautifully made-up, his face very pale, with finely applied black eyeliner, pearly eyeshadow, and sensitively drawn eyebrows. His lips are richly painted (crimson?); his hair is short and softly curled. An article written just six years after this debut as a leading man praised Helpmann's attributes as a *danseur noble*: "there is no living dancer who can convey the romantic decadence of the early nineteenth century as he does. He excels, above all, in the intimate detailed portraiture of the poet-aesthete, with his melancholy and sensuously gentle temperament."[73] In both appearance and interpretation, Helpmann's Albrecht surely informed his created role of The Poet in Ashton's *Apparitions* (1936), a work of considerable significance to the development of the Vic-Wells Ballet? (See plate 6) The ballet marked the first flowering of Frederick Ashton's creative partnership with his life-long muse, Margot Fonteyn (partnered, of course, by Helpmann).[74] Set to the music of Franz Liszt (arranged by Gordon Jacobs), the libretto was by Constant Lambert, inspired by Berlioz's *Symphonie fantastique*. The glamorous and Romantic designs were by Cecil Beaton.

It is fascinating to compare Helpmann's facial appearance as Albrecht, which remains fairly constant in the photographic record from 1934 onwards, with that of his first interpretation of the Prince in *The Sleeping Princess* in 1939. A pale skin and delicate eyebrows still formed the basis of the later make-up, but the eyes were now delineated by a darker eyeshadow on the lids, while below the eyes soft (grey?) lines gave a dream-like appearance to the face. The lips were less strongly tinted, to suit the lighter-coloured hair and costume. The production designs by Nadia Benois had been unpopular with the dancers and critics alike; Mary Clarke wrote bluntly that *The Sleeping Princess* "suffered from truly hideous wigs. Helpmann [...] was afflicted with a blond page-boy affair that flapped as he danced, and it is still a matter of surprise that the combined wig and headdress for the Blue Bird did not lead to mass resignations among the male dancers forced to wear it".[75] Perhaps by softening his facial make-up so markedly, Helpmann had attempted to accommodate the seventeenth-century style suggested by the blond sheets of hair framing his Princely face. (See plates 8 and 9)

These poetic studies make an instructive contrast with Helpmann's equally beauteous, but rather more dashing Prince Florimund in the post-war production of Petipa's masterpiece. Here, the Prince's skin-tone appears to be a more robust colour; his eyeliner is bolder, with jaunty little lines opening up the outside of the eyes. The lips are firmer – the upper lip less curved than before – but painted in a strong colour, probably chosen to work with Florimund's splendid scarlet coat. The Sadler's Wells Ballet re-opened Covent Garden's Opera House after the war with this lauded production, once more called by its original name of *The Sleeping Beauty*, and given sumptuous new designs by Oliver Messel. Robert Helpmann – already much celebrated for his versatility – outdid himself by miming the grotesque role of Carabosse in the first half of the ballet, only to reappear later as the elegant Prince Florimund in Acts II and III of the same performance.

Wartime exigencies had already led to Helpmann performing the dual roles of the Prince and Carabosse in a reduced version of *The Sleeping Princess*, presented during a short London season in 1941, when he apparently "enjoyed himself hugely in a grotesque make-up".[76] By the time these characters arrived at the Royal Opera House, a splendid 'beauty spot' had graced the face of the Prince; the very same which now appeared on the sour-faced Fairy Carabosse – an effective signature touch on the part of their creator, linking the opposing roles with wit and irony by a telling detail of stage make-up. (See plates 41 and 42) Helpmann's audacious *tour de force* was entirely in keeping with the traditions of the ballet, as he himself would certainly have been aware.[77] Sorley Walker described Helpmann's dual characterisations in glowing terms: "An elegant dowager-witch endowed with great power but no comic capering, his Carabosse was unforgettable. As Florimund he was a stylish eighteenth-century prince and a superb partner for Fonteyn."[78]

Joyce Beagarie, a renowned make-up artist and former head of the Wig Department of the National Theatre, recreated several of Helpmann's make-ups for the Helpmann Symposium held at The Royal Ballet School in 2013.[79] She found that there were interesting points of comparison between Helpmann's facial make-ups for the wicked Fairy Carabosse and Shakespeare's villainous Richard III. Helpmann played an impressively wide range of Shakespearian roles at the Old Vic during the 1956-57 season,[80] including an interpretation of Richard III, which presented him as a predatory spider biding his time at the centre of a large web. Interestingly, Sorley Walker reports that "Richard III had an opening night that lacked pace and light, and for once, Helpmann got his make-up wrong. [...] Later, changes were made, and the characterisation emerged as a very individual Richard, played with vigour, irony and a bitter honesty that could encompass the grim self-knowledge of Bosworth Eve."[81] A powerful photographic portrait by Angus McBean shows Helpmann as Richard III, presumably wearing the later version of the make-up. (See plate 64) His face is certainly arresting, but the make-up for his left hand is truly startling; the middle fingers appear fused together in a stump, echoing Richard's rancorous description of himself as "Deformed, unfinished, sent before my time /Into this breathing world, scarce half made up".[82] Beagarie pointed out how Helpmann painted Richard's eyebrows well below the actual brow line, giving him a petulant and angry scowl. There is an altogether different intensity in the face of his Carabosse, whose eyebrows sweep 'up and away', while the corners of her eyes and mouth turn markedly down. Further comparison shows a sensual note in the way that both characters' lips are delineated: Carabosse is given a full lower lip, with her upper-lip painted as a Cupid's bow, emphasising both her sullen resentment and her vanity, while Richard's full lips are wholly voluptuous and greedy for power.

David Vaughan, writing about Frederick Ashton's 1948 ballet, *Cinderella*,[83] pointed to the fact that while Helpmann and Ashton had both given notable performances in the *travestie* role of Carabosse, it was the ugly Stepsisters[84] who were "their crowning achievement in this genre". He explained: "Both Ashton and Helpmann were brilliant mimics, who frequently entertained their friends and colleagues with impromptu turns at parties or to enliven the tedium of train-calls or backstage waits."[85] Kavanagh describes many such incidents in her biography of Ashton, but she also suggests that he and Helpmann "were the original Ugly Sisters, whose relationship had always been spiked with petty rivalries".[86] Certainly, the war years had given rise to further tension between the pair, with Ashton feeling threatened in his absence while on R.A.F. service, by Helpmann's increasing influence as the Company's headline-grabbing performer and choreographer. In *Cinderella* their gift for mimicry and ongoing rivalry played out magnificently in their characterisations of the Stepsisters – as did the purely practical concerns of the choreographer. According to Vaughan, Ashton "had to leave his part until last, and he told Helpmann that he would make himself the foil to Helpmann's more domineering sister, and further decided to be 'addled and forgetful' so that if in fact he forgot what came next in performance it would just seem like part of his character".[87] Mary Clarke emphasised how naturally the roles suited their original creators:

> Helpmann's portrait of the extrovert, rapacious younger sister, continually hogging the largest men and the largest oranges, was uproariously funny. Ashton's cowering and timorous elder sister, defeated always in the battle for men and finery [...] was such a perfect study of insecurity that it became touching as well as funny.[88]

The costumes, wigs and make-up for the Stepsisters were carefully coordinated, and should be considered together. Comparison also arises between the original production of 1948, designed by Jean-Denis Malclès, and the revival of 1965, with new costumes by David Walker and sets by Henry Bardon.[89] Ashton was in his early sixties (and Helpmann five years younger) when the pair reprised their roles in the fresh designs, so it is interesting to see that their coiffure and make-up had not fundamentally altered during the intervening years. (See plate 73) Each sister still sported an elongated nose, Ashton's slightly drooping, and Helpmann's absurdly snubbed; each wore bright lipstick, Ashton's applied in a pursed bow, and Helpmann's in a ghastly smear. Ashton's eyebrows now dipped, giving him an anxious look (his earlier make-up had used arched brows), while Helpmann's still featured two high arcs, emphasising his bossy flamboyance. The colours and effects of the original designs were memorably described by the critic of the *New Statesman* in a review published in January 1949:

> There is a timid one (Frederick Ashton) dressed in the sourest possible shade of greenish-yellow, who peeps apprehensively out from beneath a tall sandy wig, for all the world like a frightened mouse peering out of a haycock; while her sister (Robert Helpmann) in furious purple and a fan (used at one moment with the extreme of archness and the next like a truncheon) is of an aggressive hauteur that baffles description.[90]

In the revival of 1965, Ashton's Stepsister wore a symphony of fussy pinks and creams, extending to the powdery pink of her make-up. Helpmann's Stepsister, meanwhile, was now dressed in a cacophony of maroon zig-zags on mustard silk, a colour reflected in the parchment-like hue of her face.

Almost twenty years had spanned the distance between the première of Ashton's *Cinderella* and its famous revival. Astonishingly, half a century separated Helpmann's first and last performances of his created role as The Red King in de Valois' most powerful ballet, *Checkmate* (1937).[91] The work depicts an allegorical game of chess, played out between Love and Death, and was intended to make a bleak analogy with the rise of fascism in Europe: a pitifully old and feeble Red King, his gentle Queen, and an honourable Red Knight are systematically overcome and destroyed by the forces of a ruthless Black Queen. *Checkmate* was first performed in Paris in 15 June 1937, exactly three years before the Nazi occupation of the city on 14 June 1940 – a poignant irony, given the prescient nature of the work. With a very different poignancy, the ballet marked Helpmann's final appearances on stage, when he performed it with the Australian Ballet in May 1986, just months before his death on 28 September. (See DVD track 6) Helpmann had first performed The Red King while still a young man in his twenties. Photographs indicate that, from the beginning, his make-up was unusually understated for the part, relying only on a bearded face and circles etched around his eyes. The high crown and long robe of a kingly chess-piece gave presence enough to the character, which Helpmann invested with "pathos and terrible vulnerability", simply by "changing the incline of his body, widening his eyes, or moving a hand to throat or chair".[92] It is possible that Helpmann's Red King was inspired by Shakespeare's King Lear, a role he never performed, but which brings striking parallels to mind. It is also interesting to draw a comparison with Helpmann's actual 'bearded' Shakespearian roles: King John and Shylock in *The Merchant of Venice*. Possibly in both instances, and certainly as Shylock, the overall make-up deployed by Helpmann was notably heavy. (See plates 40, 61 and 62) For The Red King, however, he chose to focus attention more on the expression of his face and body. Williamson likened Helpmann's nuanced approach towards The Red King to the realisation of his character, Adam Zero:

> As in *Checkmate*, when his doomed Red King, cowering at the back of the stage, dominated the action by a compelling expression of age broken by fear, Helpmann as Adam Zero conveys age less by make-up than by subtle but characteristic visual details: a quiver of lip or finger, a tired line of the shoulder blade, a shrunken withdrawal within what, by the actor's force of suggestion, appears to be an emaciated physical frame.[93]

It is paradoxical that for the first ballet that Helpmann choreographed for the huge stage of the Royal Opera House, *Adam Zero* (1946),[94] he used relatively little make-up to amplify his character. Adam, an Everyman figure portrayed by Helpmann, passes through scenes depicting the passage of his life, which are redolent of Shakespeare's "seven ages of man". This experimental work "incorporated changing costumes, make-up and scenery in view of the audience so that the action would be continuous", ideas which had "grown out of a study of Japanese Noh plays as well as from the stimulus of Cocteau films and Thornton Wilder's *The Skin of Our Teeth*".[95] A series of photographs taken by Baron forms a compelling record of Helpmann's *Adam Zero*, and shows that a minimal application of sketched facial lines sufficed to suggest the central character's advancing years, aided only by a short, white wig. This economy was, perhaps, determined by the fact that Helpmann's make-up was at times "performed" in view of the audience – in itself an intriguing idea, and clearly integral to the concept of the work. (See plates 44 and 45)

After a career in which Helpmann had made up, in the sense of having invented, a multitude of resounding – and often triumphant – theatrical characterisations, it may seem perverse to conclude with one of his least successful creations. But it is Helpmann's relative failure with *Adam Zero* which makes it so significant: Caryl Brahms described the work as "a diffuse and obscure biography with a very serious intent and a very muddled content" – but she rightly insisted that an "experimentalist is indeed a coward [...] who never over-reaches himself",[96] reminding us that theatrical innovators must be allowed to "miscalculate" (her word) if the theatre is to progress.[97] Helpmann was no theatrical coward, but an inveterate experimentalist and innovator in all aspects of his stagecraft, among which the use of make-up was just one fascinating element. An article, written in 1950, described Helpmann as "brilliant at the art of make-up", ascribing to him a "chameleon-like dexterity [with which] he assumes a dozen diverse colours and before our very eyes changes his character a hundred times".[98] Helpmann's mastery of theatrical make-up helped to invest each of his characterisations with a unique appearance; his many faces have taken their rightful place in a magnificent theatrical lineage, and remain indelibly stamped on our collective imaginations.

Endnotes

1   Audrey Williamson, "Some Dancers" in Peter Noble (ed.), *British Ballet* (London: Skelton Robinson, 1949), p.142.

2   Sorley Walker dates Helpmann's first fully professional appearance to 1926; his last was in 1986. See Kathrine Sorley Walker, *Robert Helpmann, A Rare Sense of the Theatre* (Alton: Dance Books, 2009), Appendix 3 – Chronology, pp. 184-196.

3   Mary Helpman, *The Helpman Family Story: 1796-1964* (Adelaide: Rigby, 1967), p.64.

4   Audrey Williamson, "Make-up and Character in Ballet" in Audrey Williamson, *Contemporary Ballet* (London: Rockliff, 1946), p.46.

5   Kathrine Sorley Walker (1920-2015) was a dance writer and critic who closely followed the progress of Helpmann's career from the 1930s onwards. She was the author of two studies of his life and work: *Robert Helpmann, Theatre World Monograph No. 9* (London: Rockcliff, 1957) as well as *Robert Helpmann, A Rare Sense of the Theatre*.

6   *Robert Helpmann, A Rare Sense of the Theatre*, pp 47-48. Sorley Walker cited three key roles here: Dr Coppélius, Mr O'Reilly, and a Stepsister in *Cinderella*.

7   Robert Helpmann, "The public has the final say. To become a cultural power Australia must train its own dancers and actors – and they'll have to be good", [Australian] *Woman*, 20 June 1955, p.155, reproduced in this volume, pp. 16-18.

8   Arnold L. Haskell, *Ballet, A Complete Guide to Appreciation*, Revised Edition (Harmondsworth: Penguin Books, 1945), p.159.

9   *Robert Helpmann, A Rare Sense of the Theatre*, p.63.

10   The revue was entitled *Swinging the Gate*. It opened on 22 May 1940 at the Ambassadors Theatre, in London's West End.

11   Gordon Anthony, "Foreword" in his *Studies of Robert Helpmann*, (London: Home & Van Thal, 1946), p.5.

12   *Robert Helpmann, A Rare Sense of the Theatre*, pp.41-42.

13   Mary Clarke (1923 – 2015) was a dance critic and writer for 65 years. She made this remark in a telephone conversation with the author, 15 October 2013, mentioning Helpmann's particularly heavy use of make-up in his portrayals of two Shakespearian characters, Shylock in *The Merchant of Venice*, and Richard III; also for that of the title role in his own ballet, *Comus*.

14   George Bartram, interview with Robert Helpmann, "Robert Helpmann – Human Dynamo", *Picturegoer,* July 3 1948, scrapbook cutting, no page number. The Royal Ballet School Collections.

15   Garry O'Connor, *Paul Scofield: The Biography* (London: Sidgwick & Jackson, 2002), p.75. O'Connor's book is based on interviews he conducted between 1999-c.2001 with Scofield (1922-2008).

16   Tatlock Miller, "Helpmann, Chameleon of the Theatre", *Dance and Dancers*, Vol.1, No. 5, May 1950, p.16. Miller gives the quotation without providing a source. Miller's full sentence reads: "That season, too, he appeared as a 'pale,

evil-purposed, red-haired fox with minatory hands' in the title role of King John and as a venomous Shylock."

17   "Make-up and Character in Ballet", p.46. Williamson is describing Helpmann's make-up as Hamlet in his first appearances in Shakespeare's play at the Old Vic, 11 Feb–8 Apr 1944; photographs of the Stratford production of 1948, in which Hamlet wore a Victorian frock coat with a wide white collar, indicate that his make-up was similarly restrained.

18   *Paul Scofield: The Biography*, p.71. O'Connor attributes the anecdote to the actor, Ronald Harwood, to whom Scofield had related it.

19   Ninette de Valois, *Come Dance with Me* (London: Hamish Hamilton, 1957; Second Revised Edition, Dance Books, 1981), p.109. "Monkey tricks" is de Valois' expression; she relates several of Helpmann's running "stories", invented to amuse the Company during journeys on "those slow wartime trains. These characters grew more and more alive in their sordid topicality, and we would await their further eccentricities with the greatest impatience."

20   *Paul Scofield: The Biography*, p.69.

21   *A Wedding Bouquet* (1937) presents a comic rendition of a provincial French wedding party. Choreography was by Frederick Ashton; the libretto, music and design were all by Lord Berners.

22   Julie Kavanagh, *Secret Muses, the Life of Frederick Ashton* (London: Faber and Faber, 1996), p. 212. Kavanagh adds tellingly: "The prettily plump Mary Honer was also wonderfully funny as the Bride – *too* funny, in the view of Helpmann, who felt upstaged by her. 'I think Bobby saw her as a rival,' remarked a colleague. 'He kept trying to put her off, telling her how frightful she was'."

23   *Façade* (1931) was choreographed by Frederick Ashton as a series of vignettes sending up the popular dances and social mores of the time. The music by William Walton was originally composed as a setting of the nonsense poems of Edith Sitwell. Designs were by John Armstrong.

24   David Vaughan, *Frederick Ashton and His Ballets* (New York: Alfred A. Knopf, 1977), p.124.

25   Mary Clarke, *The Sadler's Wells Ballet, A History and An Appreciation* (London: Adam and Charles Black, 1955), p.112.

26   *Robert Helpmann, A Rare Sense of the Theatre*, p.47.

27   Clement Crisp, *Financial Times*, 24 May 1979, cited in *Robert Helpmann, A Rare Sense of the Theatre*, p.153.

28   *The Helpman Family Story: 1796 – 1964*, p. 87. Mary Helpman relates that her son's telling of the story continued with an apocryphal flourish: "'Ah well,' said Bayliss (sic), 'he's got a nice little bottom.'"

29   Ninette de Valois, "Robert Helpmann, His Place in the Theatre", in Gordon Anthony, *Studies of Robert Helpmann*, p. 9. The entire article is also reproduced in Ninette de Valois, *Step by Step* (London: W.H.Allen, 1977).

30   Ibid. p. 9.

31   *The Helpman Family Story: 1796-1964*, pp. 58.

32   Caryl Brahms, *Robert Helpmann* . Second Edition (London: B.T. Batsford, 1945), p.21. Brahms is referring to Helpmann's Dr Coppélius in the Vic-Wells

Ballet revival of *Coppélia*, redesigned by William Chappell in 1940. Helpmann first assumed the romantic lead as Frantz, going on to re-define the role of Coppélius the following year. Helpmann's appearance as Coppélius in the film *The Tales of Hoffmann* (1951) was distinguished by a completely different make-up and wig. See Geraldine Morris's essay in this volume, "Robert Helpmann: Chameleon of the Screen", pp. 184-194, and compare plate 20 with 52 and 53.

33   *Robert Helpmann, A Rare Sense of the Theatre*, p.63.

34   P.W. Manchester, *Vic-Wells Ballet: A Ballet Progress* (London: Victor Gollancz, 1947), pp. 47-48. *The Prospect Before Us* (1940), choreographed by Ninette de Valois, was based on a story of two rival theatre managers in Georgian London. Set to music by William Boyce, arranged by Constant Lambert; the designs were by Roger Furse. Manchester thought the ballet owed its popularity to Helpmann's performance: "Helpmann's Mr O'Reilly is the sort of wine which needs no bush. On the first night his solo burst upon us with all the violence of a high explosive (only vastly more pleasant), and turned into an outstanding success a ballet which, until that moment, had bewildered as much as it delighted." *The Prospect Before Us* was revived by Birmingham Royal Ballet in 1998, to mark de Valois' 100th birthday.

35   *Robert Helpmann*, p.21. Brahms cites two examples of Massine's most popular characters in his own ballets: the Barman in *Union Pacific* (1934) and The Peruvian in *Gaîté Parisienne* (1938).

36   "Robert Helpmann, His Place in the Theatre", p. 9. De Valois later relented, allowing Stanley Holden to perform the role of Mr O'Reilly with the Sadler's Wells Theatre Ballet during the 1950s.

37   Joseph Grimaldi (1778-1837) was the great pantomime clown of Sadler's Wells at the turn of the 18th/19th century; his legacy is part of the fabric of that historic theatre. Marking the 50th Anniversary of her Companies at the 'Wells, de Valois reflected on this in an article she wrote for a souvenir theatre programme of the Sadler's Wells Royal Ballet, 1 April 1981: "In the past, it is said that Grimaldi ran across the Islington marshland from Drury Lane Theatre to Sadler's Wells [...] so as to make his second stage appearance on that particular evening. Some years ago, Alexander Grant and another male dancer were scheduled to leave Covent Garden by taxi [...] for an appearance at the Wells. The taxi broke down so they boarded a bus, only to be ordered off it owing to their startling make-up and costumes. They decided to run the rest of the distance so as to arrive on time for the show. So does time revive in thought and action all our yesterdays." Indeed, the story is reminiscent of Helpmann's own dash from the 'Wells to take part in West End revue!

38   Williamson is referring here to Helpmann's ballet version of *Hamlet* (1942).

39   "Make-up and Character in Ballet", p.46.

40   Ninette de Valois, "Introduction" in *Studies of Robert Helpmann*, p.14.

41   *Robert Helpmann, A Rare Sense of the Theatre*, p. 18. Also see Elizabeth Schafer's essay, "Taming, Shaming and Displaying: Robert Helpmann and Katharine Hepburns' Trousers, Australia 1955", pp. 195-211.

42   Robert Helpmann, "Learning to be a Good Dancer", *Old Vic and Sadler's*

Wells Magazine, April 1934, p.4. See also Chapter 1 of this volume, pp. 1-20.

43   Cyril W. Beaumont, *Complete Book of Ballets* (London: Putnam, 1937), p.936.

44   See *Studies of Robert Helpmann*, plates III and IV.

45   For example, Bela Lugosi's long, pointed nails in his iconic performance as Count Dracula in the film, *Dracula*, directed by Tod Browning (United States, 1931).

46   Kathrine Sorley Walker, *Ninette de Valois, Idealist Without Illusions* (London: Hamish Hamilton, 1987), p.138.

47   *Job* is subtitled 'A masque for dancing in 8 scenes'; choreographed by Ninette de Valois, the scenario was by Geoffrey Keynes with music by Vaughan Williams. Sets and costumes were designed by Gwendolen Raverat after William Blake, with wigs and masks by Hedley Briggs. It was first performed by the Camargo Society, Cambridge Theatre, London, 5 July 1931, with Anton Dolin in the role of Satan.

48   His most widely known "evil" character was, of course, that of the Child Catcher in the film *Chitty Chitty Bang Bang*, directed by Ken Hughes (United States, 1968). See Libby Worth's essay, "Robert Helpmann and the Making of an On-screen Villain", pp. 169-183.

49   "Introduction" in *Studies of Robert Helpmann*, p.8.

50   *British Ballet*, p.142.

51   The character of Satan wore a tightly curled, short wig, designed by Hedley Briggs after the drawings by William Blake. The design for make-up was not attributed, but was probably devised collaboratively between dancer, choreographer and designer.

52   "Some Dancers", p.142.

53   *The Rake's Progress* (1935) was choreographed by Ninette de Valois, with music and libretto by Gavin Gordon and designs by Rex Whistler. De Valois created the role of the Rake with Helpmann in mind and they began to rehearse it together, but at the time of the ballet's first scheduled performances he was given leave to perform in revue at London's Adelphi Theatre. Walter Gore danced the première on 20 May 1935, and Helpmann took over the role from 27 September of the same year. See *Ninette de Valois, Idealist Without Illusions*, pp. 21-22.

54   "Make-up and Character in Ballet", p.45.

55   Gordon Anthony's images have a theatrical flamboyance well suited to Helpmann's own. As de Valois' brother, Anthony was uniquely well placed to observe Helpmann's career from its earliest days with the Vic-Wells Ballet. His visual record of the Company during the 1930s and '40s, when Helpmann was its undisputed leading man, is uniquely comprehensive.

56   *The Helpman Family Story: 1796-1964*, pp. 87-88.

57   *Comus* (1942) shared this in common with de Valois' *The Prospect Before Us* (1940), which had derived its title and subject matter from an illustration by Thomas Rowlandson, inscribed: "*The Prospect Before Us. No.2*. Respectfully dedicated to those Singers, Dancers and Musical Professors who are fortunately

engaged with the proprietor of the King's Theatre at the Pantheon, 13 Jan 1791."

58   Margot Fonteyn, *The Magic of Dance* (New York: Alfred A. Knopf, 1979), p.306.

59   Robert Helpmann, "British Choreography and its Critics" in Peter Noble, (ed.), *British Ballet* (London: Skelton Robinson, 1949), p.36, reproduced in this volume, pp. 11-12.

60   *Robert Helpmann*, pp.22-24.

61   "Introduction" in *Studies of Robert Helpmann*, p.12.

62   Audrey Williamson, "Robert Helpmann as Choreographer" in Audrey Williamson, *Contemporary Ballet* (London: Rockliff, 1946), p.90.

63   "The Sitter Out" [usually attributed to P.J.S. Richardson], *Dancing Times*, new series no. 377, February 1942, p.242.

64   Marked tendril-like curls drawn above the inner eyebrows were an embellishment of Helpmann's make-up for Comus, as seen in the photographs by Russell Sedgwick in Caryl Brahms, *Robert Helpmann*, plates 13 – 30 inclusive.

65   *Studies of Robert Helpmann*, plates IX and X; and see plate 21 in this volume.

66   *Vic-Wells Ballet: A Ballet Progress*, p.92.

67   *Ballet, A Complete Guide to Appreciation*, p.159.

68   The Camargo Society was founded by Arnold Haskell and P.J.S. Richardson in 1930. It facilitated performances of new ballets, with choreography, music and design commissioned from British artists. Funded by subscription, it featured dancers from Rambert's and de Valois' establishments. When the Society closed in 1933, several of its ballets entered the repertoire of the Vic-Wells Ballet.

69   The allusion is to Sadler's Wells Theatre. See Alexander Bland, *The Royal Ballet, the First 50 Years* (London: Threshold Books, 1981), p.36.

70   "Some Dancers", p.141.

71   Gordon Anthony, *Camera Studies, The Vic-Wells Ballet* (London: Geoffrey Bles, 1938), Robert Helpmann as Albrecht in *Giselle*, plate 22.

72   Gordon Anthony, *The Sleeping Princess* (London: George Routledge & Sons, 1940), Robert Helpmann as The Prince Charming, plate 37.

73   Elizabeth Partriege and lan M. Storey, "Robert Helpmann, A Study", *Dancing Times*, new series no. 362, November 1940, pp.63-65.

74   Helpmann was Fonteyn's principal partner throughout the formative years of her career, c. 1935-49; she acknowledged that his powerful command of the stage and great skill in *pas de deux* played a vital part in her own development as an artist. After the war ended in 1945, Michael Somes was favoured by Ashton, gradually superseding Helpmann as Fonteyn's leading partner. The arrival of Rudolf Nureyev at The Royal Ballet in 1962 heralded Fonteyn's third great partnership.

75   *The Sadler's Wells Ballet, A History and An Appreciation*, p.142.

76   Ibid. p.166.

77   In the first performances of *The Sleeping Beauty* (1890), Enrico Cecchetti performed the roles of both Carabosse (a mimed role) and the Bluebird (who dances a classical *pas de deux* with Princess Florine). Sergeyev and de Valois

had first-hand knowledge of Cecchetti's supremacy as a mime and classical virtuoso; they evidently felt that Helpmann was a fine enough artist to merit this comparison.

78   *Ninette de Valois, Idealist Without Illusions*, p.78.

79   The roles for which Joyce Beagarie recreated Helpmann's make-up (in a live demonstration) were: Richard III, Mr O'Reilly, Prince Florimund and Carabosse.

80   Sorley Walker records: "His roles were Shylock [in *The Merchant of Venice*], Launce in *The Two Gentlemen of Verona* directed by Michael Langham, Saturninus in *Titus Andronicus*, and Dr Pinch in *The Comedy of Errors* (a double bill directed by Walter Hudd), and Richard III (directed by Douglas Seal)." See *Robert Helpmann, A Rare Sense of the Theatre*, p.114. (See plates 61, 62, 64 and 65)

81   *Robert Helpmann, A Rare Sense of the Theatre*, p. 115.

82   William Shakespeare, *Richard III*, 1.1.20-21.

83   *Cinderella* (1948) was choreographed by Frederick Ashton to the score by Serge Prokofiev (written between 1940-44); sets and costumes were by Jean-Denis Malclès. This three-act ballet was the first full-length work made for the Sadler's Wells Ballet.

84   As Sorley Walker points out, they were initially programmed as the Stepsisters, not as the Ugly Sisters.

85   *Frederick Ashton and His Ballets*, p.233.

86   *Secret Muses, the Life of Frederick Ashton*, p. 303.

87   *Frederick Ashton and His Ballets*, p.234.

88   *The Sadler's Wells Ballet, A History and An Appreciation*, p.231.

89   The new designs by Bardon and Walker featured in a televised recording of The Royal Ballet in *Cinderella* (Prokofiev/Ashton), BBC Television, directed by John Vernon (1969). Antoinette Sibley and Anthony Dowell danced as Cinderella and the Prince; Ashton and Helpmann were the Ugly Sisters with Georgina Parkinson as the Fairy Godmother and Alexander Grant as the Jester.

90   Anon, *New Statesman*, 1 January 1949, cited in *Robert Helpmann, A Rare Sense of the Theatre*, p. 92.

91   *Checkmate* (1937) was choreographed by Ninette de Valois, with music and libretto by Arthur Bliss and designs by Edward McKnight Kauffer. June Brae was The Black Queen, with Harold Turner as The Red Knight, Robert Helpmann as The Red King and Pamela May as The Red Queen.

92   Mary Emery, *The Australian*, 8 May 1986, cited in *Ninette de Valois, Idealist Without Illusions*, p.202.

93   "Some Dancers", p.143.

94   *Adam Zero* (1946) was choreographed by Robert Helpmann to music by Arthur Bliss; the designs were by Roger Furse. The ballet was the first work created for the Sadler's Wells Ballet at the Royal Opera House, Covent Garden.

95   *Robert Helpmann, A Rare Sense of the Theatre*, p. 79. Sorley Walker continues: "This play had been staged in London in May 1945 by the Oliviers [...] and the designer had been Roger Furse. Now Helpmann and Furse together planned the scenic development of *Adam Zero*."

96   Caryl Brahms, "British Choreographers" in Peter Noble (ed.). *British Ballet* (London: Skelton Robinson, 1949), p.59.

97   Caryl Brahms (1901-1982) was a notable critic, journalist and novelist, writing about ballet, opera and the drama throughout her life. She was the author of *Robert Helpmann, Choreographer* (London: B. T. Batsford, 1943) and *A Seat at the Ballet* (Bristol: Evans Brothers, 1951). Brahms collaborated with S.J. Simon on a number of satirical novels including *A Bullet in the Ballet* (1937); and later with Ned Sherrin on a variety of projects for theatre and television.

98   "Helpmann, Chameleon of the Theatre", pp. 10-11, 16.

Robert Helpmann

(an essay published in 1950)

Audrey Williamson

That Robert Helpmann is the outstanding actor-mime in English ballet has long been recognised. If he is less unanimously accepted as a fine classical dancer this is, I think, partly because too many ballet-goers think of male technique solely in terms of quantity and speed of pirouette (a criterion they would never think of applying exclusively to a ballerina), and partly because few outside the teaching profession have a quick enough eye to notice accuracy of detail in the performance of steps.

Today when so much male dancing, both foreign and English, has a slovenliness of execution, line and finish, which would not be tolerated in a female dancer, Helpmann in his classical performances at Covent Garden – unfortunately rare in view of the standard they could have set – has shown us an example of the mature *danseur noble* of the older classical tradition.[1]

Let us examine just what this means, from the critical point of view. To become a judge of good dancing one must have certain standards of style and performance, viewing the effect of the dance as a whole as well as the execution of certain types of steps. This judgement springs partly from instinctive good taste – a natural "visual sense", particularly valuable in the assessment of a dancer's line and general style – and partly from knowledge gained by study. The final criticism *must*, however, be based on the dancer's performance *on the stage*, not on his technical feats in class which, until they are definitely employed by a choreographer, are a matter only of speculative interest. This means, in Helpmann's case, that one must judge his standard of dancing by his performances in *Giselle*, which sets the most difficult task for the male dancer in pure classical technique, and not by what he may or may not have been able to do in some more acrobatic modern ballets, had he been called upon to dance in them.

Quality, not quantity, in a dancer's performance is, I fully believe, the highest requirement. This means, for me, what Ninette de Valois, in connection with Helpmann's dancing, has referred to as "perfection of detail".[2] However facile his pirouettes, I am not interested in a "classical" dancer with a turned-in legline, insufficiently pointed feet, an undignified carriage and badly-placed head and limbs. Nor am I interested in a dancer who performs *entrechats* and other *batterie* steps with the beat on the heels, and the toes pointing outwards to the wings – it is amazing the number of dancers who do this today to applause. The feet must contact correctly, the ball striking the instep with the toes pointing to the floor. Certain male dancers today contrive an easier *entrechat* beat by taking off from the second position, with the feet apart (indeed some classical solos have been rearranged in this way); this, too, is a form of cheating – permissible in class to help strengthen the dancer's beat, but academically incorrect on the stage, where the feet should be together at the start and finish of the step.

I am not, finally, impressed by the dancer who achieves his extra pirouettes at the expense of a balanced or secure finish, or the natural requirements of the music; who performs double turns in the air with his feet apart; whose quality of movement is flaccid, lacking precision and attack; whose face is without expression, and who in partnering makes one conscious of his hands, or fails to parallel the ballerina's line.

I think it can reasonably be asserted that Helpmann has none of these faults, except that his double turns in the air – once the most fluent on our stage – occasionally now show signs of strain,[3] partly through decreased elevation (he does, however, at his best still finish them cleanly – on his feet and not on his knees, which has lately become an ingenious method of masking the dancer's inability to complete the second turn). His pace and quantity of turn and beat have never been above a good average; but his footwork – like, indeed, his whole body – has always been beautifully placed, and he dances invariably within his powers. (Eglevsky[4] and Babilée[5], both stronger technicians than Helpmann in the quantitative sense, and Skibine[6], not technically yet at his height, are almost the only male dancers today to do this, but it is a mark of the finished artist.) A phenomenal balance helps him to achieve the most difficult *adagio* movements and a steady finish to every dance. He has, moreover, a musicianship that gives the dance a flowing unity, and a grace which is never boneless, although he lacks great physical strength. He is an extremely light dancer, supple in limb, symmetrically built (with the arched foot of the true classicist) and a perfect stylist. "A beautiful dancer", as one of his teachers has called him, rather than a brilliant one; a dancer in whom technique is a means to an end, and whose smoothness enables one to watch the dance with pleasure, unconscious of difficulties. This, to my mind, is true command of technique. (See plates 6, 7, 28 and 48)

Dancing apart, what are the other qualities that have put Helpmann in the top rank of his profession? His sense of style – that is, his clean line and nobility of carriage, plus expert timing, the ability to keep his hands out of sight, attack and careful judgement – have made him an outstanding classical partner. Margot Fonteyn, in her *pas de deux* work, continues to owe much to him.[7] His mime – in the sense of classical gesture – upholds an aristocratic tradition: he has the right-shaped hands, with long, slender fingers, and again his feeling for music helps the precision and fluency of his gesture (too many are clumsy and inaccurate in this form of mime, which has a subtle technique of its own). Above all his brain, his theatrical instinct, his sense of fun and eye for character have combined to form him as an actor who does not need the aid of speech (though he has used it finely on occasion in the legitimate theatre) to make his parts live.

Intelligence is a necessary gift in any dancer who is to achieve a position above that of the acrobat; but Helpmann's intelligence is exceptional, and gives a special quality to his work. "He learns more in one lesson than the average dancer does in twenty," said a famous teacher. "He is a delight to teach because he is so *interested* – so bright-eyed, eager to learn and quick to grasp what you want, and do it. You never have to explain anything twice."[8]

It is this quality of being *interested* that has, I think, made Helpmann a varied actor. He is intensely impressionable, and his passion for the stage – fostered from an early age by a Shakespearean-minded mother, who acted the balcony scene from *Romeo and Juliet* with him literally over the rails of his cot – has been backed by technical study, and by watching the best players of our time. (He went to see Danny Kaye, and Edith Evans in *Daphne Laureola*, again and again, fascinated by the technique of their performances.[9]) When creating his ballet *Miracle in the Gorbals*, he lingered at slum street corners, making mental notes of public-house types; and his acting, too, is based on observation of character, both in books (he is an admirer of Dickens, and certain psychological studies of literature) and in life.

This explains his versatility, and something of his imagination and skill in make-up. His mobile actor's face is a gift of nature, but the details of his performance – the uneasy hands and ravaged face of the Card Player in *The Rake's Progress*, Dr. Coppélius' mouth dropping at the corners in senile sleep, the exaggerated flick of a hand in the classical burlesque of *A Wedding Bouquet*, the feeble shuffle and rounded shoulders of the aged Adam Zero, the sense of draining strength, of physical exhaustion, as he raises the Suicide in *Miracle in the Gorbals*, the crazed eyes of Don Quixote suddenly clouded by sanity and disillusion – these are the result of thought, and his own natural wit and intelligence.[10] He has a gift of humorous invention in the tradition of the great stage clowns, and he shares with them the alert, monkeyish mask – half-wistful, half-comic – of many born comedians. But characteristically he can make this strange face of his, with its medieval set of eyes and chin, romantic and tragic at will. His power of projecting atmosphere is as strong in classical ballet as in dance-drama; with a bewildered expression and bemused gesture, in *Giselle* or *The Sleeping Beauty*, he can make his partner seem a wraith who has slipped intangibly through his fingers.[11] He acts these classical Princes as if he believed in them, giving them an aristocracy and tenderness, and a kind of oblique pain, that are more effective here than the robuster passion which he tends, temperamentally, to lack.

The strongest personality, apart from Massine,[12] on the ballet stage of our time, Helpmann has disciplined that personality until it sinks naturally into the identity of whichever character he is playing. This discipline is the final hallmark of his talent; it gives him restraint, without impairing the vitality of expression, the controlled breadth of gesture, that enable his work to carry to the back of the theatre. Helpmann – unlike many mimes in large theatres – never grimaces, and his acting can be seen from the front row of the stalls without losing its sincerity or reality.

Fokine[13] recognised Helpmann's powers of expression, and wanted to use him in *Petrouchka*[14] and *Les Sylphides*,[15] but it was in English ballet that Helpmann chose to remain and the dramatic development of our choreography and dancers owed much to the example of his work. Today, when ballet is turning away from the expressive ideal, that example needs special critical re-emphasis.

Endnotes

1   By 1950, when this essay was first published (in Cyril Swinson's edited volume, *Dancers and Critics*, published by A. & C. Black) Helpmann's dance performances at Covent Garden were increasingly limited in number because of his frequent appearances in plays, films and on radio, though he took part in the tours by the Company to Paris (1948) and to Florence, Copenhagen, America and Canada (1949). He still regularly partnered Fonteyn and created new roles for Ashton in *Don Juan* and *Cinderella* (1948) and for de Valois in *Don Quixote* (1950). Helpmann resigned from the Sadler's Wells Ballet in November 1950 during their tour of the States.

2   "His [Helpmann's] technical acquisition does not follow the virtuosity lines of spectacular execution, but favours that form representing perfection of detail in both simple and complex movement." See Ninette de Valois, "Robert Helpmann: His Place in the Theatre", in Gordon Anthony, *Studies of Robert Helpmann* (London: Home and Van Thal, 1946), p.10.

3   An original footnote here reads: "As Helpmann at the time of writing is forty years of age, some deterioration of technique is to be expected in the future; but that will not affect this assessment of his dancing in his prime."

4   André Eglevsky (1917-1977), though Russian born, studied with amongst others, Egorova, Preobrajenska and Woizikovski in Paris and Legat in London. He danced with a range of companies, including de Basil's Ballet Russe de Monte Carlo, Balanchine's American Ballet Theatre, the Grand Ballet du Marquis de Cuevas and New York City Ballet. He was noted for his disciplined approach to his roles in classical ballet and his style is continued in the Company bearing his name, which he founded in 1958.

5   Jean Babilée (1923-2014) studied at the Paris Opera Ballet School and danced chiefly with Les Ballets des Champs Elysées and Les Ballets de Paris. He was famed for his spectacular leaps and, like Helpmann, for the brilliance of his characterisations, notably in Petit and Cocteau's *Le Jeune Homme et la Mort* (1946), which he danced into his sixties. He is generally considered amongst the finest of French male dancers: sensuous, daring, an embodiment onstage of complete grace and ease.

6   George Skibine (1920-1981) grew up with Diaghilev's Ballets Russes, of which his father was a member; he trained with many senior members of that Company, performed with numerous companies in Europe and America, before settling with his wife, Marjorie Tallchief, in the Paris Opera Ballet, where he served as Artistic Director (1958-1961). Later, he moved to America and became Artistic Director of the Dallas Civic Ballet. Like Helpmann, he excelled as Albrecht in *Giselle*, because he explored the potential for complexities of characterisation within the role. He was noted for the simplicity and honesty of his technique rather than for showy virtuosity.

7   A debt Fonteyn always acknowledged. Beryl Grey also speaks warmly of Helpmann's skills as a partner within this publication (DVD Track 1). As early as 1933, Gordon Anthony described his partnering as "always romantic,

sympathetic, completely reliable and chivalrous". (Cited in Anna Bemrose, *Robert Helpmann: A Servant of Art* (Queensland: University of Queensland Press, 2008), p.54.) And in 1940 Elizabeth Partriege and Alan M. Storey in "Robert Helpmann – A Study" observe: "Particular appreciation should be given for his splendid partnering, a branch of classical work so difficult to acquire, and offering so little obvious reward" (*Dancing Times*, November 1940, p.64). Similarly, P.W. Manchester in *Vic-Wells: A Ballet Progress* (London: Gollancz, 1947) observed that Helpmann's skills in partnering made him "irreplaceable in the Company" and "indispensable in the classical ballets (pp.91 and 92).

8   The precise identity of this teacher is not known. When consulted on the matter, Henry Danton, a younger contemporary of Helpmann's in the Company, suggested Vera Volkova as the likely source. In his biography of Volkova, the Danish writer, Alexander Meinertz, gives an interesting comparison between Helpmann and Fonteyn in Volkova's classes: "Volkova said to Gilbert Vernon that it was joy to teach Robert Helpmann. He got everything right away... but he had always forgotten it by the next day! With Fonteyn it was different: like 'dripping water on a stone: it takes a long time, but once it's there it is there forever'." (Gilbert Vernon, "Margot Fonteyn: A Personal Tribute", *Dance Chronicle*, 1991, cited in Alexander Meinertz, *Vera Volkova, a Biography* translated by Alexander Meinertz and Paula Hostrup-Jessen (Alton: Dance Books, 2007), p.66).

9   James Bridie's play, *Daphne Laureola*, had first been staged by Laurence Olivier with Edith Evans and Peter Finch at the Old Vic in 1949 and then re-staged at the Music Box Theatre on Broadway with Evans and Danny Kaye in September 1950, where it ran for only 56 performances. Helpmann would have seen the play during the Sadler's Wells Ballet's tour of America, starting 28 September, when the Company was based at the Metropolitan Opera House.

10   Helpmann first danced the Rake in a revival of de Valois's *The Rake's Progress* in 1935; his impersonation of Dr. Coppélius in *Coppélia* began in 1941 (previously he had taken the role of Franz in several revivals); Ashton's *A Wedding Bouquet* was first staged in 1937 with Helpmann in the role of The Bridegroom; his own ballets, *Adam Zero* and *Miracle in the Gorbals* where he took the central character were choreographed in 1946 and 1944 respectively; and he danced Don Quixote in de Valois' version to a score by Roberto Gerhard from February 1950, to which Williamson is referring here (he was later to play the Don in the Petipa/Nureyev version to Minkus's music with Australian Ballet in 1970).

11   Helpmann first danced the role of Albrecht to Markova's Giselle in October 1934 and that of Prince Charming to Fonteyn's Princess Aurora in *The Sleeping Princess* in February 1939.

12   Léonide Massine (1896-1979) is best known for his "symphonic" ballets, such as *Les Présages* (1933) and *Choreartium* (1933) and for the comic characterisations he contributed to his own ballets, such as the Can-Can Dancer in *La Boutique Fantasque* (1919) and the Peruvian in *Gaîté Parisienne* (1938). He appeared with Helpmann in the films, *The Red Shoes* (1948) and *The Tales of Hoffmann* (1951). Significantly, writing about Helpmann as a performer often

brings Massine to de Valois' mind.

13   Michael Fokine (1880-1942), though a notable dancer is best known as a choreographer of prodigious range and versatility who was Diaghilev's first resident choreographer with the Ballets Russes. Many of his works hold a permanent place in the repertoires of companies world-wide, particularly *Les Sylphides* (1909), *Schéhérazade* (1910), *Le Carnaval* (1910), *The Firebird* (1910), *Le Spectre de la Rose* (1911) and *Petrouchka* (1912), which all exploited the technical brilliance of Nijinsky. By the Twenties Fokine was teaching and dancing in New York and founded a company, American Ballet. In 1936 while searching for dancers to appear with either Blum's Ballets de Monte-Carlo or with de Basil's Ballets Russes de Monte Carlo, Fokine personally rehearsed Helpmann in *Les Sylphides* and as Petrouchka; but Helpmann never subsequently appeared as a guest with either company.

14   *Petrushka* or *Petrouchka* was choreographed by Fokine to music by Stravinsky following a scenario by Benois; the ballet is set in a Russian shrove-tide fair and tells of the complicated loves of three puppets, a melancholy Clown (Petrushka), a Doll and a Moor, which climaxes in the latter's killing Petrushka. The Clown's ghost haunts the Magician/Showman above his booth theatre as the curtain falls. The ballet is modernist in its games with exploration of the border between reality (the fair which is realistically presented) and artistic fiction (the world of the puppets). Nijinsky, who could command a fragile, otherworldly stage persona, excelled as the puppet Clown; Helpmann's attempt finally in 1958 with The Royal Ballet was not one of his successes.

15   *Les Sylphides* is a short *ballet-blanc*, set to Chopin's music, which depicts a group of white-clad sylphs who dance in a moonlit, woodland glade as muses to a romantic poet (the one male role). The muted design was by Benois. Fokine's choreographic focus throughout is on a mood of profound reverie and ethereal grace. Helpmann first danced the role of the Poet in 1934.

Introduction to DVD Track 1: filmed recollections of Robert Helpmann as a colleague, performer and choreographer

Beryl Grey interviewed by Richard Allen Cave; Maina Gielgud interviewed by Rupert Christiansen

Richard Allen Cave

Dame Beryl Grey had a prodigious and sure-fire technique in classical ballet from her earliest years: by the age of ten she had won a scholarship to the Vic-Wells School in 1937, joined the Sadler's Wells Ballet at fourteen, danced her first Odette/Odile on her fifteenth birthday, Giselle at sixteen and Princess Aurora three years later. As a freelance artist, after leaving The Royal Ballet in January 1957, she was famously the first English dancer to appear with the Bolshoi Ballet (1957-1958) and later with the Peking Ballet Company (1964). On her retirement from performing, she became the Artistic Director of London's Festival Ballet (1968-1979).

Dame Beryl's association with Robert Helpmann was long and varied: he was the first to partner her in *Le Lac des cygnes* in 1942, and helped de Valois coach her for the demanding central role. She appeared as the Lady in revivals of his ballet, *Comus* (her natural warmth and sincerity giving her the distinctive moral authority that the role requires); and he choreographed *The Birds* and especially the central, highly technically challenging but lyrical role of the Nightingale as a vehicle for her, while for Moyra Fraser he created (as a foil for Grey) the comic role of the Hen, who absurdly endeavours to ape the Nightingale's passionate identity. (Helpmann found ingenious ways to suggest the intensity and brilliance of the Nightingale's song through movement, particularly of the arms and hands.) Later Grey's remarkable technical exactitude, and the deployment of her long limbs in a fierce and fearless attack, made her an ideal Black Queen to oppose Helpmann's ailing Red King in revivals of de Valois' *Checkmate*. In this filmed interview, recorded on 2 October 2013, she talks of Helpmann as performer and choreographer, of his skills and steadying influence as a partner, his fine-tuned comedic gifts, his meticulous and subtle artistry in mime, and his wit (often subversive, but always supportive) as a fellow Company member.

Maina Gielgud, born in 1945, was a generation younger than Dame Beryl. By the time that she began to study ballet in earnest in London, Paris and Monte Carlo with a sequence of brilliant teachers, including Olga

Preobrajenska, Tamara Karsavina, Lydia Kyasht, Stanislas Idzikovski, Julia Sedova and Rosella Hightower, Ninette de Valois' Company had moved into Covent Garden and the early years of the Vic-Wells Ballet had already become a part of history and myth. By the time she became a Principal Artist with the Sadler's Wells Royal Ballet in 1976, Helpmann had long-since left The Royal Ballet and established a new career in Australia. In the years between joining the *corps de ballet* of the Ballet de Roland Petit in 1961 and the seasons she spent with Sadler's Wells Royal Ballet in the late 1970s, Gielgud danced with numerous French companies (notably the Ballet de l'Etoile de Milorad Miskovitch and the Grand Ballet Classique de France) until she became Principal Artist with Maurice Béjart's Ballet XXème Siècle (1967-1971), with the Staatsoper Ballet Berlin (1971-1972) and London Festival Ballet (1972-1976). After 1978 she pursued a freelance career as guest artist with some eleven companies world-wide until her retirement from performing in 1981. After a short spell as Rehearsal Director for London City Ballet, Gielgud became in 1983 Artistic Director of The Australian Ballet, a position she sustained for fourteen years. Following a period as Artistic Director of the Danish Royal Ballet (1997-1999), she has continued to work as an international coach, teacher and stager of works, chiefly from the classical repertoire.

For Sadler's Wells Royal Ballet Gielgud excelled in the role of the Black Queen in de Valois' *Checkmate*, Swanhilda in *Coppélia*, the Gypsy Girl in Ashton's *The Two Pigeons* and the Siren in Balanchine's *The Prodigal Son*. All the roles are noted for presenting an intelligent, witty or cunning, forthright, independent woman with a commanding stage presence. In this filmed interview, recorded on 3 September 2013, it is therefore no surprise to find her talking enthusiastically about Helpmann's theatricality; the powerful expressiveness of his eyes; his joy in communicating ("sharing") with an audience and, related to that, his absolute dedication to serving the demands of a given role; the courage and the daring that underlay all his performances.

Much of what Maina Gielgud claims about Helpmann is substantiated by two short recorded sequences from his appearances with her in *Steps, Notes and Squeaks* (a series of masterclasses with performances, which she devised and toured from 1978 till 1981), which are included here at the close of the interview. (Gielgud recently posted the full recordings on YouTube.) The first shows Helpmann being rehearsed by Ninette de Valois in one of the Red King's solos from *Checkmate* (recorded 1979), while in the second (recorded 1978) he tutors Gielgud in one of the mimed "conversations" between Odette and the Prince in *Swan Lake*, where he recalls Karsavina's advice to him about how to approach mime. The latter extract shows how expert a teacher

Helpmann could be and also shows what many of his contemporaries recall about his approach to choreography: that he talked, told stories, discussed motivations and the feelings that define character, thereby creating a context which his dancers then had to embody to his satisfaction. It was a clever process to bring a performer to inhabit a role and perhaps conveys an insight into how Helpmann himself shaped similar contexts throughout his career to help him delineate the complex psychology he sensed within the roles he undertook.

The Actor, Robert Helpmann:
voice, text and theatrical intelligence

Richard Allen Cave

> It will be useless in future for Mr Robert Helpmann to pretend that he is
> exclusively a dancer of the first rank. Certainly his dancing gives strength
> to his Oberon; he glides into imagined invisibility; but that is not all: his
> verse sings with his thought, his Oberon flashes with power, and presides, as
> Oberons do rarely, over the whole magic of the wood.[1]

The critic for the *Times* was clearly impressed by Helpmann's professional
debut in a Shakespearean production at the Old Vic in 1937. The terms
in which his praise is couched are worth close attention. The elegance of
movement was to be expected from "a dancer of the first rank", less so,
perhaps, was his ability to switch off a projected charisma to become
invisible to spectators (the critic's use of the epithet, "imagined", shows
that the effect of Helpmann's appearing invisible was a technical feat; his
body remained in view but his *presence* was removed). What was less to be
expected by contemporary readers of the review was praise of Helpmann's
verse speaking. Again the terms in which the critic couches his comment are
revealing: Helpmann's voice encompassed a melodic excellence ("sings"),
but it was no parade of elocutionary tricks (the *voice beautiful* for its own
sake that results in empty, usually overly breathy poeticising). Aesthetic
beauty was not pursued at the expense of the meaning of the lines; rather,
Helpmann discovered the expressive power inherent in an attention to syntax
("his verse sings with his *thought*"). His Oberon was elegant, otherworldly,
expressive and intelligent, which resulted in his communicating a superb
authority onstage; Helpmann, both in his role and as a performer relating
to spectators, was a figure in unquestionable control. (See plates 10 and 11)

For a first attempt at a major acting part (and one he secured in
competition with Laurence Olivier, since Vivien Leigh was to play Titania)[2],
this was a remarkable success and one he had won in an audition with
the director, Tyrone Guthrie, by virtue of being unexpected and *different*.[3]
Though well-established by 1937 as a *danseur noble* with Ninette de Valois'
Vic-Wells Ballet Company, Helpmann had surprised Guthrie by remaining
absolutely still throughout his audition speech. Asked why he had not called
on his movement skills in evoking Oberon, he replied: "I don't think you have
to move to create magic. I think if you've got it in your voice, the magic is

1. Robert Helpmann in ENSA uniform c.1945. Photo: Harcourt © Studio Harcourt, Paris. Source: Victoria and Albert Museum, London

2. Robert Helpmann as Satan in the Vic-Wells Ballet's 1933 revival of Ninette de Valois' *Job* (1931). Photo: Edward Mandinian © Victoria and Albert Museum, London

3. Robert Helpmann as The Rake before his downfall, Ninette de Valois' *The Rake's Progress* (1935). Photo: Gordon Anthony © Victoria and Albert Museum, London. Source: The Royal Ballet School Special Collections

174.

4. Ninette de Valois as the Tight-Rope Walker and Robert Helpmann as the Cook's Man in the 1935 Vic-Wells revival of de Valois' ballet *Douanes* (1932). Photo: J. W. Debenham © Victoria and Albert Museum, London. Source: The Royal Ballet School Special Collections

5. Robert Helpmann in his created role of Paris in *The Judgement of Paris*, a short-lived ballet made by Frederick Ashton for a royal fundraising gala in memory of Lilian Baylis (Vic-Wells Ballet, 1938). Photo: Gordon Anthony © Victoria and Albert Museum, London

6. Robert Helpmann in his created role of The Poet in Frederick Ashton's *Apparitions* (Vic-Wells Ballet, Feb. 1936). Photo: Gordon Anthony © Victoria and Albert Museum, London

7. Robert Helpmann in his created role of A Young Man in Frederick Ashton's *Nocturne* (Vic-Wells Ballet, Nov. 1936). Helpmann's innate sense of classical line is evident in both these images. Photo: Gordon Anthony © Victoria and Albert Museum, London. Source: The Royal Ballet School Special Collections

8. Robert Helpmann as Albrecht in *Giselle* (Vic-Wells Ballet, c.1934). Photo: Gordon Anthony © Victoria and Albert Museum, London (Norman McCann Collection)

9. Robert Helpmann as Prince Charming in *The Sleeping Princess* (Vic-Wells Ballet, 1939). Photo: Gordon Anthony © Victoria and Albert Museum, London

10. Robert Helpmann as Oberon in Shakespeare's *A Midsummer Night's Dream*, directed by Tyrone Guthrie, with designs by Oliver Messel (Old Vic Theatre, 1937). Photo: Gordon Anthony © Victoria and Albert Museum, London

11. The same production, with Ralph Richardson as Bottom and Vivien Leigh as Titania. Helpmann as Oberon with Gordon Miller as Puck are 'invisible' upstage. Photo: Gordon Anthony © Victoria and Albert Museum, London. Source: The Royal Ballet School Special Collections

12. Constant Lambert, Ninette de Valois and Robert Helpmann backstage at Bronson Albery's New Theatre, in London's West End, which became the wartime home of the Sadler's Wells Ballet Company from January 1941. Photo: J. W. Debenham © Victoria and Albert Museum, London. Source: The Royal Ballet School Special Collections

13. Robert Helpmann and Margot Fonteyn in Frederick Ashton's *Dante Sonata* (Vic-Wells Ballet, January 1940). Photo: Gordon Anthony © Victoria and Albert Museum, London. Source: The Royal Ballet School Special Collections

14. Robert Helpmann impersonating the actress, Margaret Rutherford, in a revue entitled 'Swinging the Gate' at the Ambasssadors Theatre, London, May 1940. Photo: Gordon Anthony © Victoria and Albert Museum, London

15. Robert Helpmann impersonating the actress, Margaret Rawlings, in the same revue. Photo: Gordon Anthony © Victoria and Albert Museum, London

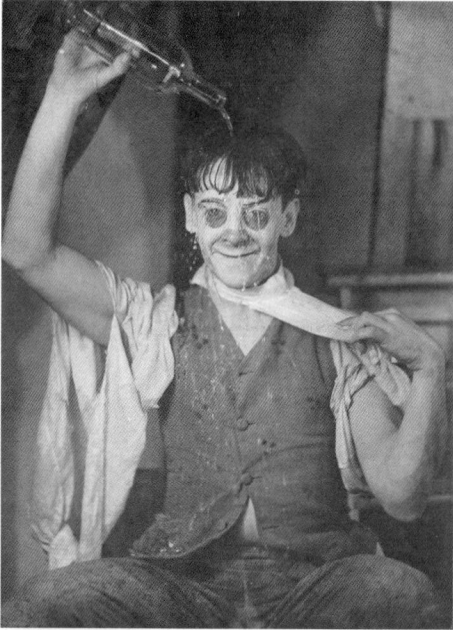

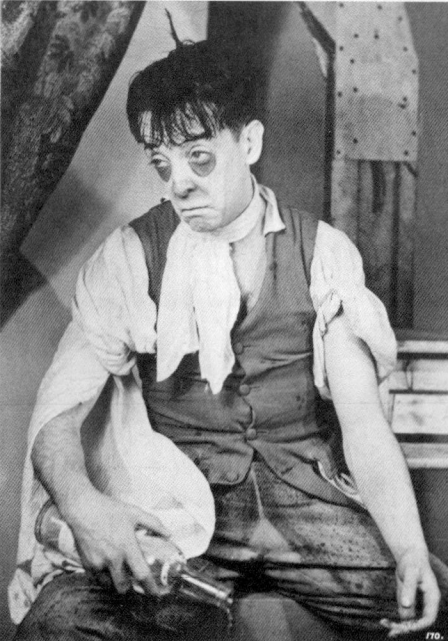

16, 17, 18. Robert Helpmann as the inebriated Mr O'Reilly in Ninette de Valois' ballet *The Prospect Before Us* (1940). Photos: Gordon Anthony © Victoria and Albert Museum, London

19. Robert Helpmann as Mr O'Reilly twirling 'en pointe'. Photo: Gordon Anthony © Victoria and Albert Museum, London. Source: The Royal Ballet School Special Collections

20. Robert Helpmann as Dr Coppélius in the popular wartime revival of
Coppélia (Vic-Wells Ballet, 1940). Verso inscribed by Gordon Anthony: 'RH
has both danced in *Coppélia* as Franz and played it as Dr. Coppélius [from 1941]
– with equal success. What other actor dancer could claim such a unique
position?' Photo: Gordon Anthony © Victoria and Albert Museum, London.
Source: The Royal Ballet School Special Collections

21. Robert Helpmann as Comus, attempting to seduce The Lady (Margot Fonteyn) in his ballet *Comus* (1942). Designed by Oliver Messel. Scenario by Helpmann and Michael Benthall, based on Milton's masque. Photographed by Tunbridge-Sedgwick. Credit: Royal Opera House/ArenaPAL

22. Depiction of the set design by Leslie Hurry for Robert Helpmann's one-act ballet *Hamlet* (1942). This painting by Martin Sutherland was made for an exhibition celebrating Hurry's career (1987). © The Royal Ballet School (Monica Mason Collection)

23. Tableau seen at the beginning and the end of Robert Helpmann's ballet *Hamlet* (Sadler's Wells Ballet, 1942). Photographed by Tunbridge-Sedgwick. Credit: Royal Opera House/ArenaPAL

24. 'Our sometime sister, now our Queen': David Paltenghi as Claudius and Celia Franca as Gertrude in Robert Helpmann's ballet *Hamlet* (Sadler's Wells Ballet, 1942). Photographed by Tunbridge-Sedgwick. Credit: Royal Opera House /ArenaPAL

25. 'A Freudian Triangle': Robert Helpmann as Hamlet with David Paltenghi as Claudius and Celia Franca as Gertrude in Helpmann's ballet *Hamlet* (Sadler's Wells Ballet, 1942). Photographed by Tunbridge-Sedgwick. Credit: Royal Opera House /ArenaPAL

26. 'Ophelia-Gertrude duplication': Robert Helpmann as Hamlet with Margot Fonteyn as Ophelia and Celia Franca as Gertrude in Helpmann's ballet *Hamlet* (Sadler's Wells Ballet, 1942). Photographed by Tunbridge-Sedgwick. Credit: Royal Opera House/ArenaPAL

there."[4] Helpmann saw that he should put his artistry solely at the service of Shakespeare's; whatever dancing qualities he brought to his impersonation were to be incidental, subsumed within the requirements of Shakespeare's dramaturgy, an insight that was to help steer him in later years through several more demanding Shakespearean characterisations.

What is remarkable about this review of Helpmann's Oberon is how it shows him establishing early in this aspect of his career many of the qualities that were to be his hallmarks as an actor: his concern with finding the right voice for the text; his ear for the music of language and for the rhythms of prose and verse; his skill in marrying his mimetic and vocal skills in the service of a given role; his maintaining a powerful authority onstage within an ensemble of performers and in rapport with his audience; and, crucially, the formidable intelligence that underpinned and shaped all he did in the theatre. One often reads of a new actor as showing promise, but in Helpmann's case that potential was fully realised from the start. Yet one could not have supposed from that performance as Oberon how diverse his range would prove, or the emotional depths that he would plumb.

The biographical facts show how important Helpmann's career as an actor was for him.[5] Excluding his performances on film, which are dealt with elsewhere in this volume, he undertook well over forty roles on the stage, on radio or television between appearances in Sydney at the age of seventeen in 1926[6] and 1985 when he appeared for two instalments in an Australian soap-opera twenty months before he died (appropriately his final stage performance was as the ailing and ill-fated Red King in a revival of de Valois' *Checkmate* with Australian Ballet in May 1986). His range as an actor seems prodigious: he proved an accomplished performer in comedy, tragedy, expressionist and existentialist drama, *commedia*, musicals, vaudeville and revue, farce, verse drama, masque, melodrama, Coward's comedy of manners and Shaw's play of ideas. Whatever he attempted, Helpmann was (to judge by most contemporary reviews) committed, inventive, original in approach and execution, stylish; he was indefatigable in extending his expertise by embracing fresh challenges. Like his one-time friend and on-stage colleague, Laurence Olivier, Helpmann could make the smallest role memorably distinctive, such as his Bishop of Ely in Olivier's film of *Henry V*. When he returned to his native Australia in 1955, it was as an actor with Michael Benthall's Old Vic Company, despite his international acclaim as a dancer and choreographer by that date. Brilliantly, Helpmann regularly accomplished roles in both performance traditions (the drama and the dance) within his schedule for a given week, commuting back and forth if necessary between London and Stratford or Edinburgh.[7] His stamina was legendary. A cursory glance through a chronological list of his acting roles might perhaps lead one to think that he seized every offer that came his way, being incapable of saying 'No' to an invitation.[8] Yet a more serious perusal reveals certain patterns emerging behind his choices that suggest a scrupulous intelligence at work tempering his enthusiasms with an exact (and exacting) awareness of his precise abilities.

If it is difficult to get a purchase on Helpmann as an actor, it is because critical writing about his performances in this art form is vastly outweighed by the volume of writing about him as a dancer and choreographer. In the field of dance history he will have an enduring place through being the first home-nurtured male dancer to lead de Valois' Company,[9] and during the time he spent with the Company he originated a number of danced roles that helped establish the modern repertory, which will always be studied when revivals occur and new dancers look to recover an appropriate sense of style. By contrast, in the field of acting, his achievements have no such afterlife. His unique impersonation of Dr Coppélius, even down to his personally devised make-up, could still nowadays be discovered in sufficient detail to effect a recreation, similarly, his Red King in de Valois' *Checkmate* (1937); but it would pose a far bigger challenge to attempt to do this with his portrayals of Shylock or Richard III, despite his considerable success in these roles.[10] Yet in the 1940s and 1950s his status as an actor, first in England and America and finally in Australia, was highly respected, and especially within acting circles. To list but some of the actors he worked with during these two decades is to appreciate why he was viewed as special: Paul Scofield, Diana Wynyard, Anthony Quayle, Laurence Olivier and Vivien Leigh, Claire Bloom, Katherine Hepburn, Keith Michell, Robert Hardy, Paul Daneman, Fay Compton, Richard Burton, Michael Hordern and Barbara Jefford. These were either already established in the highest ranks or were part of a younger generation soon comfortably to reach those ranks. That he attracted extended critical attention from reviewers while playing with such performers shows that, as an actor, he was deemed to be their equal. To gauge on what that reputation rested, it is necessary to look closely at the terms in which Helpmann's artistry as an actor was discussed.

When Helpmann first appeared in 1937 as an actor at the Old Vic playing Oberon, Audrey Williamson, who had long admired his work as a dancer, could not withhold her surprise:

> Now he flashed forth not merely as an actor of imagination and grace, but as a speaker of poetic fire. His voice proved musical, clear, strong enough for authority and sensitively attuned to rhythm and mood.[11]

Caryl Brahms was later, in 1943, to list the strengths he brought to his performance as Hamlet in his own balletic version – and they apply equally well to his strengths in performing Shakespeare's character, as scrutiny of the reviews of the two productions of the play in which he appeared will endorse: "pace, elegance, a lovely line of arm and shoulder, faultless timing and an unerring sense of the dramatic".[12] One quality that neither mentions, but one that was to feature continually in future reviews, was Helpmann's *intelligence*; it was to recur in contexts that steadily brought considerable complexities of meaning to the term that help us today gain a degree of access to his relation with a role and to his audiences. It is Kathrine Sorley Walker, who perhaps best defines Helpmann's creative intelligence, whether as performer, choreographer or director, when she describes him as possessing "a mind ably attuned to its subject".[13] This is to define intelligence as wide-ranging in its sympathies and understanding and as a kind of scrupulous tact: a placing one's self at the service of one's artistry and the material with which it works. Fully to achieve such a state of mind requires a degree of discipline and a developed skill in self-appraisal, which is precisely what the critic of the *New Statesman* valued in Helpmann's performance as Shakespeare's Hamlet at Stratford in 1948: "one felt that he had taken the exact measure of his own particular talent and played that to its uttermost without ever trying to exceed it", which resulted for this reviewer in a "vivid, quicksilver conception" of the role that was "a considered and persuasive whole".[14] It takes intelligence, honesty and humility to know the measure of one's abilities at a given point in one's career, however ambitious one might be to expand one's technical expertise.

To realise an ambition to develop as a performer requires not only the level of self-awareness that Helpmann demonstrated for that particular reviewer, but continuing hard work, tenacity of purpose and constant, selfless assessment of one's progress. Reviews of Helpmann's performances in drama, as distinct from dance, show that he must have committed himself to just such levels of application. For any one-time dancer seeking to re-invent himself as an actor, a major issue to be faced is the nature of one's voice and the physical mechanisms of its production (one's breathing patterns and one's natural or preferred register). The demands are greater and more searching if one's chief objective is to appear confidently speaking Renaissance texts. The physical elevation required of dancers inevitably situates their vocal registers such that the resonance chambers of the head and throat tend to dominate in delivery; and this usually results in a high, reedy timbre. (Christopher Gable exemplifies this pattern and his roles as an actor were noticeably limited in range and confined principally to film and television rather than the stage; and this was similarly the case with Moira Shearer.[15]) It was fortunate that Helpmann came to professional acting through the good offices of Margaret Rawlings, whose company he joined on its tour of Australia in 1932 with *The Barretts of Wimpole Street*; she had a magnificent vocal range encompassing a rich contralto, and a sensitively tuned ear for poetic rhythm.[16] Whatever tuition she gave Helpmann in his early months in her company was supplemented by classes with the noted voice coach, Beatrice Wilson, in London and by conversation and practice with his partner, Michael Benthall, and the director, Tyrone Guthrie.[17] It is clear that Helpmann worked extensively to develop and sustain a newly pitched voice by opening up the potentials in his lower chest resonances considerably to extend his range and flexibility. Extensive runs in particular plays also allowed Helpmann the chance to use his voice in performance mode and so advance his mastery of suppleness and strength of volume.[18] By the time that Helpmann came to play in a second production of *Hamlet* in 1948, J.C. Trewin was moved to comment on his expertise:

> The actor knew the range of his own voice to a semi-tone, and though the range was not wide it was used with fastidious skill. This was a beautifully spoken Hamlet, just as it was beautifully poised.[19]

Clearly Helpmann possessed a great capacity to learn by experience, and that is the mark of a very open intelligence. (See plates 37, 38 and 39)

But there is more to the speaking of classical text than vocal quality, important though that obviously is: there is a need for a developed sense of rhythm, musicality and the ability to give all these elements their due weight while subsuming them within the demands of the given dramatic situation. These additional qualities are matters of personal taste and judgement rather than technical expertise. All Helpmann's biographers stress the importance of his mother's instilling both an appreciation of such qualities in him from his earliest years and a delight in accomplishing them (playing scenes from Shakespeare with his mother was neither an embarrassment nor a chore for such a precocious child). It hardly needs stating that his training in dance would extend his appreciation of rhythmic variety and experiment and his awareness of the dramatic effects to be obtained by handling the stresses that make for rhythm, either with weight or more lightly. Considerable time must have been spent in experimenting to achieve the effects spectators and critics admired in his performance-style: however effortless they may appear in delivery, they are the product of considerable exploration and selection, of judgement, taste and tact, of creativity and intelligent selection. Herbert Farjeon wrote that his 1937-38 Oberon at the Old Vic "speaks his verse better than almost anyone else in the company".[20] W.A. Darlington wrote approvingly of the partnership of Vivien Leigh and Helpmann as the fairy consorts, and then added the interesting rider: "The odd thing is that he, a dancer, speaks the verse rather better than she does."[21]

Praise of Helpmann's handling of dramatic verse continued over the years (even when critics disliked his overall interpretations). A full and detailed account of Helpmann's vocal mastery comes in a review of his first *Hamlet* in 1944, written by James Redfern for the *Spectator*:

> [Helpmann's is] the best Hamlet I have ever seen. [... Though he is] by no means ideally endowed by nature for the part, he is tremendously impressive and the chief reason for his success is not merely his intelligence [...] but the truth and sincerity of his conception of the part. [...There is] none of the usual sham Shakespearean ranting in the production. Mr. Helpmann speaks quietly, always distinctly, and with nowhere a false emphasis. [...] He has chosen to suggest rather than to underline, and nearly all actors make the fatal mistake of underlining and exaggerating when they speak poetry [...] whereas Mr. Helpmann, by concentrating on truth rather than beauty, convinces by his sincere and natural (but oh! how exceedingly difficult to achieve!) simplicity.[22]

A further, notable accolade about Helpmann's handling of verse dialogue came from George Rylands, founder of the Cambridge University's Marlowe Society and tutor in verse speaking to such influential future figures as Peter Hall and John Barton. He reviewed the production of Shakespeare's *Antony and Cleopatra*, directed by Benthall, which Laurence Olivier and Vivien Leigh mounted as part of the celebrations for the Festival of Britain in 1951. (It was played in tandem with Shaw's *Caesar and Cleopatra*, in which Helpmann played Apollodorus.) The critics unanimously praised Helpmann's portrayal of Octavius Caesar as all "thin-lipped precision, bloodless but formidably efficient", agreeing it would add much to his standing as an actor.[23] Rylands' review focused on whether or not actors in the Shakespearean tragedy used the dynamics of the verse to generate, underpin and sustain their particular characterisations. He was adversely critical of the Oliviers on this score, but considered Helpmann exemplary: he "made every pause and syllable tell, every flicker of his lid and finger; a cold-blooded youth who had never been a boy; and how formidable!"[24] In his summing-up, he opined that, but for Helpmann, the production would have missed the necessary political dimension: "Helpmann's outstanding performance conveyed Shakespeare's intention that the play be presented as not only a love story but as an imperial theme."[25] Whether or not he was influenced by Benthall in this, Helpmann was highly perceptive not only of the demands of the role but of its particular function within the overarching dramatic structure of the tragedy.

Intelligence was not simply the hallmark of Helpmann's handling of a role, it may also be discerned in his choice of roles to play. Though many and various, those roles on a close survey share a common feature: they are all *outsider* figures. To list just the Shakespearean roles he played (Oberon, Hamlet, the Bishop of Ely (in Olivier's film of *Henry V*), Shylock, King John, Octavius Caesar, Richard III, Launce, Pinch, Gremio, Saturninus, Angelo, Petruchio, see plates 58-65) is to see the force of this: they are all by various means and with varying degrees of success struggling to impose their will on, or to come to terms with, a social world that seeks either to marginalise, question, or inhibit the full and free expression of their inherent selves, which throws their *otherness* into sharp relief. The recurrence of this type of character argues that a careful principle underlay their selection. Helpmann himself fitted that classification as outsider in life on many counts: an Australian in England; an aesthetically driven, artistic temperament in the macho or gender-conformist environment of Australia; a homosexual, who was cheerfully "out" in what were repressive times for much of his life in England; and now as a performer he was choosing to appear as a dancer amongst actors. Anna Bemrose and Elizabeth Salter, two of his biographers, have shown how he could be both outrageous and daring; some degree of both attitudes was required in all the ways in which Helpmann manifested as an outsider.[26] But in the final category, as a dancing actor or actor-dancer, intelligence had to take the major control; and I would argue that a meticulous awareness of himself as dancer influenced his choice of acting parts. No dancer can shed the impact of their training on their physique; nor can they ever quite elude an audience's expectations of them as dancers. Spectators will always be alert to a dancer's trained grace and ease of movement, the effortlessly sustained carriage, the unconscious sense of *line* in how the body is presented to others, whatever the mode of performance or the context on or off stage in which that dancer is seen. Place that dancer in a cast of actors, and he or she will invariably stand out as *different*, and markedly so. In Helpmann's case, to choose to play outsiders – all individuals different from the play worlds they inhabit – was a brilliant decision: it placed him in performance situations where his dance experience fully supported and integrated with his objectives as an actor.

The risk would always be to play for outright sympathy by presenting these outsiders as victims; but, though Helpmann suffered indignities in his life, such as the Bondi beach episode commented on by Elizabeth Schafer in this volume,[27] and not infrequent setbacks in his career even as a dancer, he possessed an indefatigable resilience (in part powered by his outrageousness and daring); and in all these portrayals he seems to have found grounds through which to develop unexpected complexities of characterisation to take audiences by surprise. His playing of Shylock in *The Merchant of Venice* is a notable example. His make-up including a prosthetic curved nose, elaborately curled wig and beard, took two hours in its application and this, together with his voluminous robes and magnificent display of jewellery verged dangerously on caricature; but the ensuing performance belied that appearance. (See plates 40 and 61) J.C. Trewin wrote the fullest account of its impact at Stratford in 1948:

> Robert Helpmann's Shylock was a gentlemanly Jew; a man of breeding to judge by his pale features and dark, thoughtful eyes, a man of taste and culture to judge by his expressive hands, a man of proud spirit to judge by his aloof bearing. This man inspired no sympathy anywhere, but a distant respect everywhere.[28]

The critic of the *Birmingham Post* summed up his impression of Helpmann's portrayal more succinctly but was clearly in agreement with Trewin: "He shows the wrongful Jew and the Jew wronged."[29] The general view was that Helpmann assumed "a commanding dignity and carried a fierce sense of wounded racial pride".[30] Frequently reviewers saw this Shylock as motivated by a prodigious, if dark intelligence: "[he was] no sombre, brooding patriarch but a keen, alert intelligence driving towards its own ends with concentrated force" and, as such, a man to be feared, not ridiculed.[31] (See plate 62) Helpmann in other words chose to play against one established theatrical tradition (though his interpretation had much in common with Henry Irving's way with the part) and against racial stereotyping, offering instead a figure of considerable authority and, for much of the play, moral dignity. The courtroom scene was his undoing, in his pursuit of "justice" beyond any point where reason, let alone charity, prevailed, though till then he had been much provoked and sinned against. Mary Clarke, writing of Helpmann's reprise of the role with the Old Vic Company as part of Benthall's five-year Folio Seasons, gives a detailed account of how the climax was handled:

> Portia allowed Shylock to come close to the merchant and even to raise his knife before she cried: *Tarry a little; there is something else.* Shylock's quick brain saw almost at once that he was trapped. *I take this offer then: pay the bond thrice, / And let the Christian go* was spoken quietly but with desperate speed. Once more money cried out – *Give me my principal, and let me go!* Thereafter he knew he had no hope and crumpled, servile, beseeching, all his former pride disappearing as he approached the Duke on his knees. With the words *I am content* his world was over [...][32]

This gave due weight to Shylock's tragic exit from the play, which tempered the joyful comedy which the final act attempted to recover: always a man apart, he remained a loner, (proud, if broken) till the last. It was a performance that eschewed sentiment and self pity.

When Helpmann played Flamineo in a revival of Webster's *The White Devil*, directed by Benthall at the Duchess Theatre in 1947, there had been no such performance tradition to negotiate, as had been the case with all his Shakespearean roles. Flamineo's dark scheming motivates much of the plot and it would have been all too easy to play him as another archetypal melodramatic villain. Helpmann presented instead a mordant-witted malcontent, a misfit with social aspirations above his station: born poor, he yet yearned to inhabit the status of a patrician, feeling he already possessed the necessary sensibility and values. There was motive in his malignity: everything was to be manipulated to feed and promote his ambition. The text ably supports this interpretation, arguing that Benthall and Helpmann had meticulously close-hand knowledge of the intimate details of Webster's dramaturgy. The result was a study of mesmerising evil, but as the critic of the *Times* argues: "Robert Helpmann makes a careful study of Flamineo, bringing out that imaginative agony which Webster gives to his greatest scoundrels."[33] James Agate considered that "his whole performance was marked by a virtuosity, a virility, and a quality of sheer verbal passion that are rare things on our stage today".[34] Reviewers' imaginations were caught by specific physical details: one noted that "Helpmann's Flamineo is a serpent. All the ruffianly refinement of the Italian Renaissance is in that depraved mask, in the twitching grace of those hands",[35] while for another, "Nothing could be more eloquent than his slow walk, waiting to pounce; or the horrified contemplation of his right hand, after he has struck the face of the dead duke."[36] The facial depravity captures Flamineo's total amorality and the cat-like stealth suggests the dangerous opportunist. The Duke, Brachiano, was Flamineo's master, to whom he had prostituted his sister, Vittoria, in the hope of advancement: his striking a superior even in death is a fine illustration of the character's desperation at the ongoing failure of his schemes and of a lingering servility that underlies and frustrates his ambition. To combine such a wealth of implication (social, psychological and emotional) within one gesture indicates a high degree of creative invention and tact. Maybe the dancer's expertise is in evidence here, but it is placed entirely at the service of Webster's dramaturgy.

Helpmann's intelligence was at work in other areas of the production as well: numerous critics quipped that his costume, which had been shaped to leave the expanse of his midriff completely exposed, was designed to show off the actor's musculature. More likely, it was a further exercise in textual insight. Lodovico, a spendthrift aristocrat down on his luck and banished, threatens in the opening scene to make "Italian cutworks" in the guts of Flamineo and his sister, whom he believes are instrumental in his exile (1, 1, 51). Late in the action he returns and gets his vengeance on the siblings precisely as he had vowed to do. "Cutwork" was the term used to describe the way material in bodices and sleeves was often slashed open to reveal the fabric lining beneath. (It was a popular upper-class fashion at the time Webster wrote his play.) Part of Webster's thematic concern in his tragedy is with the way evil generates greater evil or festers over time in the imaginations of perpetrators, completely eroding any spiritual values they might have espoused. Lodovico particularly illustrates this theme; but it is not easy for an audience to bring the links and their significance to mind, when idea and action are separated by the duration of the play. Subconsciously Helpmann's costume must have helped to sustain the idea of Lodovico's revenge and his chosen method of achieving it. (See plate 49) Helpmann's was the only costume in the piece to be designed in this way, so its difference from the rest would have prompted consideration of a possible function. The climactic action drew all these preparations into a horrifying image: "...for a dénouement, Robert Helpmann, strung up by the wrists, sagging slowly to death with the effect of five dagger thrusts reddening his abdomen".[37] It is at this moment that Webster gives Flamineo a magnificently phrased vision of death and the void that awaits him beyond:

> I recover like a spent taper, for a flash,
> And instantly go out. [...]
> My life was a black charnel. I have caught
> An everlasting cold; I have lost my voice
> Most irrecoverably.   (5, 6, 258-259; 264-266)

The wit that undercuts the cynicism of this, the jocular grasping at the mundane in the face of physical pain and metaphysical annihilation, endows Flamineo, for all the enormity of evil he has perpetrated throughout the play, with a stoical heroism: here is a bitter self-reckoning but one courageously accepted ("My life was a black charnel"). This is a prescribed and inevitable end, anticipated in the opening speeches of the play and part of Webster's metaphysical argument about the nature of evil. That such a seemingly incidental matter as the designing of a costume should become central to the presentation of Webster's dramaturgical scheme shows to what a remarkable degree Helpmann, doubtless with Benthall, understood how Webster's theatricality (that gruesome, spectacular death; the vivid death-speech in which Flamineo, a man who has proved himself a consummate actor in his relations with others, envisages a future where he is voiceless and deprived of all his customary means of expression) has to be appreciated as the correlative of his profound metaphysical engagement with his characters. This is acting at the level of the finest dramatic criticism.

The emphasis in this chapter has until now been very much on the serious and tragic sides of Helpmann's performances as an actor. Even when he appeared in such Shakespearean comedies as *The Merchant of Venice* and *A Midsummer Night's Dream*, it was the dark aspect of his characterisations that impressed itself on audiences. Shylock verged, as we have seen, on the tragic, while Helpmann's Oberon encompassed many tones and shades of significance, becoming by turns "a majestic, *ominous* and most romantic figure".[38] (Oberon is the figure in the fairy world who has most power; if his will is transgressed, he is dangerously threatening; the resolution of the comedy is entirely under his control, which he stage-manages with an exacting precision. This dimension to his character is not always explored by actors in the role, who wish to stress the Mendelssohnian charm of the fairy world; but not Helpmann, who clearly examined the full implications of the text.) Dance had given lee-way to Helpmann's comic gifts with his portrayals of Coppélius or the ever-inebriated Mr O'Reilly in Ninette de Valois' *The Prospect Before Us* (1940). It was after Benthall became the Artistic Director of the Old Vic and initiated his plan in 1953 to stage all the plays in the Shakespearean First Folio that Helpmann got an opening to develop in drama his gift for inventive clowning, and particularly in the fourth season, 1956-57, when he played Launce with his misbehaving dog in *The Two Gentlemen of Verona* and the weird magician, Doctor Pinch, in *The Comedy of Errors*. Kenneth Tynan described his performance as Pinch as "a riveting intervention" that left audiences limp with laughter: dressed like "one of the less inhibited members of the Chinese Classical Theatre", he tripped over his extended beard and struggled with the weight of his enormous book of magic, while toothlessly mouthing dire incantations.[39] Again, it was the closely thought-out integration of effects that compelled audiences' rapt attention: the costume, the make-up, the gestures, the facial dynamics (all supporting a meticulously spoken text with calculatedly pitched voice) that created a compelling, because wholly unified, invention. (See plate 65)

Reviewers tend to be less detailed in their appraisals of Helpmann's comic performances as an actor, preferring to measure the degree of merriment they inspired. There is one notable exception: Audrey Williamson's account of one of his first appearances in a farce-like role as the Tailor in Tyrone Guthrie's production of *The Taming of the Shrew* (Old Vic, 1939):

> The only other actor to emerge triumphantly [...] was Robert Helpmann [...] with a clever, decrepit and rather pathetic Gremio and a virtuoso performance in the small part of the Tailor. This was a brilliantly mimed piece of outraged dandyism, with an affected accent, an excess of brilliantine and a quite revolting centre parting. This figure of effete fun listened to Petruchio's railing with indifference, until the insult, "Thou remnant!" pierced his

professional heart and he departed in high dudgeon and in tears.[40]

This gives an immediate sense of the completeness of Helpmann's interpretation, the chosen appearance (clothes, wig, make-up) and the matching voice; but it is notable in being a rare instance that includes an example of his self-control and careful restraint in the timing of effects. The Tailor is a tiny role and, wanting to make an impact, numerous actors in the part have tended to "milk" the scene, exploiting an array of postures, expostulations and facial contortions expressive of horror and outrage at being so defamed by Petruchio. Helpmann noticeably bides his time, standing quietly impervious, as if all-too-accustomed to haggling or fault-finding customers, until Petruchio's final salvo cuts him to the quick. The chosen term, 'remnant', undermines his professionalism, his masculinity, his social standing, his pride in his craft: the devastation of the man is total. (It is interesting, as Elizabeth Schafer has observed, that all the terms of Audrey Williamson's review intimate that Helpmann played the character as gay, though she never states so openly.) What Helpmann did is remarkable in not drawing spectators' focus exclusively to himself as actor, but rather in directing attention to the way that the text builds towards the comic climax: the artistry may be Helpmann's but the honours are shared with Shakespeare's dramatic skill. A deep appreciation of the techniques by which comedy is generated on stage underlies this example and, in tandem with it, as profound an insight into the comic strategies within the text.[41]

Theatre historians are much reliant on the reviews of critics in writing an essay like this; they give a good sense of how a particular performance was received. However, they tend to offer responses to finished effects and whatever a historian reads into their assessments verges on hypothesis, however carefully that reading is inflected. We cannot know precisely an actor's intentions with a given role, many of which are probably subconscious, especially where potential influences are concerned. It is rare that one gets a glimpse of an actor's processes of invention, all that which precedes and underlies the finished effect. Much has been claimed in this essay about Helpmann's intelligence, his tact, his insight into the strategies underpinning a spoken text, but in all cases these have been judged from the standpoint of communicated effects. Remarkably, traces remain to show how one such notable effect was achieved by Helpmann: these centre on reading a sequence of promptbook entries for his 1948 Hamlet at the Shakespeare Memorial Theatre in Stratford alongside reviews of the resulting performances. The sequence occurs in the fifth scene of the opening act: the scene where the Ghost of Hamlet senior tells his son of his murder at Claudius's hand and the hellish consequences he has since undergone in the afterlife. It is a grim episode that both provides the mechanism for the tragedy which ensues and starts a division in Hamlet's psyche, which shapes the complexities of his characterisation. Most of the stage time is devoted to the Ghost's narrative; Hamlet's lines are few; and yet the whole focus of the scene is on his reactions to the circumstances of his father's death, the overwhelming idea of Claudius's fratricide, troubling doubts about his mother's complicity in the deed; and dread at what this might require of him. Much of this whirling activity in Hamlet's brain is revealed to audiences only after the Ghost's departure, but his responses, as perceived by an audience, need to prepare for his later close analysis of himself, if that analysis of his mind and emotions is to be credible.

Traditionally at this time a member of stage management at Stratford wrote all the blocking throughout the rehearsal period into a heavy tome that would eventually become the prompt copy.[42] The text is pasted to the recto of the pages, while the adjacent verso page is used for manuscript entries concerning movements and blocking on stage; cues for preparatory calls for actors about to enter or music and lighting effects soon to be required are entered into parallel columns situated in the margins of the recto pages to the right of the text, headed "WARN". At the start of each scene the characters needed within it are listed in the left hand margin of the page containing the text. Details of blocking on the verso pages are quite cursory and surprisingly minimal; groupings are usually depicted by a series of crosses with each cross carrying an abbreviation of the characters' names with a further similar diagram, if there is any change in the disposition of the actors on the stage. This is the appearance of most of the prompt copy for Benthall's production of *Hamlet*. The exception is what stage management records for Hamlet's scene with the Ghost: for a spread of three verso pages detailed descriptive directions for movements between the two performers are listed; they are pencilled in holograph and a number keys each direction into a precise position in the text where the same number is also inscribed as a tally. There are seven, eight and ten such entries on the three pages respectively. There is nothing akin to this anywhere else in the prompt copy, so it is worth following the sequence through to determine what these seemingly special directions reveal about the stagecraft deployed.

The directions begin with an instruction to strike the brazier (around which Hamlet met with the soldiers on sentry duty until the arrival of the Ghost) and fly in an arrangements of chains; then: "GHOST enters D[own] L[eft] lower steps entrance, moves slowly down steps, HAMLET following, holding sword, like cross, in front of him. GHOST D[own] R[ight] C[entre] as HAM [LET] reaches top step". Kenneth Tynan was much impressed by Esmond Knight's Ghost:

This overwhelming performance sent terror and alarm into one's very stomach: consternation rippled across the whole audience as it listened to Mr Knight's ghastly care in reaching after breath, an agonized inhaling as if he were scouring up the deepest fumes of hell to bear the noxious pain of his message to Hamlet's ears.

If ever thou didst thy dear father love
(intake of breath)
Revenge his foul and most unnatural MURDER
(the voice rising to a shriek)
         HAMLET: *MURDER?* (A horrified yell)
GHOST: *MURDER – most foul as in the best it is....*

Those three full-volume 'Murders' and their endless echoing down corridors and along galleries of pillars, sent the scene swimming up to a climax of [...] horror. I was out of my seat for fright.[43]

As Helpmann's Hamlet was stirred with pity for his father ("*Alas, poor ghost!*"), so he moved closer to Knight and knelt before him.[44] When the echoes Tynan describes occurred with the first mention of revenge, Hamlet "looks round and above him" before he "puts sword down" with the Ghost's claim on their close kindred: "*I am thy father's spirit*". The Ghost's account of the purgatorial miseries he must endure forced a horrified Hamlet to his knees "in front of <u>GHOST</u>", while the apparition's urgent demand that Hamlet "*list*" carefully to him compelled Hamlet to "stretch out his hands" to his father. When the Ghost finally revealed the purpose of his strange visit ("*Revenge his foul and most unnatural murder*") and Hamlet reiterated that last ominous word, he "leant back – R[ight] hand stretched upwards", as if to ward off fears beyond his immediate imagining. But on his injunction to the Ghost to tell him all ("*Haste me to know it*"), the directions indicate that Hamlet was to "rise on to knees", which is how he is positioned to learn of Claudius's guilt. When the Ghost mourns the loss of his Queen, when Gertrude's love was "*won to his shameful lust*", Hamlet was to "crouch on ground". Imparting the full details of his murder, the Ghost is seen "leaning down to Ham[let]" and later places "hand up to R[ight] ear" on describing how the poison, entering by that orifice, soon destroyed him by causing "*a vile and loathsome crust*" to erupt over his body. When thought of the sin perpetrated against him proves too much, the Ghost retreats into self-pity ("*O, horrible! O, horrible! most horrible!*"), and a shocked Hamlet "falls on ground"; but he kneels up again bringing "hands to head", as the Ghost begins to outline how his son should avenge him and the polluted "*royal bed of Denmark*". Urging Hamlet not to be infected by the evils that surround him and the duty now imposed on him ("*Taint not thy mind*"), the "GHOST passes his hand above HAM[LET]'s head". Perceiving the approach of dawn, the Ghost starts "moving backwards u[p]/s[tage] R[ight]". Alone, Hamlet invokes "*O all you host of heaven!*" and "collapses on ground, head towards audience". "Ham[let] rises slowly to sitting position" while he thinks over details of the Ghost's tale, the "*commandment*" that he must remember his father's appearance to him, and his role of avenger, until his mind eventually settles on the enormity that is Claudius ("*O villain, villain, smiling, damned villain!*"). "Ham[let] rises to sitting position – beating ground". Presumably his beating his hands on the ground was timed to coincide with each reiterated exclamation of "villain", and while so doing he "finds sword – and picks it up".[45] He repeats his promise to his father to remember him and ends with a solemn vow: "*I have sworn't*", which he made still kneeling but now "holding sword in front of him", which is how Horatio and the returning soldiers find him.

Helpmann, to judge by these annotated directions, physicalised the whole experience of the scene but allowed changing movement patterns to mark Hamlet's changing emotions and psychological shocks. He started and ended the scene with the same image (holding the sword before him) but where initially he held it like a cross, at the end it is held taut and forward as a weapon (this is a hypothesis, but there is no reference here to a cross formation; and the annotator is very precise, if curt, in detailing what was performed by the actor). What a wealth of horrifying experience has intervened between those two images, which has brought Hamlet from a troubled innocence to knowing experience! One has to ask: could an actor have sustained that slow fall to lying prone, the half risings and subsidings before steadily rising up for the final oath? Paul Scofield alternated the role of Hamlet with Helpmann throughout the run; photographs show that the two actors handled the same scenes very differently and critics were quick to draw comparisons and contrasts from this; instructions, chiefly for lighting and music in the right hand column of the recto pages often give two sets of directions, one for Helpmann, the other for Scofield. Interestingly no reviewer commented on Scofield in this scene with the Ghost, but several did on Helpmann's performance here.[46] It would be difficult, if not physically trained in ways that Scofield was not, to accomplish this movement sequence with the controlled grace necessary to suit the dominant tragic tenor of the episode, that slow fall and rise that are the correlative of the character's mental progress that defines a complete transformation, changing Hamlet from naïve scholar, indulging in grief, to a man absolute for revenge. Rather, a dancer's skills must be deployed adequately to support what would appear to be Helpmann's reading of the text. It is difficult in the playing to secure balance within the audience's focus of awareness between the Ghost and Hamlet: both points of focus are crucial; both define characters who are "other". The Ghost is otherworldly; Hamlet is transfixed almost in a trance as he undergoes a psychological crisis; Esmond Knight deployed limited physical action, choosing to define his character by surreal vocal effects as the correlative of his character's inner torment; Hamlet is all but silent, but Helpmann defined his inner trauma by a simple but potently evocative mime.

Here are all the hallmarks of Helpmann's acting style that this essay has sought to determine: his shrewd matching of his trained physical expertise with a scrupulous attention to the text; a careful selection of possible skills for maximum effectiveness by the minimum of means, a humility before the author he is interpreting and whose complex artistry he seeks to convey through his own varied resources as a performer; and above all his intelligence at work in bringing all these potentials into a meaningful symbiosis.[47] Robert Helpmann may be best known from performance histories as a dancer and choreographer; his achievements in the different art of acting deserve to be better known and be fully and precisely acknowledged. The deeper one probes into Helpmann's roles as an actor and the reception they generally evoked from critics, the more one is inclined to agree with the reviewer for the *New York Daily News*, who in summing up his responses to Helpmann's appearances as Octavius and as Apollodorus with the Oliviers' Company, could not stint his admiration:

> When one considers that Helpmann also has been a leading dancer with the Sadler's Wells Ballet, one must admit that he is a man of astonishing talent.[48]

Endnotes

1   Review of the Old Vic production of *A Midsummer Night's Dream* in the *Times*, 28 December 1937.

2   For an account of Olivier's attempt to secure the role of Oberon, see Elizabeth Salter, *Helpmann: The Authorised Biography* (Brighton: Angus and Robertson, 1978), p.84.

3   Helpmann had played in musical comedy and in revue in Australia earlier in his career, but chiefly as a dancer. Before travelling to England in 1932, he was a member of the Toyne/Rawlings Company, playing Septimus in *The Barretts of Wimpole Street*. His first, minor roles for de Valois and the Vic-Wells Ballet the following year were undertaken alongside small parts in plays at the Gate Theatre and the Lyric Theatre Hammersmith. With the start of the autumn season in 1933 de Valois promoted Helpmann to major roles, starting with Satan in her *Job* on 26 September. During his early years with de Valois' Company he continued to appear in plays but invariably as a dancer, "arranger of dances" or the occasional role that drew heavily on his dancing abilities, such as A Person of the Ballet in *The Fantasticks* (1933). Often these jobs were secured for him by de Valois, who was undertaking the choreography for the production.

4   Helpmann in interview with Hazel de Berg, 27 May 1974. Cited in Anna Bemrose, *Robert Helpmann: A Servant of Art* (St Lucia: University of Queensland Press, 2008), p.74.

5   J. Logan Gourlay, while preparing an album celebrating Helpmann's diverse talents, posed his subject a question about the future, to which he received a significant reply: "Robert Helpmann confesses his greatest ambition is to be a classical actor." See J. Logan Gourlay (ed.) *Robert Helpmann: Album* (Glasgow: Stage and Screen Press, Ltd., 1948), p.36.

6   Helpmann had earlier performed as a child actor while still in his infancy as a fairy in an amateur production of Shakespeare's *A Midsummer Night's Dream.*

7   Helpmann even brought his developed vocal skills into the world of dance when, in his staging of *Comus* (1942) for Sadler's Wells Ballet, he introduced the titular character's two great speeches from Milton's masque directly into what was otherwise wholly danced action, shaping the choreography to allow him the required breathing-space to both speak and dance. See also p. 4 of this volume.

8   For an exhaustive list, arranged alphabetically, of Helpmann's "roles as an actor on stage, film or TV; and work as a stage director apart from choreography", see Kathrine Sorley Walker, *Robert Helpmann: A Rare Sense of the Theatre* (Alton: Dance Books, 2009), Appendix 2, pp.179-183.

9   Helpmann was not a graduate of the Vic-Wells School, but his limited ballet technique was carefully strengthened under de Valois's eye within the Vic-Wells Company.

10   I have chosen the examples carefully to offset character roles in the dance with those in drama: each instance required a complete transformation of his appearance, facial features and stage persona. Like Olivier in his older years,

Helpmann possessed from a far younger age a chameleon-like ability to recreate himself unerringly to match the demands of a particular role. A notable exception to the generalisation here is Helpmann's portrayal of The Old Man in Strindberg's *The Ghost Sonata*, which was made for a BBC television broadcast (16 March 1962) and so was recorded for posterity.

11   Audrey Williamson, *Old Vic Drama* (London: Rockliff, 1948), p.79.

12   Caryl Brahms, *Robert Helpmann: Choreographer* (London: Batsford, 1943), p.28. Helpmann essayed the role in Shakespeare's tragedy under Tyrone Guthrie's direction for the Old Vic Company at the New Theatre, London, in 1944; and again in 1948 at the Shakespeare Memorial Theatre, Stratford-upon-Avon, where he was directed by Michael Benthall.

13   Kathrine Sorley Walker, *Brief for Ballet* (London: Pitfield, 1947), p.119.

14   Review of *Hamlet* in the *New Statesman*, 1 May 1948, included as a headed cutting in *Theatre Records* (Shakespeare Memorial Theatre), Vol. 36 (28 April 1947-3 November 1949), p.103, to be found in the library of the Shakespeare Centre, Stratford-upon-Avon.

15   Christopher Gable (1940-1998) was for many years Lynn Seymour's partner with The Royal Ballet till a rheumatoid condition of the feet terminated his career in ballet in 1967. He appeared notably as an actor in Peter Brook's production of *A Midsummer Night's Dream* as Lysander throughout the initial run in Stratford in 1970 and in 1974 in a West End production of Priestley's *The Good Companions*, but is better known for his numerous appearances in Ken Russell's films for television and cinema, starting with his portrayal of Eric Fenby in *Song of Summer* (1968), Russell's tribute to Delius. Gable founded the Central School of Ballet in 1982 with Ann Stannard, and in 1987 became Artistic Director of Northern Ballet Theatre. He returned to dancing at Gillian Lynne's invitation to appear as L.S. Lowry in her study of the artist, *A Simple Man* (1987), when he partnered first Moira Shearer and later Lynn Seymour in the role of Lowry's mother. Moira Shearer (1926-2006), a pupil of Nicolai Legat, danced with Mona Inglesby's International Ballet before joining de Valois' Sadler's Wells Company (1941-1953). Though she regularly took roles in Classical ballet from 1946 and was one of the original Soloists in Ashton's *Symphonic Variations* (1946), it was for her appearance as Victoria Page in the film of *The Red Shoes* (1948) that she became (and continues to be) best known. She starred in six further films; played Titania to Robert Helpmann's Oberon in Edinburgh and in America (1954); toured as Sally Bowles in *I Am A Camera* in 1955; danced and sang under Helpmann's direction as Morgan le Fay in his production of *Camelot* at Drury Lane Theatre (1964); and was an announcer on occasions for BBC television and radio. She possessed a clear, distinctive speaking voice, but it lacked the range and depth of resonance that Helpmann developed, which enabled him to undertake "big" acting challenges.

16   Rawlings encouraged Helpmann to come to England and subsequently introduced him to Ninette de Valois, who had choreographed Rawlings' dance in a production of Wilde's *Salome* in 1931 and remained a good friend. Though Rawlings made her name playing in Shaw's comedies, she excelled in performing

in verse drama, particularly Greek tragedy and in Racine's *Phèdre*. Her skills in speaking poetry, learned from John Masefield in her youth, allowed her in her later years to give numerous popular verse recitals.

17   Beatrice Wilson had acted with Sybil Thorndike and Lewis Casson at the Old Vic and was a member of their first joint Company; she was a particularly notable Andromache to Thorndike's Hecuba in *The Trojan Women* (Old Vic, 1919-1920).

18   Audrey Williamson records how noticeably Helpmann's voice developed throughout the run of *Hamlet* in 1944 in her review of the production included in Old Vic Drama, pp.165-171. See especially p.168.

19   Thomas C. Kemp and J.C. Trewin, *The Stratford Festival* (Birmingham: Cornish Brothers, 1953), p.228. Alan Dent, the theatre critic, noted that over the weekend following Helpmann's appearances at Stratford as King John and as Shylock, one could "hear everybody agreeing on all sides how Helpmann had strikingly improved in vocal range and resonance". See Alan Dent, "Robert Helpmann, Actor: An Appreciation" in J. Logan Gourlay (ed.) *Robert Helpmann: Album* (Glasgow: Stage and Screen Press, Ltd., 1948), p.24.

20   *Bystander*, 12 January 1938. The production opened in December 1937.

21   *The Daily Telegraph and Morning Post*, 28 December 1937.

22   *Spectator*, 18 February 1944. Sydney Carroll writing for the *Sunday Chronicle* (12 December 1944) heartily concurred with this view but was less precise than Redfern in his detailed description of the qualities of Helpmann's voice: "He has a lovely speaking voice, distinct, variable, capable of shades of inflexion and tone."

23   The words quoted here are from the review in the *Times*, 12 May 1951; but similar descriptions of Helpmann's playing the role recur throughout the reviews along with assertions about its likely effect on his reputation. The impact of his Caesar was heightened by the contrast it posed with his athletic and humorous interpretation of Apollodorus.

24   George Rylands, "Festival Shakespeare in the West End" in Allardyce Nicoll (ed.), *Shakespeare Survey 6* (Cambridge: Cambridge University Press, 1953), p.142.

25   Ibid, p.145.

26   See Anna Bemrose, *Robert Helpmann: A Servant of Art* and Elizabeth Salter, *Helpmann: The Authorised Biography*. See too Monica Mason's story of the cloak in *Elektra* in this volume (p.231) for Helpmann's ability to combine outrageousness with self-deflating irony.

27   See Chapter 16.

28   *The Stratford Festival*, p.226.

29   *Birmingham Post*, 20 April 1948.

30   *The Daily Mail*, 20 April 1948.

31   *The Stage*, 22 April 1948.

32   Mary Clarke, *Shakespeare at the Old Vic: Fourth Season* (London: Hamish Hamilton, 1957), unpaginated (but pp. 4-5 of textual section on *The Merchant of Venice*).

33 *Times*, 7 March 1947.

34 *The Sunday Times*, 25 June 1947.

35 From an undated newspaper cutting assigned to Stephen Williams included in the Robert Helpmann Biographical File (Box 47 – Personal) in the Theatre & Performance Collections, Victoria and Albert Museum.

36 From a newspaper cutting assigned to Stephen Potter and dated 6 March 1947 (nature of cutting obliterates details of source), also included in the Robert Helpmann Biographical File (Box 47 – Personal) in the Theatre & Performance Collections, Victoria and Albert Museum.

37 Undated and unacknowledged newspaper cutting included in the Robert Helpmann Biographical File (Box 47 – Personal) in the Theatre & Performance Collections, Victoria and Albert Museum. The quotations from *The White Devil* are from D. Gundy et al (eds.), *The Works of John Webster*, Vol. 1 (Cambridge: Cambridge University Press, 1995).

38 Herbert Farjeon, *The Shakespearean Scene. Dramatic Criticisms* (London: Hutchinson, 1948), p.47. (My emphasis.) The review had appeared originally in *Bystander*, 12 January 1938.

39 Tynan's review appeared in the *Observer* and is cited in Mary Clarke, *Shakespeare at the Old Vic: Fourth Season*, unpaginated (but p.6 of textual section on *Titus Andronicus* and *The Comedy of Errors*).

40 Audrey Williamson, *Old Vic Drama*, p.120.

41 It might be questioned how much of all this was Helpmann's work and how much a director's. It is obviously difficult at this point in time to draw distinctions and, say, suppose that Helpmann did the invention and left his director to assert an element of discipline. But this would be wholly hypothetical. Most frequently and especially in the roles being analysed here, Helpmann worked with Guthrie or Benthall with whom he clearly discussed his contribution to their various productions at length, often prior to rehearsals. In comic ballets de Valois, a notable disciplinarian, certainly delighted in and encouraged his zany creativity, perhaps because she knew he could be relied on with roles like Coppélius and O'Reilly to instil unexpected moments of pathos into the fun that kept his performances under control.

42 All the prompt copies for the Shakespeare Memorial Theatre as for the Royal Shakespeare Company are stored in the library of the Shakespeare Centre at Stratford. That for the 1948 *Hamlet* carries the Box Reference: 264 – 501.

43 Kenneth Tynan, *A View of the English Stage* (London: Davis-Poynter, 1975), p.78. This account exactly matches the experience of the critic of the *Warwick County News* (1 May 1948): "Esmond Knight's Ghost was venomous and revengeful, a fiery spirit breeding hate in Hamlet's distracted mind".

44 In this account of Helpmann's performance, I have used italics to distinguish quotation of Shakespeare's text (in this case the version used for the production, which is pasted onto the recto pages) from the holograph stage directions, which are given here in standard font. Most of the stage directions use theatre abbreviations (R. for right; C. for centre etc.) but for the benefit of those unfamiliar with such usage, I have completed the words within square

brackets ("R[ight]"; "C[entre]").

45   It is interesting to compare this with an episode in Helpmann's balletic staging of *Hamlet*, which the critic Audrey Williamson listed as demonstrating "unusual imagination": "Hamlet's accelerated crawl forward to the footlights, his face taut with horror at the Ghost's revelation, his hands pounding the floor". See Audrey Williamson, *Contemporary Ballet* (London: Salisbury Square, 1946), pp. 92 and 93.

46   See, for example, the reviewer in the *Coventry Standard* (1 May 1948): "Economy marked his movement and no Hamlet of the future is likely to surpass his impressive and magnificent collapse after the Ghost's revelation".

47   There were dissenters from this view with every one of his appearances as an actor, since some critics felt that this subtle approach to his acting was made too apparent for the spectator because carried too self-consciously, so that one was left "admiring an accomplished piece of virtuosity" (*Spectator*, 30 April 1948).

48   *New York Daily News*, 21 December 1951.

Introduction to DVD Track 2: Excerpts taken from Lynne Wake's film made for the ROH Collections, *Dancing in the Dark – the Royal Ballet during the Second World War*

Anna Meadmore

In this short compilation of excerpts from *Dancing in the Dark (2007)*, a documentary film about the Sadler's Wells (later The Royal) Ballet during World War II, four of Robert Helpmann's former colleagues recall their experiences of working alongside him during that intense period. Leo Kersley, Beryl Grey, Jean Bedells and Julia Farron consider Helpmann's artistic impact on the Sadler's Wells Ballet, and his vital role in raising the Company's spirits during wartime touring, which could be both tough and very tedious. The full documentary (not shown here) is half an hour long: directed by Lynne Wake, formerly a dancer with the Sadler's Wells Ballet, and edited by Christopher Bird, it was produced by Christina Franchi for The Royal Ballet, in association with the Imperial War Museum, London. The film was commissioned for the exhibition, *Dancing Through the War: The Royal Ballet 1939-1946*, which ran at the Churchill Museum and Cabinet War Rooms from 16 February to 20 May, 2007.

Leo Kersley (1920 – 2012) was born in Watford. He was trained by Marie Rambert and Stanislas Idzikowski, and danced with Ballet Rambert between 1936-9 and 1940-41; the Sadler's Wells Ballet from 1941-42; and the Anglo-Polish Ballet from 1942-43, before becoming a founder-member of the Sadler's Wells Theatre Ballet (now Birmingham Royal Ballet) between 1946-51. Early during the war, he registered as a conscientious objector, spending some time in prison before undertaking civilian service in hospitals, which he combined with his life as a professional dancer. He was married to the dancer Celia Franca, but they divorced in the late 1940s. After periods of teaching and dancing in the US and Holland, in 1959 Leo Kersley and his second wife, Janet Sinclair, established the Harlow School of Ballet in Essex. They also co-wrote *A Dictionary of Ballet Terms* (London, several editions 1952-97), and many articles based on their shared love of ballet, opera, music and the theatre.

See pp. 153-154 for biographies of Jean Bedells and Julia Farron, who also appear in Michael Byrne's film documenting David Drew's project to revive Helpmann's wartime ballet, *Miracle in the Gorbals* (1944). **See DVD Track 3.** Biography of Beryl Grey on p. 63.

Choreographic Gestures: seeing the narratives in Helpmann's *Hamlet* (1942)

Jennifer Jackson

Robert Helpmann's ballet *Hamlet* was premièred at the New Theatre in wartime London's West End on 19 May 1942, just five months after *Comus*, his first choreography for the Sadler's Wells Ballet. According to Caryl Brahms, *Hamlet* was "heralded by the heaviest doubts".[1] How was Helpmann to render the action of Shakespeare's longest play (of four hours' duration, if played in full) within the eighteen minutes of Tchaikovsky's music – his *Hamlet Overture Fantasia*, begun as a suite of incidental music for the play but which the composer completed as a "symphonic abstract" study of the hero.[2] Helpmann may have been pondering the potential of using Shakespeare's work as subject matter for some time; in 1938 he had written about the "close relationship"[3] he perceived between Shakespeare and ballet.[4] For his adaptation of Milton's *Comus*, Helpmann had included two speeches from the masque, which with deft theatrical flair he also recited, from centre-stage.[5] In discussion with his close friend and theatre director Michael Benthall, Helpmann decided to stage *Hamlet* as a flashback.[6] And unlike *Comus*, *Hamlet* was conceived as "A Ballet in One Scene",[7] without spoken text.

Hamlet is one of the most analysed of Shakepeare's plays. The ballet is likewise rich, and there are many ways of viewing it. It was last staged by The Royal Ballet at Covent Garden in 1981; dancing in the title role were Anthony Dowell, Stephen Jeffries and a young Michael Batchelor – who went on to be the muse for Kenneth MacMillan's 1988 "chamber" version of *Hamlet*, entitled *Sea of Troubles*.[8] The choreographic analysis that follows draws on rehearsal footage from the 1981 *Hamlet* revival, with Dowell and Antoinette Sibley as Hamlet and Ophelia; but primarily on a film (1964) by Edmée Wood[9] of a stage rehearsal in costume. Rudolf Nureyev is Hamlet and Lynn Seymour is Ophelia. Monica Mason is Gertrude in both the 1964 and 1981 revivals. References to the original production derive from photographs, programmes and fliers, as well as commentary by the critic and author Caryl Brahms, and Lionel Bradley's hand-written *Ballet Bulletin*.[10] Bradley made detailed entries in his notebooks after seeing *Hamlet* on at least five occasions during the Company's Spring Season in 1942. Caryl Brahms' book *Robert Helpmann: Choreographer,* published in 1943, is also a rich source of vibrant description and comment about the ballet in its historical context.

In his overview of The Royal Ballet's first fifty years, Alexander Bland calls *Hamlet* a "powerful example of mime-drama".[11] Around the time of its creation, the legendary mime and pedagogue, Jacques Lecoq (1921-1999), was beginning his own experiments combining movement and theatre, in 1944 post-liberation France. Lecoq analysed the links between "how the human body functions in space" and the "structure of drama"[12] and this work was articulated at the end of his life in his posthumously published book, *The Moving Body* (2000).[13] His theories speak of the drama to be found in the dimensions of movement in space and are highly apposite to a choreographic analysis that investigates the construction of narrative and meaning. Here, I am interested in exploring the underpinning choreographic structure as it relates to dramatic use of stage space, what Lecoq calls "the terrain of the broad emotions of melodrama";[14] the dance gesture and characterisation in *Hamlet*; the themes from the play that the ballet overtly explores, and those that it points to but cannot explicitly present (for example: political intrigue, secrecy and surveillance). Such a close reading also invites consideration of Helpmann's choreographic legacy, especially in relation to MacMillan, who picked up on similar themes for his own Hamlet-inspired work in 1988.

Choreographic Structures: Lines in Space

The ballet opens in the seconds after the play ends, as Hamlet's body is borne away by Fortinbras's four captains. It takes as a point of departure, lines from the famous "To be or not to be" soliloquy, which are quoted in the programme:

> For in that sleep of death what dreams may come
> When we have shuffled off this mortal coil
> Must give us pause
> (Shakespeare, *Hamlet*, 3, 1, 66-68)

In terms of the structural arc of the work in time and space, this same scene frames the beginning and end – and death is centre-stage. Hamlet is carried, his head dropped back towards the audience, so we see his face lit and eerily suspended "upside-down" in space. The image of the Prince of Denmark aloft, and the slow projection of the pall-bearers' movement upstage, indicate dimensions of space and time – the vertical line between heaven and earth and movement towards the future. (See plate 23) The stage is cut down the middle, defining both the space and the singular central theme of the play along which the ballet unfolds – Hamlet's tragic indecision.

Helpmann assumes an audience's familiarity with the play, and makes the ballet from an actor's analytic understanding of the title role. The action – intense, speedy, hectic, confused – takes place as if it is Hamlet thinking. It feels like a death wish, a "not to be". The ballet "gives us pause" to expand the moment of death itself; we live the suspense of the debate in Hamlet's soliloquy. The tensions of the broader political setting – Denmark is internally unstable after the King's death, and under threat of invasion – are 'unseen', but they are mirrored by the way in which Hamlet's personal torture and doubts are evoked. How does he act? How can he know the truth?

Lecoq proposes that movement lines in space infer dramatic intention and meaning:

> Vertical movement situates man between heaven and earth, between zenith and nadir, in a tragic event. As for the diagonal, it is sentimental, it flies off and we cannot tell where it will come down.[15]

After beginning in the vertical with the certainty of death, the ballet moves into the unstable world of human sentiment and relations. For the entrance of the Ghost of Hamlet's father, Helpmann chooses a shallow diagonal with the figures of the dead King and the uncertain Prince on opposite sides of the stage. Hamlet draws back and then ventures forward with slow lunges, his arms steadying as if on a tightrope that bridges the distance between them. Another balletic exchange between the living and the dead is evoked – the 'sinister' line from downstage-left to upstage-right with which ballet-goers are familiar in *Giselle* Act II, leading Albrecht towards Giselle's grave, and along which Hilarion is dispatched to his death by the Wilis. In the next scene of *Hamlet*, the *corps de ballet* makes its appearance as couples[16] and they form a diagonal pathway with an elaborate longwise dance for the entrance of Laertes and Polonius. All the courtiers are on ground level, and with a precise quarter turn they are in position for a formal bow to greet the entrance of the new King, Claudius (Hamlet's Uncle), and the Queen (Gertrude, his Mother), who are at the top of the steps on stage left, elevated. (See plates 24 and 25) A hierarchical world is established where power and status is clearly defined. Helpmann then divides the *corps* couples into male and female. The men run to frame Claudius; the women provide a diagonal avenue that focuses attention on Ophelia, now entering to stand beside the Queen, and also creates a striking juxtaposition – that of this young woman, Hamlet's lover, with Gertrude, his mother.

The swift re-grouping delineates an underlying theme that the choreography seems to reveal: confusion in the mapping of the boundaries around sexual intimacy – which renders Hamlet unable to love, unable to act. Mother and lover appear and disappear in the same frame, and then a few moments later they alternate in lunging across his line of vision. A tightly choreographed sequence follows to conjure further darkness and deception, in which Gertrude and Ophelia dance the illusion of being the same person: back to back, they make a two faced being, and spin round in half circles; their movement is both precisely accented and fluent, the arm and leg gestures insinuating through the whole body, each woman held tightly in the intensity of Hamlet's eye-line.

Helpmann makes strong use of the diagonal in establishing the relationships between the principal characters. Then for the 'play within the play'[17] he balances the stage picture; the *corps* dancers enter from each side and form symmetrical groupings to create a stable architecture that evokes the scales of justice. A 'set within the set' is created, where the action is framed, and the attention of Claudius, Gertrude and their attendants is focused away from Hamlet, and onto the play. He retreats to one side; as Bradley notes, this suggests that the action is in his mind, as "something he has heard rumoured".[18] No longer centre-stage Hamlet is free to observe and to "catch the conscience of the King" (Hamlet 2, 2).

Until this moment an order, albeit malevolent, prevails. Once the evidence of Claudius' guilt and Gertrude's complicity is revealed – the speed and drama with which the "Player" royals, and the real King Claudius and Queen Gertrude, are dispatched by the chorus, underlines Hamlet's isolation in the confusing web of intrigue. A chaotic unraveling of events follows – madness, drowning, dueling, and more death. Seeing the ballet for the third time on May 25 1942, Bradley writes: "I was more impressed than ever by the bewildering continuity of the action which hardly leaves one time to think or breathe".

Dance gesture and characterisation

The groupings, framing, and the hectic pace of the action, suggest Hamlet's psychological turmoil, and circumstances that spiral out of control. The choreographed sequences follow the events of the play, but Helpmann uses theatrical devices to point to the sexual ambiguities, uncertainties and paranoia that are themes in the play, with clever merging of characters and dance gesture. The Gravedigger[19] appears after the opening tableau, wearing the skull of Yorick. This is the first of the ballet's duplications and it establishes the strangeness of the stage world that Helpmann creates. Brahms captures its significance:

Hamlet, about to die, recalls two certainties of death from his recent experience. The Gravedigger. And his recent shock at seeing the skull of Yorick. The pace of the recollection merges these two images, so that in the speed of the dream they are indivisible.[20]

In terms of choreographic statement and construction of meaning, the interchanging of Ophelia and Gertrude is the most significant of all the duplications. Bradley thought that it "marks Hamlet's obsession with his mother in his attitude to Ophelia and the fact that in his mind they have become one".[21] This reading is coherent with the duplication that is effected (See plate 26) for "the play within the play", where the Ghost of Hamlet's father takes the role of the "Player King" and Ophelia, wearing an elaborate cartoon-like crown, is the "Player Queen".

Almost every possible permutation of Hamlet's sexual identity has been explored in different productions of the play on stage and film[22] and the merging of characters in the ballet reflects many of them. Does Hamlet hate all women including Ophelia, whom he used to love, because his mother has married his uncle, whom he despises? Or is he in love with Gertrude and therefore cannot love Ophelia? Or, in his feigned madness, does he confuse the two? To what extent the choreography suggests incestuous relationships, not only between Hamlet and his mother but between Ophelia and her brother, excited comment at the time. Bradley notes in his entry for 25 May: "The scene between brother and sister is certainly affectionate enough to justify the odd blunder of *The Times* critic who says that Laertes 'courts' Ophelia, but I do not think that any incestuous suggestion is intended." Brahms also writes about a member of the audience who, having gestured in the "direction of the vast field of action which is Mr Hurry's backcloth, was heard saying: 'All This and Incest, Too!'".[23] The ballet may well have influenced Laurence Olivier's 1948 film of *Hamlet*, which "strongly implied that Hamlet has incestuous relations with his mother".[24]

Much was made of the lack of dancing in the work. Although a "very clever and exciting ballet, it hasn't got much real dancing in it" comments Bradley, after seeing *Hamlet* for the second time in performance on 19 May 1942. But the danced passages are intimate and revealing in terms of structure and meaning. A review in *The New Statesman* includes the following:

> Some of the detail is brilliant... Ophelia, beautifully danced by Margot Fonteyn acquires a new significance. Not only do sweetness and madness go better in dance, but other aspects emerge; her attachment to Laertes is almost as strong as Hamlet's love for his mother. [25]

In Seymour's rendering of Ophelia, I notice her attention to a charming detail of interwoven hand gestures (*entrelacé*), with the arms held in 5th position, combined with a light travelling *pas de basque* step in the first encounter with Hamlet. This gesture is echoed in her deranged play with the flower garland in her entrance later in the ballet. And thus the choreographic structure again references the shocking betrayal of innocence signified in Giselle's mad scene, when she returns to the memory of the daisy petals and realises Albrecht's perfidy: 'he loves me, he loves me not'. Helpmann also seems carefully to construct the dancing to underline confusion around sexual boundaries. In Ophelia's first duet with Hamlet there is a striking promenade sequence that is repeated later in the action, with Laertes. Ophelia's upper body leans into the man's, the spine elongated so her head finds rest on his shoulder, left arm cupped around his head, opposite leg in low *attitude derrière*, her body against his, spooning, intimate.

The dance language thus mixes gesture and ballet vocabulary, cleverly delineating status and character. Bradley notes how "practically every movement is relevant and significant".[26] For example, the Gravedigger enters with small turned-in steps on bent knees. His posture hunched, he measures the spade against the length of his leg and turns to take a swig from his bottle before pointing towards Hamlet's entrance. His movement lacks the fluid elegance of Hamlet's posture and line. The duet that follows comprises bound gestures with Hamlet reaching, blindly but compelled, for a skull, which the Gravedigger thrusts into his line of vision. Then the movement of Hamlet's arms, crossing at the wrists and raised above the head as if to strike with the balletic mime gesture for "kill" or "die", leads into *attitude renversé* – a yearning action of opposing movements of the upper body and the legs.

Once he has entered into his "dream", Hamlet never leaves the stage. The *corps de ballet* provides the architecture for the main characters to enact their parts, and in the dynamic of the diagonal lines drawn between characters there is a sense of movement and unpredictability that is coherent with Lecoq's analysis. Helpmann's focus is on Hamlet's inner life – and close family relations – rather than those of the nation state. Yet the context and atmosphere of surveillance and secrecy is conveyed in the choreography for the *corps*. This body of dancers forms a hybrid – a Greek chorus arranged with dancerly attention to geometry and line, both to comment on and amplify the action. Brahms highlights their "strongly dramatic" character.[27] "[Helpmann's] groups fall naturally and dramatically into the punctuation of his story, [...] each conveys a concerted comment on the progress of the situation."[28] As if passing messages, they echo the dance movements of the principal characters; their mimetic gestures are spliced into the moving canvas that becomes Hamlet's nightmare. They mime "no"; and "hiding the head" – in shame, in horror, in sadness, to indicate not seeing, denial, secrecy, the truth veiled. The dance medium stages these ambiguities. Helpmann knows how to make the gestures intelligible as drama, however this is not "realistic" ensemble playing: the crowd is balleticised, the geometry of their groupings precisely structured in space to evoke unseen worlds outside the ordinary. The life of this court is of an 'unnatural', or 'extra-ordinary' order that is at once attentive to the laws of the theatre and dance, the human and beyond.

Theatre and dance

Helpmann moved fluidly between the conventions of theatre and ballet. His appreciation of both is evident in his musing about the potential of collaboration between choreographer and producer on a Shakespeare production. He writes:

> I do not mean that the verse in any way should be sacrificed, but if the movements, groupings and climaxes are produced on some of the principles generally thought applicable only to choreography, the dramatic value of such movements should only enhance the verse.[29]

His abilities as an actor and a dancer were clearly integrated in his presence as a performer. Bradley remarks on 19 May 1942 that Helpmann's Hamlet "is a great *tour de force*", which dominates all the action. His entry on 25 May testifies to a different quality, the agility of Helpmann's performance: "It is difficult to describe but anyone who knows what a fine actor he is will appreciate how he revels in these quick changes of emotion." These are qualities that he evidently shared with fellow members of his original cast, and arguably led to the successful creation of character in the work, as Bradley notes:

> Many of the dancers, whether by native wit or by instruction from the choreographer do present characters which are not just lay figures, but rounded subtle personalities.[30]

Beryl Grey talks of Helpmann's knowing "exactly what he wanted" and how his incisiveness as a choreographer grew from keen observation of human behaviour,[31] an attribute that was fully exploited in his ground-breaking ballet of 1944, *Miracle in the Gorbals*. The redemptive theme of this ballet set in the Glasgow slums where a mysterious Christ-like figure saves a suicide, is indicative of Helpmann's humanity and feeling for others – and the generosity and kindness described by many who worked with him. Indeed, Helpmann's personal identity as both an actor and a dancer seems to underpin his skill as a choreographer, and the synthesis in choreographic form of these differing driving factors appears to be significant in how the ballet conveys many complex themes in the play.

What of the broader historical context for the ballet? Rex Gibson writes of *Hamlet*, the play, as "sponge-like". He suggests that, "just as Hamlet described the purpose of playing as to show 'the very age and body of the time his form and pressure', so every society produces *Hamlet* to mirror itself".[32] Despite careful characterisation, Helpmann's *Hamlet* cannot provide the detail of political intrigue from different perspectives. However the ballet does point outside itself to its historical setting in a compelling way. In 1942, like Shakespeare's Denmark, England was under threat of invasion; men were being dispatched, perhaps to their deaths. We in the twenty-first century, see from a distance a unified drive towards national victory, in which the Sadler's Wells Ballet prospered through its important role in boosting morale, not the lived realities – the inner struggle and confusion that arises in times of personal and national upheaval. Indeed ballet and opera attract strong emotions that find expression on and off stage[33] and *Hamlet* was immediately popular. Bland makes the point that Helpmann's "highly emphatic style fitted perfectly into the expressionist mood".[34] At the première, Bradley comments: "It lasts 18 minutes, [and] caused nearly as much excitement as the first performance of *Dante* [*Sonata*]." His skill as a collaborator was evidenced in Leslie Hurry's *décor* and costumes which Bradley thought "conspicuously successful for a first attempt at stage design". (See plate 22) It provided interesting roles for Celia Franca as Gertrude, and Fonteyn as Ophelia. In parallel with my reading across choreographic texts, Bradley notes that Fonteyn's dancing in Helpmann's work is a reprise of her *Giselle*, thus suggesting that there are parallel relationships between roles, which are discoverable only through performance.

Brahms highlights how in the prevailing context of the "draining and unaccustomed conditions" of war, Helpmann emerged as a "choreographer of first importance".[35] In discussing his merit as a choreographer she leads from a consideration of his dancing which is characterised by elegance rather than technical virtuosity. She draws attention to the inherent human and dramatic expression in the quality of movement he creates: "Drama, expressed in exquisite line, is Helpmann's *forte.*"[36] Her description of line in the aesthetic context of dramatic gesture, rather than beauty of form, strikes a fresh note for today's ballet-goer. The post-Balanchine perception that narrative-driven dance and "abstract" dance are separate forms of expression, governed by different rules, often characterises how choreography is made and viewed. Today, the taste for spectacle and athletic values tends to attribute innovation to physical or mechanical feats – often driven by exploration of technology or the body's capacities for extraordinary movement itself. Helpmann's integration of dramatic and balletic features in 1940s ballet was considered innovative. Brahms regards Helpmann as daring and highlights how his "sense of situation [...] intellectual grasp and masterly treatment of technical difficulties"[37] underpinned his theatrical experiment. And he brooked controversy. Whilst Brahms endorsed the integration of dramatic line in choreographic structure on its own terms, Bradley criticised mimetic elements in Helpmann's realisation and choice of subject matter: "one cannot convey the poetry of Shakespeare's conception by grimaces and writhings on the ground."[38] *Hamlet* also fed debate about the nature of ballet and the use of music, as well as the balance of dancing and drama as choreography. At the time so-called "symphonic" ballets were seen as new and controversial because of the absence of literary or narrative subject matter. Massine had opened up new territory with his extended abstract dance works; *Les Présages* (1933), and the much more ambitious *Choreartium* (1933), set to Brahms' Fourth Symphony, had been heralded by the balletomane and writer, Arnold Haskell, as "the birth and the triumph of pure dancing".[39] *Hamlet* is in stark contrast. To quote the *Dancing Times* – "one is faced with a ballet in which dancing, the principal ingredient of ballet, is scarcely present". The difficulty that the *Dancing Times* identifies is the choice of Tchaikovsky's music, "which depicts the climax of each episode but does not paint the action leading up to that climax".[40] However, whilst also acknowledging that "dancing" is not central to this ballet, *The Times* newspaper suggests that Tchaikovsky's music underpins the cleverly staged choreography: "[Helpmann's] designs are drawn from the symphonic-poem which forms the musical half of the composite art of ballet."[41] But his *Hamlet* appears to be driven less by the formal questions about dancing that Massine was exploring in his symphonic ballets, than by the potential of movement to express the psychology of characters.

Brahms claims that Helpmann influenced the ballet of the time more than any other dancer, apart from Massine.[42] What of his influence on the subsequent generations of dancers and choreographers in the Sadler's Wells and Royal Ballet Companies? Lynn Seymour[43] speaks about Helpmann's kindness and intelligence and how "he opened you out [...] made it all pertinent". Donald McLeary, talking about the creation of *Le Baiser de la Fée* (1960) with Kenneth MacMillan, comments on Helpmann's understanding of the underpinning drama in ballet movement (he was partnering Seymour on tour at the time):

> We didn't just want to do the steps. We wanted to do more – we were curious. The person who really got me into the drama of it was Robert Helpmann. He coached Lynn and I in *Swan Lake*. He danced on the Opera House stage, he partnered Margot Fonteyn, he acted at Stratford. This was a serious, good, theatre person. [44]

These testimonies also suggest that Helpmann's importance as a choreo-grapher lies in his links with the theatre and his contribution to the tradition of characterisation and storytelling in British ballet, that de Valois espoused and promoted, for example in her own works and through her nurturing of Kenneth MacMillan and John Cranko. More subtle underpinnings of her vision of dance as a branch of theatre can be traced in her commissioning of Massine to work with the Company and The Royal Ballet School. Also noted for his rich characterisation in such ballets as *The Three Cornered Hat* (1919), Massine re-staged this work and others for the Sadler's Wells Ballet during the 1940s.[45] Much later, he became a guest teacher of choreographic composition at The Royal Ballet School (1968-76),[46] after which he published his findings in a theoretical volume, *Massine on Choreography; Theory and Exercises in Choreography* (London: Faber & Faber, 1976).

In analysing Helpmann's *Hamlet* I am struck by Brahms' and Bradley's vivid writing about the work in its own time, and how their comments illuminate differences that shed light on the focus of dancing in our own age. The risks that Helpmann took were motivated by different social and aesthetic drives from those of today. The extreme physicality, hyper-mobility and athleticism which characterise dancing today are perhaps an inverse mirror to the expression of extreme emotions in the experience of war. Helpmann's choreographic language seems to spring from an interest in character and human understanding. It makes me especially curious about Helpmann's influence on MacMillan, who explores his "perennial concerns of family relations and their 'Freudian implications'"[47] in *Sea of Troubles* (1988). This chamber work, written for Dance Advance (see endnote 8), is a compelling return to many themes that Helpmann explores, and MacMillan renders these in dancing which is a sophisticated refinement of dramatic line in dance gesture, and very much of its own time. In the authorised biography of MacMillan, Jann Parry writes that he deliberately avoided comparisons[48] but there are striking structural similarities. Both works begin from Hamlet's famous soliloquy to evoke the state of Hamlet's mind. MacMillan's own duplication of characters is more radical and concise than Helpmann's, but is nevertheless a key structuring device which was also pragmatic: writing for a cast of only six dancers he refined the list of characters and each of the dancers played all the parts in different scenes – the three men taking on Hamlet/Claudius/Ghost/Polonius while the three female dancers dance Gertrude/Ophelia. Their identity is distinguished by simple and naïve "pretend" props: daisy-chain wreaths and felt crowns. Was Helpmann's imagination similarly liberated and constrained by the numbers of dancers when he chose to merge the Ghost and "Player King", or the Gravedigger with Yorick?

This close reading of *Hamlet* has considered Helpmann as a choreographer and how his work reflected contemporaneous concerns. In her 2013 article for *New Republic*, Jennifer Homans[49] bemoans a lack of intellectual and emotional courage in ballet choreography today. Brahms identifies how Helpmann's intellect and mastery results in "great inventiveness and even greater skill in characterisation".[50] As a dancer, Helpmann captured his audience by virtue of artistry rather than technique. The links that a choreographic analysis establishes with experimental practitioners such as Lecoq confirms Brahms' view that Helpmann's choreography is grounded in his being firstly "a man in love with the theatre"[51] – and furthermore, with an intuitive grasp of its inner dramatic structures and their crafting in dance. *Hamlet* invites deeper analysis, for the traces of influence – and for how Helpmann speaks to the power and range in balletic expression from then into the now.[52]

Endnotes

1   Caryl Brahms, *Robert Helpmann: Choreographer* (London: Batsford, 1943), p.28.

2   Stephen Walsh *BBC3 – CD Review:* "Building a Library: Hamlet Fantasy Overture" (22 February 2014).

3   Robert Helpmann "Shakespeare and the Ballet", *The Old Vic and Sadler's Wells Magazine*, January 1938, p. 5. Reproduced in this volume, p. 2.

4   Discussion of "Shakespeare and the Dance" is picked up by John Bryson writing in the magazine *Ballet* in 1946 (vol. 2, no. 6). On page 29, he says this: "Surely a star danced in Warwickshire skies when Shakespeare was born, for the dance has its share in his art. [...] Time and its elements are a dance; the planets move to harmony and the stars dance in their courses".

5   For *Comus* Helpmann uses music by Henry Purcell, and as with *Hamlet*, he tackles an established work of literature.

6   Alexander Bland, *The Royal Ballet: The First 50 Years* (Sotheby Park Bernet: Threshold Books, 1981), p.68.

7   As listed in the 1942 theatre programmes.

8   *Sea of Troubles* was commissioned by Dance Advance, a small-scale, artist-led Company committed to making and touring new choreography from a ballet base with live music. It premièred on March 17 1988 at the Gardner Centre, Brighton. The Company was led by dancers who had recently left Sadler's Wells Royal Ballet – Michael Batchelor, Susan Crow, Sheila Styles and Jennifer Jackson. Batchelor's early death of an AIDS-related illness in 1991 robbed audiences of one of the finest actor-dancers of his generation. For further discussion about *Sea of Troubles*, see Jennifer Jackson's paper, "Problems of Perception: *A Sea of Troubles.* Looking at MacMillan's work from the inside out and the outside in", *Revealing MacMillan: Conference Papers* (Royal Academy of Dance, 2004), pp.52-60. *Sea of Troubles* was recently revived at the Edinburgh International Festival, and again by the Yorke Dance Project at the Lilian Baylis Studio, London, October 2016. (See Gerald Dowler, "From Page to Stage", *Dancing Times*, October 2016, Vol. 107, Issue 1274, pp.40-43.)

9   Edmeé Wood's film of the rehearsal was screened at *The Many Faces of Robert Helpmann* Symposium, The Royal Ballet School, October 27 2013.

10   For an account of Lionel Bradley's *Ballet Bulletin*, see Jane Pritchard's essay in this volume, p. 115.

11   *The Royal Ballet: The First 50 Years*, p.68.

12   Simon McBurney, cited in Jacques LeCoq (in collaboration with Jean-Gabriel Carasso and Jean-Claude Lallias), *The Moving Body (Le Corps poétique): Teaching Creative Theatre* (London: Methuen, 2000), pp. ix.

13   In *The Moving Body* (2000) Lecoq articulates the principles and philosophy underpinning the teaching of creative theatre at the International Theatre School he founded in Paris.

14   Ibid, p.87.

15   Ibid, p.87.

16   In the film and video footage of the revivals at Covent Garden the *corps* comprises male and female dancers. According to photographic records and the cast-list in the programme for the first performances in the 1942 season at the New Theatre, it is all female. This must have reflected the lack of men within the Company due to military service rather than a choreographic decision.

17   Hamlet is uncertain whether he can trust the Ghost and his motives for revenge, if he is evil. He uses the visit of a band of travelling players to act out a murder in front of Claudius, in which he will observe and discern if his Uncle Claudius is responsible for the death of his Father and if his Mother was complicit in this.

18   Lionel Bradley *Ballet Bulletin* [May 25, 1942] Theatre & Performance Collections Victoria and Albert Museum, GV1645. Manuscript.

19   This role was created by Leo Kersley. See a short biography on p. 87 of this volume.

20   *Robert Helpmann: Choreographer*, p. 29.

21   Lionel Bradley *Ballet Bulletin* [May 19, 1942].

22.   Richard Andrews and Rex Gibson (eds,) *Hamlet* in *The Cambridge School Shakespeare Series*, (Cambridge: Cambridge University Press, Second Edition, 2005), p.256.

23   *Robert Helpmann: Choreographer*, p. 30.

24.   Richard Andrews and Rex Gibson (eds.) *Hamlet*, p.274.

25   *Robert Helpmann: Choreographer*, p.31.

26   Lionel Bradley *Ballet Bulletin* [May 25, 1942].

27   *Robert Helpmann: Choreographer*, p.28.

28   Ibid, p.22.

29   "Shakespeare and the Ballet", p.5, reproduced in this volume, p.2.

30   Lionel Bradley *Ballet Bulletin* [May 25, 1942]

31   See *Tales of Helpmann: A Profile of Sir Robert Helpmann* (dir. Don Featherstone; script Alan Sievewright; ed. Melvyn Bragg), a *South Bank Show* film produced by London Weekend Television for ITV, in association with Australian Broadcasting Corporation (1990). In the film Beryl Grey relates an incident which illustrates Helpmann's interest in everyday human movement as a source for choreographic realism. They were sitting in a café on tour in Bournemouth, Helpmann urged Fonteyn to observe the distinctive hand gestures of a deranged woman seated at an adjacent table and these made their way later into Ophelia's dancing.

32   Richard Andrews and Rex Gibson (eds.) *Hamlet*, p.242.

33   Was there ever a lyric theatre without its intrigue? The acid-throwing crime at the Bolshoi Theatre in the 2012-13 season testifies to the political intrigue, passion and personal ambition that ballet can attract.

34   *The Royal Ballet: The First 50 Years*, p.68.

35   *Robert Helpmann: Choreographer*, p.5.

36   Ibid, p.22.

37   Ibid, p.22.

38   Lionel Bradley *Ballet Bulletin* [July 18, 1942].

39   Arnold Haskell *Balletomania: The Story of an Obsession* (London: Victor

Gollancz, 1934), p.250.

40   The *Dancing Times*, cited in *Robert Helpmann: Choreographer*, p.34.

41   Ibid, *The Times*, cited on p.35.

42   Ibid, p.17.

43   Lynn Seymour, in conversation with Jennifer Jackson (24 January 2014).

44   Donald MacLeary in *Kenneth MacMillan: New Wave Ballet (1952-1962)*, film, dir. Lynne Wake (2003).

45   In 1948 Massine choreographed a new work, *Clock Symphony*, for the Sadler's Wells Company at Covent Garden, with music by Haydn and décor by Parisian designer, Christian Bérard. Bland (1981) reports that this much-anticipated ballet was not well received.

46   Choreographer Kate Flatt was a student of Massine's at The Royal Ballet School and she contributed an essay, "De Valois' invitation to Léonide Massine to teach Dance Composition", to *Ninette de Valois: Adventurous Traditionalist* (Alton: Dance Books 2012). The fruits of her study with Massine also manifest in the curriculum for the current choreography programme at The Royal Ballet School, which Flatt and I developed in collaboration between 1999-2015.

47   Jann Parry, *Different Drummer: The Life of Kenneth MacMillan* (London: Faber & Faber, 2009), p.638.

48   Ibid, p.638.

49   Jennifer Homans *New Republic* www.newrepublic.com/article/114707/crisis-contemporary-ballet-essay-jennifer-homans (2013).

50   *Robert Helpmann: Choreographer*, p.22.

51   Ibid. p. IX.

52   It is interesting to note that in May 1977 Frederick Ashton created a *pas de deux* for Margot Fonteyn and Rudolf Nureyev, entitled *Hamlet Prelude*. Set to the "Hamlet" symphonic study by Franz Liszt, Alexander Bland (in *Fonteyn and Nureyev: the Story of a Partnership* (London: Orbis, 1979), p.207) suggested that for this short gala piece, Ashton "chose characters who were manifestly linked to those of the dancers – Ophelia [Fonteyn] with her tragic tenderness and Hamlet [Nureyev], a mixture of irony and passion". Parallels were drawn at the time between the fifty-eight year-old Fonteyn's portrayal of Ophelia for Ashton with her much earlier creation of the role for Helpmann; and with Nureyev's brooding interpretation in Helpmann's *Hamlet*, which had been revived especially for him in 1964.

The Creative Partnership of Michael Benthall and Robert Helpmann

Jann Parry

Michael Benthall's is not a name or reputation that resonates these days. Yet he was a considerable figure in British theatre and, thanks to his life partnership with Robert Helpmann, in the development of British ballet. It was Benthall's experience of Glasgow as a serving soldier in World War II that determined the setting of *Miracle in the Gorbals* (1944) and his experience of wartime devastation in Holland that influenced *Adam Zero* (1946). Benthall advised Helpmann on *Comus* and on *Hamlet* as a ballet (both 1942), and he prepared at least two other ballet scenarios that never came to fruition. He made his career as a well-respected director in the theatre in the 1940s, 1950s and 1960s at Stratford, the Old Vic, the West End, and on Broadway. Yet he has been relegated to a footnote in theatre and ballet histories, overshadowed by his more famous partner.

Born in London in 1919, Michael Pickersgill Benthall was the only child of a well-to-do upper class family. His father, Sir Edward Benthall, came from a family that had owned Benthall Hall in Shropshire from the Middle Ages. When Michael inherited the Hall in 1961, he handed it over to the National Trust. His uncle's family still lived there until very recently – the Benthall clan is a large one, including members who established the well-known Bentall's department stores in the nineteenth century. His mother was the Honourable Ruth McCarthy Cable, the only daughter of Ernest Cable (Baron Cable) and Lilian Sparkes. Michael Benthall's second name, Pickersgill, was the surname of Lord Cable's mother. The Pickersgill clan were portrait painters – many of their paintings now hang in Benthall Hall, bequeathed by Michael in his will.

Michael Benthall was expected to follow his father into family business interests connected with India, but he was theatre-mad. He had been educated at Eton and Oxford, but he never graduated, leaving Christ Church within a year, aged 19. He had just met Robert Helpmann (then 29) who was on tour with the Sadler's Wells Ballet in Oxford. It was June 1938, the end of the academic year; and Helpmann was performing the title role in Ninette de Valois' ballet, *The Rake's Progress*. Young Michael fell asleep and had to bluff his way through compliments at the after-show party. He had acted and designed sets for the Oxford University Drama Society, and was determined on a career in the theatre. He reckoned Helpmann was the man to give him an *entrée* to the profession. (Helpmann had recently acted in

Tyrone Guthrie's 1937 production of *A Midsummer Night's Dream*.) On the way home to his parents in Devon, Michael stopped off in Bournemouth, where the Sadler's Wells Ballet was on tour, and sought Helpmann's aid.

A few months later, Benthall was in a play in Newcastle that transferred to the West End. There, Helpmann introduced him to Tyrone Guthrie, who gave him a small part in *The Taming of the Shrew* during the 1939 Old Vic season. Helpmann was playing Gremio, alternating with Charles Hawtrey (and with his ballet roles). Benthall was noted in a review as "very young and very good looking".[1] He did not have long as an actor, however, before war broke out. He enlisted in the Royal Artillery, soon became an officer, and was initially quartered at Dover. He offered his Ebury Mews flat in Victoria to Helpmann. From then on, they shared the same addresses and telephone numbers.

So they lived together as a couple, although homosexuality was illegal until 1967. Common enough in the theatre, such relationships had to be discreet in the wider world. Later on, at other, grander addresses in Knightsbridge and Belgravia, Benthall and Helpmann were described as sharing a housekeeper, a cook, two chihuahuas and a secretary.[2] Evidently, Michael's parents had come to terms with his profession and his relationship with Robert, since – at first – their establishments must have been funded with Benthall money. The theatrical Helpmann family had no problems with their son's life style.

During the war, Benthall was only occasionally at home. Helpmann did not serve, though other Australians in the Sadler's Wells Ballet did. He was too vital to Ninette de Valois's Company, which had to uplift and entertain the war-battered populace, and later the soldiers abroad. Helpmann began to choreograph, discussing his ideas with Benthall when he was home on leave. Benthall encouraged the mix of words and movement in *Comus* (1942), and had some input into Helpmann's hallucinatory *Hamlet* ballet, made later in the same year. While still at Eton, young Michael had acted as Hamlet; he would co-direct Helpmann in the title role of the play in 1944, and a number of other actors in later Old Vic revivals, including Richard Burton and John Neville.

Benthall's first credit as a ballet scenarist was for Helpmann's *Miracle in the Gorbals*, given its première at the Prince's Theatre in London, in October 1944. (See plate 36) According to Arnold Haskell's monograph about the ballet:

> It was born as a long and detailed scenario and the author must share to the full in the success of the work [...] Benthall's scenario was worked out in full detail, his characters and their reactions clear from the start. With rare skill, he avoided the pitfalls of novelising his story. Everything that he put down could be made clear in balletic action and was discussed with Helpmann in detail.[3]

The idea for *Miracle in the Gorbals* apparently came to Benthall while he was in Glasgow, deployed there by the army to establish an anti-aircraft battery. That must have been early on in the war, since he subsequently served in France;[4] Benthall actually did not see the ballet until 1945, while he was still stationed in France and the Sadler's Wells Ballet was on an ENSA tour of liberated countries. Haskell had commented on Benthall's skill in setting the story of Christ's return to earth in a Glasgow slum, where the inhabitants danced socially, in dance halls and on Saturday nights in the Palais.[5] There were thirty-two acting and dancing roles, all of which Helpmann acted out for the Company as he told them the story of his ballet.

Benthall must have been confident that Helpmann could bring off the role of the Christ figure without (in Haskell's words) being "mawkish or offending religious sensibility". (See plate 31) Michael Somes took over the role of the Stranger when the ballet was given in Edinburgh in 1945. Interestingly, it was left off the programme for a visit to Glasgow, maybe for "fear of moral indignation or inciting gang violence" (Haskell again). This shows that the work was taken seriously at the time as a possible provocation. After Benthall finally saw the ballet in performance, he suggested a modification: at the end, the Stranger should be left alone on stage with just the Beggar beside him. All the others should leave, as if in fear of being mixed up in a killing. It seems sound theatrical advice.

When Benthall wrote about dance-drama, some years later in a Sadler's Wells Ballet Book (No.3, London 1949; see Appendix III of this volume), he stated that dramatic ballets should not need programme notes. But he acknowledged that audiences often missed "the fascinating psychological comment" that Helpmann made on Shakespeare's *Hamlet*, and the social comment embodied in the character of the Official in *Miracle in the Gorbals*. He was somewhat ambivalent about Helpmann's *Adam Zero*, for which he also contributed the scenario.

> A universal theme with an existentialist flavour has been tackled and it is an attempt to introduce philosophy and psychology into the dance. As a new avenue for the dance-drama this can only lead to a dead end, for these ologies and isms are matters for verbal discussion and not for mime.[6]

Adam Zero was the first new ballet on the Covent Garden stage, first performed in 1946, shortly before Ashton's *Symphonic Variations* (which the critic Audrey Williamson reckoned would not last, while *Adam Zero* would).[7] The first version of the scenario was for an abstract ballet about a man's life cycle, with scenery that represented creation, achievement and decay. Helpmann then felt the theme would be too like one of Massine's symphonic ballets, so Benthall's second scenario introduced real-life characters who were also symbolic: Helpmann's role was both Adam/Everyman and the Principal Dancer of a ballet company; the leading female role encompassed the Creator/Choreographer, the Wife/Mistress/Ballerina, and finally Death in a huge red cloak. (See plates 44 and 45) There were references to politics, and the devastation caused by war. As Benthall showed in his dance-drama essay, he was aware that the ballet was overcharged with allusions, incidents and possible meanings.

Helpmann was injured during the performances. As Adam, he had to fling himself from a height into the arms of his friends: he miscalculated and was badly enough hurt to have to retire. He then had a physical breakdown after endless touring, suffering next from a bad infection, which was followed by an abscess resulting from injections: he had to be immobilised for months, presumably looked after by Benthall, back from army service. Undeterred as a scenarist by *Adam Zero*, Benthall prepared Oscar Wilde's *The Picture of Dorian Gray* as a ballet for Helpmann,[8] and later a scenario based on Kafka's *The Trial*,[9] but neither was realised.

By 1946, Benthall had been demobbed, having reached the rank of major and been mentioned in despatches. He bought a house for himself and Helpmann in 23 Trevor Place, near Sloane Square. They enlisted the services of Mrs Sheila Stead as what would now be called their Personal Assistant. Their telephone number, SLO 7942, appears in Laurence Olivier's diaries,[10] always under the name Bobbie. "Bobbie and Michael" were frequently invited to lunch and to weekends at Notley, the Oliviers' country house, where Bobbie, in particular, entertained Vivien Leigh – he was described as her court favourite.[11] Benthall, by now in his late twenties, pursued a career as a director of plays, operas and, later, of musicals. As a side-line in 1948, he was asked by Ninette de Valois to be the lighting designer for the first revival of her 1931 ballet *Job* on the Covent Garden stage (with Helpmann as Satan).[12]

In 1947, Benthall and Helpmann set up a drama company together, called Trevor Productions after the street in which they lived. They had been offered the small Duchess Theatre in the West End by its owner, Marianne Davis. Benthall directed Helpmann as Flamineo in Webster's *The White Devil*; the second production, *He Who Gets Slapped*, directed by Tyrone Guthrie, had a disastrous first night when an elderly actor forgot his lines, and the play closed after two weeks. Benthall went off to Stratford, alternating with Anthony Quayle in the 1947 and 1948 seasons as director of numerous Shakespeare plays including *The Merchant of Venice*, *The Taming of the Shrew*, *King John* and *Hamlet*. Helpmann, while still performing with the Sadler's Wells Ballet, appeared in leading roles in Benthall's productions of *King John* and *The Merchant of Venice*. In that same 1948 season, he also shared the role of Hamlet with Paul Scofield, alongside a seventeen-year-old Claire Bloom as Ophelia.[13] (See plates 37, 39 and 40)

Over these same years, Benthall also directed operas at Covent Garden (*Turandot* in 1947 and *Aida* in 1948) and plays such as Ibsen's *The Wild Duck* in the West End and Goldsmith's *She Stoops to Conquer* for the Old Vic. The setting for this was based on Rowlandson's cartoons, used as backdrops and as a tableau before each scene: echoes, surely, of Ninette de Valois' use of Hogarth's etchings in her ballet, *The Rake's Progress*, and of Rowlandson's cartoons in *The Prospect Before Us*, which Benthall knew well, since both were devised to feature Helpmann in the central role. His reputation was evidently strong enough by 1949 for the Theatre Guild of New York to ask him to meet Katharine Hepburn and persuade her to play Rosalind in *As You Like It*. Benthall flew to California – a very long journey in those days – and according to Hepburn's biographer, Anne Edwards, "his sensitivity and urbane wit made a good impression".[14] He duly directed her in *As You Like It* on tour in the States and on Broadway (January-June, 1950). He must have overlapped with Helpmann, as the Sadler's Wells Ballet was on its famous inaugural American tour of 1949. Helpmann told his biographer, Elisabeth Salter, that he was initially resentful of the closeness between Michael and Kate Hepburn: "When we were all together, a sort of tension grew up between the three of us. I didn't feel at ease with her. I don't think she felt at ease with me."[15] That would change with Benthall's production of Shaw's *The Millionairess* in 1952, when Helpmann was the Egyptian doctor to Hepburn's heiress (see plate 55). By then, Helpmann had abruptly left de Valois' Company in the middle of its second American tour (November 1950). He met up with the Oliviers, Laurence and Vivien Leigh, in California. They had just been on a long Australian tour and were no longer involved with the Old Vic. The Oliviers decided to set up their own company, leasing the St James's Theatre in London during the Festival of Britain in 1951, with Benthall directing both of them in Shakespeare's *Antony and Cleopatra*, and Shaw's *Caesar and Cleopatra*. (Olivier preferred not to direct, so that he could give Vivien his full attention). The two productions transferred to the Ziegfeld Theatre on Broadway from 19 December of that year.

Meanwhile, Benthall and Helpmann had been involved in a South African musical by John Toré, called *Golden City*, at the Adelphi Theatre in London. Benthall directed and Helpmann choreographed "Zulu" dances. It ran for 140 performances in 1950. They also collaborated on a production of *A Midsummer Night's Dream* for the Edinburgh Festival (1954). Benthall directed while Helpmann, cast as Oberon, also did much of the choreography – with the notable exception of a *pas de deux* for Titania and Oberon (Moira Shearer and Helpmann), created by Frederick Ashton.[16] The text was cut, to make way for Mendelssohn's music and the ballet. Sol Hurok then toured the production around the United States for six months, insisting that Shearer appear at every performance, even when she was injured and the *pas de deux* had to be omitted.[17]

Benthall became Artistic Director of the Old Vic from 1953 to 1962, succeeding Tyrone Guthrie. (See plate 35) He launched a five-year project to stage all thirty-six plays in the Shakespeare First Folio, though not in chronological order, performing them in repertory. Benthall was placing the Old Vic as the National Theatre for Shakespeare in London, hoping for a substantial Arts Council grant and for regular subscriptions. It was an ambitious plan, which ended up requiring Benthall to direct many more plays than he had originally intended in order to save money. Funding was always a problem, which led to lengthy Old Vic tours of Australia under the aegis of the Australian theatrical agency, J.C. Williamson Theatres Ltd.[18] – hence the tours Benthall arranged with Helpmann and Katharine Hepburn in 1955 (see plates 54, 56-63), and with Vivien Leigh in 1961, after her divorce from Olivier.

In the 1960s, the Old Vic productions became eclipsed by the rival Shakespeare Company at Stratford, eventually known as the Royal Shakespeare Company (RSC), under innovative directors such as Peter Brook and Peter Hall. However, John Lambert, music director at the Old Vic from 1958-1962, paid Benthall this tribute:

> In the latter days of his reign at The Old Vic, when it became fashionable to decry nearly every production, his wit and wonderful insight kept the place going. If he sensed talent, he used it boldly, disregarding the counsels of the timid. He had an uncanny skill in picking actors, directors, designers, members of back and front-stage staff. He knew them all and was loved by all.[19]

Benthall and the Old Vic also lost out to rival schemes for a National Theatre, a contest eventually won by Laurence Olivier – though that enterprise took some fourteen years to come to fruition in a new building on the South Bank. The Old Vic Theatre was taken over by the National Theatre Company in 1963, after Benthall had resigned as Artistic Director, following the death of his father in 1961. Michael was then ostensibly in charge of the Benthall family business interests, though he continued to direct plays and musicals – some for the British Council, one for the Chichester Festival, others on Broadway.

He and Helpmann were now sharing a garden flat at 72 Eaton Square, where they had a cook, a housekeeper, Mary Power, and the ever-loyal Sheila Stead, who ran their lives for them. (See plate 68) Her son, Barrie

Stead, remembers picture windows, mirrors, light green damask walls, gilt decorations, and sculptures in the garden.[20] Alan Sievewright, in the Australian TV documentary, *The Tales of Helpmann,*[21] recalled theatrical summer parties in the Belgravia garden. From the mid-1960s onwards, however, Helpmann spent more and more of his time in Australia, where he was increasingly involved with the Adelaide Festival and The Australian Ballet (see **DVD track 6**).

In 1969, Benthall was memorably involved in directing Katharine Hepburn in a Broadway musical, *Coco*, based on the life of Coco Chanel. The book was by Alan Jay Lerner, the music by André Previn and the choreography by Michael Bennett. Cecil Beaton's set proved to be a complicated piece of machinery that frequently malfunctioned and was difficult for the cast to manoeuvre. Hepburn insisted the theatre's thermostat be set at 60 degrees, and the exterior doors left open; as a result most of the cast became ill due to the unusually cold September weather. After forty previews, the Broadway production opened on 18 December 1969 and ran for 329 performances. At the time, it was the most expensive show in Broadway history. Benthall was nominated (unsuccessfully in the event) for a Tony award for the best director of a musical. Hepburn then headed the cast of the US national tour. Frederick Bresson, the producer of *Coco*, gossiped to Cecil Beaton about how ghastly Hepburn was on tour: "Even her best friend, Michael Benthall, told Fred that the best place for her was Bellevue Hospital in a straitjacket."[22] The original cast recording of *Coco*, with Hepburn "singing" nearly every song in a restricted range, is a collector's item.

Benthall's subsequent career as a director of American musicals was not a success. He died in London of cirrhosis of the liver on 6 September 1974, evidently alcoholic. Helpmann was with him at the end, having returned from Australia during Benthall's final illness. He wrote Mrs Stead a very touching letter about mourning Michael's death. She continued to work for Helpmann – whose London address remained the same after Benthall died – until she retired in 1980, with a pension from Trevor Productions after forty years' loyal service.[23] Benthall, who was awarded an OBE, although not a knighthood like Helpmann, has a plaque in the "actors' church", St Paul's in Covent Garden, but scarcely features in theatre histories. He flourished in the wrong era, the overlooked 1950s, and was overshadowed by the radical theatre directors of the 1960s.

Michael Benthall has also been obscured in ballet histories by the greater renown of Robert Helpmann. At this distance, one can only guess at the dynamics of their long relationship, which seems to have underpinned both their lives for at least thirty years. The initial attraction was obvious: Michael was young, handsome, rich and passionate about the theatre, including ballet. Although he may have started, at nineteen, as Bobbie's *protégé* in the theatre, he matured rapidly during the war. His *Miracle in the Gorbals* scenario was remarkably assured for a novice, and his 1949 essay about dance-drama could have been written as advice for Kenneth MacMillan or Matthew Bourne.

Helpmann respected Benthall's ideas and advice, and was willing to take direction from him as an actor from 1944 (when Michael was just twenty-five) onwards. Although Benthall was Tyrone Guthrie's *protégé* as a young director, his own directorial style was obviously influenced by his exposure, through Helpmann, to ballet. There are comments in reviews that some of his productions were choreographed like ballet-fantasies and he was criticised for giving greater importance to the visual elements of a production, the movement and music, than to the verse speaking.

Benthall and Helpmann complemented each other creatively and personally, as equals in spite of the ten-year gap in their ages, which mattered less as they grew older. Helpmann was quoted as saying:

> You know an artist can't function without emotion and for me, I find emotion in my relationships far more important than sex. It's the emotion of what I feel and the stimulus that I get from other people that helps me go forward.[24]

Benthall seems to have been the stable, reliable fixture in Helpmann's life and career, even when their theatre activities took them in different directions and to different continents. Elizabeth Salter, author of Helpmann's authorised biography, assumes that Benthall, because of his privileged background, was reserved and conventional, needing extrovert, extravagant Helpmann to liberate him. Yet actors relished Benthall's dry wit. Joss Ackland described its effect in rehearsal:

> He could accomplish more with an inflection, the suspicion of a smile or the raising of an eyebrow than many directors can mange after hours of heavy discussion. He could achieve effortless rapport but also be wicked, scathing and easily capable of knocking one down to size.[25]

The professional partnership between Benthall and Helpmann was an extension of their personal, private lives. They lived together for some twenty five years during dangerous decades for homosexuals: same-sex relationships between consenting adults were only cautiously acknowledged in 1967 as no longer a criminal offence. Though the theatrical milieu in which they moved accepted homosexuality, actors and dancers were vulnerable targets for politicians' and newspapers' witchhunts. John Gielgud was arrested in 1953 for importuning, as was the choreographer John Cranko in 1959. An editorial in the *Daily Express* (9 April 1959) fulminated against the "West End vice", claiming that the theatre was too full of people belonging to a "secret brotherhood" of homosexuals. Yet Helpmann and Benthall, living and entertaining in affluent Mayfair, were regarded as respectable and admired members of their professions. Benthall's background may have protected him; Helpmann, flamboyantly gay, defied censure. Their living arrangements went unremarked in contemporary publicity about them. Only now, in a more tolerant age, can they be seen as effectively a married couple until their lives went in separate directions.

Endnotes

1   Unidentified newspaper cutting in the Theatre and Performance Collections of the Victoria and Albert Museum, Michael Benthall Archive 1935-1968 ref. no THM/69 barcode -654097 online: <archiveshub.ac.uk/data/gb71-thm/69>.

2   See Elizabeth Salter: *Helpmann, the authorised biography* (Australia: Angus & Robertson, 1978), p.207.

3   Arnold Haskell, *A Study of "Miracle in the Gorbals"* (London: The Albyn Press, 1946). All quotations and factual information about the genesis of the ballet in this and the subsequent paragraph are drawn from this volume.

4   See Kathrine Sorley Walker, *Robert Helpmann: A Rare Sense of the Theatre* (London: Dance Books, 2009), p.68.

5   *A Study of "Miracle in the Gorbals"*, pp.15-17. For further information about the inspiration for Benthall's scenario, see "Designs for Robert Helpmann's Wartime Ballets" in this volume p. 14. and p. 128 note 4.

6   Michael Benthall, "The Dance-Drama" in Arnold L. Haskell (ed.), *Hamlet & Miracle in the Gorbals*, Sadler's Wells Ballet Book, no 3 (London: The Bodley Head, 1949), reproduced in this volume, Appendix III.

7   Audrey Williamson, *Contemporary Ballet* (London: Rockliff, 1946), pp. 86 and 97.

8   Ibid, p.167.

9   Mentioned in Michael Benthall's theatre materials in the Theatre and Performance Collections of the Victoria and Albert Museum.

10   Laurence Olivier diaries in the British Library, Add MS79766-Add MS79894.

11   Alexander Walker, *Vivien: the Life of Vivien Leigh* (New York: Weidenfeld & Nicolson, 1987), p.101.

12   Benthall was commended by Richard Buckle in his magazine, *Ballet*: "Benthall's lighting increases immeasurably both the beauty of the settings and the impact of the drama..." Quoted in *Robert Helpmann: A Rare Sense of the Theatre*, p.116.

13   For a fuller description of this aspect of Helpmann's acting career, see Richard Cave's essay in this volume, pp. 66-86.

14   Anne Edwards: *A Remarkable Woman: a Biography of Katharine Hepburn* (London: Hodder & Stoughton, 1986).

15   *Helpmann, the authorised biography*, p. 159.

16   It is interesting to speculate whether Ashton may have had Shearer and Helpmann in mind when he created the Sibley/Dowell roles in his ballet, *The Dream* (1964). His Titania is certainly as glamorous as a film star, while Oberon is famously androgynous (as Helpmann could be).

17   Jane Nicholas, Moira Shearer's understudy, in an interview with Jann Parry, 2014.

18   The agency owned many theatres throughout Australia until 1974.

19   John Lambert: letter to *The Times* 10 September 1974 (commenting on their obituary for Benthall).

20   Barrie Stead in an interview with Jann Parry, 2014.

21   *The Tales of Helpmann,* TV documentary, directed by Don Featherstone, made for Australian television, shown in the UK on ITV's *The South Bank Show,* 1990. Also quoted in Anna Bemrose, *Robert Helpmann A Servant of Art* (Australia: University of Queensland Press, 2008), p. 81. See transcript reproduced in this volume, Appendix V.

22   Hugo Vickers (ed.), *The Unexpurgated Cecil Beaton Diaries* (London: Phoenix Paperback, 2003). p.106.

23   In Benthall's will he left £352,804 net, some to the staff of the Eaton Square flat, most of it to Helpmann; his furniture and paintings (together with some funds) were bequeathed to the National Trust, specifically for Benthall Hall, where they remain today. He left his theatre collection of cuttings, programmes and photographs to the Theatre Museum, now part of the Theatre and Performance Collections of the Victoria and Albert Museum (in 13 boxes, unsorted).

24   *Helpmann, the authorised biography,* p.156.

25   Joss Ackland: letter to *The Times,* 10 September 1974 (commenting on their obituary of Benthall).

Information on the Old Vic Theatre from George Rowell, *The Old Vic Theatre: a History* (Cambridge: Cambridge University Press, 1993), passim.

Designs for Robert Helpmann's Wartime Ballets, drawing primarily on the resources of the Victoria and Albert Museum

Jane Pritchard

As a choreographer and director, it is hard to imagine any novice in the world of ballet who was as innovative as Robert Helpmann in his choices of designers for his earliest ballets. Undoubtedly he benefited from his experiences during the previous decade as a dancer and actor on the London stage and from his partnership with director Michael Benthall, who frequently also served as his librettist, but it is extraordinary for an inexperienced choreographer to collaborate on his first four major ballets with such varied and important designers as Helpmann achieved. Each was ideal for the production he designed, revealing that, even if Helpmann may not be classed as a great choreographer, he had consummate skill as a producer/director. During the years 1942-1944 Robert Helpmann invited artists ranging from the established master Oliver Messel for his first ballet, *Comus* (January 1942), to the absolute novice theatre designer, Leslie Hurry, for his second, *Hamlet* (May 1942). For the third and fourth it is hard to think of a greater contrast than that between the delicate pastoral sets and costumes by the Chinese illustrator Chiang Yee for *The Birds* (November 1942) and the almost brutal urban world created by Edward Burra for *Miracle in the Gorbals* (1944). Significantly all four designers were recognised as artists in the world of fine art as well as theatre, and in selecting this range of designers to enhance his productions, Helpmann reveals that he was a true man of the theatre.

It should be acknowledged that Helpmann had taken his first steps as a choreographer working in revues,[1] but during World War II, after Frederick Ashton had been called up in June 1941, the Sadler's Wells Ballet was in need of a second choreographer to take the pressure off Ninette de Valois. During the war her creations, notably *The Prospect Before Us* (1940) and *Promenade* (1943) had been works in a light, comic style. Helpmann seized his opportunity; three of his ballets were dramatic and all very different from those choreographed by Ashton, who had previously provided choreographic contrast for the Sadler's Wells' repertoire. For Ashton the choreography came first, supporting any narrative or idea, while for Helpmann it was the theatrical subject that dominated, and the steps served to support his ideas.

Although Oliver Messel and Leslie Hurry would go on to become closely associated with the Sadler's Wells Ballet, designing notable and frequently revived/revised productions of, respectively, *The Sleeping Beauty* (1946) and *Swan Lake* (as *Le Lac de cygnes* 1943), their experiences on *Comus* and *Hamlet* began their collaborations with the Company. Of the four designers, only Edward Burra had previously worked with the Vic-Wells Ballet designing Ashton's *A Day in a Southern Port* (later retitled *Rio Grande*) and de Valois's *Barabau*.[2] Burra had studied along with dancer-designer, William Chappell, at the Chelsea Art School and was identified more with the circle around Ashton and Chappell than that of Helpmann, who was clearly making his own choices rather than using the designers most closely associated with the Company. Although between Helpmann's creation of *The Birds* and *Miracle in the Gorbals* he had invited Sophie Fedorovitch (Ashton's faithful collaborator) to design his proposed *The Picture of Dorian Gray*, this ballet fell by the wayside apparently as the composer, Clifton Parker, never completed the score.

For his first two ballets Helpmann was drawn to established theatrical texts which he reworked as dance presentations, while the second pair were, perhaps, less obvious and therefore more original subjects for the 1940s. Helpmann was familiar with Shakespeare's *Hamlet*. It has been claimed that he created the ballet so that theatre producer Tyrone Guthrie would recognise Helpmann's appropriateness for the lead in the play[3] and he did indeed go on to perform the title role in Shakespeare's *Hamlet* with the Old Vic Company in February 1944. The idea of choreographing a version of *Comus* was apparently suggested by Benthall, but both Benthall and Helpmann, who had danced at the Open Air Theatre, Regents Park, in 1934, must have been aware of The Theatre in the Park's production of John Milton's masque, which had been presented for four consecutive summer seasons from 1934 to 1937 (initially to mark the tercentenary of the work's creation). For his third and fourth works Helpmann was employing new narratives, although the identity of the characters for *The Birds* came from the music selected by Respighi for earlier productions in Italy on the theme of birds. *Miracle in the Gorbals* was an original plot, although it had clear parallels with Jerome K. Jerome's *The Passing of the Third Floor Back*, which he had conceived as a dramatic vehicle for the English actor-manager, Johnston Forbes-Robertson in 1908. In both, a Christ-like stranger inspires new attitudes in an unhappy community, which ultimately turns against him.[4]

In discussing these four ballets it is worth noting that the war years were a period of devoted "fandom" for ballet, and in particular for dancers of the Sadler's Wells Ballet. In spite of paper rationing in the 1940s Helpmann's work as a choreographer became the subject of a series of books either concerning one individual ballet or a group of them; thus his creations are well documented. However, in discussing the four ballets this chapter privileges the writing of dance enthusiast, Lionel Bradley, still only available in its original manuscript in the Theatre & Performance Collections of the Victoria and Albert Museum.[5] Bradley was present at the first nights of all four productions, noting the excitement of the occasions and faithfully describing what he saw on stage. He would return as often as possible, witnessing repeat performances of the ballets, recording how well dancers settled into their roles, and how the productions evolved and changed. An observant member of the audience, Bradley was not handicapped in his writing by newspaper deadlines or word counts. He describes the ballets without using technical terminology for the choreography and music, but importantly for this chapter he gives detailed descriptions of sets and costumes, which he discusses in terms of effect and colour.

Lionel Bradley (1898-1953) was a Manchester-born librarian, who on moving to London in 1936 attended as many dance performances, concerts and operas as he could, and compiled "Bulletins" which were sent around to four or five friends. Bradley would have loved the immediacy of sharing information with his friends by keeping a "blog", but in the 1930s-1950s it was necessary to put pen to paper to detail what he saw and post the reports to his friends. It now seems a miracle that the General Post Office collaborated in the Bulletins being mailed from one reader to the next (often with their date of receipt) and then back to Bradley. On Bradley's death the Bulletins passed to his friend Rex Hillson (one of the original recipients), who passed all Bradley's dance material to Cyril Beaumont for the London Archives of the Dance,[6] of which Bradley had been an active supporter. That complete archive has now been subsumed into the V&A. Bradley's concert and opera material was eventually acquired by the Royal College of Music.[7]

During the war Helpmann was adored by his fans and many eulogies to his work exist, but Bradley was not amongst his devotees. However his repeated visits to the Company's performances reveal Bradley's growing admiration for certain ballets, while finding he disliked or lost interest in others. In respect of Helpmann's dramatic works Bradley was sometimes stymied as to accepting such mimetic works as "ballets", although through repeated viewings he did accept that classification. Of course Bradley had his personal "favourites" among the dance fraternity, and if his heart belonged to one company it was Ballet Rambert. However, in 1942 Rambert was not active, and there were far fewer dance companies seen in London than in other years, so Bradley focused more fully on the Sadler's Wells Ballet in the year Helpmann emerged as a major choreographer.[8]

Bradley's reports are enhanced by other resources in the V&A. Of particular relevance are set models for *Comus* (scene 2), *Hamlet* and

Miracle in the Gorbals. If the V&A lacks original material for *The Birds* (the designs by the Chinese artist Chiang Yee are in the collections of the Dance Professionals Fund, formerly The Royal Ballet Benevolent Fund, held by The Royal Opera House), it is worth noting that the V&A has recently made a significant acquisition of drawings by Yee. The collector James Gordon owns the costume designs for *Hamlet* and the design for Burra's front cloth for *Miracle* and some of his costume "ideas". The V&A holds rich collections of black and white photographs of all four ballets taken by Gordon Anthony; of *Comus, Hamlet* and *The Birds* by Tunbridge Sedgwick; and of *Miracle* by Edward Mandinian. There are also images by the Graphic Photo Union for this work; the 1957 performances of *Miracle* were photographed by Zoë Dominic. Finally, it should be noted that the V&A holds the Michael Benthall Collection.[9]

Before considering the four productions individually, two observations may be useful. The artist-designers Helpmann commissioned may be categorised as either neo-Romantic or on the fringes of being Surrealist or both. Indeed the two genres lent themselves to theatre. Secondly Helpmann's wartime works provide a significant link in the development of dance-drama, coming as they do between the work of Kurt Jooss and Ninette de Valois in the 1930s and the emergence of Roland Petit with such creations as *Le Rendezvous* (1945), and *Le Jeune homme et la mort* (1946) immediately after the war. Also they prefigure the contribution made by several British choreographers, most notably Peter Darrell and Kenneth MacMillan, in the second half of the twentieth century.

Comus

Frederick Ashton's absence from the Sadler's Wells Company gave Helpmann the opportunity to create his first complete ballet in two scenes. *Comus*, a masque by John Milton originally presented with music by Henry Lawes at Ludlow Castle in 1634, was apparently suggested by Michael Benthall, who helped to prepare the scenario. Helpmann's production involved dance, mime and voice, preserving two of Milton's speeches to be delivered by Helpmann in the title role. Bradley noted that some critics disliked the speeches and "suggested that the cessation of movement & introduction of speech breaks the tension, but to my mind, delivered as well as Helpmann delivers them they made useful focal points in the action". However by the end of 1942 Bradley regretted that "Helpmann's speaking is becoming rather too stereotyped & [...] he is beginning to forget the meaning of his words".

Constant Lambert arranged the score, drawing on seven theatrical works by Henry Purcell, and Oliver Messel (1904-1978) was invited to undertake the designs, work that had to be carried out on one of his brief periods of leave from the army. Helpmann had previously worked with Messel, who had designed the Old Vic's production of *A Midsummer Night's Dream* in 1937 in which he acted Oberon to Vivien Leigh's Titania. (See plates 10 and 11) Helpmann recognised Messel was in sympathy with the traditions of the English masque and could create appropriate sets and costumes to evoke the Stuart world of the seventeenth century. Bradley compares the costumes for the two brothers with those worn in paintings by Anthony van Dyck. In his report he initially refers to the portrait of the Duke of Buckingham and his brother in the National Gallery but then adds a correction that it is the portrait of *Lord John Stuart and his Brother Lord Bernard Stuart* (c.1638) that appears to be the source of inspiration. With Messel came one of his regular collaborators, Hugh Skillen, to make the masks and headdresses, including the animal masks for the Rout of Comus's followers. (Skillen would also be involved subsequently in making headdresses for *Hamlet*.)

Bradley was present at the première of *Comus* at the New Theatre, London, 14 January 1942, and saw it repeatedly during the four wartime years in which it was presented 120 times. After several viewings he repeated his initial comment:

> The first thing to say about *Comus* is that it is an enchanting spectacle. Oliver Messel has surpassed himself & it is no disparagement to Helpmann's first sustained effort as a choreographer to say that the honours went to the designer.

The plot concerned a Lady (originally Margot Fonteyn), who is seduced by Comus (Helpmann) and then tempted to drink the potion that will transform her into one of his grotesque and bestial creatures. (See plate 21) She is rescued by her Brothers (John Hart and David Paltenghi), guided by the Attendant Spirit (Margaret Dale), who summons up the River Goddess, Sabrina (Moyra Fraser) and her Attendants; the production ends with the Triumph of Chastity over Vice.

> For the first scene the backcloth was a moonlit view of the river (in a blue rather than green) with the winding stream, bosky woods & a distant jutting hill which struck me as being like a landscape by Rubens. The wings gave us more feathery, more delicately painted trees than is usual in the somewhat crude forests we have had at the Wells & the whole was enclosed in a frame (like an engraved book-page or a sculptural box) somewhat similar in style to the lamented frame which Rex Whistler designed for the Wise Virgins.[10] In the second scene the wood was hidden by the tall pillars & window tracery of a ruined abbey which extended over more than half the backcloth and was fronted by a curiously decorated table.

Bradley was clearly familiar with the works of Milton, as is evident from his comments when re-visiting *Comus* for the fourth time on 31 January 1942:

> The décor & costumes are undeniably most beautiful and appropriate and though Milton's Masque has lost a great deal in content by the transference to the (almost) silent stage, enough of the story remains to be fairly plausible. And where the characterisation suffers from the absence of Milton's language & the give and take of the dialogue, it is filled out to some extent by the choreography & by the art & the personality of the dancers, tho' for instance the contrast between the temperaments of the two brothers goes for nothing. I am not sure, either, whether it is correct for the creatures of the Rout to appear, as they do in the ballet, to be happy accomplices in his orgy rather than unwilling victims but this does usefully underline the contrast between virtue & vice.

> Margot Fonteyn's first entrance & dance is very well contrived to express her temporary doubts & inner purity & certainty by a skilful use of dance movements which are almost mimetic. The scene in which Comus disguised as a countryman (he no longer wears a cloke [sic] for this) meets the Lady & lures her to his Palace on pretence of seeking shelter is quite subtly carried out, as Comus's expression & gesture changes from ingratiating [sic].

> I regard the entrance of Sabrina as one of the most effective & perhaps most original features of the ballet. The manner in which her nymphs manipulate their long piece of gauze round her really does convey an impression that she has been washed by the river of which she is the goddess, which then recedes leaving her alone on dry land.

Bradley confirms his view of the "enchanting spectacle", when he attends a performance of the Sadler's Wells Ballet on 14 September 1942 at the Royal Court Theatre, Liverpool:

> I suspect that its chief choreographic merit lies in the dances given to the Attendant Spirit, which if not quite Miltonic are a perfect vehicle for the art of Margaret Dale.

Comus was "always a feast to the eye", an escape to another place, so welcome in the war years and presumably one that made a lasting impact on viewers for, as Zoë Anderson has noted, the ballet is referred to in Agatha Christie's 1951 thriller, *They Came to Bagdad*, which was published six years after the production was last seen.[11] *Comus* was a production Bradley hesitated to call a "ballet" but he eventually noted that "in spite of some critics, [it] seems to me to have passages of real choreographic merit".

Hamlet

Helpmann's second ballet, *Hamlet*, was also a feast for the eye and without any doubt a highlight of ballet creation during the war. Rather than attempt to retell Shakespeare's play, Helpmann created a tight-knit evocation of experiences flashing through Hamlet's mind at the point of his death, or as Bradley described it in his entry for 21 May 1942:

> The idea of the ballet, which begins and ends with the carrying out of the body of the Prince of Denmark, is to embroider the suggestion made in Shakespeare's words printed in the programme:

> "For in that sleep of death what dreams may come
> When we have shuffled off this mortal coil
> Must give us pause."

Certainly, "dreams" and "death" provided the keys to Helpmann's production. The eighteen-minute length was dictated by using Piotr Tchaikovsky's *Hamlet Fantasie-Overture* (Opus 67a), which had been recommended by Constant Lambert. Lambert appears to have suggested two possible scores, but the alternative by Franz Liszt was too short, being only ten minutes in playing time, while the Tchaikovsky worked well with the impressionistic ideas Helpmann proposed. The score not only inspired Helpmann but, once Leslie Hurry (1909-1978) was part of the team, it was absorbed, along with Shakespeare's text, by the ballet's designer.

Hurry was discovered by Helpmann during a visit to the Redfern Gallery in London where his paintings were displayed. Hurry was recovering from depression, and the somewhat disturbing quality and colouring of the works captured the mood Helpmann hoped his dream-ballet would express. Initially nervous of the project, Hurry secured the promise that he could pull out if it did not seem to him to work; but *Hamlet* launched him on a second career as one of Britain's most brilliant twentieth-century stage designers. According to the address Helpmann delivered at Hurry's Service of thanksgiving, the set was completed in a week.[12] Predominantly red, orange and crimson, the setting was given a deliberately distorted perspective, encapsulating the whole narrative and dwarfing the characters. It is rare for such a busy set to work to a production's advantage, but it does here. (See plates 22 and 23)

Bradley was present at the gala opening of *Hamlet*, in aid of Mrs Churchill's Red Cross Aid to Russia Fund at the New Theatre 19 May 1942, and noted the stir it created, causing "nearly as much excitement as the first performance of *Dante Sonata*" by Frederick Ashton. He described the audience: "I had the Russian Ambassador & his wife and Mrs Churchill &

other notables in front of me & Sarah Churchill on my right" but delayed writing his description until after his second viewing of *Hamlet*:

> We are shown a large hall in a baroque palace, in a colour scheme of violent red & orange which suggest hatred & bloodshed. On either side is an archway approached by steps but that on the left is surmounted by a hand holding a dagger. The backcloth shows on the right, a broad staircase leading up to a lofty landing, in the centre are steps leading to a colonnade or passage, but on the left is the menacing figure of a fury brandishing a sword. We must believe that vengeance, swords & daggers are dominant in Hamlet's mind.
>
> When the curtain goes up, Hamlet (Helpmann in the traditional black, relieved by a gold belt etc, and with a silver crucifix, above his left breast, lying on his open neck), is being lifted up and carried away by four hooded pall-bearers. At the foot of the steps on the left is stretched the body of Claudius ([David] Paltenghi – in crimson tights & gold and crimson decorated doublet with a rather Henry VIII beard). In front of him kneels the page (Margaret Dale) holding the foils. Below the steps on the right lie Laertes ([John] Hart in green tights etc) & Gertrude (Celia Franca in a rich green dress) while 10 Court Ladies (in crimson and gold) huddle up the steps & round the doorway. As the bearers reach the backcloth with their burden the light fades & goes up again to reveal an empty stage, on which are to be enacted with all the confusions of a nightmare, the principal incidents of the play.

Bradley is sure he has missed some details in such a rich short ballet:

> The confusion is established at the outset by the entrance of the Grave Digger ([Leo] Kersley) who crosses the stage brandishing his spade. For he is clad in parti-coloured tights and wears an elaborate fool's hat so that it is clear that in Hamlet's mind Yorick and Grave Digger have become one....

Bradley also noted the inclusion of scenes between Laertes and Ophelia which were outside Hamlet's personal experience and comments further on these after a performance on 25 May 1942:

> I noted that the two scenes, which are not in Hamlet's own experience (Ophelia and Laertes & Ophelia mad), are played while Hamlet sits or lies with his back to them. Is this a subtle way of showing that this is in his mind merely as something he has heard & not something he has seen?

Bradley's comments show that he really considered all aspects of productions he commented on, adding in the same entry that: "The absence of Horatio has probably no more than a personal significance (This Hamlet has no friends)." He recognised the work as "a great tour de force. (And, rather oddly, I felt I would like to see [Serge] Lifar do it)". At that performance

Bradley concluded: "I was more impressed than ever by the bewildering continuity of the action which hardly leaves one time to think or breathe."

Seeing *Hamlet* at Royal Court Theatre, Liverpool, on 10 September 1942, he mused:

> Now that I have seen the ballet 10 times I am inclined to regard it as a ballet & as a successful one. It is true that there is more miming in it than dancing, but the movements fit the music so perfectly and are so expressive of character that I don't now feel justified in raising objections which may be merely academic and pedantic. It isn't obscure if you know the play & such obscurity as remains may be set down to its being a nightmare. Certainly the action very fitly matches the febrile character of the music [...]. I am even beginning to feel that some of the detail has a touch of genius in it.

Many other critics admired Hurry's sets and costumes, agreeing they were "conspicuously successful for a first attempt at stage design", and *Hamlet* withstood considerable enlargement for the Royal Opera House stage, with revivals up to The Royal Ballet's fiftieth anniversary in 1981.

The Birds

Helpmann's third creation, *The Birds,* had a much shorter life albeit still receiving fifty performances over two seasons, but in choreographing a light-hearted fantasy Helpmann was clearly tackling a different subject from his usual dramatic work. Loving versatility, he recognised it was an opportunity to broaden his skills. The ballet responded to the need for a new light production for the repertory, and the need to keep younger dancers in the Company stimulated. Instead of commissioning a score or arrangement, Helpmann used a suite of seventeenth- and eighteenth-century compositions orchestrated by Ottorino Respighi which, according to Bradley, had been used at least twice before as the basis of ballets in Italy. Always an enthusiastic music-lover, Bradley's accounts can be useful as he details the music choreographers use. In respect of *The Birds*, he recorded on 24 November 1942 that the score:

> [...] includes a Prelude and The Cuckoo after Pasquini, The Dove after J. de Gallot, The Hen after Rameau and The Nightingale after an anonymous English composer [...]. It was proceeded by Lambert's overture, *The Bird Actors* (Op.1), which a critic has described as an essay in the manner of Stravinsky, & which is cheerful & jaunty enough but not so accordant with the music that follows as is Weber's *Abu Hassan* overture, which now regularly comes before [Ashton's] *Les Rendezvous*.

According to Chiang Yee (1903-1977), it was Constant Lambert who introduced him to Helpmann. His work was also quite different from other designers of the 1940s and the invitation to design *The Birds* was, as Yee wrote, "an unusual request for, from my experience, a Chinese artist's work is not found on the Western stage even if a play or ballet has a Chinese setting".[13] Yee is most frequently categorised as a poet and an adventurer, who enjoyed new experiences. He settled in London in 1933 and contributed to the growing fascination with modern Chinese art. Disillusioned by the new regime in China, he left his family (it had been an arranged marriage) and a career in administration to travel to London where he became one of the first Chinese nationals to publish widely in Britain, both poetry and travel books, giving a fascinating Chinese perspective on his adopted country. Yee's links with British theatre developed from sharing a Hampstead flat with the Chinese playwright Hsiung Sh-I, whose *Lady Precious Stream* found success in 1934.[14] Yee provided illustrations to the published text. Chiang Yee's famous series of books, *The Silent Traveller* (1937-1972), presented a Chinese perspective on well-known places including the Lake District and London. These included delicate pen and ink illustrations of Lakeland fells and London parks. It was hardly surprising that the setting for *The Birds* was quite unlike others in the Sadler's Wells Ballet's repertory. Yee explained that he created his designs after discussions with Helpmann, listening to the score and watching rehearsals. As he wrote:

> At first, I thought *The Birds* admirably suited to go with a flower painting or a landscape by our Sung masters, very simple and full of imaginative intuition [...]. However, after further consideration of the dancing I felt that such a backcloth would be too simple, so I painted instead a rather detailed, leafy wood.

Interestingly Yee suggests no one helped him understand the needs of stage lighting so the set, to his cyc, "became too bright". That Yee did not design other productions should not suggest his work was ineffective, and it appears from an unidentified press cutting in the V&A that in 1955 Helpmann hoped he would collaborate again with Chiang Yee, as it was announced that he would design the costumes for Shakespeare's *As You Like It* at the Old Vic, which Helpmann was directing. However, the whole production (sets and costumes) were eventually designed by Domenico Gnoli.

Lionel Bradley clearly enjoyed *The Birds* and admired Chiang Yee's scenery and costumes (See plate 30):

> The backcloth & wings represent trees & flowers – perhaps in a paddock, whatever that may be – the trees being chiefly of a peculiarly vivid green & the flowers large & red. These plant forms are slightly conventualised but

are treated in a detail which verges on the practice of the pre-Raphaelites.

The brightly-coloured costumes for the avian creatures were reminiscent of late nineteenth century costumes for fantasy ballets (such as those designed by the great Wilhelm for pantomimes and ballets in London at the Alhambra and Empire, Leicester Square).[15] But they certainly capture the likeness of the various birds with only the Nightingale (a role created by Beryl Grey) and her attendant doves (Anne Lascelles, Moira Shearer, Pauline Clayden and Lorna Mossford) in short fluffy tutus.[16]

The use of masks (always a challenge for dancers) was avoided with elaborate make-up, accentuating the oval of the eyes, and the use of "closefitting 'jockey' caps with a peak in the shape of a pointed beak". The Cuckoo (Gordon Hamilton) was in shades of blue with yellow beak and legs and he carried his "close fitting brown wings, not unlike a tailcoat". The two mischievous sparrows (Margaret Dale and Joan Sheldon) were similarly dressed but in grey with brown feathers, with shorter, more rounded wings and yellow "beaks" and stockings. The most elaborate costumes were worn by the Dove (Alexis Rassine) and the comic Hen (Moyra Fraser). The Dove, the *premier danseur* in the ballet, who performed a *pas de deux* with the ballerina-Nightingale wears a "coat of slaty-blue with a pattern on it, his cap is of the same colour with a pink beak". Bradley continues:

> He wears pale blue tights and pink stockings. He wears also what looks like a green neckcloth, which (I am told) is really a green waistcoat. For his wings and tail feathers he wears a sort of scalloped skirt, almost like a tonnelet of a darker blue edged and lined with pink. [...] [The Hen's costume] has a suggestion of the female bathing costume of Victorian days. She is a brown and white speckled hen, with a red comb on her head, round eyes, two red tufts hanging from her chin, fluffy white feathery pantaloons & a tuft of tail feathers sticking up at the back. She too has yellow stockings. (See plate 29)

Within the choreography the dancers adopted bird-like movements and characteristics; the hen had a "strutting gate & a jerky movement of the body from the waist", the sparrows had a "stiff hop". The narrative concerns the Dove and Nightingale with the Cuckoo impersonating the Dove to try and win the Nightingale and deceiving the Hen who was also in love with the Dove. At the opening performance, 24 November 1942, Bradley was doubtful of its success as the dancers were still finding their way in quite complex roles, and the more classical scenes seemed over-ambitious. Nevertheless the audience "displayed the usual first night hysteria & yelled the place down for Helpmann as though he had produced a masterpiece". Clearly the ballet improved as the dancers became more confident in their characterisation so that the Hen became a "little masterpiece of melancholy humour", the Cuckoo a "presentation of conceited bad temper & fussiness" with the Sparrows adding "a touch of pert gaiety".[17]

Miracle in the Gorbals

Throughout the war Helpmann moved effortlessly between dance, drama, film and radio, and his final ballet creation for the Sadler's Wells Ballet during that period coincided with his return to dance after a spell as an actor. *Miracle in the Gorbals* was a full-company drama with half a dozen principal characters created for a season at the Prince's Theatre and first performed on 26 October 1944. The Prince's stage was slightly larger than that at the New Theatre, which had been the main London performance-base for the Company during the war; its slightly larger scale would help when, after the war, it was presented at the Royal Opera House, Covent Garden, until 1950 (with a brief revival for five performances in 1958).

In 2014 Gillian Lynne, who danced in Helpmann's original, created a new version of the largely forgotten ballet for Birmingham Royal Ballet using the score and a reconstruction of the original sets.[18] This alerted new audiences to the significance of Helpmann as a pioneer of dance-drama and encouraged interest in choreography of the 1940s, which placed a recognisable society on stage in dramatic works. Productions in that decade reveal a much bleaker world than was portrayed in 'up-to-date' ballets of previous generations; in part the new trend may have derived from portrayals of urban life by Kurt Jooss in the 1930s. Andrée Howard's dramatic ballet, *The Fugitive* (1944) for Ballet Rambert, concerning sibling rivalry and the suicide of a man on the run, was premièred within weeks of Helpmann's ballet. *Miracle*'s lineage as a collaboratively created drama with original choreography, design and score, follows in the tradition of Mikhail Fokine's *Petrouchka* (1911) and Ninette de Valois' *The Rake's Progress* (1935). The critic, Arnold Haskell, was satisfied that the precepts of Noverre and Fokine were being followed, creating a clearly structured work with detailed characterisation.[19] Several critics added that the impact of *Miracle* was enhanced by being performed in contemporary dress. Once again it was Helpmann's partner, Michael Benthall, who had been posted to an anti-aircraft gun battery in the Gorbals, who came up with the idea for the plot and wrote a detailed scenario re-locating Jerome's novel/play/film to a notorious slum area of Glasgow south of the Clyde. By choice the ballet had no programme note; its title gave the audience enough detail of its subject as was needed.

For the first time Helpmann was working with a commissioned score from Arthur Bliss, who looked to compose more ballets after his success in

1937 with his score for de Valois' *Checkmate*, a symbolic work portraying the conflict between Love and Death as a game of chess. Bliss had hoped to build on the success of *Checkmate*, but it was not until he resigned as Director of Music for the BBC in May 1944 that he had time to compose again. The dramatic narrative appealed to Bliss: "it gave the Sadler's Wells Ballet a great chance to show their powers of characterisation and realistic action", and Helpmann was quoted as saying that Bliss's score was "very modern indeed and contained all sorts of rhythms, like the rumba and the palais glide".[20]

Miracle presented the crowd as a gullible group. A young girl commits suicide, but is apparently resurrected by a Christ-like Stranger. The Stranger is consequently idolised by the people until a jealous Official, who according to the librettist, Michael Benthall should be seen as a representative of the "organised Church" not just "petty officialdom",[21] provokes a lynching, after he has seen the Stranger visiting the Prostitute. As Bradley recalled: "At the end the half-witted beggar, penitent prostitute & restored suicide are the only three who retain their faith in & worship the miracle-working Stranger."

Jane Stevenson, Edward Burra's biographer, has suggested that Helpmann chose the designer for his "unique ability to produce intensely dramatic images of people in cheap clothes",[22] while *Miracle* is described by her as the first English ballet to have a contemporary working-class setting. Burra (1905-1976) was an artist with experience in design for dance. A life-long friend of dancer, designer and director William Chappell, Burra had designed, as noted earlier, for Frederick Ashton and Ninette de Valois. While the score's overture is played, the ballet's location is established by a powerful front cloth showing the hull of a ship in dry dock, surrounded by cranes and industrial chimneys belching smoke to evoke the ship-building industry of Clydebank. (See plate 34) Chimneystacks appear in the distance in the stylised and symmetrical single set, showing the exterior of tenement buildings complete with open balcony-landings on the stairs and the Shamrock Bar and Mac's Fish Shop opening on to the street. (See plate 32)

Once again Bradley attended the première of *Miracle* (26 October 1944) and noted that the ballet had too much detail to take in on one viewing. He also observed that "advanced information about the plot was a trifle misleading". As was his usual practice, his first account described the setting, noting the use of a practical landing on the first floor of the tenement, "lit by the opening of the prostitute's door". He continued with the costumes (which are familiar to us now only from black and white photographs): Burra's designs served only as suggestions of the appearance he wished to attain for costumes which, despite the wartime clothing rationing, were bought "off the peg" and, if necessary, adapted.[23] The Suicide (Pauline Clayden) wore a black dress while the Prostitute (Celia Franca) was in a figure-hugging red dress, described variously as being scarlet or flame. The Official, (David Paltenghi) wore a coffee-coloured straight-coat revealing a dog collar and narrow trousers, appearing as a figure of menace recognisable from Burra's paintings. The Stranger (Helpmann) wore "a nondescript grey coat and trousers with an open-necked shirt". (See plates 31-33) Leslie Edwards played a memorable cameo role as the Beggar "depicted as a poor old man in a long shabby coat, probably half-witted, & legalising his profession by some mandolin-like instrument".

> The crowd of 22 slum dwellers of various types – street boys & a few small girls, tough young men in caps (rather like the young men in [Kurt Jooss's 1932 ballet] "Big City", tho' with some less sombre suits – a brightish blue & a crimson one among them) their girls in varied finery – to their generation belong the pair of lovers & the "gang" is led by Messrs Burke, Franklin, White and Danton – & their elders matronly women & bedraggled red-nosed harridans – the usual teeming life of a slum. Like "Petrouchka" it is a ballet in which the crowd plays an important part and its movements tho' casual enough in appearance are doubtless cunningly contrived.

Although the symmetry of setting and movement suggests the formal nature of the work, Bradley voiced some reservations:

> [S]ome of the movements seem too stylised & even too uniform – but for the interweaving & orchestration of the movements only the highest praise is possible [...]. The whole thing is very well knit, the various transitions, emptyings and fillings of the stage have an air of natural casualness which makes everything fall into place with the same inevitability that [Helpmann] showed in his Hamlet.

Once again Bradley mused on how to categorise *Miracle*: "If any sort of ordered movement constitutes a ballet, it is a good ballet & it is certainly a piece of very effective 'Theatre'."

Through Bradley's eyes it is possible to gain an insight into the designs of Helpmann's productions and understand how they evolved through the war. Outside the parameters of this essay, the Bulletins also enable historians to appreciate the impact of changes of cast on the ballets. Helpmann's focus on drama over technical demands enabled his productions to continue in performance even though many of the men were called up for war service. Helpmann welcomed the opportunities the war gave him to develop as a choreographer. Later he had fewer chances to create for the Sadler's Wells Ballet but he continued to be involved in a wide range of productions in which he could collaborate with interesting designers. Of his first designers Messel and Burra would remain actively involved in the theatre for a further decade, bringing their individual styles to the stage. It was, however, Leslie Hurry for whom the door was really opened with *Hamlet.* He was launched on a second career as a stage designer which ran parallel to his painting; Hurry went on to design more than sixty productions covering dance, opera and drama.[24] For all four artists, Messel, Hurry, Yee and Burra, working with Helpmann was a positive experience that in turn enhanced the pleasure of audience members, including Lionel Bradley, who found a great deal to enjoy in the ballets they designed.

Endnotes

1   For four consecutive years from 1936-1939, Helpmann had arranged the dances and ensembles in Cambridge University Footlights Dramatic Club's June revues; *Turn over a New Leaf* (1936), *Full Swing* (1937), *Pure and Simple* (1938) and *The All-Male Revue* (1939). He had begun to choreograph *La Danse* (completed by Wendy Toye) for the Royal Academy of Dance Production Club (1939), and choreographed "The Old Shoemaker" for *Fun and Games* at the Saville Theatre in 1941.

2   In addition to *A Day in a Southern Port* (created for the Camargo Society on 29 November 1931, renamed *Rio Grande* for the Vic-Wells Ballet 26 March 1935), *Barabau* (17 April 1936) and *Miracle in the Gorbals*, Burra's work as a theatre designer was for the Royal Opera's *Carmen* (14 January 1947), Frederick Ashton's *Don Juan* (25 November 1948), de Valois' *Don Quixote* (20 February 1950), Ballet Rambert's contribution to the Festival of Britain, *Canterbury Prologue*, choreographed by David Paltenghi and given its first public preview at Harrogate 15 October 1951 and the 'negro musical comedy' *Simply Heavenly* at the Adelphi, London (20 May 1958).

3   Kathrine Sorley Walker, *Robert Helpmann A Rare Sense of the Theatre* (Alton: Dance Books, 2009), p.51.

4   Jerome created the play in 1908 out of his short story of the same title written a year earlier. The popularity of the production led to its being used as the basis for a film by Herbert Brenon in 1918 and again by Berthold Viertel in 1935, starring Conrad Viedt, Anna Lee and Frank Cellier. Veidt's film was voted the fourth best British movie of 1936 and, most likely, was seen by Benthall and Helpmann, given its much publicised success.

5   Material from Lionel Bradley's Ballet Bulletins is quoted by kind permission of Mrs Christine Angel.

6   The London Archives of the Dance (THM/238) was founded under a trust deed on 9 January 1945 to provide documentary resources for the study of dance. At its heart was the collection of books, programmes, photographs, souvenirs and ephemera gathered by the Ballet Guild during the war. It included the Jacobi and Bolitho music-based collections (THM/140 and THM/99) and the Margaret Rolfe collection of Marie Taglioni ephemera. The Archive was active for a decade but the lack of independent premises and sufficient funding resulted in the collection being put into storage. The Archive as a separate organisation was wound up in 1968 and acquired by the V&A but parts had become inextricably mixed with Beaumont's Collection, which came to the museum after his death in 1976. While some papers and collections are catalogued as LAD, the books, programmes and photographs have largely been subsumed into the core collection of the Theatre & Performance Collections.

7   On 9 October 2012, BBC Radio 4 broadcast *One Man's War* on Bradley and his experiences of attending concerts and ballet during the 1939-45 War; and in 2013 Paul Banks gave a number of presentations on Benjamin Britten's music through Bradley's eyes.

8   In 1942 Bradley attended 52 performances by the Sadler's Wells Ballet. He also attended performances by Russian Opera & Ballet later called New Russian Ballet (4), Ballet Guild (3), International Ballet (3), Anglo-Polish Ballet (2) and single performances by Albion Opera (for which dancers from Rambert were performing) and Kyasht Ballet and saw ballet again in *Moscow Bells* at the London Coliseum. In the spring he was also housebound because of illness for seven weeks.

9   The Michael Benthall Archive THM/69 focuses on his Shakespearean productions at Stratford-upon-Avon and at the Old Vic and includes typescripts, minute books, press cuttings albums (1935-1968), programmes, scores. See http://archiveshub.ac.uk/data/gb71-thm/69

10   The reference is to Ashton's ballet, *The Wise Virgins* (1940), which was set to music by J.S. Bach (orchestrated by William Walton) with designs by Whistler. After seeing a matinée performance at the New Theatre, London, on 16 January 1941, Bradley was shocked to find that "the admirable curtain and scenery by Rex Whistler which did so much to establish the atmosphere of the work" had been discarded; he repeatedly returned to this theme in his writing.

11   Christie's novel was published by Collins (London: 1951); this information is noted in Zoë Anderson, *The Royal Ballet 75 Years* (London: Faber, 2006), p.78.

12   Helpmann's address, delivered at Leslie Hurry's Thanksgiving Service at St Paul's Church, Covent Garden on 24 May 1979, is reproduced in Daniel Ladell (ed.), *Leslie Hurry: A Painter for the Stage* (Stratford, Ontario: Stratford Festival and Gallery, 1984).

13   Chiang Yee, "What can I say about Ballet", in Arnold Haskell (ed.) *The Ballet Annual: A Record and Year Book of the Ballet* (London: Black, 1948, second issue), p.113. For an edited version of the essay, see Appendix II.

14   *Lady Precious Stream*, described as "A Traditional Chinese Play in Four Acts", was first produced at the Little Theatre 28 November 1934, revived the following year and transferred to the Savoy Theatre on 13 April 1936, where it had a total run of 733 performances. For this the stage was undecorated, leaving the décor to the imagination of the audience; and the stage management worked in full view of the audience. The play was also successfully staged in New York in 1936.

15   Wilhelm [William John Charles Pitcher] (1856-1925) was an English artist and costume and set designer. His meticulous designs include a number for fantasy characters, butterflies, flowers and birds. Among his most famous birds were those for the 1883 revival of *A Trip to the Moon* and *The Swans* (1886), both for the Alhambra, London.

16   For further discussion of Beryl Grey's involvement with *The Birds*, see DVD Track 1.

17   For an extensive discussion of the movement designed for *The Birds*, see Audrey Williamson, *Contemporary Ballet* (London: Rockliff, 1946), pp. 95-97.

18   See DVD Track 3: *Miracle in the Gorbals*, reconstruction workshops; and DVD Track 4: An Interview with Gillian Lynne.

19   Arnold I. Haskell, *Miracle in the Gorbals, A Study* (Edinburgh: The Albyn

Press, 1946, pp.12 – 13.

20   Helpmann in interview with H.R. Jeans, *Manchester Daily Mail*, 31 August 1944.

21   Michael Benthall, "The Dance-Drama" in Arnold Haskell (ed.), *Sadler's Wells Ballet Books No. 3: Hamlet and Miracle in the Gorbals* (London: Bodley Head, 1949), p.11. For the full text of this essay, see Appendix III.

22   Jane Stevenson, *Edward Burra: Twentieth-Century Eye* (London: Pimlico, 2007), p.283.

23   Acknowledging the "found" nature of the costumes in the original production, the 2014 staging was clothed by purchases from charity shops. This explains why some outfits looked more modern than the 1940s look that might have been expected. See DVD Track 2: Interviews with Jean Bedells and Julia Farron about their costumes for the original production (1944).

 24   For a full account of Hurry's activities as designer, see Raymond Ingram, *The Stage Designs of Leslie Hurry*, Theatre in Focus Series (Cambridge: Chadwyck-Healey, 1990); and Daniel Ladell (ed.) *Leslie Hurry: A Painter for the Stage* (Stratford, Ontario: Stratford Festival and Gallery, 1984).

27. Robert Helpmann as Prince
Siegfried and Margot Fonteyn
as Odette in the 1943 revival
of *Swan Lake*, designed by Leslie
Hurry (Sadler's Wells Ballet, New
Theatre).

28. This full-length portrait of
Helpmann (from the same production)
shows he possessed a fine classical
physique.

Both photos: Tunbridge-Sedgwick.
Sources: Victoria and Albert Museum,
London/The Royal Ballet School
Special Collections

29. The opening scene of Robert Helpmann's *The Birds* (1942), with the Hen (Moyra Fraser) being mocked by the Sparrows. Designed by Chiang Yee. Photographed by Tunbridge-Sedgwick. Credit: Royal Opera House/ArenaPAL

30. Robert Helpmann's *The Birds* (1942) with Beryl Grey as the Nightingale partnered by Alexis Rassine as the Dove. Chiang Yee's full set can be seen in the upper illustration. Photographed by Tunbridge-Sedgwick. Credit: Royal Opera House/ArenaPAL

31. Robert Helpmann as the Christ-like 'Stranger' in his ballet, *Miracle in the Gorbals* (Sadler's Wells Ballet, Princes Theatre, 1944). Helpmann based the hand gestures for this role on the religious paintings of El Greco. Contact sheet photos: Gordon Anthony © Victoria and Albert Museum, London

Miracle in the Gorbals.

32. Posed stage photograph of Robert Helpmann's *Miracle in the Gorbals*, showing the set design by Edward Burra (Sadler's Wells Ballet, Princes Theatre, 1944). Postcard annotated with the names of the cast. Photo: Edward Mandinian © Victoria and Albert Museum, London. Source: The Royal Ballet School Special Collections (Reeves Collection)

33. The 'resurrection scene' from Gillian Lynne's re-creation of Robert Helpmann's 1944 ballet, *Miracle in the Gorbals* (Birmingham Royal Ballet, 2014). Photo: Bill Cooper/ArenaPAL

34. Reproduction of Edward Burra's original front cloth depicting the Clydeside docks; the ship's hull and chain were painted deep red against a grey background. From Gillian Lynne's re-creation of Robert Helpmann's 1944 ballet, *Miracle in the Gorbals* (Birmingham Royal Ballet, 2014). Photo: Bill Cooper/ArenaPAL

35. Michael Benthall at work in a theatre, undated. Benthall wrote the libretto for several Helpmann ballets; his military posting to Glasgow during WWII inspired the location of *Miracle in the Gorbals* (1944). Photographer unknown. Source: Victoria and Albert Museum, London

36. Robert Helpmann and Michael Benthall c.1942-46, described in the original photograph caption as 'Choreographer and Scenarist'. Reproduced from Audrey Williamson, Contemporary Ballet (London: Salisbury Square, 1946), plate 29. Photo: Baron

37. Robert Helpmann as Shakespeare's Hamlet, musing over Yorick's skull. Directed by Michael Benthall (Shakespeare Memorial Theatre, Stratford-upon-Avon, 1948). Angus McBean Photograph © Houghton Library, Harvard University. Source: Victoria and Albert Museum, London

38. *Below left:* Robert Helpmann in the title role of Shakespeare's Hamlet, during the "O what a rogue and peasant slave am I" soliloquy that culminates in his decision to kill Claudius. Directed by Tyrone Guthrie (Old Vic Company, New Theatre, 1944). Photo: Edward Mandinian © Victoria and Albert Museum, London

39. *Opposite above:* Robert Helpmann as Hamlet in the same soliloquy in a later production, directed by Michael Benthall (Shakespeare Memorial Theatre, Stratford-upon-Avon, 1948). Photo: Angus McBean. Credit: University of Bristol. Source: Victoria and Albert Museum, London

40. Robert Helpmann as Shylock in Shakespeare's The Merchant of Venice, directed by Michael Benthall (Shakespeare Memorial Theatre, Stratford-upon-Avon, 1948). Angus McBean Photograph © Houghton Library, Harvard University. Source: Victoria and Albert Museum, London

41. Robert Helpmann as Prince Florimund, in Act II of the Royal Opera House production of *The Sleeping Beauty* (Sadler's Wells Ballet, Feb.1946). Photo: Gordon Anthony © Victoria and Albert Museum, London

42. Robert Helpmann as the Fairy Carabosse, in the Prologue of the Royal Opera House production of *The Sleeping Beauty* (Sadler's Wells Ballet, Feb.1946). Photo: Gordon Anthony © Victoria and Albert Museum, London

43. Robert Helpmann making up for the role of the Fairy Carabosse in *The Sleeping Beauty* (Sadler's Wells Ballet, ROH, 1946). The drawing above his dressing table (see top image) shows Carabosse's make-up, and may have been provided for reference by the production's designer, Oliver Messel. Photographer unknown. Source: Victoria and Albert Museum, London

44. Robert Helpmann as the elderly Adam Zero/ Principal Dancer in his ballet *Adam Zero* (Sadler's Wells Ballet, ROH, April 1946). The multi-layered work referenced Shakespeare's "Seven Ages of Man". Photo: Baron. Source: The Philip Richardson Library, Royal Academy of Dance

45. Robert Helpmann as the young Adam in his ballet *Adam Zero*, in a "classical" pas de deux with June Brae as the Choreographer-Ballerina/ First Love-Wife-Mistress/ Death (Sadler's Wells Ballet, ROH, April 1946). Photo: Baron. Source: The Royal Ballet School Special Collections

46. Portrait of Robert Helpmann as Wycroft in the film *Caravan*, and 47. (*below*) in a scene from the same film with the actor Brooks Turner (dir. Arthur Crabtree, UK, April 1946). Photos: Rank Films © ITV/REX/Shutterstock

48. Robert Helpmann in his created role of Adelino Canberra in *Les Sirènes*, a humorous ballet by Frederick Ashton (Sadler's Wells Ballet, ROH, Nov.1946). Helpmann's pose echoes the neo-classicism of Ashton's *Symphonic Variations*, which had premièred earlier that year. Photo: Gordon Anthony © Victoria and Albert Museum, London

49. Robert Helpmann as Flamineo with Margaret Rawlings as Vittoria Corombona, in John Webster's play, *The White Devil*. Costumes designed by Audrey Cruddas; directed by Michael Benthall (Duchess Theatre, 1947). Angus McBean Photograph © Houghton Library, Harvard University. Source: Victoria and Albert Museum, London

50. Robert Helpmann with Margot Fonteyn in her dressing room, and 51. (*below*) in rehearsal with Fonteyn and Moira Shearer (Edinburgh, September 1948). Photographers unknown. Credit: Evening Dispatch. Source: The Royal Ballet School Special Collections

52. and 53. Film stills of Robert Helpmann as the malign Coppélius, seen in close-up, and in action with Moira Shearer as the hapless doll, Olympia. From *The Tales of Hoffmann* (dir. Powell and Pressburger, UK, 1951). Photographers unknown. Credit: Ronald Grant/ArenaPAL

The (re)Generation of *Miracle in the Gorbals* (1944)

Michael Byrne

> [Helpmann's] lined hands and tired eyes were reminders of the long years the dancer has spent on stages around the world. But age has not withered his genius.[1]

"The trouble with ballet", declared Robert Helpmann, "is that everybody is constantly watching their age, afraid of getting old."[2] Having reprised his performance as the rickety Red King in his late seventies – almost half a century since originating the role in Ninette de Valois's *Checkmate* in 1937 – Helpmann's longevity as an actor-dancer and director-choreographer serves as a useful springboard for questioning debates around ageing and re-creativity in dance.[3] Judith Mackrell insists that it is "a profound faultline in ballet that the point at which dancers are maturing as artists is also the point at which their bodies – at least by the exacting standards of the art form – are on the decline".[4] Few can dispute that Classical ballet places an unjust premium on youth, overvaluing athleticism and physical prowess whilst dismissing the ageing body as a site of technical and expressive limitation. Nowhere was the subject of "degeneration in dance" better represented on stage than in Helpmann's post-war production of *Adam Zero* – a confusing Shakespearean allegory that sees in "old age no compensation of wisdom or geniality".[5] The ballet's 1946 programme-note outlined a pessimistic philosophy that described how "[m]an is born, makes a success in his own particular sphere, loses his position to a younger generation, sees his world crumble before his eyes, and only finds peace in death".[6] Furthermore, the narrative unfolded as Brechtian "ballet within a ballet", allowing shifting scenery to dress and denude the vast Covent Garden stage as a means of depicting a "[c]ompany creating a ballet and calling on all the resources of the theatre to do so".[7] Despite such a perplexing plot, *Adam Zero*'s twinned themes of ageing and ballet-making resonate forcefully throughout the contemporary reconstruction of Helpmann's earlier dance-drama *Miracle in the Gorbals*, engendering a renewed optimism for the senior artist as a creative agent – on and off stage.

In 2011, David Drew[8] embarked on a four-year preservation project that is best described by Ann Dils as a "compelling scavenger hunt, an act of scholarship and an artistic venture,"[9] aiming to recreate Helpmann's progressive ballet as it first appeared to audiences at the Prince's (now Shaftesbury) Theatre in London:

[T]his is a tale from the war years, 1944 to be exact. I was a 19 year old [...] sitting on hard benches, peering down at tiny forms on the stage far below, happily enjoying and criticising the performances. [T]hat first night the girl, danced by Pauline Clayden, achieved perfection in an adage, a wonderful combination of technique, timing and inspiration – an ecstasy, which has remained with me to this day. After the grim end, possibly as a relief from tension, the "gods" went wild! And, I went wild with them! We clapped, we shouted, we shrieked, we threw anything we had onto the stage below, and we wouldn't, couldn't stop, however many curtain calls the cast took. [...] As I lie in my bed, 85 and not far to go, my muscles tense up and in my mind I can still see and feel that moment when I was privileged to see a tiny part of absolute perfection.[10]

In Buss Jackson's poignant account above, she details the reception received by the Sadler's Wells Ballet at the première of *Miracle in the Gorbals* on 26 October 1944, praising Pauline Clayden for her affecting performance in the role of the Suicide Girl. Such adulation continued during the Company's debut tour to North America in 1949, with a New York critic exclaiming how Helpmann's ballet "accomplished one of those rare moments at the [Metropolitan Opera House]. For a long while the audience was just too stunned to applaud. And then, the house fairly exploded".[11] Whilst the international presence of *Miracle* affirmed the production's status as an exemplar of British dance-theatre and creativity, the appetite for Helpmann's gritty melodrama was not shared by all. Many critics were underwhelmed by the production's lack of choreographic invention, compelling ballet impresario Lincoln Kirstein to pen his disapproval: "The Gorbals program. Well, mother. All is forgiven, but *never* do it again."[12] This curt cautioning seemed prophetic when *Miracle* disappeared from the Company's permanent repertoire in 1958, falling victim to what Helen Thomas describes as the "history of lost dances", an inventory of vanished works.[13]

Arthur Bliss's composition, Michael Benthall's scenario, and Edward Burra's designs remain today as vestiges from Helpmann's wartime original; however, the affective textures and dramatic impulses behind the choreography can only continue to exist within the memories of those who originally performed in the production itself. David Drew's determination to reconstruct *Miracle*, therefore, highlighted certain archival frictions, for without dance notation or a video recording, the ballet's 're-assembly' was contingent on the living histories of first-generation cast members – all aged in their eighties and nineties. Audrey Williamson, writing on the "Future of the Ballet in England" in 1944, reminded her readers that "[b]allet, more than any other art, is dependent on its instruments, the dancers, since in the absence of a satisfactory system of recording ballets the work of the choreographer can only be seen and judged in actual performance".[14] In this regard, the circulation of creativity in dance tended to rely less on such objects as scripts, scores or paintings, but rather on the body's capacity – as a corporeal museum – to collect, archive, preserve, curate and re-exhibit movement. The transmission of choreography from generation to generation can, therefore, be viewed as a form of "social technology", using the practice of performance as a systematic means to retain and re-distribute embodied works. Drew initiated the remaking of *Miracle* by arranging a series of multi-generational rehearsals with five surviving cast members – Pauline Clayden, Jean Bedells, Henry Danton, Julia Farron and Gillian Lynne.[15]

To "remember the past is, whether we like it or not, to perform a creative act in the present".[16] This essay presents a confluence of short interviews – or "creative acts" – with these inspiring senior artists, affording all respondents the opportunity to illuminate Helpmann's "extinct" production through their own voices and personal commentaries. The discussions filmed by Nigel Hodgson and me over the last few years have been transcribed, conflated and edited into three sections, each seeking to celebrate the mature dancer as an essential distributor of historical, cultural and creative knowledge: Section I explores the narrative framework behind Helpmann's "slice of social realism",[17] and allows Drew to outline the key developments that foreshadowed the restaging of *Miracle* by Birmingham Royal Ballet (BRB) in 2014. It is worth noting here that David Bintley's Company proved the ideal collaborator in advancing Drew's desires for an authentic recreation, as the size, ethos and itinerant schedule of BRB best represented the touring model, led by de Valois through the turbulent years of war. Having first performed in the ballet as a teenager, Gillian Lynne was tasked with re-choreographing *Miracle* for BRB at the age of eighty-eight, thereby subverting many of the ageist norms in dance that "prescribe (and proscribe) who is legitimated to do what, where and when".[18]

Section II is shaped by the context of war, providing a platform for Bedells, Clayden, Danton, Farron and Lynne to reflect collectively on the importance of characterisation within Helpmann's work, and to address the frailties of memory when reclaiming 'lost' choreography. Particular attention is directed towards the re-performance and re-teaching of Clayden's Suicide solo, which contradicts a prevailing assumption that not a single step from the original 1944 ballet can be remembered (or reused).[19] Accordingly, former cast members unite in Section III to discuss the value of maintaining idiosyncratic works within the Classical ballet repertoire, and to assess how *Miracle* has the creative potential to enrich a new generation of performers today. Above all, this conversational "triple-bill" champions the tacit knowledge, embodied heritage and artistry of the mature dancer and, in doing so, encourages future choreographic projects that "refute our expectations of athleticism and technical expertise".[20] Helpmann's final appearance on stage in 1986 inflects these convictions:

> [W]ith rolling eyes, a few grand gestures, and a moving moment in which he shows the defiance of his distant youth, Helpmann's tottering Red King compels the attention in a way that none of his highly charged young colleagues could equal.[21]

To enliven the key themes presented in this essay, each section will include a short postscript discussion. Supporting information relating to performers' biographies and workshop days can be found in the Introduction to the documentary film (DVD track 3), which follows this essay and should be viewed in tandem with it.

Section I: Creative Context

In conversation with David Drew

Michael Byrne (MB): Before exploring some of the dramatic tensions within *Miracle in the Gorbals,* could you describe your earliest experiences of Robert Helpmann and how these led to your involvement with his ballet?

David Drew (DD): The first production I ever saw at Covent Garden was *Swan Lake* with Margot Fonteyn and Robert Helpmann in the principal roles. It was Easter 1951; I was just thirteen; and Helpmann entered the performance space, seeming to reach the centre within only a few strides: this was my introduction to the hypnotic power of his stage presence. Three years later, I left Bristol to join The Royal Ballet School, and my dancing teacher presented me with a good luck gift – a copy of Gordon Anthony's *Studies of Robert Helpmann* (1946). The range of characters depicted in Anthony's photographs was chameleonic: from Carabosse in *The Sleeping Beauty* to Dr Coppélius in *Coppélia*, Satan in *Job* to the Christ-figure in *Miracle in the Gorbals*. Ninette de Valois' perceptive introduction to the anthology described how *Miracle* had shaken the Parisian public to the core, and how Boris Kochno had declared that the "English Ballet had taught [him] something new".[22] This presentation in France was one of many performances of *Miracle* staged locally and internationally between the period of 1944 and 1950. I joined the Company in 1955, and was cast some years later as a member of the Gorbals' razor gang that attacks and murders Helpmann's character at the end of the ballet.

MB: Responding to the social evils and brutality in *Miracle*, the *New York Daily News* exclaimed that "it was impossible to believe that a ballet of superior beauty and superb force [could] be fashioned out of such ingredients as criminal violence, slum poverty and psychopathic sadism".[23] Why were these themes so provocative for Classical ballet at the time?

DD: This was a work that appealed to ordinary people; it was not a highfalutin', fantastical piece, or some "pretty-pretty" ballet – it was set in tenement slums, depicting real people on stage. The ballet is essentially a one-act dance-drama about Christ appearing in the twentieth century, with his Passion and death providing the context for a modern Miracle Play. Michael Benthall, a theatre director, deserved the credit for giving the ballet's initial theme an almost mythic quality.[24] His premise was that mankind throughout the ages will inevitably destroy a Christ-like figure; it is his vision that gives the ballet its unique theatrical power. Having been garrisoned in Glasgow at the start of World War II, Benthall adapted the ballet's scenario from a 1907 short story by Jerome K. Jerome, *The Passing of the Third Floor Back*, but decided to relocate the ballet to the Gorbals, which were at the time ruled by ruthless razor gangs and considered the most notorious slums in Europe.[25] Not only did Benthall transplant the action from the play's original setting in Bloomsbury to the grittiness of Glasgow, but he also sought inspiration in the Bible. Mary Magdalene is represented by the character of the Prostitute whom Christ accepts into his fold; Lazarus becomes the character called the Suicide, who throws herself into the river and is subsequently restored to life. Caiaphas, Jerusalem's high Priest, becomes the Minister, who is envious of Christ's power over the people and incites them to murder him.

MB: In Brinson and van Praagh's seminal book on *The Choreographic Art*, I discovered that Benthall had in fact directed some of the final rehearsals for *Miracle*, and that, by allowing the theatre director such influence in the dance-making process, Helpmann had effectively "introduced for the first time to English choreography the idea of using a producer".[26] The authors also proposed that the survival of any ballet is dependent on the unity of a "good scenario and a good score".[27] Was it the dramatic complexity of Benthall's narrative, combined with Bliss's climactic music, that motivated you to consider *Miracle* as a feasible reconstruction project?

DD: Surprisingly, a prompt to revisit this production emerged during an exhibition about Ninette de Valois at Manchester's Lowry Gallery: I was unexpectedly reunited with Edward Burra's atmospheric drop cloth, depicting the bow of a huge ship in the Clydeside docks.[28] (See plate 34) It was apparent then that the ballet's creative architects – Bobby [Helpmann], Benthall, Bliss and Burra – had become neglected over the years, and I wanted to remedy this. However, recreating a lost ballet like *Miracle in the Gorbals* is very difficult because – whilst the score, the designs and the scenario may be re-used – the spirit of how it was performed can only continue to exist in the memory of those who were originally in it. This project therefore began in earnest by assembling a handful of original cast members to review archival photographs from the Royal Opera House Collections: Jean Bedells, Pauline Clayden, Henry Danton, Julia Farron and Gillian Lynne. We were entirely reliant upon this group of remarkable people to keep the production alive, and all involved felt that we were reawakening something very important, for, if this generation of cast members died, the ballet died. Having consulted Arthur Bliss's score with Henry Roche,[29] we rehearsed several vignettes in The Royal Ballet studios under Gillian's choreographic leadership, followed by an intensive day-long workshop at The Royal Ballet School at White Lodge, Richmond. These efforts contributed to the strong belief that it would be possible to bring together a faithful re-imagining of what that first performance on 26 October 1944 at the Prince's Theatre entailed. Our ambitions were achieved, when Birmingham Royal Ballet decided to remount the ballet in 2014.

MB: You conferred upon the surviving cast members of *Miracle* the affectionate title of "The Fab Five". What were their contributions in Helpmann's ballet?

DD: The role of the Mother was originally played by Jean Bedells, who appeared up on a tenement balcony, yelling at her daughter (Moira Shearer) to come inside immediately and have nothing to do with that 'ne'er do well' boyfriend (Alexis Rassine). Shearer was very soon lured away to star in *The Red Shoes* with Helpmann and Léonide Massine, thereby enabling Gillian Lynne – who had been in the *corps de ballet* originally – to take over the character of the Young Lover. Julia Farron had also been in the *corps* – having joined the Company on her fourteenth birthday – and when Celia Franca left in 1946, she inherited the role of the Prostitute, seducing the up-tight local Minister (David Paltenghi). The part of the Suicide girl was created by the astonishing Pauline Clayden, who performed the role in almost one hundred and fifty consecutive shows. Touchingly, Julia and Pauline have remained the greatest of friends; they were eight when they first met and have both recently celebrated their ninetieth birthdays. The final member of this extraordinary quintet is Henry Danton, for it was whilst in the army – aged nineteen at the time – that he first experienced ballet at Covent Garden.

From that moment he resolved to become a dancer, eventually becoming a member of the razor gang in *Miracle,* before going on to create the third man in Fredrick Ashton's masterpiece, *Symphonic Variations* (1946). In fairness, Peter Franklin White[30] should also be acknowledged for he was an original gang member, who murdered the Christ-like figure. During an interview with Peter a few years ago, he revealed that the stage-door keeper at the time had introduced him to actual Glaswegian gang members whilst on tour with *Miracle.* From this encounter he claimed that he learnt how to wield the [imaginary] razor blade he kept concealed in the peak of his cap, a technique that he subsequently included in Helpmann's ballet.

MB: I can recall the moment when Peter rose from his chair to demonstrate these flick-knife actions, seeming to "reawaken in himself" some physical traces from Helpmann's choreographic landscape. Even if he was unable to reclaim specific steps, the theatrical intentions behind the movement remained within.

DD: Yes, it must be remembered that, although Helpmann produced an undeniably dramatic piece full of idiosyncratic characterisations, *Miracle* in fact contained very little choreography. Mere "steps" were not Bobby's forte, nor indeed his main interest. He was essentially a story-teller, who knew how to involve his audience in a living drama. Those familiar with his brilliantly condensed, balletic version of *Hamlet* (1942) will appreciate this approach. Helpmann created drama and narrative; he created everything theatrical, but not really steps.[31] Therefore you have this strange situation of a ballet with few Classical ballet movements. So, is it really a ballet at all? This is one of the reasons why I felt it was so important that we should bring *Miracle* back, because I believe that – and I hope that many others now agree – it is still a ballet even though it seems to have so few formalised steps.

MB: Arnold Haskell confronts the conceptual clash between dance and drama, insisting that the term, "ballet", is all-inclusive, provided the choreographer and dancer support their work with the formality of Classical ballet training:

> Let us scotch that absurdity once and for all that such a work as *Miracle in the Gorbals* has more acting than dancing. It is all dancing and can be nothing else.[32]

Haskell amusingly suggests that a mere "eyebrow lift" qualifies as a choreographic gesture and that, to convey the harsh realities of the slums, Helpmann prioritised characterisation and acting above the traditional,

Classical dance vocabulary.[33] Do you think that in privileging drama over definitive "steps", *Miracle in the Gorbals* represented his personal balletic statement?

DD: Helpmann's work makes us question our own assumptions about what the art form is. Ballet is recognised as a combination of the arts; Serge Diaghilev saw it as a mutual creation by a triumvirate of choreographer, designer and composer. Through his choreography of *Miracle in the Gorbals, Hamlet, Adam Zero* and his own performances, Helpmann highlighted the fourth essential ingredient: "theatricality". His general inclination on stage was to be outrageous and way over the top, and by today's performance standards he would have been considered melodramatic in the extreme. However, one of the most remarkable things about his characterisation as the enigmatic Stranger was that he was totally still and controlled, he was convincing and natural in his presentation – the audience didn't perceive any sense of acting at all. In fact, Helpmann's portrayal of this Christ-like figure was so compelling that, when I came off stage, I believed that I had just murdered a truly holy man. The potency of this dramatic situation lived with me throughout the rest of my career with The Royal Ballet.

Michael Byrne (Postscript to above conversation): Attending to Helpmann's interpretative abilities as a performer, it is worth noting that his histrionic displays were heightened further when playing elderly characters on stage, evidenced by the stupefying senility of his Dr Coppélius (*Coppélia*), his bewildered optimism as Cervantes's Knight (*Don Quixote*), the haggard malevolence of his Carabosse (*The Sleeping Beauty*), his pernicious foil to Frederick Ashton's demure Stepsister (*Cinderella*), and the tottering fragility of his Red King (*Checkmate*). Audrey Williamson describes "his drollery and busy invention, particularly in the creation of old men, being of that now rare type in which the Grimaldi clown and character comedian meet in a riot of mingled folly, caricature and acute human observation".[34] However, as noted by Drew, all forms of pantomimic gilding were stripped away from his performance as the "Christ-like figure" in *Miracle*, allowing for an expression of character that was more nuanced, unaffected and subtle in style. In 1958 *The Dancing Times* described how it was the "simplicity and economy of gesture of Helpmann as The Stranger that made him tower over the younger members of an excellent cast".[35] In light of such minimal choreography, all thirty-five members of the Sadler's Wells Ballet were required to deliver "first-rate acting performances" in a production that – according to Cyril Beaumont – was better suited for "the legitimate stage" than the domain of dance.[36]

Although the revival of *Miracle* by Birmingham Royal Ballet exists as a detailed re-imagining of the 1944 original, I propose that Drew's reconstruction workshops in 2011 advanced the ambitions of Helpmann by creating an environment where ballet and drama could integrate seamlessly. This is best demonstrated by the decision to cast professional actors, Judith Paris and Jack Rebaldi, in the lead roles of the Prostitute and the Minister.[37] The involvement of these mature 'non-dancers' inspired me to question whether Helpmann's creation would still constitute dance if the National Theatre, the Old Vic or the Royal Shakespeare Company had revived *Miracle* instead? Helpmann's response – I believe – would be an assured "yes", as his commentary about the art forms reveals:

> These are particularly interesting times in that they are bringing an increasing affinity between ballet and drama – a highly desirable development, because the two mediums can give useful assistance one to the other. I believe that all dancers should train to be actors and all actors as dancers. Dancers should know how to play a scene as well as how to dance it, and actors should know how to move a scene as well as how to follow its basic script requirements.[38]

With less emphasis placed on physical and technical prowess, Paris and Rebaldi illustrate how dance-dramas like *Miracle* have the potential for performers to express and enhance their dramatic sensibilities as they continue to age. Looking at the ballet's more structured sequences of steps (e.g., the Suicide Solo), Pauline Clayden's extraordinary ability to present the choreography in her late eighties proves that when "youth is no longer the uppermost quality, resilience and knowledge and experience come to the fore, each quality being revealed on stage through movement and gesture".[39] The process of restoring Clayden's solo to the stage – discussed in greater detail during the section to follow – shows that athleticism and youth are not necessarily preeminent criteria in the field of Western Classical dance. Rather, the unity of dramatic and emotional expression operates as a locus of creativity. It is ironic, however, that the reconstruction *Miracle*, relying on the performance experiences of senior artists, has the potential to challenge the melodramatic and caricatured representations of age that Helpmann himself allowed to predominate in the discipline throughout his career.

Section II: The Cast of 1944

In conversation with Jean Bedells, Pauline Clayden, Henry Danton, Julia Farron and Gillian Lynne[40]

Michael Byrne (MB): When the Sadler's Wells Ballet performed *Miracle* in 1944, critics seemed unsettled by the harsh realities depicted on stage. The *Dancing Times* cautioned audiences that Helpmann's production was "not for the fastidious ballet-goer looking for the niceties of Classical technique and the dainty subtleties of porcelain dancers".[41] As first-generation cast members, how did you respond to this form of dramatic work?

Julia Farron (JF): There were, of course, those who didn't think that the production was quite right: ballet after all was meant to be about pretty tutus and wands. However, for us at the time, this type of work was a new thing and the Company fell into it – it was like a breath of fresh air. Instead of just being dancers going around on *pointe*, we were required to act more than dance. It was also unusual at the time for the wardrobe department to insist that we go out ourselves and acquire cheap shoes for the ballet. Armed with a coupon, I gaily went to Oxford Street and found myself a pair to match my purple dress on stage. The designs by Edward Burra were completely naturalistic; there wasn't any deference to stage costume – we were dressed in brash, rather ordinary clothes.

Pauline Clayden (PC): We were all excited to present *Miracle* because so many people described the ballet as something completely different.

Gillian Lynne (GL): It was pithy! We found the ballet's dramatic content thrilling and it proved an inspired contrast to our work at the time. Our repertoire contained beautiful ballets – all very Classical or *demi-caractère* based – however the Company had few dance-dramas that allowed for such rich characterisation. We found it thrilling!

JF: Greater freedom was given to us: far more than we normally had in other repertoire. In between the set dance movements we were on our own – we had to rely on our own imaginations. Ballet technique during the war was not particularly strong, and Bobby seemed mindful of this. It was the emotion and the story that was of utmost importance – he would rarely correct us on the specifics or technicalities of the actual dancing. The foundations of Classical mime had no place in this ballet because Bobby encouraged an approach that was more realistic. Our body language was critical, the way we stood, the way we moved – he wanted us to be real, rough people. Being faced with an opportunity to break away from pure Classicism must have been a release for him, and in this sense, *Miracle in the Gorbals* was as beneficial for him as it was for us.

Jean Bedells (JB): As a great actor-dancer, Bobby stimulated a creative response from the members of the Company, many of whom came from rather different backgrounds and did not necessarily have comprehensive or comparable training.

Henry Danton (HD): *Miracle* marked the first opportunity that we had of getting out and acting. I was startled to receive a write-up that claimed, "Danton was good as a dockworker", [42] and such praise seemed ridiculous, particularly since I was only in the *corps de ballet* at the time. As for Helpmann himself, he had a way of affecting people, and a way of bringing out something special in them – he was way ahead of his time with this ballet in attempting to deal with the kind of television realism we see today. He wanted us to collaborate creatively, and that's why I was able to give my own interpretation to the character, giving the dockworker a heavy, weighted way of walking. Helpmann didn't just create choreography, he explained what he was trying to get us to do – it was about the feeling and emotion. Further inspiration came from his affection for the compositions and the use of hands in El Greco's works. We were encouraged to study these elements, and I remember going to the National Gallery where I bought postcards of the paintings – I still have them. (See plate 31)

JF: I was also in the *corps* initially, and I recall standing backstage at the bottom of the stairs after a *Miracle in the Gorbals* performance, when down came Bobby's great chums – Vivien Leigh and Laurence Olivier! Bobby emerged from his dressing room to greet them and I overheard Olivier say – looking straight at me – "There she is, that girl, that girl in purple". I nearly fell about, for I was just a member of the *corps de ballet* then. Bobby said to me afterwards, "He thought you were very good".

MB: I have been told that the barometer for gauging a ballet's success was the sound of a theatre seat closing during a performance, indicating that an audience member had left the auditorium dissatisfied. When *Miracle* was being performed during the war, however, the thud of a collapsing seat was seldom heard. Was this true?

GL: Yes, I remember us taking *Miracle* with ENSA[43] to the continent where, unsurprisingly, we encountered troops, who had never experienced ballet before and who probably would have preferred the entertainment of something else (had it been available). Instead, they had the Sadler's Wells Ballet. The unexpected realism of *Miracle* was something that they could grip onto, and they ended up loving it. (See Appendix I)

MB: With so little "structured" choreography in the production, one critic insisted that *Miracle* was hardly a true ballet, except for the part of the Suicide solo.[44] I had the privilege of watching Pauline [Clayden] eliciting strands of this emotive sequence during workshops at The Royal Ballet's Fonteyn Studio in 2011. Having not performed Helpmann's movements in over sixty years, I am curious as to how you, Pauline, managed to reclaim elements of this choreography with such assurance and ease?

PC: The first thing that I could remember about that Suicide solo was that I could hum the music – it was the rhythm that I could remember, and so much of the movement was on the beat. I could visualise the piece and have carried it with me throughout the years. The choreography of some ballets escapes me completely, but movements like that of the Suicide Girl's solo that remain firmly on the musical beat and have a pulse, I seem to recollect.

MB: Suggestions were also made at the time of the ballet's première in 1944 that audiences were "afforded no clue" as to why the Suicide Girl wished to take her life.[45] Can you provide any insight into the motivation behind Helpmann's choreography on stage?

PC: Bobby left it to us to interpret what his movements were to mean. As the character of the Suicide I was never told *why* I was committing suicide; however, there were slight hints in the choreography that lent themselves to the belief that – in my mind – the piece must have been related to the death of the character's mother. The choreography included the folded mime gestures for "mother", and that it is how I interpreted it. I never felt that the character truly belonged in the Gorbals: she was a country girl, destitute, begging for help from the old hags near her, and she conveyed a sense of revulsion for the man who tried to kiss her during the routine. These provided some clues as to the shape and characterisation of the role. For my own inspiration in the performance I drew upon past experience: I visited a small tea-shop when on tour with the Company, and when I went upstairs, I can remember very distinctly seeing a little round table with a wizened old lady seated behind it. She started talking: "Do you see visions?

I can see angels with a coach floating across the sky." Although this was a peculiar encounter, this woman painted such a vivid picture in my mind of these flying cherubs, wafting this carriage along, that I stored it throughout the years. When the Suicide solo was choreographed, I incorporated this mental imagery as I looked across the audience in despair. During Bobby's death as the Stranger at the very end of the ballet, Julia and I had to hurry downstage. The only instruction I can remember was that we were to run forward and see him, to turn, and then to crumble and cry. The scene was trying to communicate a moment of nothingness before the realisation of the Stranger's death. However, Bobby was explicit in the kind of reaction we should give; I just felt completely stunned by the vision of death before me.

MB: Following Drew's successful revival workshops in London, a BBC television documentary replicated the teaching of the Suicide solo to Birmingham Royal Ballet principal, Natasha Oughtred, who expressed her astonishment at Pauline's ability to retain such "clarity on the ballet after so many years".[46] I'd like to quote from the *Ballet Annual* of 1947, which revealed that another member of "The Fab Five" was well-known for her impressive ability to remember choreography:

> Jean [Bedells] has a photographic memory for ballets, and only occasionally makes a written record. On one occasion, when *Miracle in the Gorbals* was in rehearsal, the group of dancers tensely watching the Suicide being dragged out of the river (off stage) had got into a considerable tangle with their timing and positions. "What's happened to that group?" Robert Helpmann called out. "You all know what you ought to be doing. Can't any of you count?" After a moment's rather sheepish pause, someone answered, "Jean's not here to-day. She usually counts for us." Although each dancer should be doing his or her own counting (keeping track of the beats or bars on which the movements of a ballet are hinged), when a dancer with a potential ballet mistress's memory and reliability is in a group, that is what idleness is liable to make happen.[47]

JB: Frustratingly, I can only remember a small amount of the Scottish dancing that appeared after the resurrection scene with Pauline as the Suicide, mainly because the music is there for it. We directed the action towards the Stranger, congratulating him for bringing the girl back to life. I was mostly up on the tenement balcony, and was therefore often not involved in the group action.

JF: As much as I adored performing in *Miracle in the Gorbals*, the choreography doesn't come out of me – it is gone, it is lost. Most of the ballets that I did

– and I performed dozens of them – I can remember; and I credit this to the steps being set. As a trained Classical dancer, this was a more natural way to retain the choreography; but, as the character of the Prostitute, I have forgotten the movement entirely. I can summon the feeling of it, but I cannot remember the steps. During The Royal Ballet School workshop, we eventually consulted the archival photographs, which were quite helpful, and linked them together to form various pictures and positions.

Michael Byrne (Postscript to above conversation): Barbara Dickinson proposes that when "considering the nature of virtuosity in older dancers, one must ask what qualities these artists possess now that were not present in their younger selves".[48] Observing the touching footage of Pauline Clayden dancing alongside Kristen McNally,[49] it is apparent that the senior performer maintains an emotional intensity that transcends the athleticism and technical expertise of her talented junior. Although Pauline's re-performance of the Suicide solo demonstrates the body's impressive capacity to function as an embodied archive, Jean's inability to remember the ballet's choreography reflects the consensus that the majority of Helpmann's movement remains irrecoverable. This may be attributed to Julia's suggestion that *Miracle* was more drama than dance-based, and that a set choreographic sequence – like the Suicide solo – is easier to recall than unstructured or mimed gestural vocabulary. However, even though most members of "The Fab Five" are unable to recreate their past performances on a virtuosic level, the dramatic intentionality behind Helpmann's movement exists within them, and could be reawakened in the context of a revival workshop. As Pina Bausch famously stated, "I'm not interested in how people move, but *what* moves them".[50] Framed by this conception, the value of the senior performer extends beyond the need to recreate specific steps with accuracy, but to recreate (and invoke) the "affect" of Helpmann's original staging. Graham Watts, reviewing the completed Birmingham Royal Ballet production in 2014, suggests that the "choreography is very much a flavour of what might have been, although – to be frank – it is not Helpmann's dance steps we need to rediscover but his intense sense of theatre, and in this regard, *Miracle in the Gorbals* is well worth having back".[51] It is the transmission and circulation of this "affective knowledge" between generations that emerges as an area of interest in the concluding conversation with cast members.

Section III: The Bridge Generation

In conversation with Pauline Clayden, David Drew, Henry Danton, Julia Farron and Gillian Lynne

Michael Byrne (MB): Joan Lawson – commenting on the 1958 revival of *Miracle in the Gorbals* – believed that it was beneficial to maintain Helpmann's work within The Royal Ballet's repertoire because it enabled the younger members of the Company to acquire "a deeper knowledge of the dramatic implications of characterisation and plot development".[52] Decades later, *Miracle* has had the same transformative effect with a different generation of dancers, illustrated by James Barton's statement (in response to the rehearsal process in 2014):

> For anyone who comes to see Birmingham Royal Ballet perform regularly, it is a chance for them to see us do something completely different, not just in the style and context of the piece but also in our individual performances. It is like nothing we have ever done before.[53]

Gillan Lynne (GL): *Miracle* is a dance-drama, and dance-dramas are very interesting for ballet companies; they are so different from what these young dancers perform normally in that the genre opens them up. Helpmann was a wonderful director, and – being such a fine actor himself – he taught us the subtext and acting required to underlie the movement. David [Drew] wanted to revive this ballet because he believed that Bobby hadn't received the adulation and credit he deserved, and I agree.

Julia Farron (JF): I learnt more from Bobby about performing and acting on stage than I did from anybody. We all felt that he taught us a great deal about not just being dancers executing steps, but that there was more to performance. Characterisation wasn't added: it was integrated.

David Drew (DD): Looking at this idea of generational influence, I am reminded of young Kristen McNally and Pauline Clayden working alongside each other: two generations performing Helpmann's choreography in unison. Kristen is a fine Soloist with The Royal Ballet, and after rehearsing the Suicide solo in the studio she commented on the value of working with Pauline, of creating something out of basic steps, and of the extra layering of theatricality needed to enhance Helpmann's movement.

GL: Bobby's ballet is after all a piece of theatre rather than a "ballet-ballet". It is all about getting into the earth, and it can be difficult for a performer to shift out of Classical technique and into feeling the strength of the floor, because we are taught the exact opposite in ballet: we are instructed to be above the floor, pulling out of it. The dancers I have worked with are so fluid and responsive that they can adjust to this different approach with relative ease – it merely takes time. When recreating this ballet, it was important to provide the dancers with the full dramatic structure and *raison d'être*.[54] An understanding of dramatic subtext is essential, and I constantly encouraged this during the rehearsals. In a way it is easier to teach Classical techniques like fifth [position, or *sauté*] jump, etc. Those structured approaches, perhaps, are simpler to absorb than teasing out our dramatic ability and a feeling of earthiness. For example, my original focus in The Royal Ballet School workshop was on where to place the arms, how to make them heavy, and how to disturb the air around the room. I was uncertain if the revival could be tackled until seeing it on its feet then – I needed to see it for myself first.

Henry Danton (HD): *Miracle* contains compelling emotions: it is about hate and frustration, about love and about desire. The younger generations have to feel that life is passionate and full of these emotions. And that is why this ballet was worthy of a revival – it reflects human feelings that have not changed. The ballet is not out of date at all – it remains contemporary. Bliss's music is powerful and Burra's sets were marvellous. When David [Drew] first approached me about this revival project, he presented me with images of the front cloth of *Miracle*. These were exciting to see because, having been behind the cloth at the start of each performance, I never had the opportunity to see or truly appreciate the design before.

MB: Those observing the multi-generational workshops and rehearsals between 2011 and 2014 have supported the reawakening of *Miracle*, deeming the ballet's revival a triumphant exercise in the restoration of a wartime dance-drama to the stage. This motivates the question as to why *Miracle* vanished from the repertoire in the first place? Was the production's disappearance attributed to changes in aesthetic taste? Did the work lose its contemporary appeal? Should Helpmann's ballet have remained in the archive, merely as a nostalgic work of its time?

HD: A production like *Miracle* can easily deteriorate when the chorographer hands it over, and is therefore reliant on a decent *régisseur* to maintain it. By shoving them and pulling things out of them, Helpmann knew how to evoke something from the Company, which often his successors were unable to achieve.

GL: Fashion and styles do change; however, I agree that the main reason for the ballet's removal from the repertoire was because the Company didn't have someone to teach it. You need an actor-choreographer to coach and awaken the dramatic undertones of the piece.

DD: Opinion may indeed be polarised as to whether *Miracle* has dated. Personally, I believe that, as an idiosyncratic work emerging during a significant historical period, this ballet was deserving of resurrection. The original was progressive for its time and subsequent dance works have reaped the reward of putting violence onto the stage: for example, the ballet can be regarded as a precursor to *West Side Story* (1957).[55] Furthermore, this reconstruction has highlighted – perhaps more than anything else – the fact that we have to call at some stage on the opinion of those people who are still alive and can provide a valuable assessment of a ballet (like *Miracle*), and advise whether or not it should be revived. The number of people who have some working knowledge of about one hundred years of ballets, created from Diaghilev to this day, are fast diminishing; and this is why Monica Mason referenced us as the "Bridge Generation", because we can speak from first-hand knowledge.

Michael Byrne (Postscript to above conversation): David Drew's unyielding resolve to reawaken *Miracle in the Gorbals* has enforced the maxim that ballet is an "art of tradition" – a vital, living force, handed down from master to student, redistributed and re-appropriated from dancer to dancer.[56] Jean Bedells, Pauline Clayden, Henry Danton, Julia Farron and Gillian Lynne have served as invaluable conduits between Helpmann's original 1944 dance-drama and the younger performers of today, shifting the emphasis of ballet-making away from a process of "reconstruction" towards a process of "re-generation". Michael Mangan argues that ballet "sets its own standards of physical perfection and will callously reject those who fail to live up to it, through being too tall, too short, too disproportioned – or, eventually, too old".[57] The involvement of "The Fab Five" illustrates that, while Western Classical dance may outwardly reflect the exuberance of youth, it is ironically the experiential knowledge of the senior artist (and the transmission of such tacit knowledge between generations) that underpins the spectacle of ballet on stage. The intergenerational relationship between dancers enables the mature body to function as a kind of corporeal museum, mediating between the past and present, and as a site of creative emergence during re-performance. This restoration enterprise has, therefore, allowed dancers from Birmingham Royal Ballet to inherit the same artistic riches that David Drew and the members The Royal Ballet received during the revival of

Miracle in 1958. Once again, the words of Joan Lawson, written over fifty years ago, still resonate today:

> To the young members of the [*Miracle in the Gorbals*] cast I would therefore say – congratulations and bring your newly gained experience of character building to other roles: it can do nothing but good [...].[58]

Endnotes

1   Valerie Lawson, "Helpmann's Last Move on the Chessboard" (Sydney: Dancelines, 2011). http://dancelines.com.au/helpmanns-last-move-on-the-chessboard, (accessed 31 July 2014).

2   Robert Muller, "The Astonishing Decision of Robert Helpmann" in *The Daily Mail*, 1958, unpaginated (London: Royal Opera House Collections).

3   Helpmann reprised his role as the Red King in *Checkmate* for Australian National Ballet in 1986.

4   Judith Mackrell, "Keep Dancing: The Ballet Stars Leaping Through The Age Barrier" (London: *The Guardian*, 2015) http://www.theguardian.com/stage/2015/jul/05/ballet-dance-age-barrier-wendy-whelan-alessandra-ferri-interview, (accessed 10 August 2015).

5   The Sitter Out, *The Dancing Times*, February 1948.

6   *Adam Zero* Programme, Royal Opera House, 1948.

7   Ibid.

8   See biography of David Drew in the Introduction to DVD track 3, pp. 152-153.

9   Helen Thomas cites Ann Dils in *The Body, Dance and Cultural Theory* (Basingstoke: Palgrave Macmillan, 2003), p.134.

10   Buss Jackson, "Perfection", (London: *Went The Day Well*, 2010) http://www.wentthedaywell.co.uk/wtdw_articles.html, (accessed 1 September 2014).

11   Robert Sylvester, *New York Daily News*, 26 October 1949, cited in Kathrine Sorley Walker, *Robert Helpmann: A Rare Sense of Theatre* (Alton: Dance Books, 2009), pp.95-96.

12   Alastair Macaulay, "Royal Ballet's Focus on British Choreography Exposes Its Limits" (New York: The New York Times, 2015) http://www.nytimes.com/2015/06/29/arts/dance/royal-ballets-focus-on-british-choreography-exposes-its-limits.html?_r=0, (accessed 12 July, 2015).

13   *The Body, Dance and Cultural Theory*, p.121.

14   Audrey Williamson, "Future of Ballet" in *Theatre World: Guide to the Sadler's Wells Ballet* (London: Practical Press, 1944), p.20.

15   Biographies for Pauline Clayden, Jean Bedells, Henry Danton, Julia Farron and Gillian Lynne can be referenced in the Introduction to DVD track 3, pp. 153-154.

16   Michael Mangan, *Staging Ageing: Theatre, Performance and the Narrative of Decline* (Bristol: Intellect, 2013), p.123.

17   Alexander Bland, *The Royal Ballet: The First Fifty Years* (London: Threshold Books, 1981), p.74.

18   Elisabeth Schwaiger, *Ageing, Gender, Embodiment and Dance: Finding a Balance* (Basingstoke: Palgrave Macmillan, 2012), p.141.

19   Reviews from the revival of *Miracle in the Gorbals* in 2014 reported that none of the ballet's original choreography could be remembered. This was an inaccuracy: Pauline Clayden managed to reclaim the specifics of her Suicide solo during a workshop held at the Royal Opera House in 2011 (and replicated the sequence of movements on numerous occasions thereafter). See documentary

footage on DVD Track 3. http://www.telegraph.co.uk/culture/theatre/dance/11150898/Shadows-of-War-BRB-review-brazenly-theatrical.html

20   Jessia Berson, "Old Dogs, New Tricks" in Valerie Barnes Lipscomb and Leni Marshall (eds.), *Staging Age: The Performance of Age in Theatre, Dance, and Film* (New York: Palgrave Macmillan, 2010), p.166.

21   The quotation describes Helpmann's performance as the Red King in Australian National Ballet's 1986 production of *Checkmate*. Jill Sykes, *Sydney Morning Herald*, 9 May, 1986, cited in *Robert Helpmann: A Rare Sense of Theatre*, p.159.

22   The quotation reads: "[*Miracle*] shook the Parisian public to the core. 'The English Ballet has taught me something new,' was Boris Kochno's brief comment when he met [de Valois] after the fall of the curtain." Gordon Anthony, *Studies of Robert Helpmann* (London: Home & Van Thal Ltd, 1946), p.12.

23   Robert Sylvester, *New York Daily News*, 26 October 1949, cited in *Robert Helpmann: A Rare Sense of Theatre*, pp.95-96.

24   For further information on Michael Benthall, see Jann Parry's essay in Chapter 8, pp. 102-112.

25   It is difficult at this point in time to establish whether it was Jerome's story, the play that he derived from it for Sir Johnston Forbes Robertson, either of the two films that were made using the text of the play in 1918 and in 1935, or some combination of these that was the prime source of Benthall's invention. The list of possible sources indicates the popularity of the subject. For further material on this issue, see "Designs for Robert Helpmann's War-time Ballets" in this volume p. 114 and p. 114, note 4.

26   Peter Brinson and Peggy van Praagh, *The Choreographic Art* (London: Adam & Charles Black, 1963), p.88, p.255.

27   Ibid. p.264.

28   The Royal Opera House Collections curated an exhibition at the Lowry Gallery in Manchester, entitled *Invitation to the Ballet: Ninette de Valois and the Story of The Royal Ballet* (October 2010-March 2011).

29   Head of Music Staff at The Royal Ballet Company, 1991-2010.

30   Peter Franklin White (1923-2013) danced with The Royal Ballet 1942-1966.

31   Drew's reference to "steps" pertains to the formal movements which form the Classical ballet vocabulary.

32   Arnold Haskell, *Miracle in the Gorbals* (Edinburgh: The Albyn Press, 1946), p.12.

33   Ibid. p.12.

34   Audrey Williamson, *Contemporary Ballet* (London: Rockliff, 1946), p.88.

35   Joan Lawson, "The Helpmann Revivals", *The Dancing Times*, May 1958, pp.371-372.

36   Mary Clarke, "Ballet in Wartime IV", *The Dancing Times*, June 1990, p. 893; Cyril W. Beaumont, *The Sadler's Wells Ballet* (London: C. W. Beaumont, 1946), p.201.

37   For further information on Judith Paris and Jack Rebaldi, see the

Introduction to DVD track 3, pp. 155-156.

38   Helpmann, "Dance and Drama" in *Bandwagon*, July 1945, cited in *Robert Helpmann: A Rare Sense of Theatre*, p.75.

39   Barbara Dickson, "Age and the Dance Artist" in Valerie Barnes Lipscomb and Leni Marshall (eds.), *Staging Age: The Performance of Age in Theatre, Dance, and Film* (New York: Palgrave Macmillan, 2010), p.204.

40   Some edited transcriptions from interviews conducted by Francesca Franchi and Patricia Linton at the *Miracle* study day at The Royal Ballet School at White Lodge, Richmond (November 2011) have been included. For extended sections of these interviews, see the accompanying documentary (DVD Track 3).

41   The Sitter Out, *The Dancing Times*, December 1944.

42   Quoted by Henry Danton during an interview in 2011.

43   In 1939 the Entertainments National Service Association (ENSA) was initiated by Basil Dean and Leslie Henson to provide entertainment for British armed forces personnel during World War II.

44   Anthony Hopkins, "The Ballet Music of Arthur Bliss" in Arnold Haskell (ed.), *The Ballet Annual* (London: A&C Black Ltd, 1947), p.104.

45   Cyril W. Beaumont, *The Sadler's Wells Ballet* (London: C. W. Beaumont, 1946), p.200.

46   Interview with Natasha Oughtred in Paul Wu's television documentary, *Ballet in the Blitz: How World War Two Made British Ballet* (BBC Four, 2014) https://www.youtube.com/watch?v=tH0pqjgOKJk

47   Eveleigh Leith, "The Ballet Music of Arthur Bliss" in Arnold Haskell (ed.), *The Ballet Annual* (London: A&C Black Ltd, 1947), p.140.

48   "Age and the Dance Artist", p.192.

49   Kristen McNally has danced with The Royal Ballet since 2002, becoming a Soloist in 2009 and Principal Character Artist in 2017.

50   Pina Bausch, *Speech* (Published by courtesy of the Inamori Foundation) http://www.pinabausch.org/en/pina/what-moves-me (accessed 7 May 2015).

51   Graham Watts, "Review: Birmingham Royal Ballet – Shadows of War – Sadler's Wells" (London: Londondance.com, 2014) http://londondance.com/articles/reviews/birmingham-royal-ballet-shadows-of-war-sadlers-wel/ (accessed 10 December, 2014).

52   "The Helpmann Revivals", pp.371-372.

53   James Barton, "James Barton on BRB and rehearsing with a legend..." (Birmingham: Birmingham Hippodrome, 2014) https://birminghamhippodrome.wordpress.com/2014/09/16/james-barton-on-brb-and-rehearsing-with-a-legend/, (accessed 22 January 2015).

54   French phrase meaning "reason for existence".

55   Choreography by Jerome Robbins: original production and film of the Leonard Bernstein musical.

56   Arnold Haskell, *Ballet,* (London: Middlesex, 1955), p. 13.

57   *Staging Ageing: Theatre, Performance and the Narrative of Decline*, p.231.

58   "The Helpmann Revivals", pp.371-372.

Introduction to DVD Track 3: *Miracle in the Gorbals* reconstruction workshops (2011). A documentary film made by David Drew, Michael Byrne and Nigel Hodgson; edited by Michael Byrne. With Pauline Clayden, Gillian Lynne, Julia Farron, Henry Danton, Jean Bedells and Henry Roche. Also to DVD Track 4: an interview with Gillian Lynne recorded by Víctor Durà-Vilà.

Anna Meadmore

David Drew MBE (1938-2015), was the driving force behind an ambitious project to revive Helpmann's *Miracle in the Gorbals* (1944), which is documented in this film (DVD Track 3). Drew had trained at Sadler's Wells Ballet School, graduating into the Company in 1955, shortly before it became The Royal Ballet. He was promoted to Soloist in 1961, Principal in 1974, and then Principal Character Artist, creating significant roles in narrative works by both Ashton and MacMillan. He made his final appearance at Covent Garden in 2011. Alongside his work as a dancer, David Drew taught *pas de deux* classes at The Royal Ballet School for many years, and assisted Norman Morrice with the School's Choreographic Course (1987-96). He had an abiding wish to preserve the history and ethos of The Royal Ballet; Drew recognised that he was part of the "bridge generation" (a term coined by his friend and colleague, Monica Mason), responsible for spanning the interval between the Company's founders, with whom they had worked directly, and the rising talent that would shape its future.

In the spring of 1958 David Drew was cast as a gang-member in the first (and only) Royal Opera House revival of *Miracle in the Gorbals*. Helpmann had returned to The Royal Ballet for the season, and was to play his original role of the Stranger. The revival seemed timely: the Bernstein/Robbins musical *West Side Story*, famously set against a background of gang violence, had opened on Broadway in September 1957, and would come to London in December 1958; meanwhile, controversial slum clearances had begun in some areas of the Gorbals. Helpmann's ballet carried new contemporary resonances. Drew's experience of performing in *Miracle* convinced him that it was a work too significant to be lost, given its wonderful score by Arthur Bliss, striking designs by Edward Burra, and a wealth of dramatic leading roles provided by Michael Benthall's scenario. His idea to attempt a revival of the ballet was partly inspired – over half a century later – by Richard Allen Cave's successful reconstruction of the W.B Yeats/Ninette de Valois collaboration, *The King of the Great Clock Tower* (1934), which Drew had seen performed to stunning effect at the culmination of the Ninette de Valois Conference (1-3 April 2011).[1] With great purpose, Drew soon secured support from the Linbury Trust, The Royal Ballet School and Company, and the Royal Opera House Collections. He also approached several members of Helpmann's original 1944 cast to help with the ballet's reconstruction:

Pauline Clayden (b. 1922) had been a student at the Cone-Ripman School in London, before dancing with Ballet Rambert, and joining the Sadler's Wells Ballet in 1942. She became a highly valued Soloist with de Valois' Company, noted for the integrity of her performances, and her popular success as Fonteyn's regular understudy in several leading roles, most notably in Ashton's *Nocturne* (1936), *Daphnis and Chloë* (1951), and in Helpmann's *Hamlet* (1942). Besides originating the part of The Suicide in Helpmann's *Miracle*, she had a range of roles created for her by de Valois, Ashton and Cranko. In 1956 she retired from the stage to start a family.

Gillian Lynne DBE (1926-2018) had also studied at the Cone-Ripman School, and danced with the Arts Theatre Ballet before joining Sadler's Wells Ballet (1943-51). She then became Principal Dancer at the London Palladium, and went on to appear in films and musicals, before starting to produce and choreograph in the commercial theatre. She is internationally celebrated as the choreographer and associate director of Andrew Lloyd Webber's innovative musical, *Cats* (1981), and also choreographed his record-breaking *Phantom of the Opera* (1986). For Northern Ballet Theatre, she created the dance drama, *A Simple Man* (1987), based on the life of the painter, L.S. Lowry; and for Birmingham Royal Ballet she staged her interpretation of Helpmann's *Miracle in the Gorbals* (2014).

Julia Farron OBE FRAD (b. 1922) also began training at the Cone-Ripman School, before entering the Vic-Wells School as its first scholarship student, and graduating in 1936. She became a leading member of the Sadler's Wells (later Royal) Ballet, known for her great versatility and dramatic ability, and continued to appear as a guest Principal Character Artist after her official retirement from the Company in 1961. She created significant roles in ballets by de Valois, Ashton, Cranko and MacMillan. From 1964 Julia Farron was a senior teacher at The Royal Ballet School; she also taught for the Royal Academy of Dancing (later Dance), becoming Director of the RAD from 1983-89.

Jean Bedells FRAD (1924-2014), was trained by her mother, the English *prima ballerina*, Phyllis Bedells, before joining the Vic-Wells School on a scholarship in 1936. She danced with the Company for ten years, leaving upon her marriage in 1947. She later taught for The Royal Ballet School, and the Royal Academy of Dancing (later Dance), becoming a Major Examiner in 1965. Recognised for her accurate recall and attention to detail, she was asked by Sadler's Wells (later Birmingham) Royal Ballet to stage important revivals of de Valois' *Job* (in 1971 and 1993) and Ashton's *Dante Sonata* (in 2000), also mounting other productions of their early works for several companies.

Henry Danton (b. 1919) began his training late, after serving in the armed forces at the outbreak of war in 1939. Blessed with a fine classical physique, and taught by two of the greatest teachers of the period, Vera Volkova and Olga Preobrajenska, he made astonishing progress. He joined Mona Inglesby's International Ballet in 1943, and Sadler's Wells Ballet the following year. Danton was in the original cast of Ashton's *Symphonic Variations* (1946), but he left de Valois' Company soon afterwards, disliking her style of directorship. He subsequently danced with several companies worldwide, including Roland Petit's Ballets des Champs-Elysées (1947-48) and Australian National Ballet (1951-52). He later settled in the USA, where he became an established teacher.

Helpmann's *Miracle in the Gorbals:* the reconstruction workshops[2]

In the summer of 2011, Pauline Clayden joined David Drew in his efforts to revive *Miracle in the Gorbals* by teaching her created role of The Suicide to Royal Ballet dancer, Kristen McNally. The resulting footage is incorporated into Byrne's documentary film, and demonstrates that Clayden clearly recalled the choreography for her central solo: not only because she performed it nearly one hundred and fifty times during the 1940s, but also because it consisted of precisely timed and structured movements – unusual in Helpmann's choreography, where expressive gesture was often prioritised over "steps". At the same time, Gillian Lynne joined Drew's team. She was not able to recall specific movements, but in the spirit of Helpmann's own dramatically truthful choreography, she set out to re-imagine the duet for The Lovers – a role she had taken over from Moira Shearer soon after the ballet's première – on Royal Ballet dancers Laura McCullough and Johannes Stepanek. This movement material was eventually discarded by Lynne, and therefore does not form part of Byrne's film, but it was a valuable exercise that confirmed the dramatic effectiveness of Bliss's score combined with

Benthall's scenario. It was decided that Lynne would attempt to revive a greater section of the work, assisted by other members of the original cast: Pauline Clayden, Julia Farron, Jean Bedells and Henry Danton, who, aged ninety-two, flew in from the USA especially for the project. David Drew, quite rightly, dubbed this astonishing group "The Fab Five".

An all-day workshop was held in the Margot Fonteyn Theatre at The Royal Ballet School, White Lodge, in November 2011. A cast of almost forty performers was assembled, with students from The Royal Ballet School, Central School of Ballet, The London Studio Centre, the Judith Harris and Dawn King Schools; they were joined by members of the Kensington Temple Pentecostal Performance Group and former Royal Ballet dancers, Oliver Symons (as the Beggar), David Yow (the Stranger), Jane Burn (the Suicide), Jennifer Jackson and Nicola Katrak (as slum-dwellers). Together with actors, Jack Rebaldi (the Minister) and Judith Paris (the Prostitute), the group spent a day recreating a major section of the ballet: starting with the discovery of The Suicide's body in the River Clyde, and ending with her apparent revival by a mysterious Stranger. A shorter, more intimate, scene was also re-imagined, depicting a searing encounter between the Minister and the Prostitute.

Byrne's film provides a record of the warm-up/casting, consultations and rehearsals that took place during the concentrated and productive workshop, but largely focuses on the final "draft" performances of the two selected sections. Choreographic reconstruction was led by Gillian Lynne, working tirelessly throughout the day in consultation with the pianist Henry Roche (Head of Music Staff at The Royal Ballet, 1991-2010), who had made a close study of Bliss's score. There was constant input from the original cast members, who prompted Lynne energetically when they remembered something about a movement, usually its rhythm, dynamic quality or dramatic purpose. Although no actual sequences could be recalled in full (other than Clayden's solo), structural elements, such as floor patterns or groupings, were often confirmed when the "Fab Five" pooled their memories. All the while, Drew referred both re-creators and cast-members to the mass of photographic images he had assembled, which showed many moments from the original production (some taken during placed stage calls, others in actual performance). Participants had been sent some of these to study in advance, and the cast had been asked – as were their forebears – to create their own costumes by raiding family wardrobes and second-hand shops. As in the original production, a dustbin and an old car-tyre were used as stage-props.

While Gillian Lynne rehearsed the large ensemble section of the reconstruction, Julia Farron spent the morning working in another studio with Guy Attew, Head Pianist at White Lodge, and the two actors playing the Minister and the Prostitute. Both actors had previously worked with Lynne, who invited them to join the *Miracle* project: Jack Rebaldi had appeared as Munkustrap in *Cats* (London and Germany casts, 1997-2010), while at the time of the workshop, Judith Paris was performing her one-woman show, *Waxing Lyrical*, at the New Diorama in London; a play about the life of Madame Tussaud, written by Paris herself, and directed by Lynne. Guided by Bliss's music, original photographs, and Farron's memories of Helpmann's dramatic intent – she had no recollection of the choreography – these experienced actors invested the psychological encounter between the repressed Minister and cynical Prostitute with a visceral physical intensity. There was also an extraordinary episode, prompted by Lynne's comment that she had always found the closing moments of the ballet to be particularly moving, when Farron and Clayden spontaneously reprising their roles as the Prostitute and the Suicide re-enacted the sequence. These performances can be seen in Byrne's film.

The power of Helpmann's allegorical piece, which had struck wartime audiences so forcefully, became evident as rehearsals progressed and culminated with a performance of the day's work. The presence of Helpmann's colleagues from the 1940s and '50s, and their extraordinary commitment to the reconstruction workshop, was a testament to the great regard in which they held both the man and his work. There was a palpable sense of theatrical endeavour and purpose that enthused all the participants in the event, both young and old, and an infectious willingness to apply Helpmann's own advice: that anyone wishing "to gain the fullest enjoyment and understanding of the choreographer's intention must shake off the detachment of the critic and try to merge himself with the spirit of the dance".[3]

The engagement with Helpmann's "lost" *Miracle* led to the realisation that a better understanding was needed of his enormous contribution to the development of The Royal Ballet; questions arose of relevance and re-evaluation, of national style and artistic identity. A decision was taken to explore Helpmann's work by means of a symposium: this was eventually held in October 2013, at The Royal Ballet School in Covent Garden. The interdisciplinary event was entitled *The Many Faces of Robert Helpmann*, and concentrated on Helpmann's multi-faceted roles as a performer, choreographer and director.[4] As part of the preparations for the symposium, a choreographic exploration of Helpmann's most problematic ballet, *Adam Zero* (1946) was instigated (see pp. 166-168, the introduction to Track 5 on the DVD that accompanies this volume).

Another hugely rewarding consequence of David Drew's *Miracle in the*

Gorbals workshops was that Gillian Lynne was invited by David Bintley to re-stage Helpmann's ballet for his *Shadows of War* triple bill, created by Birmingham Royal Ballet to mark the centenary of the 1914-18 War. Significantly, October 2014 marked precisely seventy years since the first performance of *Miracle* took place in the depths of World War II. In her programme notes for the revival, premièred on 8 October 2014,[5] Lynne wrote: "Directing and choreographing David Bintley's exceptionally talented company during the rehearsals for *Miracle* has been a joy. I hope I have instilled this same acting approach that Bobby [Helpmann] found quite naturally – the drama of realness; nothing for him was ever danced without reason, without passion, without knowledge and without dare. I owe him a lot."[6]

DVD Track 4: an interview with Gillian Lynne recorded by Víctor Durà-Vilà
This short film allows the viewer to hear Gillian Lynne discussing the influence of Robert Helpmann upon her work; it is a three minute edit of an interview given at Lynne's home in London on 16 October 2013, filmed and conducted by Víctor Durà-Vilà.

Endnotes

1   The half-hour performance of Cave's reconstruction of *The King of the Great Clock Tower* (1934) was performed in the Margot Fonteyn Theatre, The Royal Ballet School, White Lodge in Richmond Park, on 3 April 2011. It was professionally filmed, and can be viewed on Track 9 of the DVD that accompanies the book based on the proceedings of the de Valois Conference, with additional essays and filmed resources: Richard Cave and Libby Worth (eds.), *Ninette de Valois: Adventurous Traditionalist* (Alton: Dance Books, 2012).

2   See also Byrne's essay, "The (re)generation of *Miracle in the Gorbals*", pp.131-151.

3   Robert Helpmann, short entry in a composite chapter, "The Spectator and the Ballet" in *Ballet Review* No. 1 (Edinburgh: The Albyn Press, 1947), pp.5-8. The full quotation runs thus: "It is generally calculated that the success of a play depends 75 per cent. on the players and 25 per cent. on the receptiveness of the audience, but in the case of ballet the audience's share of responsibility for its own entertainment and appreciation is considerably higher. A ballet-goer who wishes to gain the fullest enjoyment [...etc]."

4   Some of the content of this volume originated as papers presented at the Robert Helpmann symposium, subsequently developed for publication. The symposium committee was chaired by Professor Richard Allen Cave, Emeritus Professor of Theatre Arts, Royal Holloway, University of London; Dr Víctor Durà-Vilà, then a Research Fellow of the Department of Philosophy, King's College London; Olwen Terris, of the British Universities Film and Video Council; Jay Jolley, then Assistant Director of The Royal Ballet School; and Anna Meadmore, then the Curator of White Lodge Museum & Ballet Resource Centre, The Royal Ballet School.

5   Mark Monahan reviewed the piece favourably, calling it "a recreation rather than a revival, pieced together by pooling memories. [...] The result is as brazenly theatrical as Helpmann himself was, a lively, oddball study in life, death, envy and crowd-mentality that's as much dance-theatre as ballet. [...] But the story – a distant forerunner of Kenneth MacMillan's *The Judas Tree* [1992] – unfolds clearly and atmospherically. Those crowd scenes are good, with the assembled multitude swaying helplessly before the Christ-like Stranger like a field of corn in the breeze, and the piece also gives BRB's leads ample chance to shine." See "Shadows of War, BRB, review" in *The Telegraph* online, posted 9 October 2014. http:// www.telegraph.co.uk/culture/theatre/dance/11150898/Shadows-of-War-BRB-review-brazenly-theatrical.html, accessed 16 October 2014 and 30 January 2017.

6   Gillian Lynne, "The Inspiration" in Birmingham Royal Ballet *Shadows of War* triple bill programme, October 2014, p.21. The programme was performed at Birmingham Hippodrome 8-11 October; Sadler's Wells Theatre, London 17-18 October; and the Theatre Royal Plymouth 28-29 October.

Reviving Helpmann's *Miracle in the Gorbals* (1944) and *Adam Zero* (1946)

Transcription of a discussion hosted by Richard Allen Cave, with Michael Byrne, Jann Parry, Andrew McNicol and Víctor Durà-Vilà

(The following is the transcript of a panel discussion held on 27 October 2013, discussing the two decidedly different approaches adopted in attempts to recreate two of Helpmann's dance-dramas. The discussion was led by Richard Allen Cave, with Michael Byrne, Víctor Durà-Vilà, Andrew McNicol and Jann Parry. It took place immediately following a workshop demonstration with students of The Royal Ballet School, in which they rehearsed and performed two excerpts from Andrew McNicol's choreographic re-imagining of *Adam Zero* (1946): a scene with Adam and The Fates and The Lovers' *pas de deux*. McNicol took as his starting points the original score by Arthur Bliss, and the original Helpmann-Benthall scenario, and he had seen a wealth of photographic material relating to the initial production; however, he avoided any attempt to recreate Helpmann's original choreography and characterisations. This approach was in marked contrast with David Drew's intention to reproduce all aspects of the original production of Helpmann's *Miracle in the Gorbals* (1944), deploying Bliss's score and Benthall's scenario).[1]

Richard Cave (RC): Thinking about reviving not only Helpmann's work from the past but potentially other choreographers from that period: we've watched memorial [i.e. from memory] reconstruction – that seemed to me to have some wonderful benefits; and we've watched a different kind of re-claiming from the past, where we have given you [Andrew McNicol] all that exists of what inspired Helpmann in the first place [the original production's score, scenario, photographic and written records] and asked you to work with it creatively. So: is there a preferable way between the two methods, would you say, from what we have experienced?

Jann Parry (JP): I've always been told by choreographers in interviews with them that they can't go back and revise a work; and I've often said, well, it wasn't a great success the first time round, so why not go back and give it another go? And I've been told, well, it doesn't work like that – that the original inspiration has gone and you can't fiddle around afterwards. You can do a re-make entirely, but you can't just adapt and mess around with something, so is there a point in trying to retrieve exactly what they intended in the first place? It's tricky: I'm thinking of MacMillan's *The Burrow* [1958], for example, which wasn't done for a long time, then Peter Wright revived it for Birmingham Royal Ballet [in 1991] and it was a completely different ballet, effectively, apart from basic designs and general arrangement and scenario – so you couldn't go back in that instance.

On the other hand, if you think about attempts to revive the original Nijinsky *Rite of Spring* [1913], which continue to be controversial, I've always enjoyed the Hodson/Archer one[2] because I've always thought, well, it must have been something rather *like* this, given that you've got the very dramatic sets, wonderful costumes, extraordinary music and the scenario. If you try and go back to that, surely you get something of the power of the first piece? Even if we don't have the exact details of how they get from left to right [*indicating intricate footwork with her hands*], or know whether the floor patterns are correct, surely that's worth doing? Yet other people say, 'No, no, this is a travesty – leave it alone. If it's not *there*, it's dead'.

RC [*addressing Michael Byrne*]: What's your view of this, having seen a different work [*Miracle in the Gorbals*] in progress?

Michael Byrne (MB): I'm looking at the wider theme of re-creativity – the broad canvas of "authenticity versus interpretivity". As far as [the re-making of] *Adam Zero* goes, there was complete freedom to have an interpretive framework, relying on the music as a sort of scaffolding for creativity. For *Miracle in the Gorbals*, I think I can speak on behalf of David Drew:[3] his goal was very much to try and recreate it as authentically as possible. I think Gillian Lynne[4] is thinking about it in a looser sense, trying to maintain some of the *feeling* of the original, but I know David is desperate to use original sources: all the photographs, all the various ephemera, to attempt to save the original. But the thing is tricky; it's a balance: if the choreographer is alive, then there is an authority. But then again, as Lynne has communicated, it's a question of handing *ownership* over to the actual performers themselves, thereby challenging notions of that "fixity", and finding some sort of breadth and freedom.

RC [*addressing Andrew McNicol*]: You were given vast quantities of photographs of the original production of *Adam Zero* by David Drew, and you talked at length with Víctor [Durà-Vilà] about the annotations to the [Bliss] score. Some of the original performers are still alive, do you think a memorial [memory-based] recreation would have been possible for you, or are you happier taking the inspiration Drew's material offered you and 'doing your own thing' with it?

Andrew McNicol (AM): Yes, absolutely, that interests me much more – and the interesting thing with *Adam Zero* was that the original idea was more of a *poetic* interpretation of the seven stages of a man's life, and I think it was only because Helpmann was concerned about it becoming too similar to Massine's 1930s symphonic ballets that he, *they* [Helpmann and Benthall], then re-looked at it and it became set in the context of "a Ballet". So, for example, "a Dresser" and "a Wardrobe Mistress" were identified with The Fates [becoming dual roles performed by the same dancers]; and, for me, I think that's one of the reasons it wasn't a huge success.

RC: Too many layers...

AM: Too many layers, yes. So now you still have the music and you still have this general outline – there is great freedom in that, and that's really what excited me to experiment and try this "work in progress".

RC: But if you'd had a lot more time than, sadly, you've actually had to work on this, could you see a way of working in other layers: philosophical layers, moral layers – the way they worked, layers upon layers, in the original story?

AM: Yes, but I don't think I would want to do that in the context of "a Ballet", like the original. But definitely with a work that deals with such complex issues about life, and being human, you can go so *far* with that – it's really limitless in that sense.

RC [*turning to Víctor Durà-Vilà*]: You have studied both [of Bliss's] scores and you've been party to a lot of the developments in terms of re-creation of both *Miracle* and *Zero*. Is there a method you prefer?

Víctor Durà-Vilà (VDV): I think that you really need to look at the specificity of each work. In the case of *Adam Zero* I can tell you with no hesitation: there are no memories [to call upon]. Julia Farron created one of The Fates – she doesn't remember *anything*; Gillian Lynne created The Daughter – she doesn't remember anything. It was only danced for nineteen performances between 1946 and 1948, that's all. So, even if Andrew really wanted to reproduce choreography from the dancers' memories, there is no option to do that. In the end, then: what do you have in front of you? You have a work that is very episodic in its musical nature; it is also a huge musical structure. Andrew is very sophisticated when it comes to music, so he's ideally placed to react to that. *How* he reacts to that and respects what is really salient to the score is up to him – and I think rightly so. *Zero* has a very clear philosophical structure. In that sense Bliss's score is a wonderful work, because it gives a choreographer a lot of direction musically. The music is very vivid, and it really "wraps" the action [*he gestures as if enclosing something with both hands*].

With *Miracle* it's very different, because there *are* memories and there are three minutes of footage at the British Film Institute – which is less than ten per cent of the whole thing – but at least we can have an insight... a little window: it shows Annette Page dancing the Suicide solo from 1958. And it is *dance*, and it is very expressive dance. So, you might think, "I want to preserve this solo". If we *can* preserve some choreographic jewels, it does make sense to try to create something which is dramatically coherent and as much related to the original as possible. But, of course, there are huge chunks of the work, where Gillian Lynne has a very good understanding of what was meant theatrically, but she has no memory of the actual steps. So each case has its own challenges, and you cannot make one blanket policy.

By contrast, just think of any choreographer these days trying to re-choreograph *Les Noces*, *Rite* or *Petrushka*:[5] their plots, the scenarios, were very different from what Benthall and Helpmann were doing,[6] so there you would have much more freedom to use the music in different ways, because you don't have the very direct, episodic and emotional nature of Bliss's music, where you have very precise directions at every stage. Again, think of Stravinsky's *Rite of Spring*: what an amazing canvas that is, but it has very little in the way of the precise direction that you get in Bliss's scores.

RC: May I give you a quotation from Arnold Haskell, talking about *Miracle in the Gorbals*? He wrote that, as a dance-drama, it met a particular "urge of self expression, the need to reconcile Helpmann the dancer and Helpmann the actor".[7] Helpmann seems quite unique as a performer in his generation – do you think we need more dancers like him? I thought it was very interesting that Julia Farron said that she felt very liberated by performing in *Miracle* because she discovered herself as an actress, and that she wanted to pursue a further career with that new knowledge. So: "actors and dancers"?

JP: I think it has happened quite frequently and particularly as dancers grow older: they find that they are more interested in the acting side than in the dancing. But one of the problems is the voice: it was quite unusual for Helpmann to have such a well-developed way of speaking, rather than having to re-train completely to get his voice down [i.e. to a lower register]. I'm thinking of Adam Cooper, switching from ballet dancing to all sorts of other things, who has a pleasing light tenor in musicals now – he changed his voice completely, and the way he spoke.[8] I think there are dancers, particularly those who moved from ballet to Gillian Lynne's *Cats*, for example, who had whole new careers just from that one production.[9]

RC: Does *Miracle* require a special kind of performer?

MB: After performing myself as a lowly spear-carrier in The Royal Ballet's production of MacMillan's *Romeo and Juliet*, I can recognise in Helpmann's ballet the importance, the real value, of having good acting, albeit in the background. Any dancer should have that instilled anyway, regardless. For example, Marianela Nuñez has a purity of technique which is embedded, it's fantastic; but that extra layering of her consummate acting is also there. I don't think it's a question of either/or; it's a fusion.

RC: Any questions from the floor?

Libby Worth (LW): A question for Andrew: I'm just curious about what you found exciting and pleasurable in this role that you've taken on – to work with materials from *Adam Zero?*

AM: A huge attraction was the music – there was so much to explore and experiment with, solely in the music. But also having to research into the original ballet, asking why *was* it a success, and why *wasn't* it a success? What should I pull out and keep, and what should I discard? A fascinating process – that was what really intrigued me. And then being able to experiment in the studio, which stimulated more and more ideas.

Endnotes

1   See Michael Byrne's essay on pp. 131-151 of this volume, and his accompanying film of the workshop reconstructions of *Miracle in the Gorbals*, DVD track 3, which the panel had viewed together earlier.

2   The original choreography for Igor Stravinsky's *Le Sacre du Printemps* [The Rite of Spring] (1913) was by Vaslav Nijinsky, with designs by Nicholas Roerich. Its first performance by the Diaghilev Ballets Russes, at the Théâtre des Champs-Elysées in Paris, was greeted by wild outrage and enthusiasm, with opposing camps causing a famous "riot". Nijinsky's choreography was subsequently performed only a few more times in Paris and London. Stravinsky's epoch-making score was later attempted by many great choreographers, including Léonide Massine (1920), Kenneth MacMillan (1962) and Pina Bausch (1975), but the legendary status of the original production never faded. In 1987 the dancer and historian Millicent Hodson was invited by Robert Joffrey to recreate Nijinsky's version of *Rite* for his company in New York. Hodson used many sources, namely contemporary photographs, drawings and accounts of the original production, interviews with surviving dancers, and a music score annotated in 1913 by Marie Rambert, who had assisted Nijinsky in rehearsals. Hodson worked closely with Kenneth Archer, who recreated Roerich's designs from surviving costumes and paintings. The reconstruction was premièred by the Joffrey Ballet on 30 September 1987, and received much acclaim, although opinion was divided as to its true authenticity.

3   David Drew was due to take part in this panel discussion, but in the event he was too unwell. From the outset, Michael Byrne was closely involved in Drew's project to reconstruct Helpmann's *Miracle in the Gorbals*, see Chapter 10 and DVD Track 3 of this volume.

4   Gillian Lynne was a central collaborator in Drew's *Miracle* project; she later went on to re-choreograph the ballet for a revival by Birmingham Royal Ballet (2014). See Chapter 10 and DVD Tracks 3 and 4, of this volume.

5   All three ballets had scores by Igor Stravinsky, and were commissioned by Serge Diaghilev for the Ballets Russes: *Les Noces* (1923) was choreographed by Bronislava Nijinska and designed by Natalia Goncharova; *The Rite of Spring* [*Le Sacre du Printemps*] (1913) was first choreographed by Vaslav Nijinsky with designs by Nicholas Roerich; and *Petrushka* [*Petrouchka*] (1911) was choreographed by Mikhail Fokine with libretto and designs by Alexandre Benois.

6   Interestingly, Jane Pritchard makes the opposite case, finding compelling parallels between the scenarios for Helpmann's *Miracle in the Gorbals* and Fokine's *Petrushka* in her programme note (p.22) written for the Birmingham Royal Ballet revival of *Miracle* in 2014: "*Miracle* has a specific story set in a fixed period, the 1940s, and place – in a slum-area of Glasgow. As such it can be seen to parallel Mikhail Fokine's dramatic Russian fair-ground ballet, *Petrushka*, with the crowd in both playing an important part; it appears casual and spontaneous but is really cunningly contrived. In both the central figure shows elements of redemption. Indeed, it is *Miracle*'s position in the lineage of narrative works

going through to Kenneth MacMillan's dramatic ballets that gives it a particular interest. It also paralleled *Petrushka* in that it was a true collaboration by its creators; choreographer, librettist, composer and designer all of whom had an on-going relationship with the Sadler's Wells Ballet."

7   Arnold Haskell, *"Miracle in the Gorbals": A Study* (Edinburgh: The Albyn Press, 1946), p.10.

8   Adam Cooper graduated from The Royal Ballet School into The Royal Ballet, becoming a Principal in 1994. He took leave of absence to create the central role of The Swan in Matthew Bourne's iconoclastic reading of Tchaikovsky's ballet, *Swan Lake* (originally choreographed by Petipa and Ivanov, 1895). Bourne's version (1995) became a worldwide sensation, making Cooper a star in London and on Broadway.

9   The musical *Cats* (opened 1981) was composed by Andrew Lloyd-Webber, with lyrics based on T.S. Eliot's *Old Possum's Book of Practical Cats*; it was directed by Trevor Nunn and Gillian Lynne. Lynne's technically demanding and ballet-based choreography was integral to the entire production. The dancers' strong classical training gave them a feline grace and power, which was a fundamental part of the show's enduring success and influence. The cats' costumes, designed by John Napier, were based on practice clothes worn by ballet dancers in daily class, such as lycra all-in-ones and leg-warmers, which were soon adopted as high street fashion accessories.

Introduction to DVD Track 5: *Adam Zero*: a rehearsal demonstration with students of The Royal Ballet School in new choreography by Andrew McNicol (2013), filmed by Michael Byrne and Nigel Hodgson; edited by Michael Byrne.

Anna Meadmore

Robert Helpmann's complex ballet, *Adam Zero* (first performed on 10 April 1946) was the first new work mounted by the Sadler's Wells Ballet after it became resident at the Royal Opera House. Zoë Anderson notes that the accolade fell to Helpmann's ballet by chance, after cast injury had postponed the première of Ashton's *Symphonic Variations*. She goes on to assess the Company's first new ballet at Covent Garden:

> It was designed to show off the capabilities of the new theatre. *Adam Zero* was bursting with technical wizardry: lifting and falling platforms, changes in lighting, costume changes and use of a moving cyclorama. Michael Benthall's allegorical scenario showed the life of a man in terms of a ballet company staging a new work [...] most dancers played roles with several aspects. June Brae played the Choreographer (Creator and Destroyer) and Ballerina (first love, wife, mistress). Between symbolism and stage effects, there was no room for dancing.[1]

Helpmann himself performed the title role of Adam Zero, dominating the stage for the forty-five minute piece, while metamorphosing from youth to old age with minimal costume changes (made in view of the audience). (See plates 44 and 45) The multi-layered ballet was set to a lavishly-orchestrated score made up of sixteen episodic movements, especially written by Arthur Bliss; the scenery and costumes were by Roger Furse. The project was highly ambitious, but its desire to explore universal themes of birth, love and death through parallel worlds and characters ultimately proved too challenging for audiences. At the end of the war, Helpmann had been riding high in both public and peer esteem, justly celebrated for his seeming ability to master any theatrical form. Bliss went so far as to declare: "Robert Helpmann breathes the dust of the theatre like hydrogen. His quickness to seize on the dramatic possibilities of music is mercurial. [...] It would seem quite natural to see him walk on to the Albert Hall platform one day to play a violin concerto."[2]

However, by most accounts, even Helpmann could not make the complexities of *Adam Zero* cohere satisfactorily, and his ballet was received with some bafflement and even ridicule. *Adam Zero* was never subsequently revived in the repertory.

The 'reclaiming' of *Adam Zero* (2013)

The theatrical concept of Helpmann's *Adam Zero* was unquestionably bold, and the work remains an intriguing episode in his career. It was one of his rare "flops", despite its magnificent score, striking designs and memorable set pieces (photographs showing the Ballerina/Death figure sweeping the stage in her long cloak pre-figure the imagery of Roland Petit's *Le Jeune homme et la mort*, which premièred in Paris just two months later, in June 1946). None of the choreography remains extant. As part of the preparations for *The Many Faces of Robert Helpmann* Symposium of 2013,[3] it was decided that there would be much to learn through practical engagement with his *Adam Zero*. The idea was largely inspired by David Drew's 2011 project to reconstruct a faithful revival of Helpmann's 1944 ballet, *Miracle in the Gorbals*.[4] By contrast, the project to re-visit *Adam Zero* took a very different approach; the choreographer Andrew McNicol was free to take only as much from the existing traces of the work as interested him creatively, while engaging with Helpmann and Benthall's original vision, and Bliss's challenging score.[5]

The film on Track 5 of the accompanying DVD records McNicol's choreographic response to selected elements of the 1946 production of *Adam Zero*, and allows viewers to see the tantalising results of this productive dialogue between the past and the present. The twelve-minute documentary film includes photographs of an initial exploratory workshop that took place with students from Central School of Ballet, held at The Royal Ballet School in Covent Garden (17 February 2013). McNicol soon decided to work with just two scenes from the ballet: "Adam and The Fates", which he set for a man and a trio of women; and a *pas de deux* for "Adam and his First Love". In the weeks leading up to the Helpmann Symposium, McNicol was then able to work with the second-year Upper School students of The Royal Ballet School, who can be seen on this film in the final demonstration performance.

Andrew McNicol is a young British choreographer. While a student of The Royal Ballet School (White Lodge), he won the MacMillan Choreographic Competition, later gaining an MA through Central School of Ballet's Choreographic Programme. He has choreographed for the National Youth Ballet, The Royal Ballet of Flanders, New English Ballet Theatre, Northern Ballet, Dance East and Juice Opera Trio. Andrew has also worked with Kim Brandstrup through the Royal Opera House Dancelines programme and at the New York Choreographic Institute. In early 2017 he launched the McNicol Ballet Collective as a vehicle for creating new work.

Endnotes

1   Zoë Anderson, *The Royal Ballet, 75 Years* (London: Faber and Faber, 2006), p.92.

2   Arthur Bliss, "Grace Notes on Ballet" in Peter Noble (ed.), *British Ballet* (London: Skelton Robinson, 1949), p.130.

3   For details of the symposium, see endnote 4, p. 158.

4   Documented in the film on Track 3 of the DVD that accompanies this volume; see also the introductory essay to the track on pp. 152-158 and "The (re)generation of *Miracle in the Gorbals*", pp. 131-134.

5   Lewis Foreman has claimed that Arthur Bliss's score for *Adam Zero* "dates from the winter of 1945-46 and [was written at] the height of Bliss's powers: it is arguably his greatest work, and certainly numbers among his half dozen finest scores. Its total neglect both on the stage and in the concert hall is amazing and incomprehensible."

Source: http:// www.musicsalesclassical.com/composer/work/7474, accessed 5 February 2017.

"There are children here somewhere, I can smell them." Robert Helpmann and the making of an on-screen villain: the Child Catcher in *Chitty Chitty Bang Bang* (1968)

Libby Worth

In 2008 *Entertainment Weekly* put out a list of the "50 Most Vile Movie Villains" with Robert Helpmann's Child Catcher from *Chitty Chitty Bang Bang* featured as No. 19 in the ratings.[1] At the 2012 London Olympic Opening Ceremony, director Danny Boyle chose to include the figure of the Child Catcher with horses and carriage, hook and net, appearing along with a host of other children's story villains. Given that the film was released in 1968, these are indicators of Helpmann's skill in the creation of an enduring image of villainy. At the time of the film's release, Australian composer Malcolm Williamson, who had become close to Helpmann through composing for Helpmann's ballet *The Display* (1964), recalls the horror his children experienced in seeing their playful friend transformed into the Child Catcher. In an interview for The South Bank Show documentary, *Tales of Helpmann: A Profile of Sir Robert Helpmann*[2] Williamson relates how his children's fear was compounded by Helpmann, with typical wicked humour, refusing to reassure them on the phone, and instead playing directly into his character and their (gleeful) terror. Even in 2014, asking groups of undergraduate students about their memory of the Child Catcher elicits collective shudders of horror.

In 1938, on the occasion of his acting the role of Oberon in *A Midsummer Night's Dream* at the Old Vic, Helpmann wrote confidently in a short article for *The Old Vic and Sadler's Wells Magazine*: "I have no desire to leave the Ballet which I love but I believe my ballet training will help me with my acting. For I realise that my past experiences as an actor have helped with regard to certain aspects of the ballet."[3] Interviewed for the *Daily Mail* in 1953, Helpmann was more explicit on the value for dancers of learning acting skills, and for actors he suggested: "a few dancing lessons would teach them, in costume plays especially, to kneel, fence, carry their clothes and move generally with grace instead of walking on and off the stage as if they were wearing diving boots".[4] This perspective on the value of multi-disciplinary training can be extended to Helpmann's later inclusion of film acting within his performance repertoire. Helpmann's early film acting took place at a time when moves were being made in the UK and US to encourage greater use of realism in actor training. It is evident in the examples selected for illustration and analysis below, that Helpmann, to some degree, resisted this move and offered performances that were rooted in ballet mime training, with facial and gestural exaggeration. This was even the case in his small role for the 1942 Powell and Pressburger[5] film, *One of our Aircraft is Missing*, which was relatively naturalistic in style. Given Helpmann's versatility and speed of learning, I suggest that this was a deliberate ploy consistent with his utter belief in the power of movement to communicate, both in support of spoken text and in its absence. Helpmann's familiarity with the dance necessities of acute rhythmic, spatial, tonal and dynamic awareness meant that he had a sophisticated variety of skills and attributes at his disposal on entering the film medium.

I argue in this chapter that it is in large part his successful exploitation of these skills that contributed to the development of his UK film roles, with particular success found in the Child Catcher. His ballet and theatre performance output was so extensive that he was not left with much time to enter fully into the film world as maker/director, but it is pertinent to note that – even within the small frame considered within this chapter – he offered distinct approaches to film acting. These have more in common with American Delsartism[6] and the Denishawn school of dance (see later in chapter for fuller discussion), with their impact on the training of the silent movie performer, than with the passion for naturalism and method acting that would dominate the later film industry. Given Helpmann's prolific output as a performer, I have selected just a few examples of film roles to analyse in detail, including the enduring role of the Child Catcher referred to above. The other smaller illustrations are from his film work within the UK; they are roles that were made for film rather than dances or plays that were subsequently filmed. Inevitably, there are overlaps between all roles created within the film medium, but the aim here is to consider how particular strategies, skills and experiences rooted in his ballet performance and choreography later inform Helpmann on entering the film terrain.

The highly collaborative nature of film-making means that it is hard to isolate individual components for examination, as becomes evident below in the short references to Helpmann's contribution to the Powell and Pressburger film, *The Red Shoes* (1948). Although he acted and danced the role of Ivan Boleslawsky, the principal dancer of the fictional ballet company, his chief contribution was as a choreographer for the famed ballet of *The Red Shoes*, performed by Moira Shearer and that was a major component within the film. The innovative film techniques displayed in this sequence suggest that Helpmann was happy to embrace the challenges such new camera work brought to the act of choreography. Prior to working on *Chitty Chitty*

Bang Bang, he was therefore, already becoming familiar with film practices, and their potential in relation to dance-making. This contributed spatial and dynamic range to his development of the role of the Child Catcher, in tandem with his intelligent and insightful incorporation of a wide range of physical skills harnessed to unsettle and disturb the intended family viewers. In the process of achieving this, it is conceivable that he offered an original approach to film performance, which both referenced back to the silent film era of heightened gestural acting, and anticipated the potential of freer flow between dance and acting techniques relevant to a cinema tiring of realism, and the type of training that supported it.

Helpmann is not primarily known as a film actor, but he worked on a clutch of films with Michael Powell and Emeric Pressburger that revealed how gifted he was in crossing readily from one arts discipline to another – and that, as with other performance outlets, he brought with him special insights on entering this new medium. It is not possible to unravel all of the many strands within Helpmann's performance training and experiences, so I have chosen to privilege his dance/movement skills over his vocal/ theatre stage skills in this examination of screen roles he undertook leading up to the Child Catcher in *Chitty Chitty Bang Bang*. He will of course have drawn from his considerable stage experience as detailed elsewhere in this volume, but it is the application of dance and mime skills that I argue offer distinctive, even original aspects to his on-screen presence, reminiscent of early twentieth-century silent film acting and experimentations in dancefilm making.

The filmmakers Powell and Pressburger are of such renown and stature that I do not propose to rehearse their achievements here. It is sufficient to note their inspirational impact on film-making in the 1940s and '50s, with ripples of influence that continued steadily onwards. Helpmann's relatively small involvement in their output is nevertheless significant because it included their few ventures into dance on film, a combination which brings with it both special artistic qualities and some severe difficulties. Maya Deren, who was making non-commercial, highly experimental, short dance films from the 1940s to 1961, when assessing the role of film within the arts in 1946, commented:

> Dance, for example, which, of all art forms, would seem to profit most by cinematic treatment, actually suffers miserably. The more successful it is as a theatrical expression, conceived in terms of a stable, stage front audience, the more its carefully wrought choreographic patterns will suffer from the restiveness of a camera which bobs about in the wings, is on stage for a close-up, etc. There *is* a potential filmic dance form, in which the choreography and movements would be designed precisely, for the mobility

and other attributes of the camera, but this, too, requires an independence from theatrical dance conceptions.[7]

In this same period, Powell and Pressburger with *The Red Shoes* (1948) *do* pay attention to just the difficulties that Deren highlights, and the example of the extended ballet sequence choreographed by Helpmann is testimony to their courage in bringing dance and film together in such an inventive manner. Amy Greenfield, in assessing the impact of Deren's seminal dancefilm, *A Study in Choreography for Camera* (1945), notes that "Even aspects of Michael Powell's formidable original dance sequences in *The Red Shoes* were influenced by *A Study*".[8] For instance in the final sequence of Deren's dancefilm, dancer Talley Beatty is instructed to spin at a constant speed whilst Deren "was smoothly hand-cranking the camera motor from 64 to 8 frames per second. Thus, the camera created the illusion that Beatty speeds up".[9] This allowed Beatty's face to stay consistently in line with his background and within the frame. Anna Bemrose notes camera director Jack Cardiff's similar use of this technique in the "Paper Dance" for *The Red Shoes* for which he "changed speed with the pirouettes so that a dance would start off at normal speed and then, as [he] changed the speed to only four frames a second, she would whirl faster and faster until she was a spinning blur".[10]

Helpmann was quick to learn that filmed dance was a special category of work, as shown by his comments in interview with Monk Gibbon, quoted in Kathrine Sorley Walker's biography:

> There is no possibility of orchestrating choreographically on the screen [...] the camera has already done the work of selection... I realised this before I even began. I realised that it would be useless and a waste of time to choreograph the parts that were not visible.[11]

Most importantly, as discussed later, Helpmann elaborated on this by saying that he "always bore in mind what *would* be happening elsewhere, even if it *wasn't* happening".[12]

This briefest of comments reveals an imaginative awareness of the filmic environment that is applicable to his technique both as a performer and a choreographer in films. George Bartram commented on Helpmann's early film involvement for the *Picturegoer* at the time of *The Red Shoes* release:

> Robert Helpmann sees immense possibilities for the screen. "I do not believe that it has yet reached the full range of its conception," he says. "It is a completely fascinating medium in which to work."
>
> "I want to make more films," he assured me. "If I could get the right parts I should particularly like to tackle comedy."[13]

When the *The Red Shoes* was taken through a meticulous process of restoration using digital technology by The Film Foundation, led by Martin Scorsese in 2009, he commented then on how significant a film it was for him: "The ballet sequence itself was like an encyclopaedia of the history of cinema. They used every possible means of expression, going back to the earliest of silent cinema."[14]

There is much written on both the film and the extended ballet sequence that does not require re-iterating, but another comment from Scorsese in its praise hints at a perspective that is not so readily discussed:

> There is something about the use of colour and the impact of the movement in the frame. It is to do with the high drama, even melodrama, within the lives of the characters and how seriously they took what they were doing. It was also their actual journey in creating something and the difficulty they faced. You could really feel the work that was being done by these dancers and by Lermontov and by the Marius Goring character (the young composer). It made it very visceral. [15]

The impact of the movement in the frame, its visceral power and a sense of the hard work being undertaken by the performers are integral to the discussion below. Clearly it needs to be acknowledged that Helpmann's contributions to *The Red Shoes* as choreographer of the ballet and in the role of principal dancer, and in *The Tales of Hoffman* (1951) in multiple roles, were significant contributions to dance on film; but there are other ways in which his background in dance equipped him to work innovatively within cinema. In particular these experiences of making dance sequences embedded an understanding of the difference between the proscenium arch stage and the film frame. For instance, if the camera focuses on a close-up of a face, then the potential for performer invention is reduced to facial movement. I will illustrate later how this can be used effectively in film acting, but only by a performer who is alert to making the most of the dynamic movement potential within each range of camera shot. Choreographing for film, therefore, allowed Helpmann a more distanced and holistic perspective on the essential integration of camera work, direction, editing and choreography, than that afforded to most dancers/performers. He was able to reinvest this knowledge in his non-dance roles for cinema in UK produced films, as discussed below.

It is noticeable, even in the minor roles Helpmann played in the early Powell and Pressburger film *One of Our Aircraft is Missing* (1942)[16] and in *Caravan* (1946),[17] directed by Arthur Crabtree, that he was experimenting with a style of acting that stands out within the context of each film, and appears to hark back to the mimetic exaggerations of early silent film.

Film and dance scholar, Erin Brannigan, in *Dancefilm: Choreography and the Moving Image* (2011), offers a rigorous analysis of the changing modes of acting in early twentieth century films. Her detailed account of the links between dance pedagogy and screen acting highlight, in particular, the importance of François Delsarte and later Ruth St Denis who, with Ted Shawn set up the Denishawn School (Los Angeles, 1915). The fact that film director D.W. Griffith gave "encouragement for his actresses to attend Denishawn classes" revealed both the experimentation taking place in this period of silent movies and that Griffith "understood the special significance of corporeal performance in silent film".[18] Although Helpmann was clearly not a part of the transitions taking place in early screen-actor training in the first part of the twentieth century, it is notable that it is his extended experience in dance and mime that underpins an unusual and playful versatility in the development of a screen-actor presence. In his first roles in cinema therefore, far from adopting the largely naturalistic style of acting of the more experienced film actors around him, he instead adapted his wide range of dance skills to re-visit the kind of melodramatic facial and bodily movement most associated with silent movie stars. The result, I suggest, is economical in the way that ballet mime is swiftly narrative through deployment of easily recognisable codified gestures, but this speed of communication buys Helpmann time to manipulate the rhythm of his movements to contribute humorous twists. For instance, he paid attention to the length of time needed to hold a gesture or expression, beyond usual everyday timing, in order to elicit the intended emotional quality.

One of Our Aircraft is Missing was made in the midst of World War II, with a narrative based on stories of ordinary Dutch villagers showing extraordinary courage. The slender plot concerns the failure of one of the British Wellington bomber aircraft to return to base. Shot down over Holland, the aircrew bail out of the burning plane and parachute-land in the countryside, where they are eventually rescued by Dutch sympathisers. Despite the inevitable constraints on the film-makers, imposed both through the requirement for it to function as propaganda and the need for it to be carefully monitored by The Ministry of Information, the film succeeds in communicating a touching story with humour and sparse dialogue. Michael Powell, in his brief memoir for Helpmann, recollected how he managed to include all the friends he admired at the time, even though they had no experience of film, in his and Pressburger's "movie" (for instance Peter Ustinov, Alec Clunes and Pamela Brown):

> Bobby Helpmann played a Dutch Quisling traitor, and had a glorious time skimming about the floor on his knees and grabbing hold of the priest's vestments in a fine piece of over-acting that scandalised all the regular West

End actors in the cast. I egged him on.[19]

Powell's comments, although brief, are revealing of his familiarity with Helpmann's performance work, prior to selecting him, and that he clearly nurtured the somewhat unusual style of performance Helpmann brought to the part. Powell's "egging" him on, chimes with de Valois' similar support for the stance Helpmann took in dancing Dr Coppélius, when in 1941 he first played the role, just a year before *One of Our Aircraft is Missing* was released. Elizabeth Salter states that "Helpmann determined to give them [Londoners and foreign troops] the kind of evening they wanted [...] to the point of offending the purists and to the delight of his audiences".[20] In response to the critics' negative reactions, Salter notes de Valois' defence: "'I am guilty of encouraging Helpmann's interpretation of Dr Coppélius up to the height of its utmost humour,' she writes. 'Great clowns are rare and Helpmann clowned Dr Coppélius with genius'."[21] This is evidence of Helpmann being chosen for the film precisely because he brought the ability to harness the melodramatic for humorous ends from his proficiency in ballet character roles. Perhaps his desire to perform in the *right* comedy parts in film stemmed from this early experience, although it clearly took him time to appreciate his own special brand of comedic film acting. Salter recounts his reaction to seeing himself on film for the first time as De Jong, the Dutch Quisling who speaks in Dutch.

His first reaction was disbelief:

> I saw this slight figure with eyes like Eddie Cantor,[22] dancing across the stage speaking some kind of gibberish, and wondered who the devil he was. The shock was like a physical blow when I realised it was me. I thought "My God they've hashed some plot to make me look terrible. Peter Ustinov looks fine, so does Eric Portman. Why have they done this to me?"

> I asked the producer, protesting vigorously. It took him some time to convince me that I, too, looked fine to them.[23]

In this small role of the traitor, who is content to collude with the Nazi occupying soldiers and betray his countrymen and the British pilots they are sheltering, Helpmann is on screen for just under five minutes. However, within this time he conveys a rapid shift from confident certainty in the backing of his Nazi masters, to wretched pleading for help to escape when he realises he has been hoodwinked by a child to appear a traitor to the German soldiers. The economy of characterisation is found in swift, decisive movements around the dining room, where the action is set, but more importantly, through a series of nine close-ups of his face that constitute a facial "ballet". Filling the screen, the viewer sees every slight movement of

Helpmann's facial muscles, and how he uses his eyes to control and direct attention around the surrounding space, in conjunction with exposure of his inner feelings. Much less naturalistic than his fellow actors, Helpmann draws on a combination of extreme eye movements and facial manipulation to demonstrate the sudden shifts in his character's position. With his long experience in ballet and the need to project facial expression into a large auditorium, he has no difficulty in adapting the technique to fill the small screen, but with swifter alterations between the steady held gaze and the anxious sideways glances and flickers that follow, as his situation within the narrative becomes unstable. Bartram sums it up as "a gem of a performance in a film which was overloaded with talent".[24]

This reliance on physical story telling is explored again in *Caravan* (1946), set in the nineteenth century, in which Helpmann plays the unpleasant sidekick Wycroft, valet to the villain, Sir Francis Castleton (Dennis Price), in an elaborate plot that has him employed to murder first Richard Darrell, the hero (Stewart Granger) and later his Spanish gypsy wife, Rosal (Jean Kent). He succeeds in neither, and spends the entire film fearfully avoiding conflict whilst avowing the opposite. Bartram notes in 1948 that it was "one of Britain's biggest ever box office successes";[25] and, although this might seem surprising to a contemporary audience, the actors did receive mainly positive reviews. The *Monthly Film Bulletin* (1946) noted particular strengths in the male performances, including the comment: "It is interesting to see Robert Helpmann in a new sphere: he makes the most of what scope is offered him in the semi-comic part of Wycroft."[26] And even from a later perspective the strength of his performance is acknowledged by Michael Brooke in his write-up of the film for *Screenonline* (2013): "*Robert Helpmann* as the sinister Wycroft reveals his Child Catcher from *Chitty Chitty Bang Bang* (d. Ken Hughes, 1968) in embryonic form."[27] (See plates 46 and 47)

Brannigan, highlighting Delsarte's important influence on very early film acting, notes that one of his insights was "how gesture pre-empts or provides the context for speech and thought, revealing the moments prior to speech where the body is already heavy with meaning".[28] This feeling for potency of gestural movement is exploited by Helpmann in *Caravan* within his role as the impotent Wycroft. He sidles along walls, vacillates from one direction to another, hugs the shadows and works with rapid contrasts between half-attempts at action and shuddering failure to carry through his intentions. Helpmann, in his interview for the magazine *Picturegoer*, asserts: "After I had read through the part I realised that it could only be played with a touch of comedy [...] I agreed to play it provided I could do it my way. I did, and got the desired result. Played as it was originally intended – and I shudder to think of the consequences."[29] In order to achieve this comedy however, Helpmann had to work hard to fill out what is a somewhat slender role within an unwieldy plot that moves between England and Spain. This is achieved in part through establishing repeated physical reference points: gestural catchphrases, which economically signal his character whilst allowing commentary and change as the film progresses. For instance, his private boxing practice is shown to be ineffectual and pretentious, signalling the disjunction between his imagined and actual ability. When confronted, or rather buffeted accidently, by "real" boxers on the boat crossing to Spain, he physically shrinks in recognition of weakness. This role of fighter is re-visited with humorous effect as he fails time and again to match up to, or even to take on, his opponents.

In the final chase scene, Wycroft finally gains courage to confront his master, who, having kidnapped the heroine, Oriana (Anne Crawford), is driving a carriage and horse in a demented, almost suicidal, frenzy and threatening to kill them all. The forcefulness and energy of Wycroft, as he rises from the back seat and attempts to force Sir Francis to slow down, anticipates Helpmann's later role as the Child Catcher where, this time, he will be in charge of clattering horse and carriage.

There is something of the weasel in the character of Wycroft that is sharpened and hardened in the role of the Child Catcher in *Chitty Chitty Bang Bang*. This family musical film in which the magical flying car of the title takes centre stage, emerged in the wake of the hugely successful *Mary Poppins* (1964), and there are many similarities that can be noted throughout. However, there is a dark edge to this primarily frothy film that was less evident in *Mary Poppins*. This is made starkly evident when the Potts family arrive at a village in the fictional country of Vulgaria to find it empty of children. The children of Vulgaria have been kidnapped or are hidden away, banned by the Baron Bomburst (Gert Frobe) in response to his wife's (Anna Quale) aversion to them. The Baron employs a Child Catcher (Robert Helpmann) to help rid the country of its offending offspring. From the minute he is called up by the Baron to hunt out the Potts children, Jemima (Heather Ripley) and Jeremy (Adrian Hall), Helpmann takes on the role as a force of nature. Dressed in black with a battered top hat and crouched over the horse as it careers down the path to the village, dragging the barred cage on the cart behind it, Helpmann moves with precision and intent. Most noticeable as he enters the village square is his command of space that makes even the soldiers scatter in disarray.

Gone is the humorous aspect of character creation evident in *Caravan;* in *Chitty Chitty Bang Bang* Helpmann adopts the chilling duplicity of the kidnapper as 'sweet seller' who entices children into a cage. Roald Dahl's screenplay and role creation cannot be underestimated as a major contributory factor in the success of the character. His subsequent series of unsentimental and disturbing character creations for his children's stories, such as *George's Marvellous Medicine* (1981), *Matilda* (1983) and *The Witches* (1988), include adult villains who hate children. However, Helpmann's attention to detail and economy in the development of the physicality of the role is surely the primary means by which this particular villain becomes so enduringly disturbing and memorable. The ability to move with ease and grace through space is a professional ballet dancer's skill, but in this instance Helpmann merges this with his awareness of the special attributes of film. That is, he knows he must communicate a great deal within each brief series of frames, and he finds this economy of communication through mime. This alone is insufficient and, building on the earlier experiences as detailed above, he works towards a layered performance where sudden changes in movement dynamic, rhythm and texture both build depth of character and reference externally to a range of story villains.

Much is made in the film of the Child Catcher's ability to sniff out children, and the large prosthetic nose he is given of course adds to the animalistic effect. This is most evident in his first foray into the village square on his mission to seek out the Potts children. But the domination of space that makes the character so unnerving is achieved primarily through his eyes that lead the movement. The characteristic swivel of his eyeballs to the furthest extremity on one side, followed by the jerking turn of the head, signal hyper alertness, a sharpness of awareness that is beyond the usual human range. (See plate 75) He moves around the village square with ease and familiarity, like an animal on home territory that will note any slight change to its terrain. The lines he delivers in the nasal and high tonal register created for the role are, as one would expect, chilling: "there are children here somewhere, I can smell them".[30] By the time he utters this line however, the information has already been conveyed in the build-up to the confrontation with the Toymaker (Benny Hill) who has hidden the Potts family in his basement as clown-like, jack-in-a-box toys. The dialogue works to reinforce the gestural information because, as Brannigan helpfully phrased it within a different context, the body is "already heavy with meaning".[31] The film viewers have seen the Child Catcher sniff the air and home in on the precise spot. They have seen his certainty in bossing the soldiers with not a fleck of hesitancy. Do viewers believe that he has been hoodwinked by the family, now concealed as toys? Or is the Child Catcher momentarily distracted and tempted away by the soldiers who have delightedly cried out that they have found Chitty Chitty Bang Bang? His eyes and his threatening "uh huh" suggest merely that he delays his pleasure of capturing the children, which, in film narrative terms, heightens the suspense.

The culmination of Helpmann's role as the Child Catcher occurs on his return to the village square, transformed as the 'sweet seller' in an apparently simple scene of child enticement within the narrative, running simultaneously with absolute clarity of evil intent, in order to repel the film viewer. For the scene to work, viewers need to be drawn into the seduction as well as the intention, and this Helpmann finds in the skipping dance he uses to cross the square accompanied by the playful, jingling melody of the musical accompaniment. Helpmann's ability in clowning movement alluded to earlier, is on full show in this scene. His props have changed from the net and hook of the first scene to lollipops and colourful cloak, but he still wields them in the manner of a performer used to incorporating props into physical extensions of himself. Such body extensions, when united with clarity and speed of movement, have the potential to increase spatial authority; knowledge that Helpmann in this role exploits to the full. Running in tandem with his calling out for children to "come taste" his sugary wares, Helpmann employs fast switches of facial expression to reveal looks of pure evil. He leaps lightly onto the village water pump, as the highest point in the square, and from this vantage point he can assert his dominance, use his sweeping gaze to stay in charge of the environment. The brightly coloured flowery costume and canopies for the cart establish his disguise as the "sweet seller" but throughout the scene, it is his determinedly consistent, restless actions that create the required clash of movement styles: the light dancing step, circling motion and swirl of the cloak, enticing gestures with his handful of lollipops and bells juxtaposed with facial contortions and twisted physical poses.

Helpmann's tripping dance in this section, reprised briefly and triumphantly when he delivers the children to the Baron, is not equivalent to the kind of "show" or break-out dances used earlier in the film. Helpmann's precision and speed of movement, as argued earlier, creates time for him to inject additional physical inflections, which in this case reference and accumulate images of evil from external children's stories and films. He employs a prodigious kinaesthetic and visual memory of stock fictional and filmic characters, to trigger precisely such resonances in his viewers, and thereby augment their experience of evil. It is worth noting that, throughout his life, Helpmann was famed off-stage as well as on, as an excellent mimic: witty, and at times ruthlessly cutting. As shown in all the films examined in this chapter, Helpmann deliberately avoided the pull of naturalism or method acting, in order to generate condensed and exaggerated movement imagery. In *Chitty Chitty Bang Bang* for instance, he uses angularity in physical poses that seem to reference early Walt Disney expressionist drawing of the evil step-mother in *Snow White and the Seven*

Dwarves (1937) and *Cinderella* (1950). The Child Catcher's long hair, cloak, high vocal register and lightness of step suggest androgyny or gender transformation that signals a witch-like character, rather than a wizard. This could summon images for parents, if not the child viewer, of well-known fairy stories, such as the witch in *Hansel and Gretel* or the wicked fairy Maleficent in *Sleeping Beauty* (Disney film, 1959). The dance out of the square is a reminder of the *Pied Piper of Hamlyn*, and the offer of the lollipops at the window where the children hide, hints at both the disguised witch of *Snow White* and the temptations of the gingerbread cottage in *Hansel and Gretel*. Helpmann's adaptation of dance and choreographic techniques to work with film importantly includes the fact that he always had "in mind what *would* be happening elsewhere, even if it *wasn't* happening".[32] This skill, combined with precise physical discipline and a playful enjoyment of mimicry, was essential for the economy of expression Helpmann required to create such a multi-referential character. As the Child Catcher leaves the village with the children in the cage hidden beneath the colourful trappings of the sweet stall that horrifically drop away the minute they are ensnared, Helpmann is crouched low over his horse, whipping it furiously on. Villagers stare in horror as Truly Scrumptious (Sally Anne Howes) runs ineffectually behind it. Through Helpmann's mimicry of a speeding frenzy the viewer is convinced that the horse is crazily galloping as it drags the caged children behind it. A careful look at this footage reveals that all the action is taking place in Helpmann's movement, and that in fact the horse is trotting quite sedately out of the square and away. (See plate 74)

At a recent conference within a Performer Training Working Group,[33] one of the most persistent questions to arise was how conservatoires and other training institutions might best support the pressing need for versatility in performers, who are frequently expected to be able to move between stage and film acting and dance/dance theatre. Helpmann, who from his teenage years, challenged the creation of boundaries between the performing arts, offers a lateral approach to this issue through his implied provocation to think again about the wealth of potential interrelationships that can be extracted from each form. Rather than a set training blueprint, Helpmann's performance output, under close scrutiny yields inventive ways to re-apply dance and acting techniques within new contexts. Helpmann's extraordinary and idiosyncratic life as a performer could hardly offer a model for others to follow closely, but his bold steps in integrating performing arts techniques is an approach worth heeding. For the contemporary performer, so often under pressure to adapt quickly to different styles, genres and media, Helpmann's process of valuing and creatively re-cycling his past performance experiences could prove useful, even liberating. His work across the performing arts and within film has its own intrinsic value within the context of performer training, but it also can be seen as a provocation not to replicate, but to keep reinventing boundary-breaking combinations and collaborations.

Endnotes

1   *Entertainment Weekly*, "50 Most Vile Movie Villains" (2nd April 2008), http://netflixcommunity.ning.com/forum/topics/1993323:Topic:58584

2   *Tales of Helpmann: A Profile of Sir Robert Helpmann* (dir. Don Featherstone; script Alan Sievewright; ed. Melvyn Bragg), a South Bank Show film produced by London Weekend Television for ITV, in association with the Australian Broadcasting Corporation (1990).

3   Robert Helpmann, "Shakespeare and the Ballet", *The Old Vic and Sadler's Wells Magazine* January 1938, p. 5, reproduced on p. 2 of this volume.

4   Cecil Wilson, "Helpmann Turns Producer", *Daily Mail* (28 March 1953) n.p.

5   English Director, Michael Powell (1905-1990) and Hungarian, Emeric Pressburger (1902-1988) collaborated on over twenty films with Powell mainly directing, Pressburger producing and both writing film scripts. They formed the Archers Film Productions (1943) and were subsequently referred to as The Archers.

6   Based on French composer and movement teacher, François Delsarte's methods of movement expression using gesture linked with emotion, American Delsartism, however, "was a distinct type of body culture and of particular relevance to the shift from pose to flow. Delsartism crossed the Atlantic in the late nineteenth century". Erin Brannigan, *Dancefilm: Choreography and the Moving Image* (Oxford: Oxford University Press, 2011), p. 30.

7   Maya Deren, *Essential Deren: Collected Writings on Film by Maya Deren*, Bruce R. Mcpherson (ed.), (New York: McPherson and Company, 2005), p. 30, 31.

8   Amy Greenfield, "The Kinesthetics of Avant-Garde Dance Film: Deren and Harris" in Judy Mitoma (ed.), *Envisioning Dance on Film and Video* (New York: Routledge, 2002), p.25.

9   Ibid. p.23.

10   Anna Bemrose, *Robert Helpmann: A Servant of Art* (St Lucia, Queensland: University of Queensland Press, 2008), p.92.

11   Kathrine Sorley Walker, *Robert Helpmann: A Rare Sense of the Theatre* (Alton: Dance Books, 2009), p. 87.

12   Ibid. p.87.

13   George Bartram, "Robert Helpmann – Human Dynamo", *Picturegoer* (3 July 1948), p. 5.

14   Martin Scorsese talking to Geoffrey Macnab, "The movie that plays in my heart", *The Independent* (15 May 2009), n.p. 2009) http://www.independent.co.uk/arts-entertainment/films/features/martin-scorsese-the-movie-that-plays-in-my-heart-1685003.html, accessed 3 September 2013.

15   Ibid. n.p.

16   *One of Our Aircraft is Missing*, Michael Powell & Emeric Pressburger (Directors), (UK, The Archers, 1942), DVD.

17   *Caravan*, Arthur Crabtree (Director), (UK: Gainsborough Melodramas, 1946). DVD.

18   *Dancefilm: Choreography and the Moving Image*, p.88.

19   Michael Powell, "Robert Helpmann", *Spectator* (4 October 1986) pp. 16-17.

20   Elizabeth Salter, *Helpmann: The Authorised Biography* (Sydney: Angus and Robertson, 1978), p. 111.

21   *Helpmann: The Authorised Biography*, p. 111.

22   It is worth looking up images for Eddie Cantor (1892-1964), American actor, comedian and singer on the internet for the full impact of this quotation.

23   *Helpmann: The Authorised Biography*, pp. 137-139.

24   "Robert Helpmann: Human Dynamo", p. 5.

25   Ibid. p. 5.

26   *Monthly Film Bulletin* (Anon.), "Caravan (1946)", (Volume 13, No.148, April 1946) p. 44.

27   Michael Brooke, "Caravan (1946)", *Screenonline* (2013-4) unpaginated. http://www.screenonline.org.uk/film/id/440361/, accessed 20 August 2014.

28   *Dancefilm: Choreography and the Moving Image*, p.77.

29   "Robert Helpmann: Human Dynamo", p. 5.

30   *Chitty Chitty Bang Bang*, Albert Broccoli (Producer), Ken Hughes (Director), (UK: Warfield Productions, 1968). DVD.

31   *Dancefilm*, p.88.

32   *Robert Helpmann: A Rare Sense of the Theatre*, p.87.

33   The Performer Training Working Group, in the Theatre and Performance Research Association (TaPRA), meets each year at the TaPRA conference and during the year at interim symposia. The theme for September 2014 was performer training for and with film/digital media and video, convened by Mark Evans, Konstantinos Thomaidis and Libby Worth and held at Royal Holloway, University of London.

Robert Helpmann: Chameleon of the Screen[1]

Geraldine Morris

> This gallimaufry of Gothicisms, this pantechnicon of palettical paroxysms, this meddle-muddle of media, this olla podrida of oddsbodikins, this massive accumulation of mighty midcult Wurlitzerisms, follows Offenbach's operetta faithfully and fills in filmically with ballet, décor and by-play, seeking moreover, an operating visual style with a total disdain of plausibility.[2]

Despite this somewhat equivocal tribute to *The Tales of Hoffmann*, Raymond Durgnant was one of the first writers to reappraise the films of Michael Powell and Emeric Pressburger. Lauded during the 1950s, their reputation had diminished during the "swinging" era of the 1960s, and Durgnant not only reinstated them as significant British film-makers but also revealed their ingenuity and creativity. In doing so, he prompted renewed interest in their two great dance films: *The Red Shoes* (1948) and *The Tales of Hoffmann* (1951). Robert Helpmann had a leading role in both. While much has now been written about *The Tales of Hoffmann* as a film, I want to consider in this chapter how Powell contrived to make Helpmann central to the film's narrative. By 1951 Helpmann was already an acclaimed actor and throughout his career performed in many films, but these two were the only ones in which he also danced.

Contemporary dance critics failed to recognise the significance of Helpmann's role in this film. Writing in the *Ballet Annual* of 1952, Arnold Haskell condemned the film for its "lack of imagination", its "restless images", "repository art, [and] chocolate box covers".[3] He exclaimed that the performers had been obliterated, were devoid of personality, and that they had been "directed into nothingness". Haskell appears to be something of a snob, but it is worth remembering that, since the Ballets Russes (1909-1929), ballet was regarded as high art and its perceived descent into cinema threatened to return it to the days of the Music Hall and popular culture. He argued that the film would probably prove popular in the "drab industrial cities", indicating his unease; but he was also scathing about the two directors, Powell and Pressburger. Of its final stamp "Made in England", he urges that it would have been "far better to have kept its origins a secret".[4] Yet the film attracted such stars as Moira Shearer, Léonide Massine, Ludmilla Tcherina and Frederick Ashton (the latter as both performer and choreographer).

Fernau Hall reserved his strongest, most barbed, criticism for Ashton:

> At no point in the film did Ashton create dance images expressive of the characters and moods of the personages involved, and this made the film as a whole into a bewildering succession of shots with little or no relation to the singing or each other. [...] Massine's superb acting in one of the central roles with his professional assurance and complete grasp of the film medium showed clearly what was wrong with Ashton's choreography.[5]

The film gave each critic a chance to air their grievances and, as the following discussion demonstrates, Hall's comments in particular are both rash and inaccurate.

The status today of *The Tales of Hoffmann* has changed: a recent re-mastering of the film by the BFI (British Film Institute, 2014) led Peter Bradshaw, film critic of *The Guardian*, to describe it as "a hothouse flower of pure orchidaceous strangeness... sensual, macabre, dreamlike and enigmatic".[6] According to the distinguished film academic, Ian Christie, it was seminal for the development of British cinema. He regards it as a summary of all Powell and Pressburger's work, writing that "the resulting film shot quickly and cheaply in the studio to a pre-recorded soundtrack, proved to be not only a unique artistic landmark in British cinema – the absolute antithesis of realism – but a virtual anthology of the Hoffmannesque themes underlying their work as a whole".[7]

Eminent film directors such as Cecil B. DeMille, George A. Romero and Martin Scorsese also found the film inspirational. Writing to the film makers, DeMille observed that, as a lover of opera, he had often been bothered by the "physical drawbacks of the average opera presentation" and remarked:

> [...] for the first time in [my] life [I] was treated to Grand Opera where the beauty, power and scope of the music was equally matched by the visual presentation. I thank you for outstanding courage and artistry in bringing to us Grand Opera as it existed until now, only in the minds of those who created it.[8]

According to Martin Scorsese, it was above all Helpmann's reaction shots during the duel scene in the second tale, "Giulietta", that most influenced his film *Raging Bull* (1980).[9] Indeed, more than sixty years later he believed that the film was so significant that he funded its re-mastering.

Helpmann was central to the film, playing a pivotal character in each of the four scenes. Powell remembered that he had indulged both Helpmann and Massine: "Massine took charge of the whole production. I was his cameraman", while Helpmann "knowing which parts Massine would grab for himself [...] made a clean sweep of all the villains".[10] Powell's shooting of Helpmann is evidence of his admiration: the camera lingers over his face, from above and below, indulging in the variety and depth of Helpmann's expressions, making them hugely memorable.

E.T.A. Hoffmann is the (fictitious) protagonist, who entertains his drinking companions with the tales of his three failed love affairs. But the film starts with the sinister Councillor Lindorf (Helpmann) who is competing with Hoffmann for the love of the ballerina, Stella (Shearer). In this opening section, Lindorf outwits Hoffmann by intercepting a note to Stella from Hoffmann. And in the last scene of the film, we realise that Lindorf has won. When Stella arrives in the tavern and finds Hoffmann drunk, she exits on Lindorf's arm.

The three main tales centre on Hoffmann's loves. The first, "Olympia", concerns a mechanical doll (Shearer), with whom Hoffmann falls in love. The second is set in Venice at carnival time, where it is Giulietta (Ludmilla Tcherina), the glamorous courtesan, who is the object of Hoffmann's adoration. Yet once again Hoffmann is thwarted, this time by the sinister magician, Dapertutto (Helpmann). The latter is portrayed as a magician-come-pimp, who attempts to destroy Hoffmann by inveigling Giulietta into stealing his reflection/soul. In the final tale, the object of Hoffmann's attention is the opera singer, Antonia, who, dying of consumption and warned against singing, is encouraged to sing again by the macabre Dr Miracle (Helpmann). Dr Miracle's motives are unclear but her singing hastens her death and, at the end of her aria, she falls lifeless into his arms.

As Councillor Lindorf, Helpmann dominates the opening shots. He bursts through the huge doors of a theatre, wearing an opera cloak and flourishing a cane, which he uses to alert the dozing doormen. The camera highlights the cloak, as Lindorf sweeps dramatically around three chairs. With this gesture, Helpmann immediately establishes his authoritative and menacing character. He moves on and pauses before a poster of the evening's performance announcing the appearance of the ballerina, Stella, in *The Dragonfly*. Helpmann's face, fine-boned, intimidating, with piercing eyes, fills the screen, as he peers at the poster through the lens of an elegant lorgnette. (A major motif of the film is the use of glass: scenes shot through coloured and spattered glass and characters who view the world through (rose-coloured) glasses, transforming it as in the tale, "Olympia".)

Even if we know nothing about the opera, Lindorf's bearing is ominously portentous, alerting us to the misfortunes that will follow. It foreshadows the narrative and Helpmann carries it off through his dramatic embodiment of evil, helped by extraordinary facial powers. It is no surprise that Powell uses Helpmann's spectacular movement, studied expressions and piercing eyes as a major focus of the film. Yet much of his activity in this opening section is clandestine, taking place back stage, in the wings or at a side table in the beer cellar, while Hoffmann is open, centre stage and first seen, pensive, sitting enraptured in the theatre stalls. Powell uses Helpmann in both close-up and long shot, and a particularly effective moment is when Lindorf is seen in the distance seemingly overseeing the drinking song in the beer cellar, to which Hoffmann has retired for the ballet's interval. Throughout the film, Lindorf, in different guises, threatens, hovers near to and defeats Hoffmann.

Ashton is present in the film, as both choreographer and performer, though he claimed not to have arranged Massine's dances.[11] The first tale, "Olympia", has most of the dancing, quite apart from the *Dragonfly* ballet. Ashton plays both Kleinsach, the dwarf in love with a beautiful maiden (also Shearer), and Cochenille, the puppet master in "Olympia".[12] His performance as the dwarf is wonderfully captured by Edwin Denby, who observes that "Ashton does it reticently, with perfect timing, the apparently tentative gesture, the absorption and the sweetness of nature of a great clown".[13] Denby is actually discussing Ashton's Ugly Sister in *Cinderella* (1948) here, but it equally applies to his performance in this film, made three years later.

His choreography for Shearer has all the bravura qualities of Olympia's aria as composed by Offenbach, but aspects of the Ballerina's first variation in *Scènes de ballet* (1948) and of Cinderella's in Act II of *Cinderella* (1948) also creep into the dance, not least the sharp upper body bends. Restless floor patterns dominate the dance as she moves back and forth in big circles or short, sharp diagonals. Her movement is mainly confined to the lower body with crisp, sprightly pointe-work and a series of virtuoso turns that end the variation. Yet, when she does use her arms, they shoot into space like sparkling arrows. The dance has all the doll-like qualities of a marionette and yet matches the virtuoso qualities of the aria. As Olympia dances she sings, Shearer mouthing the words to the voice of the pre-recorded soprano (Dorothy Bond).[14]

Ashton, as well as being a great artist, was a great craftsman and even in this limited dance, his craft is to the fore. The dance centres on sharp footwork, performed close to the body, and on multiple turns, *renversés*, *fouettés*, *pirouettes*, all executed at breath-taking speed. Yet it is economical in its use of movement and Ashton was not tempted to deluge the dance with spectacular steps. Later, in the waltz section, Olympia's movement flows, becoming more exuberant but still somewhat contained, in that her limbs do not always extend into the space, remaining close to the body. She begins the waltz with Spalanzani (Massine) before being passed on to Hoffmann. Cochenille, the puppet master (Ashton), is responsible for unfurling the huge staircase (a painted conceit) down which Olympia and Hoffmann waltz. But disaster strikes, waltzing faster and faster, Hoffmann loses control, his glasses fall off, and he totters off the edge of the stairs to end prostrate on Olympia's swinging bed, apparently lifeless. Olympia continues waltzing and, lured by

Coppélius (Helpmann), waltzes into his clutches.

Helpmann, as Coppélius, though manipulative, is initially less threatening in this tale. Unlike in the ballet, *Coppélia*, he is not the doll maker but the more creepy maker of eyes. (See plate 52) His argument is with Spalanzani, the mechanical toy maker, as to who is the legitimate creator, and thus owner, of Olympia. She can only move once Coppélius has fitted her eyes, yet without the mechanics and the doll, there would be nothing into which to fix the eyes. The pair conspire to get Hoffmann to marry Olympia, with which he willingly, if unwittingly, colludes. Yet, he is thwarted. Having fitted Hoffmann with Coppélius's magic spectacles, which, like 3D glasses, transform the world and make Olympia appear real flesh and blood, Spalanzani has tricked him into believing she is real. Sitting astride a chair, Spalanzani plays the harp to which Olympia dances her bravura variation. Supper is called and the marionettes (opera chorus and observers) proceed to the dining room, leaving Hoffmann alone to woo Olympia. Here Shearer is woodenly brilliant; when he tries to embrace her, she marches up and down angrily, just like Swanhilda in the ballet, *Coppélia*. Initially taken by surprise, he nevertheless proclaims his love, believing it to be reciprocated. The exuberant waltz follows, leading Hoffmann to his fate.

With Hoffmann seemingly unconscious, Spalanzani hands Coppélius the promised cheque which, when presented at the bank, bounces. Coppélius vows revenge. As Hoffmann recovers, he awakes to see Coppélius tearing Olympia limb from limb. The sudden realisation that he has been duped is dramatised by his mournful cry, "it's automatic". All that is left is the eye-blinking head and a fluttering leg. The viciousness with which Coppélius tears Olympia apart is breath-taking (even more chilling perhaps than Vicky's leap to her death in *The Red Shoes*). Coppélius's face becomes contorted and his eyes appear to leap from their sockets. (See plate 53) It is the first time in this tale that he becomes more than an eccentric elderly man but it is an abiding image. "Olympia" finishes with Cochenille mourning the destruction of the doll and stroking its lifeless hand. It is a macabre end to a seemingly frivolous tale.

Set in Venice and beginning with the lilting, if beguiling, rhythm of the Barcarolle that opens and closes the section, the second tale, "Giulietta", materialises in the next frame. The singers' dialogue gives clues as to the narrative but, equally, Dapertutto's (Helpmann) make-up and opulent clothes ominously warn of the events to follow. Accompanied by Giulietta, dressed in black, gold and green, Dapertutto has green shadowed eyes which end in an upward curl, matched by a twisted scroll of green down the right cheek. Each of the green lines is stopped by a small, glittering jewel. We have left the sunny, youthful, yellow abode of Olympia, to enter the erotic and highly charged world of the Venetian carnival. We assume it is carnival time because of the physical abandon, the licentiousness, hedonism and apparent sexual excess of the scene that follows.

In this opening *Barcarolle* section, the camera pauses over the main protagonists. First Dapertutto and Giulietta, reclining in a gondola, their faces filling the screen; this is followed by a younger looking and bearded Hoffmann, gazing down from a bridge. Dapertutto, hardly moving, motions to Giulietta and Hoffmann bows in recognition. Finally we see Schlemil (Massine), the white-faced soldier and former lover of Giulietta. She has robbed him of his shadow, hence his colourless appearance and black suit. The camera lingers briefly, and then in close-up we see him fingering a key; the key to Giulietta's bedroom. In time with the Barcarolle, the camera drifts over each character. It is extremely beautiful but spine-chilling and disturbing. Apart from Hoffmann, the participants are richly dressed in black, silver, gold and green. Powell and his designer Hein Heckroth, exploited not only the opulence and sensuousness of Venice but also its more grotesque and eerie elements. This opening scene, with the gondola moving to the lilting *Barcarolle*, is both portentous and compelling.

Leaving the canal, we enter a world of sexual fantasy and eroticism. It is almost as though we had moved on to 1999 and the world of Stanley Kubrick's *Eyes Wide Shut*. The orgy taking place in this Venetian palace omits the nude bodies but otherwise connects with the later film. Not that *The Tales of Hoffmann* has any of the subliminal Masonic elements of Kubrick's film, but the use of masks for disguise and the magical atmosphere are all apparent in *Hoffmann*.

Inside the brothel, we observe the lone Dapertutto as he coaxes the dripping candle wax into jewels. Diamonds, sapphires, rubies and emeralds are forged from the wax into a glittering necklace. It is a bribe for Giulietta, but Dapertutto's dance as he fashions the necklace creates an ironic contrast with his actions. It is fluid, elegant and circular, comprising slow turns to the knee and sustained leg extensions. He seems more like a Prince from a nineteenth-century ballet than the malicious Dapertutto. The appearance is of old-fashioned courtesy but the reality is infinitely more threatening. Dapertutto is a protean Mephistopheles, who can change shape and character at will. Ashton picks up on this in the dance he made for Helpmann, showing him to be both prince and pimp. When Giulietta is offered the necklace, she is beguiled and demands to know "what [she] must do to merit such a prize?" The price is to obtain Hoffmann's reflection. In nineteenth-century fairy tales, to lose your reflection was to lose your soul or, as Jack Zipes puts it, "lose oneself".[15] Giulietta accepts the bribe.

Bribery is another significant theme in the film. We first encounter it when Lindorf is seen bribing Andres, Stella's servant, in the wings of the opera house. On payment of several gold coins, Andres hands to Lindorf Stella's *billet doux*, a love note meant for Hoffmann, who never receives it. In the first tale, Spalanzani bribes Coppélius to hand over Olympia; and in the final tale, "Antonia", set on a Greek island, there is an undertone of bribery, since both Hoffmann and Doctor Miracle clandestinely gain access to the closely protected Antonia.

Beyond striking some sensual poses, Giulietta has little dancing. She plays the siren, a temptress, who values wealth over creativity and freedom. Zipes makes the point that many of E.T.A. Hoffmann's tales concerned the "battle between the forces of rationalism, utilitarianism and repression and the forces of creativity, imagination and freedom"[16] This notion of the battle between materialism and art is perhaps most clearly reflected in this particular tale. In Powell's *The Red Shoes,* there is something of this too. It is a world where Vicky (Shearer) is made to decide between art and life, but she has become a puppet in the hands of the two male protagonists, Boris Lermontov and Julian Craster, and rather than choose one or the other, she opts for death.

In *The Tales of Hoffmann*, Giulietta opts for the necklace and agrees to steal Hoffmann's reflection. Hoffmann has vowed not to be seduced by her but is powerless on seeing her again. He is captivated and they swear undying love. Not only does he then lose his reflection but he is also tricked into thinking that she will await him in her boudoir. Giulietta advises him that Schlemil has the key, knowing he will refuse to part with it. Hoffmann tries to force the key from Schlemil but he resists; instead, he challenges him to a duel. It takes place on board a gondola where Schlemil is killed. By the time Hoffmann returns and enters the boudoir, Giulietta has already departed. But this allows Hoffmann to redeem his soul: in fury he throws the key at the looking glass, which shatters only to materialise into his reflection.[17]

Powell bolsters the image of evil in the final scene of this tale. Hovering over the departing couple, Giulietta and Dapertutto, is a vision of Giulietta, dressed in a virginal white sari embroidered with gold. But the image confounds: as the camera pans down to the rocks, it focuses on Giulietta's jewelled toes and gold-painted toenails; she is both a whore and a virgin, the traditional phallocentric image of women.

The final tale "Antonia" has little dancing. Helpmann, as Doctor Miracle, has a major singing role (sung by Bruce Dargavel). Kathrine Sorley Walker observed in her monograph on Helpmann that, despite having a very different physique from his bass-baritone character, he performed outstandingly.[18] His stance is convincing, particularly in the scene where he conjures up Antonia's mother. Set on a Greek island, the tale is again dominated by Helpmann. Dressed in black with pale face and silvered hair, he seems not only malevolent but also dangerous. Yet, this time, there is little reason for him to destroy Antonia, beyond the fact that (as Lindorf) he is still attempting to wreck Hoffmann's chances. When Antonia dies, she falls into Doctor Miracle's arms and, as he holds her, he peels off a series of masks: Doctor Miracle, Coppélius, Dapertutto, till his real identity as Councillor Lindorf is revealed.

Helpmann has played the villain in different guises throughout and yet remains both compelling and appealing. So what is it about his performance that captivates us? Is it because of Powell's direction? Powell was also a friend and admirer of Helpmann. In an earlier film, *One of Our Aircraft is Missing* (1942), Powell mentions that Helpmann "did a splendid piece of overacting which shocked the other, less naked and more reserved, actors. I encouraged it. I loved Bobby's overacting."[19] He does overact in *The Tales of Hoffmann*, but his performance is not one dimensional. As Lindorf, he is suave, elegant even courteous, while his Coppélius is elderly and malign. He plays Dapertutto as a somewhat enigmatic character and his fluid dancing provides several layers to what might simply be a villainous pimp. We are left with the final image of the quack Doctor Miracle and here he seems otherworldly, vampire-like with his pale face and red-rimmed eyes. Doctor Miracle is perhaps the wickedest of all the characters, as it is only in this tale that he causes the death of a human character. The camera focuses on his eyes, malicious and threatening. The role has few nuances and perhaps it is because Helpmann plays it as a straightforward villain that he succeeds.

The Tales of Hoffmann is an "unworldly, otherworldly" film, "hallucinatory and dreamlike".[20] It was initially misunderstood and may have seemed strange, even kitsch, which is what the ballet press focused on. But it was ahead of its time and is now justifiably recognised as a great classic. It certainly repays close attention, as does the work of the designer Hein Heckroth, which would need a separate chapter. (In the field of modern dance, he is perhaps best known for his expressionist designs for *The Green Table* (1932) by Kurt Jooss.) But as Nanette Aldred remarked, the film served to "reassert the freedom of the imagination and the possibilities of art within a popular mode – an achievement that would have been impossible without Hein Heckroth".[21]

These "ballet" films of Powell and Pressburger are essentially about art and the nature of art, particularly in cinema. When asked why *The Red Shoes* became such a success worldwide, Powell observed "that [...] we had all been told for ten years to go out and die for freedom and democracy [...] and now that the war was over, *The Red Shoes* told us to go and die for art".[22] This, of course, Antonia does in *Hoffmann*, so the notion continued into the 1950s. As Zipes observed of the fairy tale, its main impulse "was at first revolutionary and progressive, not escapist".[23] The same can be said of these two films by Powell and Pressburger. As Ian Christie puts it, they had "a vision of film-making as the synthesis of all the arts [...] realised in *The Red Shoes* and *The Tales of Hoffmann*".[24]

Endnotes

1   An anonymous article in the *Dancing Times* described Helpmann as "The Chameleon of the Theatre". See "Robert Helpmann: A Portrait", *Dancing Times*, June 1953, p.539.

2   Raymond Durgnant, "Durgnant on Powell and Pressburger", in Ian Christie (ed.), *Powell, Pressburger and Others*, (London: BFI, 1978), pp. 65-78.

3   Arnold Haskell, "*The Tales of Hoffman* (sic): Carlton Cinema", in Haskell (ed.), *The Ballet Annual* (London: A. and C. Black, 1952), pp. 26-27.

4   When Sir Thomas Beecham, who conducted the performance, is shown at the end of the film, he closes the score and stamps it with "Made In England". Haskell erroneously writes, "Made in Britain".

5   Quoted in Vicente Garcia-Márquez, *Massine: A Biography* (London: Nick Hern Books, 1996) pp. 332- 333.

6   Peter Bradshaw, "*The Tales of Hoffmann* – Powell and Pressburger's other magic ballet film", review, 26 February, online at: http://www.the guardian. com/film/2015/feb/26/tales-of-hoffmann-r.

7   Ian Christie, *Arrows of Desire* (London and Boston: Faber and Faber, 1994), p. 68.

8   Quoted in website, *The Powell and Pressburger Pages*: www.powell-pressburger. org/

9   Martin Scorsese, "Forward", in Ian Christie, *Arrows of Desire*, (London and Boston: Faber and Faber, 1994), p. xvii.

10   Quoted in Julie Kavanagh, *Secret Muses: The Life of Frederick Ashton* (London: Faber and Faber, 1999), p. 395.

11   Ibid, p. 394.

12   The Kleinsach scene comes just before "Olympia". In the opera Hoffmann tells the tale of a hunchbacked dwarf who woos a beautiful maiden and tries to entice her with money. But for the film, the story was slightly altered and Kleinsach is shamed when he has to look at his reflection in a mirror. Either way, it is a somewhat cautionary tale.

13   Edwin Denby, *Dance Writings* (London: Dance Books, 1986), p. 359.

14   Shearer, however, forgets to sing as the dance becomes more demanding, though this is less noticeable as she performs multiple and varied turns.

15   Jack Zipes, *Breaking the Magic Spell: Radical Theories of Folk and Fairy Tales* (London: Heinemann, 1979), p. 38.

16   Ibid.

17   A similar scene occurs in *The Red Shoes* when Lermontov smashes the looking glass in his hotel.

18   Kathrine Sorley Walker, *Robert Helpmann: A Rare Sense of the Theatre* (Alton: Dance Books, 2009), p. 102.

19   Michael Powell, *A Life in Movies* (London: Mandarin, 1986), p. 395. See "Robert Helpmann and the Making of an On-Screen Villain" pp. 174-175.

20   Peter Bradshaw, "*The Tales of Hoffmann* – Powell and Pressburger's other magic ballet film".

21   Nanette Aldred, "Hein Heckroth and The Archers", in Ian Christie and Andrew Moor (eds.) *The Cinema of Michael Powell: International Perspectives on an English Film-Maker* (London: BFI, 2005), pp. 187-206.

22   *A Life in Movies*, p.653.

23   *Breaking the Magic Spell: Radical Theories of Folk and Fairy Tales*, p. 36.

24   *Arrows of Desire*, p. 12.

54. Michael Benthall, Katharine Hepburn and Robert Helpmann stride along a beach – all wearing trousers. Publicity shot for the Old Vic Company's Australian Tour, May-November 1955. Photo: Australian Consolidated Press. Source: Victoria and Albert Museum, London

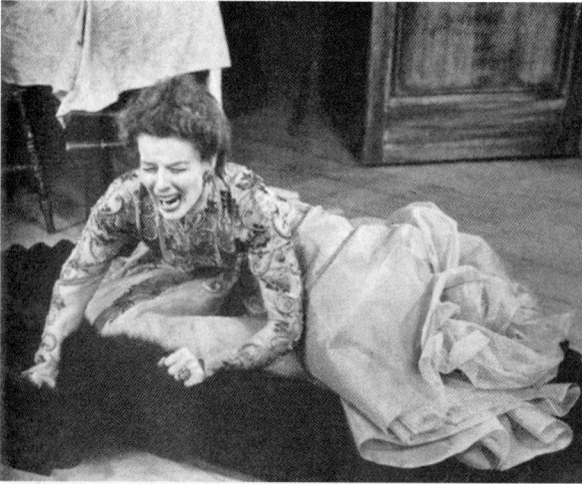

Epifania: You brute! You have killed me.

In a towering rage Epifania flings herself on the floor and continues her tantrums vociferously.

The Doctor: What's the matter? What is going on here?

Epifania: Who the devil are you?

The arrival of a quiet, shabby, unemotional gentleman in a fez creates a new interest. Epifania, learning that he is a doctor, demands to be his patient, but he is not interested.

55. Katharine Hepburn as Epifania and Robert Helpmann as the Egyptian Doctor in George Bernard Shaw's *The Millionairess*, directed by Michael Benthall (New Theatre, London). *Theatre World*, August 1952, p. 6. Angus McBean Photographs © Houghton Library, Harvard University. Source: The Royal Ballet School Special Collections

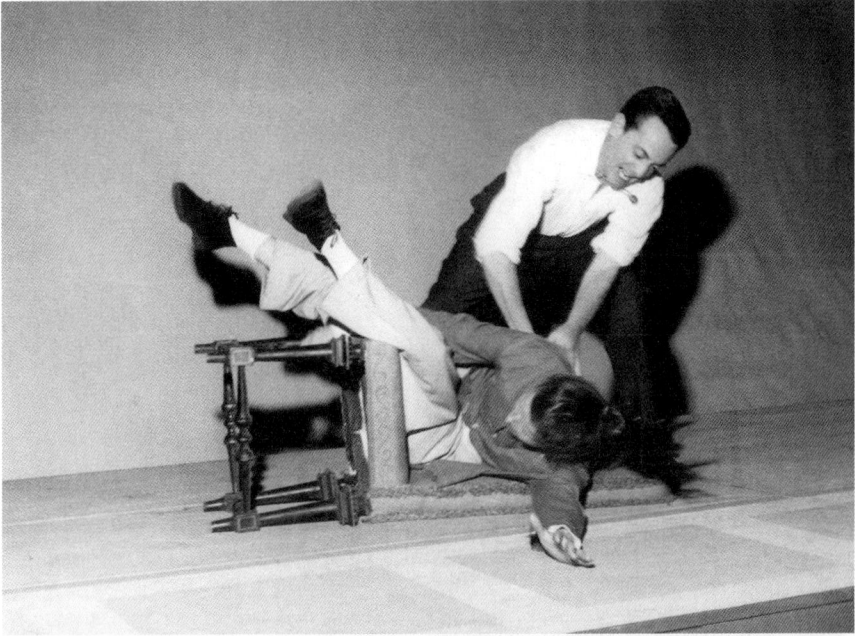

56. and 57. Robert Helpmann as Petruchio and Katharine Hepburn as Kate, rehearsing and performing scenes of 'comic violence' in Shakespeare's *The Taming of the Shrew* (Old Vic Company, Tivoli Theatre, Sydney; Australian Tour, May-November 1955). Photo: Australian Consolidated Press. Credit: University of Bristol/ArenaPAL

58. Robert Helpmann as Petruchio in Shakespeare's *The Taming of the Shrew* (Old Vic Company, Australian Tour, May-November 1955). Photo: G.R. Flack, Australian Consolidated Press. Source: Victoria and Albert Museum, London

59. Robert Helpmann exuding an 'exaggerated masculinity' as Petruchio, in the same production. Photo: Australian Consolidated Press. Credit: University of Bristol/ ArenaPAL

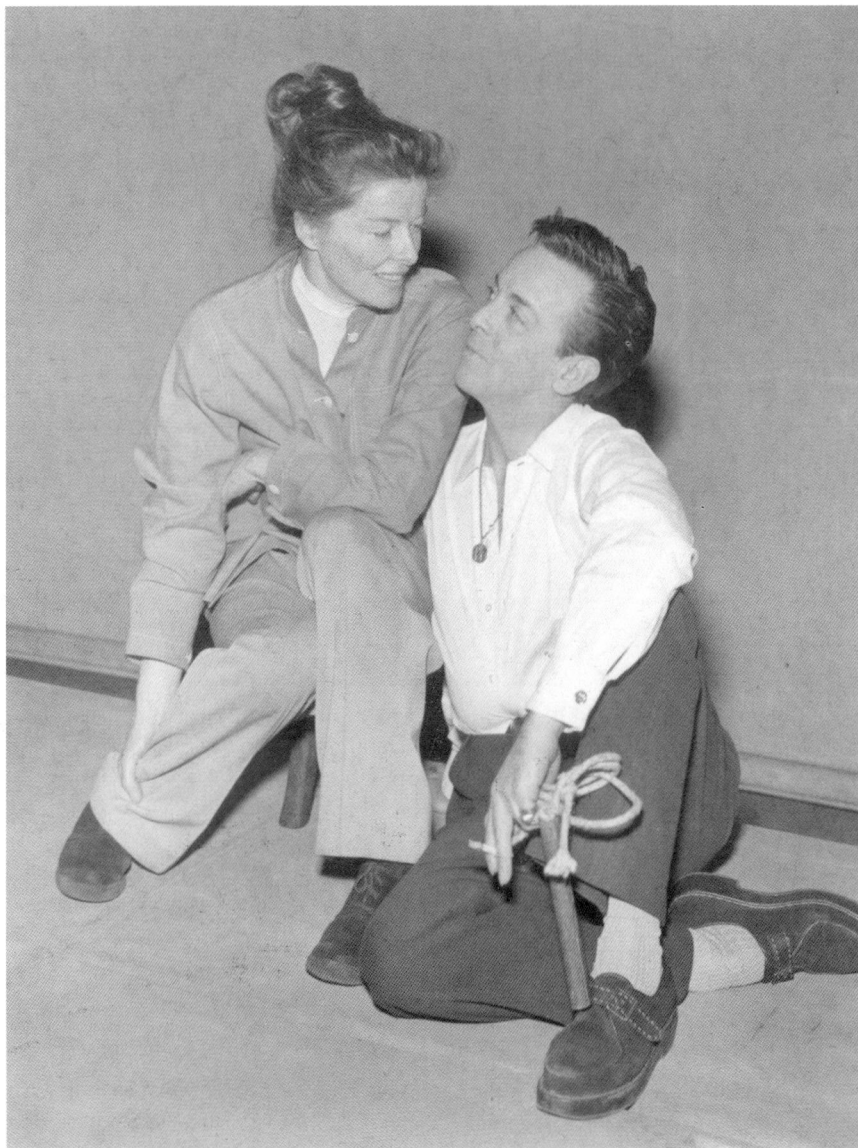

60. Robert Helpmann and Katharine Hepburn during a break in rehearsals for the Old Vic Company's Australian Tour, 1955. Photo: Australian Consolidated Press. Credit: University of Bristol/ArenaPAL

61. Robert Helpmann making up for the role of Shylock in Shakespeare's *The Merchant of Venice* (Old Vic Company, Australian Tour, May-November 1955). Photo: Australian Consolidated Press. Source: Victoria and Albert Museum, London

62. (Opposite page) Robert Helpmann as Shylock in Shakespeare's *The Merchant of Venice* (Old Vic Company, Australian Tour, May-November 1955). The image demonstrates how Helpmann brought to his acting the 'sustained carriage' of a trained dancer. Photographed by Doug Kerrigan and Noel Rubie. Credit: University of Bristol/ArenaPAL

63. Robert Helpmann as Angelo in Shakespeare's *Measure For Measure* (Old Vic Company, Australian Tour, May-November 1955). Photographed by Allan Studios. Credit: University of Bristol/ArenaPAL

64. Robert Helpmann in the title role of Shakespeare's Richard III, directed
by Douglas Searle, with designs by Leslie Hurry (Old Vic Theatre, 1957). As
Richard, Duke of Gloucester, Helpmann spoke the opening soliloquy before the
backdrop of a spider's web. Angus McBean Photograph © Houghton Library,
Harvard University. Source: Victoria and Albert Museum, London

65. Robert Helpmann as Doctor Pinch, a schoolmaster and 'conjuror', in Shakespeare's *The Comedy of Errors* (Old Vic Theatre, 1957). With Pinch's great book of spells open on the floor, Helpmann's interpretation appears to reference the ballet-mime of Dr Coppélius. Angus McBean Photograph © Houghton Library, Harvard University. Source: Victoria and Albert Museum, London

66. Robert Helpmann, 'nude with violin', at the time of his appearance in Noël Coward's comedy of that title (Globe Theatre, London, 1957, and on tour in Australia and New Zealand, 1958). Angus McBean Photograph © Houghton Library, Harvard University. Source: Victoria and Albert Museum, London

67. Robert Helpmann at an informal event in Melbourne, undated. Photo: Australian Consolidated Press. Source: The Royal Ballet School Special Collections

68. Robert Helpmann and Michael Benthall in a domestic setting, probably their home in Eaton Square c.1960. Photographer unknown. Source: Victoria and Albert Museum, London (Kathrine Sorley Walker Collection).

69. Robert Helpmann's expanded revival of his ballet *Elektra* (Australian Ballet, 1966), designed by the Australian artist Arthur Boyd. The image captures one of the acrobatic 'throws' where the Erinyes (the Furies) attack Elektra (Kathleen Geldard). Photo: Australian News and Information Bureau. Source: The National Archives of Australia

70. Joseph Janusaitis as a Fury in Helpmann's *Elektra* (Australian Ballet, 1966). The cast all wore individually designed make-up referencing the face and body-painting traditions of the Australian indigenous peoples. Photo: Walter Stringer. Source: The National Library of Australia

71. Janet Karin as Klytemnestra [Helpmann's preferred spelling of the name], and Warren de Maria as Aegisthus in *Elektra* (Australian Ballet, Melbourne 1966). Photo: Walter Stringer. Source: The National Library of Australia

72. Action shot of the scene in which Elektra (here, Kathleen Gorham, prone on the floor) persuades Orestes (Brian Lawrence, leaping) to murder their mother Klytemnestra (Janet Karin), seen here with a cloak (Australian Ballet, 1966). Photo: Australian News and Information Bureau. Source: The National Archives of Australia

73. Robert Helpmann and Frederick Ashton reprising their created roles of the Stepsisters in the 1965 revival of Frederick Ashton's *Cinderella* (1948). This major revival by The Royal Ballet featured new costumes and scenery by David Walker and Henry Bardon. Photo: Donald Southern © Royal Opera House. By kind permission Royal Opera House Collections

74. and 75. Robert Helpmann as the Child Catcher in *Chitty Chitty Bang Bang* (dir. Ken Hughes, UK, 1968). These film stills reveal Helpmann's distinctive use of his body on camera; while creating the illusion of a 'speeding frenzy' (above), or 'leading the movement' with his eyes (below). Credits: Christophel/ ArenaPAL (above) and Ronald Grant/ ArenaPAL (below)

76. A portrait of Robert Helpmann (1909–1986) in later life (signed print, undated). Photo: Anthony Crickmay © Victoria and Albert Museum, London

Taming, Shaming and Displaying: Robert Helpmann and Katharine Hepburn's trousers, Australia 1955

Elizabeth Schafer

Robert Helpmann's 1964 deeply Australian – but also deeply troubling – ballet, *The Display*, critiques as well as displays dominant contemporary Australian gender stereotypes.[1] It asks tough questions about links between physical prowess, violence and sexuality. It also features a remarkable courtship "display" by a dancer performing the role of a male Superb Lyrebird. *The Display* is dedicated to Helpmann's close friend, Katharine Hepburn, and Helpmann gave two reasons for this: firstly, because during the Old Vic tour of Australia in 1955, starring Helpmann and Hepburn in *The Merchant of Venice*, *Measure for Measure* and *The Taming of the Shrew*, Hepburn insisted that Helpmann take her to look for lyrebirds.[2] They visited Sherbrooke Forest, a temperate rainforest area in the Dandenong Mountain ranges, forty kilometres east of Melbourne and, after some perseverance, Helpmann and Hepburn succeeded in seeing male lyrebirds dancing.[3] Secondly, Helpmann claimed that *The Display* was partly inspired by a dream he had which featured Hepburn standing naked, surrounded by lyrebirds.[4] *The Display*, however, also connects allusively with the 1955 production of *The Taming of the Shrew*; indeed that production might be seen as part of the imaginative archive Helpmann drew on when he choreographed *The Display*. This chapter explores the 1955 Helpmann and Hepburn *Shrew* in detail, and places it alongside the public displays performed by both Helpmann and Hepburn offstage during the 1955 tour; displays which were refracted and inflected by Hepburn's much reported, gender-troubling and iconic trousers.

The critical point of contact between *The Shrew* and *The Display* is the motif of taming by means of violence. In Shakespeare's play, Paduan society hands Katherina over to Petruchio for taming and correction: her shrewish behaviour is deemed unacceptable and she is punished for it. In *The Display* two central characters are subjected to violent punishment because they do not abide by societal norms: The Outsider and The Girl. The ballet is set at a picnic where the men strut around, play Australian Rules Football, drink beer and display their athleticism; meanwhile the women organise the picnic. The Outsider is beaten up by the men after he flirts with the girlfriend of The Leader. The Girl is intrigued and attracted by The Outsider but, raging after the humiliation of his beating, The Outsider later attacks/punishes her.

In a deeply ambiguous piece of choreography, The Girl also encounters the Lyrebird, who looms over her and then enfolds her by means of his splendid tail feathers; this sequence is based on the actual dancing display of male lyrebirds.[5] Kathrine Sorley Walker reads the choreography optimistically: "To the deserted girl, the returning lyrebird symbolised both love and fulfilment."[6] A darker reading of the choreography might see The Outsider as attempting to rape The Girl, with The Male lyrebird then threatening as much as consoling her.

The "taming" sequence in the 1955 Old Vic *Shrew*, in which Helpmann played Petruchio and Hepburn played Katherina, was a largely conventional piece of staging. Directed by Helpmann's long-term partner and Artistic Director of the Old Vic, Michael Benthall, Hepburn's Katherina was energetically, comprehensively and indubitably tamed; there was no question of any complexity in her final "submission" speech, although others playing Katherina had been undercutting, resisting and subverting the speech for a long time.[7] Outside the theatre, the trouser-wearing "Katie" and the dapper "Bobby" were creating a series of rather different displays, offering memorable, if ambiguous, images of performance, concealment, and un-tamedness.

In 1955 the tamer Petruchio was a new "face" for Helpmann. He had played several major Shakespearian roles previously – Hamlet, Shylock and King John[8] – but he was not, at least initially, enthusiastic about playing Petruchio. Helpmann felt "unsuited" to the role and *The Taming of the Shrew* was a play he knew well;[9] he had previously played Gremio, Nicholas and a camp tailor in a 1939 Tyrone Guthrie Old Vic production. The Australian reviewers tended to endorse Helpmann's reservations, suggesting he "lacked manliness, which alone makes [Petruchio] plausible";[10] he "lacked the physique to make the role convincing", and looked "as juvenile as a schoolboy";[11] although his Petruchio was a "witty, purposeful figure", he was "none too happily cast".[12] (See plates 58 and 59) *Shrew* was chosen primarily as a vehicle for Hepburn; *Merchant of Venice* was there to give Helpmann his chance to shine. Helpmann also wanted to take *Hamlet* to Australia but, as Hepburn did not want to play Gertrude, the compromise play was the relatively unknown *Measure For Measure*.[13]

It is possible to put together an impression of the 1955 *Shrew*, as there is a substantial, if scattered, archive.[14] The Bristol Theatre Collection holds the prompt copy, programme, reviews, photographs, and clippings. The Theatre and Performance Collections, V&A Museum, also hold a range of material, much of it collected by the Vic-Wells Association. These sources indicate that Benthall's *Shrew* was firmly in the tradition of the popular, and very farcical, Lynn Fontanne/Alfred Lunt *Shrew* of 1935, a production which traded in exaggerated masculinity, gags, stage 'business' and comic violence. This *Shrew* also inspired Cole Porter's 1948 musical, *Kiss Me, Kate*. Helpmann met Lunt and Fontanne in 1934, and they became good friends, so he would have been aware of their critical and box office success with Shakespeare's play. Helpmann was certainly following in Lunt's footsteps when his Petruchio spanked Katherina (a piece of stage business that becomes critical to the plot line in *Kiss Me, Kate*).[15] However, when he cracked a whip, Helpmann was using traditional comic business that went back to the eighteenth century.[16] Helpmann's lion-tamer Petruchio also made Katherina trot around the stage jumping over small pieces of furniture.[17]

Despite all the broad comedy, Helpmann stated that Hepburn and he "both feel [*Shrew*] should be played more as a romantic comedy and less as a knockabout farce"; however, he saw the first scene between Katherina and Petruchio (2.1.165-313) as "practically an acrobatic dance",[18] and a glimpse of Helpmann's choreography for this sequence can be excavated from the prompt copy and production photographs:

> Petruchio, onstage alone, considers what tactics he should adopt. He practises bowing but decides against this approach. Katherina rushes in, followed by Baptista, and runs straight out again. Baptista pushes Katherina on again (left) and locks the door behind him. Katherina tries the door (right). As Petruchio is looking for her on his left, he doesn't see her. Katherina moves softly to a position behind a chair. Petruchio continues to look right and still doesn't see her. Then he looks left and sees her peering round the end of the chair. He introduces himself and bows to her; she stamps on his foot. She sticks out her tongue at him. He grabs her and sits her on his knee on "Come sit on me" (l.194) and then stands up so she falls. He hits her with his whip handle. At "in sooth you scape not so" (l.230) he overturns the chair, and holds her down over it. She bites him on "very liar" (l.234). On "Why does the world report that Kate doth limp?" (l.242) she kicks him and he grabs her by her foot; she hops in circles around him until her shoe comes off. At "keep you warm" (l.255) she grabs a cloak, rushes at him and puts the cloak over his head. He pulls the cloak from her at "your father hath consented" (l.258) and covers her with it. At "Here comes your father" (l.268) he catches her by the hair and, as the prompt copy specifies, hits "her bottom". Once Baptista, Gremio and Tranio are on, Katherina is kept on the floor, confined under blankets although she kicks out from under them and at "Be patient, gentlemen" (l.291) she manages to put her head out between Petruchio's legs. At "curstest shrew" (l.302) there is "tiger biz". The sequence concludes as Katherina falls in a faint at "Give me thy hand, Kate" (l.303).

At the end of this lively, physically demanding sequence, it might appear that Petruchio has already tamed the prostrate Katherina. Despite Hepburn's maverick, independent, fiery red-head public persona, her Katherina contained not a whiff of feminism; indeed, in the final scene of the play, Hepburn's Katherina, on recommending "true obedience" (5.2.153) to other women, tenderly held Baptista's hand against her cheek. Hepburn was proud of her father-centric interpretation:

> I'm sorry that I never did *The Taming of the Shrew* in New York. It was a good production and I think I had a really good basic idea there: that Kate was devoted to her father and had a hard time transferring her affection to Petruchio.[19]

The narrative being played out onstage in the Old Vic *Shrew* was deeply conservative, but two slightly different versions of Helpmann's "acrobatic dance" between Petruchio and Katherina emerge when the two different sets of publicity photographs documenting the choreography are put side by side.[20]

The first sequence consists of rehearsal shots. Although the aesthetic is rough and ready, suggestive of the hard work of rehearsal, the choreography is clearly well advanced. Crucially, in this sequence Hepburn wears trousers. The second set of photographs probably documents a specially staged photo shoot, but it purports to reflect actual performance, in costume, on set.[21] The images I have selected for reproduction here (See plates 56 and 57) reflect the comic violence of the "acrobatic dance" but, to me, the taming appears more complete in the costumed photograph than in the rehearsal photograph, even though there is no question who is in control in either sequence: Helpmann's Petruchio.

In the rehearsal photograph (See plate 56), Hepburn looks ready for action and, despite Helpmann's position of dominance, he appears to be having to put effort into achieving this dominance, something suggested particularly in the tension in his face. The potential for a relatively equal fight is suggested by Hepburn's practical clothes and sensible shoes, which are very similar to Helpmann's attire. Hepburn's shoes look as if they could administer a hefty kick the moment she has a chance. Meanwhile Helpmann's flying medallion looks as if it might damage the wearer. The photographs are very unflattering to Hepburn in terms of conventional feminine good looks and she is choosing to flout convention, displaying herself as a down-to-earth tomboy rather than a Hollywood star. She is shown working hard, not caring what she looks like, and being a good sport, but the flailing legs look dangerous. There is a strong sense of movement, energy and a suggestion that the tables could turn.

Kathrine Sorley Walker describes the "fast, gymnastic and tightly choreographed domestic fight" as "the talking point" of the production and the rehearsal photographs, which were used for advance publicity, as "delightful".[22] But, for me, the roughness, the blurring, the obscuring of Hepburn's face, alongside the tension in the muscles of Helpmann's face, all allow the untamed Katharine Hepburn to modify the tamedness of Katherina. By contrast, in the costumed photographs representing the actual performance, Katherina is tamed by her costume as much as by Petruchio. (See plate 57) Katherina is handicapped by her cumbersome, hyper-feminine, flouncy gown which not only conceals the kicking legs, making her appear less dangerous, but also makes effective kicking impossible. Katherina's dainty slippers also contrast starkly with Petruchio's hefty boots. While most of what is visible of Katherina during the "acrobatic dance" is her disabling dress, Petruchio is unencumbered, more dignified, strategic. Petruchio is a controlling lion/shrew-tamer; by contrast, Katherina is floundering in feminine finery. Later, at the end of the wedding scene (3.2.), yet another sumptuous frock, Katherina's bridal dress, quite literally becomes the cause of her downfall; Petruchio catches Katherina in her dress-train, before wrapping her up in it, and dragging her across the stage. Petruchio then "hoists Kate on his shoulder and carries her off", cave-man style.[23]

The displays by Helpmann and Hepburn performed in the two sequences of publicity photographs for *The Taming of the Shrew* also worked alongside the displays performed in the offstage photo-calls. In order to explore these displays it is important to remember the clichés and gender stereotypes in circulation in 1955, particularly in relation to Hepburn's enthusiasm for wearing trousers at almost every public event. Even though during both World Wars, many women had worn trousers and overalls in factories, Hepburn – along with Marlene Dietrich – was notorious for her trouser wearing.[24] Although mainstream Australia then, as now, was obsessed with sport, and women routinely wore trousers for horse riding, cycling and golf, Hepburn's trousers garnered extensive press coverage. It was news if Hepburn wore trousers and it was news if she did not; while one newspaper noted that Hepburn was "in slacks as usual",[25] another carried the headline "Katie in a Dress!"[26] Hepburn explained that she wore "slacks and sweater" because "comfort is the only thing that counts with me",[27] and her view was that a suit is "more comfortable than a dress".[28] Nevertheless, loaded language was used to discuss her attire; Hepburn's suits were "mannish",[29] "man-tailored",[30] and of "mannish cut";[31] one reporter also commented that Hepburn wore "what look like men's shoes".[32] This masculinised display suited Hepburn's persona as an independent, sporty woman who didn't stick to the rules; for some, it raised questions about her sexuality.[33]

Andrew Britton devotes a whole chapter of his study of Hepburn to "Gender and Bisexuality", and attributes Hepburn's significance to the "contradiction" she is able to generate "within narrative structures that are committed overall to the reaffirmation of bourgeois-patriarchal norms".[34] I would argue that Hepburn generated such contradictions on the 1955 tour, and ultimately that her actual sexuality was irrelevant; what was important was that questions were asked – and continue to be asked – around her behaviour, or displays, onstage, on film, and in the photo calls. But even when viewed through the lens of normative heterosexuality, Hepburn, unlike the tamed Katherina Minola of Shakespeare's play, might be imagined to be the sort of woman who would wear the metaphorical trousers in any relationship. This is important because of the constant speculation during the 1955 tour about Hepburn's relationship with Helpmann. Onstage, Helpmann's Petruchio, despite his lack of what the Australian press considered to be 'manliness', tamed Hepburn's Katherina totally and flamboyantly. Offstage Hepburn, the untamed shrew, was frequently constructed as a potential wife for Helpmann. (See plate 60)

Hepburn's reputation for shrewishness was partly the result of a series of film roles in which she played a feisty woman who, the films intimate, needs to be tamed by a man such as Cary Grant's Dexter Haven in the 1940 classic, *The Philadelphia Story*, who tames Hepburn's Tracy Lord.[35] By 1955 Hepburn had reached a stage in her film career where she often played an older spinster figure: recent films included *Adam's Rib* (1949), *The African Queen* (1951), *Pat and Mike* (1952) and *Summertime* (1955), released during the Old Vic tour. These "spinster roles" intersected with the unmarried, and potentially unmarriageable, aspect of Hepburn's rather mature Katherina. But, in addition, Hepburn had a reputation for behaving shrewishly towards photographers and reporters who annoyed her, and she was outspoken on issues she was passionate about; indeed the tour of Australia came at a time when Hepburn's film career was suffering because of the House for Un-American Activities Committee's interest in her, on account of her liberal politics. These politics were discussed in a profile of Hepburn by James Lyell, exploring Hepburn's unconventionally feminist background: her mother was "one of America's earliest suffragettes".[36] Meanwhile "her father scandalised his generation by leading crusades for birth control and social hygiene". The reader was left to infer that it was no wonder that the daughter of such parents, as a girl, was "one of the toughest tomboys in her district" who "cropped her hair short, to prevent the boys getting a grip on it". The article headline: "Katie tames the critics", with its explicit play on Hepburn's performance as Katherina, also hints that she might present a challenge if any man – Helpmann being the likeliest candidate – were brave enough to consider marrying her.

The bejewelled Helpmann, who was accompanying the betrousered Hepburn, was returning to his native Australia after an absence of over twenty years. Despite the fact that it was reported that "In England Helpmann shares his pretty Knightsbridge house with another English bachelor, Michael Benthall, a director of the Old Vic",[37] the speculation about Helpmann, Hepburn and marriage was considerable. In Sydney, Helpmann commented: "I have been asked three times since I arrived [...] here several hours ago, whether I am going to marry Kate. Could be. Could be".[38] Helpmann stated he was touring Australia with "the one woman I can ever imagine being married to",[39] but this assertion needs to be contextualised: the Old Vic Company was touring an Australia where, under the Prime Ministership of Robert Menzies, entrenched conservatism ruled. It was during 1955, whilst on tour playing Orsino in *Twelfth Night*, that Barry Humphries first developed the character of Mrs Edna Everage, and began using her to satirise the prejudices of contemporary suburban Australia. Although it took nearly two decades for Edna to evolve into the spectacular, opinionated megastar she later became, it is easy to imagine what Edna, in 1955, would have had to say about Hepburn's trousers.

Furthermore, 1955 was a watershed year in Australia, theatrically speaking. In October, overlapping with the Old Vic tour, which began in Sydney on 14 May and concluded in Perth 12 November, expatriate star actress, Judith Anderson (like Helpmann, an Adelaide-born star returning home), began touring Australia in a production of *Medea*.[40] But more indicative of the faultlines that were beginning to appear in Menzies' Australia was the première of Ray Lawler's *The Summer of the Seventeenth Doll* on 28 November 1955, two weeks after the end of the Old Vic tour. *The Doll* realistically portrays working class, inner city, Melbourne life and, unconventionally for the time, allows its gutsy heroine, Olive, to walk away from a seventeen-year relationship with the cane-cutter, Roo, when he proposes marriage. *The Doll* predates Britain's equivalent play, John Osborne's *Look Back in Anger* (1956), and anticipates that play's angry realism, if not its more reactionary gender politics:[41] in *The Doll* it is the barmaid Olive who becomes angry when she is asked to settle down and become a wife. Olive destroys the collection of dolls that decorate her home, and which symbolise her relationship with Roo, who has bought her a new doll every year they have been together. The dolls are all *kewpie* dolls on a stick, with huge, brightly coloured *tulle* skirts, which in 1950s Australia were given out as prizes at Carnivals and events like the Melbourne Royal Show.[42] In Australia they are associated with a day out at the fair but also, because of the *tulle*, they evoke the world of ballet. Olive smashes the dolls to pieces in her fury and anguish at being asked to become a wife. At the end of *The Summer of the Seventeenth Doll* Olive is an untamed shrew, refusing to compromise on her ideas of happiness.

The spectacular success of *The Doll* – which Laurence Olivier brought to the UK in 1957, and which was made into a film in 1959 – displayed an Australia that had not been seen in mainstream theatre before: it was gritty and realistic in its treatment of working-class, inner-city life. Compared with *The Summer of the Seventeenth Doll*, Michael Benthall's *The Taming of the Shrew* must have seemed stylised, busy and slightly camp. Indeed the realistic portrayal of urban working life portrayed in *The Doll* connects more with the 1944 Benthall/Helpmann collaboration on *Miracle in the Gorbals*, with its crowd of realistically characterised and individualised slum dwellers, than with the 1955 Old Vic Shakespearean revivals. But Helpmann, Benthall and Hepburn connect with Lawler's heroine, Olive, in refusing to do what society expected and get married.

The Taming of the Shrew was generally reviewed positively, and many appreciated the "beauty of the staging and costume" and "the design of movement".[43] Hepburn got her best reviews of the tour for *Shrew*, but there were complaints about Benthall's interventionist approach. [44] One commented: "if a conductor took as many liberties with a score as Michael Benthall did with *The Taming of the Shrew* there would be a roar from the musical pundits";[45] another complained that "there was vastly too much distracting business in the first half".[46] Benthall's staging priorities are made clear in a detailed report in the *Sydney Herald* on the Old Vic Company in rehearsal: Hepburn suggests a staging change to Benthall, "Because it is pretty isn't it?". Benthall responds "Lovely, charming," and the change is accepted. A further alteration is then rejected by Benthall as "Not as nice".[47] Prioritising loveliness and charm in *The Shrew* predictably resulted in the cutting of Shakespeare's opening scenes, which feature the drunken tinker, Christopher Sly. After being thrown out of a tavern, Sly is then made the subject of an elaborate jest and deceived into believing he is a lord watching a play set in Padua. Shakespeare's play opens in a realistic and contemporary Warwickshire; Benthall's production went straight to a Candyfloss version of Padua, where Katherina and Bianca made their first entrance in exotic sedan chairs.

Helpmann's published views on producing Shakespeare aligned with Benthall's in stressing the composition of stage pictures. In an essay written in 1938, Helpmann comments:

> I believe that in the production of Shakespeare the collaboration of a producer and a choreographer would have very interesting results.[48]

He adds that "movements, grouping and climaxes" should be "produced on some of the principles generally thought applicable only to choreography". Choreography involving "movements, grouping and climaxes" does not always produce prettiness and, as in *Miracle in the Gorbals*, can result in something challenging and cutting-edge. However, the term "choreography" was certainly used pejoratively in the most antagonistic review that the Old Vic Company received on the 1955 Australian tour; the *Argus* reviewer described *The Merchant of Venice* as "one of the most devastatingly bad productions I have ever seen", as too "pretty" and as reducing the text to "a mere scenario for balletic choreography".[49] By contrast in 1954, in a "Personality of the month" profile in *Plays and Players*, Benthall was identified as a "fine manipulator of actors", who "is able to compose compelling groups, placing his actors in just the right place at the right moment. He brings pageantry, colour and pace to every play he undertakes." But *Plays and Players* did have doubts about Benthall's ability to handle verse:

> The one quality he has so far lacked is the feeling for poetry which makes a Shakespearian production really memorable. The assets of colour, movement, design and speed are incidental. They do not compensate for the glory of the verse. [50]

Australian reviewers also had doubts about the verse speaking, although this was often linked to audibility; the Company were playing very large theatres compared with the relatively compact Old Vic.

Despite the *Argus*' denunciation of *The Merchant of Venice*, in general, Helpmann's Shylock was admired and it was a role he had great success with: Helpmann had played Shylock under Benthall's direction at Stratford in 1948; later he returned to the role at the Old Vic in London in 1956-7; and he chose to be painted as Shylock by James William Govett in 1966.[51] In 1955 *Plays and Players* thought Helpmann's interpretation was "complex and subtle".[52] The Australian press judged Helpmann's performance to be "wonderfully impressive", evoking "a proud man of distinguished bearing" who "talks with a high-pitched lisp that throbs with racial pride";[53] a Shylock "raw with racial pride, with contempt for the new-come Venice".[54] (See plate 62) In May the Melbourne-based *Age* offered its readers – who had to wait until August before they got a chance to see the production – a preview by means of a digest of the Sydney reviews:[55] "Helpmannn gives Shylock a towering dignity and passion"; "Helpmann stole the show"; "He was an unorthodox and magnificent Shylock". Meanwhile the *Daily Mirror* reported on Helpmannn's make-up and costume – which took 105 minutes to get ready – publishing photographs that took the reader step by step through the process.[56] (See plate 61) There were some who objected to the performance's use of stereotype, the "vots and vys of the music-hall Jew", which were dropped in the court scene.[57]

Helpmann's use of an accent and a lisp in *Merchant* helped indicate that "Shylock would always be an alien in Venice."[58] Shylock is also a character who is tamed: thwarted, designated socially unacceptable, and made to conform to the dominant group's rules, something which might connect forward to *The Display*, with its character of the chastised Outsider. But the recurring motif of the alien (or outsider) in Helpmann's work also links with one of the most frequently related anecdotes about his life in Australia: the humiliation at Bondi Beach. This incident identified Helpmann as an outsider in Australian society, one who was punished and made to look ridiculous because of his deviation from the dominant norm. Elizabeth Salter, Helpmann's "authorised" biographer, who often narrates incidents as if quoting directly from Helpmann himself, relates the episode in detail: once when the youthful but "resplendent" Helpmann (with plucked eyebrows, and wearing red nail varnish, loose, baggy trousers, or Oxford bags, with a "pink shirt and purple tie") was walking along the beach at Bondi, in the company of Esmé Cannon, a girl Helpmann "imagined himself to be in love with", he was picked up and dumped in the sea by a group of lifeguards. Salter claims after this ignominy:

> The rage that boiled within him then took a lifetime to disperse. He had worn the bright plumes of the showman and been thrown into the ocean. He knew that he must show his prosaic countrymen that they could not cut him down to size [...]. He must leave Australia and make his name abroad.[59]

As Salter's biography was published in 1978, her account of the anecdote had travelled a long way from its originating moment (circa 1929-30) in this retelling, but presumably Helpmann was happy with and "authorised" Salter's rendition. The crucial point is that, for Salter, the punishment of Helpmann (in effect for his "display") directly resulted in him leaving Australia.

Anna Bemrose relates the Bondi anecdote to Helpmann's ability to "draw attention to himself through comportment and/or dress whether on or off the stage",[60] and in the 1969 retelling from which she is quoting, Helpmann identified the item of clothing that enraged the lifeguards as "a pair of suede shoes". Bemrose also locates the incident as taking place when Helpmann was fifteen, that is, 1924, rather than Salter's "not long before his departure" from Australia (he left for Europe in December 1932).[61] In yet another account by Bill Akers, the incendiary item of clothing is identified as "plus fours". Michelle Potter notes that Akers:

> who created the dappled lighting for [*The Display*], recalled in an oral history

interview in 2002 that as a youth Helpmann was thrown into the sea at Bondi by a gang who thought his clothing was "sissy". He was, according to Akers, wearing plus fours at the time. Akers suggested that *The Display* reflected Helpmann's feeling that he had always been an outsider in society.[62]

The critical point here is not what happened and when, but the fact that this anecdote is told over and over again. Jacky Bratton has encouraged theatre historians to acknowledge the cultural work that theatrical anecdotes perform, as there is "a world of historical meaning in what they say", whether or not there is "tangible proof" of an anecdote's "truth".[63] The Bondi anecdote, in its tellings, retellings and variations, says much about the policing of gender boundaries, gender display and violence towards those who do not conform. And it certainly seems significant that one of the first things Helpmann did on arriving back in Australia on 5 May 1955, after more than twenty years away, was to star in a photo-call at Bondi, along with Hepburn and Benthall.[64] (See plate 54) Salter discerns "an intensely personal fulfilment" in a photograph of "Benthall, Hepburn and Helpmann, walking along Bondi Beach, beside that same sea in which, not long before his departure, he had been so ignominiously ducked".[65] But Helpmann's very public return to Bondi, accompanied by a press entourage, with the betrousered Hepburn on his arm and with his partner, Benthall, by his side, is an image of some complexity. One reading might see the lifeguards' attempted taming of Helpmann for his predilection for unorthodox display as a failure: Helpmann was back again displaying unconventionally at Bondi. In another sense, the display offered to the press at Bondi might be seen as a taming because Helpmann, instead of inspiring outrage in lifeguards, was performing, and being read rather conventionally as a potential husband for Hepburn.

In *The Display* Helpmann appears to be excoriating an Australian society that – like the Bondi lifeguards – preferred its men to be exclusively macho, heterosexual and not "outside" the norm. However, the display of the flamboyantly feathered, dancing male Superb Lyrebird also offers a particularly multivalent image in relation to the flamboyant and multi-talented Helpmann; something wittily picked up in the title of Tyler Coppin's one-man play about Helpmann, *The Lyrebird: Tales of Helpmann*.[66] The lyrebird not only clears its own space in the forest, and creates a stage to perform on, but it is an expert at mimicry, and can "pass" aurally as chainsaws and car alarms as well as kookaburras. "Passing" describes a performance by a member of a particular group – in terms of, for example, ethnicity, gender, sexuality – which is successful in convincing those around him or her that he or she belongs to another group. Helpmann, even when standing alongside Benthall, "passed" as a potential husband for Hepburn: at the photo-call at Bondi, at the lavish, and extensively reported, Old Vic first night galas, and at a host of glittering social events.

Helpmann's Petruchio was also a kind of "passing", as the role he originally wanted to play in *The Shrew* was Katherina. In 1947, eight years before the Old Vic tour, Michael Benthall proposed to Barry Jackson, who was then running the Shakespeare Memorial Theatre at Stratford, that Benthall should direct an all-male production of *The Taming of the Shrew*, starring Helpmann as Katherina.[67] *Variety* reported that the proposal was rejected as "decadent"[68] (a loaded description in 1947), and Sally Beauman's history of the Royal Shakespeare Company claims one reason that Jackson was ousted from Stratford, after setting out to make it "another Salzburg", is because Jackson did not reject this proposal quickly enough.[69] Stratford-upon-Avon could be as conservative as Bondi.

One of Helpmann's signature Shakespearian roles can also be constructed as including a taming dynamic: Oberon, the Fairy King, in *A Midsummer Night's Dream*.[70] Oberon tames his wife Titania and makes her do his bidding – specifically to yield up her beloved Indian boy – after humiliating her as comprehensively as Petruchio ever humiliates Katherina. Oberon was Helpmann's crucial ballet-to-acting crossover role, and Salter claims that Helpmann actually secured the role of Oberon to Vivien Leigh's Titania, in the 1937 Old Vic production of *The Dream*, despite the fact that Leigh's then lover, Laurence Olivier, wanted the part.[71] Given that the 1937 *Dream* was retro Victorian, gauzy and balletic, Helpmann was probably better suited to the production than the less obviously sexually ambiguous Olivier. Helpmann's appearance as Oberon in terms of make-up and costume was exotic, otherworldly and not traditionally masculine; he was not conventionally sexualised in the way that Vivien Leigh as Titania clearly *was*. (See plates 10 and 11) Helpmann returned to Oberon in Purcell's version of the play, *The Fairy Queen*, at Covent Garden in 1946, with Margaret Rawlings as his Titania; Helpmann also reprised Shakespeare's Oberon in 1954, in a production directed by Michael Benthall, with Moira Shearer as Titania, a production which owed something of its marketability on Broadway to the success of Helpmann and Shearer in the 1948 film of *The Red Shoes*.[72] Stills and publicity shots indicate that, across all three productions, Helpmann's Oberons were darkly ominous, suggestive of a decorated insect or bird. Or, perhaps, of "The Spider and the Fly": the dance that Salter claims "triggered [Helpmann's] move to London", which featured a spider menacing its victim.[73] But the glittering, other-than-human appearance of Helpmann's Oberon also connects again with the role of The Male/Superb Lyrebird in *The Display*; and, like Oberon, The Male inhabits a sylvan realm, which is invaded by human beings who need to learn important lessons from their visit to the green world of the forest.

In 2001, Live Performance Australia inaugurated an annual award ceremony that confers the equivalent of the London Olivier or the New York Tony Awards. The awards are called "The Helpmanns".[74] While it is entirely appropriate that the awards should be named after an Australian who reached the heights of not one but several performing arts disciplines – dancing, acting, choreography, directing – it is also important to keep in mind the complexity of Helpmann's relationship with his homeland. A "Helpmann" award invokes virtuosity, excellence, extraordinary and dazzling talent. But a "Helpmann" might also suggest a display in public that is effective, entertaining and a magnificent artifice. For me, this is emblematised by the multivalent image of Katharine Hepburn, in trousers, as featured in the press coverage of the 1955 Old Vic tour and, rather more dynamically, as featured, in the rehearsal photographs of *The Taming of the Shrew*: here, Hepburn's betrousered Katherina performs being tamed by the Petruchio of Robert Helpmann, the man who would have preferred to play Katherina. I am not claiming that the creative network of "tamings", "displays" and "outsiders" I have traced here constitute direct source material for *The Display*; but they must, especially the 1955 Old Vic *Shrew*, have contributed to the imaginative archive that Helpmann drew on when he choreographed *The Display*. As a lyrebird picks out shells, leaves, flowers, stones, feathers and anything that catches its eye to decorate its nest, so Helpmann could return to and pick out gems from the tamings, shamings and displays he had choreographed and performed, in Shakespeare and in real life, across many years.

Endnotes

1   First performed by the Australian Ballet in 1964, *The Display* came to Scotland in 1965 for the Commonwealth Arts Festival. It was revived by the Australian Ballet in 2012.

2   The tour was very profitable. The *Daily Telegraph* (21 November 1955) reports profits of £24,000. The *Times* (26 November 1955) puts the profit at £20,000.

3   Elizabeth Salter quotes Helpmann as stating improbably: "We had to wait in our sleeping bags for ten long nights before we saw them." See Elizabeth Salter, *Helpmann: The authorised biography of Sir Robert Helpmann, CBE*, with a foreword by Katharine Hepburn (Sydney: Angus and Robertson, 1978), pp.182-3.

4   Publicity for the 2012 revival of the ballet by the Australian Ballet featured this anecdote. See Michelle Potter, 'Robert Helpmann's Ballet "The Display"'http://michellepotter.org/articles/robert-helpmanns-ballet-the-display (accessed 18 December 2013).

5   The Lyrebird role is simply called "The Male". Potter, 'Robert Helpmann's Ballet "The Display"', records that Helpmann "included a note in a program for *The Display* in which he maintained that the movements he eventually choreographed for the character of the lyrebird in his ballet were those 'learned after many hours of watching this beautiful creature'".

6   Kathrine Sorley Walker in *Robert Helpmann, A Rare Sense of Theatre* (Alton: Dance Press, 2009) p.125.

7   Mary Pickford popularised the notion of subverting Katherina's submission when she winked before delivering her final speech in Sam Taylor's 1929 film of *The Taming of the Shrew*.

8   See Richard Cave's essay for more on Helpmann's Shakespearean roles, pp. 66-86.

9   See Anna Bemrose, *Robert Helpmann, a Servant of Art* (St Lucia: University of Queensland Press, 2008) p. 98.

10   Sydney *Sun* 25 May 1955.

11   *ABC Weekly* 11 June 1955.

12   *Truth* 25 May 1955.

13   Bemrose, pp. 96-8 details the process by which the choice of plays was negotiated. The other play suggested was the "Shaw", that is, *The Millionairess* which in 1952, directed by Benthall, had been a success for Hepburn, but less of a success for Helpmann. (See plate 55, which juxtaposes a vigorously physical Hepburn with a monumentally still Helpmann) As late as 31 December 1954, the *Sunday Telegraph* was reporting *Merchant* and *Shrew* as definites but the third play was yet to be decided. It was the end of January before the *Herald* (26 January 1955) confirmed the repertoire. The compromise play, *Measure for Measure*, was the least favourably reviewed of the tour.

14   The National Library of Australia also have substantial Helpmann holdings.

15   See Sorley Walker p.18 and Salter, p.59-61 for Helpmann's friendship with

Lunt and Fontanne.

16   Whip-cracking Petruchios originated with J.P. Kemble. See Elizabeth Schafer (ed.), *The Taming of the Shrew: Shakespeare in Production* (Cambridge: Cambridge University Press, 2002) p.11.

17   *Bulletin* 1 June 1955.

18   *Sydney Herald* 4 May 1955.

19   Katharine Hepburn, *Me: Stories of My Life* (London: Random House, 1991), p.270.

20   The rehearsal photographs were taken in England and appeared in the *Sun* (21 and 24 March 1955) and the *Mirror* (24 March 1955). Four are reproduced by Bemrose (p.104).

21   Barbara Hodgdon draws attention to different fashions in theatre photography in "Photography, Theater, Mnemonics; or, Thirteen Ways of looking at a Still" in W.B.Worthern with Peter Holland (eds), *Theorizing Practice: Redefining Theatre History*, (Basingstoke & New York: Palgrave MacMillan, 2003), pp. 88-119. In 1955 using rehearsal photographs for publicity was not as usual as it is now.

22   Kathrine Sorley Walker, *Robert Helpmann*, p.111.

23   Prompt copy, Bristol Theatre Collection. This traditional business was, presumably, relatively easy for Helpmann, accustomed as he was to lifting his dancing partners.

24   British *Vogue* featured women's trousers on a cover for the first time on 17 May 1939.

25   *Adelaide News* 11 March 1955.

26   Sydney *Sun* 9 May 1955.

27   *Woman's Day and Home* 21 March 1955.

28   *Sydney Herald* 14 May 1955.

29   *Australian Woman's Weekly* 4 May 1955.

30   *Argus* 12 August 1955.

31   *Age* 12 August 1955.

32   *Herald* 12 August 1955.

33   Andrew Britton, *Katharine Hepburn: Star as Feminist* (London: Studio Vista, 1995) pp.19-20. Hepburn's predilection for masculine attire has also been linked to the trauma she experienced when, as a young teenager, she discovered her brother hanged.

34   Ibid, p.7.

35   Ibid. pp. 51-3. Britton comments on how some of these tamings – for example, the containment of Hepburn's Jo, in Cukor's *Little Women*, by marriage to Professsor Bhaer (p. 51-3) – problematise as much as resolve matters.

36   James Lyell, "Katie Tames the Critics" *Woman's Day and Home* 21 March 1955. Technically, Hepburn's mother was a suffragist rather than suffragette.

37   *Listener In* 14 May 1955.

38   *Sydney Herald* 14 May 1955. *The Australasian Post* (26 May 1955) reported it as "Four times".

39   Salter, p.183. Photographs of a joyous reunion between Hepburn and

Helpmann appeared in some newspapers in support of such suggestions and Salter reproduces one such photograph (p.176).

40   Today Anderson is mostly remembered for her Mrs Danvers in Alfred Hitchcock's 1940s film *Rebecca*. She was reprising Medea, which she had played before in 1947 under the direction of John Gielgud. For the Australian tour see http://www.ausstage.edu.au/pages/browse/#, (accessed 9 January 2014).

41   *Look Back in Anger* and its kitchen sink heralded a fashion in the 1950s for "angry young men" characters like the play's lead role, Jimmy Porter. *The Doll* is more working class than *Look Back in Anger* but just as "kitchen sink" in its realism.

42   A sense of how iconic *kewpie* dolls were, and still are, in Australia can be gauged from their massed presence, in giant form, as part of the closing ceremony of the Sydney Olympic Games. The derivation of the word "kewpie" is from "Cupid".

43   *Advocate* 29 September 1955.

44   Before the Old Vic tour, Hepburn had only ever performed in one Shakespeare: as Rosalind in 1950 in 145 performances of Benthall's Broadway production of *As You Like It*.

45   *ABC Weekly* 11 June 1955.

46   *Farrago* 13 September 1955.

47   *Sydney Herald*, 4 May 1955.

48   Robert Helpmann, "Shakespeare and the Ballet", *The Old Vic and Sadler's Wells Magazine* January 1938 reproduced in this volume, p. 2.

49   *Argus* 15 August 1955.

50   *Plays and Players* September 1954.

51   For more on this production, see Penny Gay's Introduction to her Bell Shakespeare edition of *The Merchant of Venice* (Sydney: Science Press, 1995), pp.57-8.

52   *Plays and Players* August 1955.

53   *Sydney Morning Herald* 16 May 1955.

54   *Daily Telegraph* 15 May 1955.

55   *Age* 16 May 1955.

56   *Daily Mirror* 16 May 1955.

57   *ABC Weekly* 28 May 1955.

58   *Farrago* 13 September 1955.

59   *Helpmann: The authorised biography*, p.40.

60   *Robert Helpmann, a Servant of Art*, p.14.

61   *Helpmann: The authorised biography*, p.177.

62   http://michellepotter.org/articles/robert-helpmanns-ballet-the-display (accessed 10 January 2014).

63   Jacky Bratton, *New Readings in Theatre History* (Cambridge: Cambridge University Press, 2003), p.131.

64   The *Adelaide News* (11 May 1955) crops Benthall out of the picture leaving Hepburn and Helpmann arm in arm; the *Sun* (9 May 1955) keeps Benthall in.

65   *Helpmann: The authorised biography*, p.177.

66 *Lyrebird* originated in 1995 and played in London in July 2000. Frank Van Straten records that Coppin, in the character of Helpmann, opened the 2001 Helpmann Awards ceremony. https://liveperformance.com.au/halloffame/roberthelpmann1.html (accessed 10 January 2014).

67 Helpmann's interest in non-masculine and travesty roles began as a child (Bemrose, p.11). He had had ongoing success as a Stepsister in Ashton's *Cinderella* (1948). (See plates 14, 15 and 73)

68 *Variety* 5 November 1947.

69 Sally Beauman, *The Royal Shakespeare Company: a History of Ten Decades* (Oxford: Oxford University Press, 1982) p.189.

70 *A Midsummer Night's Dream* also provided Helpmann with his first professional appearance, at the age of six, when he appeared as a child fairy in Adelaide.

71 *Helpmann: The authorised biography*, p.84.

72 For the 1937-38 production the choreography was by Ninette de Valois (Salter, p.84). Helpmann choreographed for the Purcell and the 1954 *Dream*.

73 *Helpmann: The authorised biography*, p.44.

74 https://liveperformance.com.au/halloffame/roberthelpmann1.html (accessed 8 February 2014).

Introduction to DVD Track 6: filmed recollections of Robert Helpmann and the Australian Ballet. Maina Gielgud interviewed by Rupert Christiansen

Richard Allen Cave

In this further interview with Rupert Christiansen, recorded on 30 September 2013, Maina Gielgud recalls her time as Artistic Director of The Australian Ballet (1983-1997), where one of her predecessors had been Robert Helpmann. This was a period in which she got to know him closely, building on the friendship established during their working together on *Steps, Notes and Squeaks* during the late 1970s. She discusses the qualities of Helpmann's partnership with Peggy van Praagh as Joint Artistic-Directors of The Australian Ballet, carefully differentiating their approaches to coaching the Company and to the art of choreography. Gielgud then speaks first of Helpmann's direction of The Australian Ballet as a time when he worked to give the dancers an identity at home and abroad; and secondly of her own time as Artistic Director, when one of the earliest expectations of her was that she oversee a revival and re-staging of Helpmann's *The Display* (1964). The choreography she admired for its dynamism rather than its technical originality; for its power to challenge audiences by taking them beyond their comfort zone and making them think about social issues, values and prejudices. She affirms that it was because of Helpmann's involvement with the Company that Ninette de Valois gave them the right to stage her enduring 1937 ballet, *Checkmate*. Its presence in the Company's repertory enabled them to bring back Helpmann to dance his created role of the Red King whenever a revival was planned. It was to be the last stage role Helpmann performed before his death. The particular revival of *Checkmate* ran from 6-24 May 1986; Helpmann died on 28 September. Maina Gielgud ends by celebrating Helpmann's exemplary commitment as a performer by outlining his lengthy preparation, where the stages of his making-up and donning of his costume were a kind of ritual in which he steadily took complete possession of the role.

Elektra: Helpmann uninhibited

Michelle Potter

"The trouble is that Helpmann can be too uninhibited."[1]

Robert Helpmann is often lauded for the theatricality that lay behind his ballets, rather than for his choreography. *Elektra*, created for The Royal Ballet and given its première performance at Covent Garden on 26 March 1963, is no exception. It was Helpmann's first ballet since his *Adam Zero* of 1946 and, writing for the influential (now-defunct) Sydney-based magazine, *The Bulletin*, shortly after *Elektra*'s London première, Craig Dodd analysed what he saw as a basic feature of *Elektra*:

> Like his ballets of sixteen and more years ago [Helpmann] uses his innate theatricality to cover up deficiencies in his ability to produce first class dances and invariably is able to do it so well that the result is such a theatrical experience as to make it a blessing rather than a curse.[2]

Helpmann's *Elektra*, with a commissioned score from Malcolm Arnold and designs by Australian artist Arthur Boyd, was a distillation of the Greek myth in which Elektra vengefully muses on her father's murder by her mother, Klytemnestra,[3] and her mother's lover, Aegisthus. She is then party to the killing of her mother and her mother's lover by Orestes, her brother. It was initially a very short work, around fifteen minutes long, and was danced by Nadia Nerina as Elektra, David Blair as Orestes, Monica Mason as Klytemnestra and Derek Rencher as Aegisthus, with a supporting cast of eight male dancers as Erinyes (Avengers of the Dead), or Furies as they were often later called. Despite the wild and prolonged applause that, according to all reports, greeted the opening night performance, *Elektra* was scathingly reviewed by critics in the United Kingdom, with its choreographic language and its blatant eroticism being lambasted:

> The most exciting moments are the music-hall tricks where [Nerina] is thrown into the air and caught by the avengers, but little actual dancing is involved. Even David Blair as Orestes is given little to do other than a few turns and some symbolic axe swinging. The avengers, unlike a Greek Chorus, intrude rather than blend into the action and much of their movement is meaningless and reminiscent of the gymnasium.[4]

[Nerina] performs a modest amount of toe dancing, strongly accented with crotch-flings which will not look unfamiliar to students of Roland Petit. [5]

> His aim is well below the belt, and his ammunition – the well-tried amalgam of blood and sex – is not compounded with much originality. It delighted the audience at Covent Garden as it delights crowds in Grand Guignol, Hammer Films or in the Biblical best-sellers from Hollywood. [6]

A few respected critics were less withering in their comments. Richard Buckle, for example, could see some value in the work and suggested it was "tremendously effective" and that Helpmann had not lost "his blazing sense of theatre". [7] Kathrine Sorley Walker, one of Helpmann's many biographers and a long-time supporter of his work, believed that *Elektra* was choreographically ahead of its time, and "a production that must be considered a success". [8] Others continued the attack:

> There is no point in beating about the bush. Robert Helpmann's new ballet – his first for more than 15 years – is the most ludicrous and the most tasteless work I have ever seen at Covent Garden. More than that, it is among the most appalling things I have ever seen anywhere. [9]

The Royal Ballet included *Elektra* in its repertoire for its North American tour, which began in April 1963, but it was a short-lived production for the Company, which apparently saw little reason to perform it again. As Company Board minutes from the Australian Ballet Foundation indicate, The Royal Ballet gifted *Elektra* to the Australian Ballet, most likely in 1965. [10] It was given its Australian Ballet première at the Adelaide Festival of Arts on 15 March 1966 as the third Helpmann ballet to enter the Company's repertoire. Helpmann's first creation for the Australian Ballet had been *The Display*, a ballet that he developed following an excursion with Katharine Hepburn in 1955 to Sherbrooke Forest in the Dandenong Ranges, where they watched the mating dance of the Australian lyrebird. The experience provided Helpmann with his inspiration for *The Display*. The ballet, which premièred in 1964, was quickly followed in 1965 by the Japanese-inspired *Yugen*.

The year 1965 was a momentous one for the Australian Ballet. Not only did it acquire a second Helpmann ballet but, in that year, Helpmann also became its co-artistic director, joining founding director Peggy van Praagh at the helm of the relatively new Company (it had given its first performance in November 1962). The importance of "strengthening the Company image by using Helpmann's name" was stressed by the Australian Ballet's administrator at the time, Geoffrey Ingram. [11] In fact, the potential value of the Helpmann name to the Company had been under discussion at Australian Ballet management meetings over several months in 1964 and 1965. [12]

The need for a boost to the Australian Ballet's image was partly a result of the dire financial straits in which the Company found itself in its early years; the first full year of its operation, 1963, was especially difficult. A long tour to New Zealand was planned to take place between June and August 1963 but was curtailed after just six weeks as a result of a series of poor houses and resulting financial losses. Although denied by Company management, there was a real threat, reported in the Australian and New Zealand press, that the Company's government subsidy would be withdrawn as a result of poor box-office takings recorded both during and before the New Zealand tour. Memos held in the archival records of the Australian Elizabethan Theatre Trust, the organisation that provided financial and institutional backing for the Company in its early years, note that losses on the seasons in Australia prior to the New Zealand tour were serious. It was such a grim situation, the Trust believed, that it called for a radical revision of plans, even perhaps an abandonment of the idea of a permanent Australian ballet company.[13] The drawcard of the Helpmann name was desperately needed.

Helpmann's appointment was also skilfully timed to coincide with the Australian Ballet's 1965–1966 tour to the Commonwealth Arts Festival and beyond, a tour that included performances in Baalbek, Nice, Liverpool, London, Glasgow, Birmingham, Paris, Copenhagen, Berlin, Los Angeles and Honolulu. In such places, Helpmann's name would clearly carry weight, and his two Australian works, *The Display* and *Yugen*, were part of the tour repertoire.

Rehearsals for the Australian Ballet production of *Elektra* began in London in 1965 during the Company's engagement there as part of the Festival, but discussions with Helpmann regarding *Elektra* had been underway in Australia at least for several months, and certainly before the Company set off on tour in August 1965. Discussions may have begun as early as January 1965, but were definitely in train by mid-May of that year when Geoffrey Ingram, and the Australian Ballet's technical director, William (Bill) Akers, began corresponding with Helpmann regarding details of production.[14] Thus, planning had begun around the same time that *Yugen* was being staged. *Yugen* had opened in Adelaide on 18 February 1965 and was performed over the following months in other Australian cities, including Melbourne, Canberra, Sydney and Brisbane. *Elektra* was clearly being welcomed as another work that would give kudos to the Company via the Helpmann name.

Though gifted by The Royal Ballet as a complete entity, the Australian production of *Elektra*, which featured Kathleen Gorham as Elektra, Bryan Lawrence as Orestes, Janet Karin as Klytemnestra and Warren de Maria as Aegisthus, differed in a number of ways from the British version. Helpmann, in fact, told his Australian dancers that he wanted the Australian production to be different,[15] although it was never quite clear to the dancers just what those differences were to be. All that Helpmann seems to have divulged is that there was nothing in the Australian production that wasn't in the original version, but that certain things had been clarified.[16]

The Australian production was around ten minutes longer than the British version (twenty-two minutes as distinct from twelve minutes at Covent Garden), necessitating additional music from Malcolm Arnold as well as additional choreography. The recollections of Janet Karin, whom Helpmann personally chose to dance the role of Klytemnestra in the Australian production, despite the fact that another dancer had initially been allocated the role, are revealing of Helpmann's manner of conducting rehearsals, and his attitude to the creation of the choreography. Karin recalls that she asked Helpmann which version of the Greek tragedy he had used when developing his original production – she wanted to do some background reading. Helpmann's response was to tell her that he didn't want her reading anything. *He* would tell her the story.

Once rehearsals began, Karin remembers:

> It was a really different way of working from the classical approach at the time, where you were taught every single move. We had a video of the old production but a lot of what Monica Mason did as Klytemnestra you couldn't see well. And Bobby didn't want to reproduce it entirely anyway. So he just said, "I want you crawling on your tummy, like a snake." So we worked that out. Then he'd say, "Well I want you to dance with Aegisthus up here and writhe around him a bit." Then he'd go off and do something else and he'd come back and say, "Yes, OK. But do that twice." That kind of thing.
>
> I had great fun but I thought, "This man isn't controlling the work, he's producing it." Of course now, especially in more contemporary styles of ballet, such as the work of William Forsythe, they do this. But we had no skills in choreography, except I had done some improvisation when I worked with Ruth Bergner as a student, so I was lucky that way. But we made up our own movement, the same as had happened in *Display*.[17]

Karin, then a Soloist with the Australian Ballet, was asked by Helpmann to take on the role of Klytemnestra after he had seen her dance the Queen of the Wilis during London performances of *Giselle*. She records that she knew that Helpmann had seen particular qualities in her interpretation of the Queen of the Wilis and was looking for something similar in her Klytemnestra.

He wanted that deep passion. My Queen of the Wilis was very much a woman, not a spirit. She had a woman's hatred and venom. The way a woman hates is different from the way a man hates and I think those things are also translated to Klytemnestra. So I knew what he was talking about. He wanted those qualities.[18]

As well as additional music and choreography, there were also a number of design changes for the Australian production, some quite substantial. Arthur Boyd's London sets, which included two dramatic backcloths as well as side screens that boxed in the space, were enlarged from a series of black and white drawings and painted under Boyd's supervision. They suggested the states of mind that emerged from the dramatic storyline – desire, vengeance, torment, passion and a host of other dark moods and emotions. (See the scenic background in plates 69 and 72) They drew on ideas Boyd was formulating in his series, *Nude with beast* – a series that he had begun shortly after arriving in London, where he had been working from early 1960, and where he had had his paintings exhibited in ground-breaking and sometimes controversial shows of Australian art, including *Recent Australian Painting* at the Whitechapel Art Gallery in 1961, and *Australian Painting – Colonial-Impressionist-Contemporary* at the Tate Gallery in early 1963. Boyd's cloths and screens had their own brand of eroticism that more than matched any "crotch-flings" and "blood and sex" that might have been apparent in Helpmann's choreography and staging. To the cloths and screens Boyd added, upstage, a flight of scarlet steps extending the width of the stage space, and a red floor cloth, which Boyd's biographer, Darleen Bungey, has likened to a river of blood spilling over the entire floor.[19] Boyd's set designs, despite the obvious sexual connotations contained in the images, were not as severely criticised in the British press as was Helpmann's input. For example, Alexander Bland wrote:

> [*Elektra*] has the advantage of the finest ballet décor to be seen at Covent Garden for a long time, a set of startling power by Arthur Boyd. His idea of backing the action with vast blown-up drawings and concentrating the colour on the red-carpeted stage was inspirational.[20]

And Richard Buckle commented, "The sets of Arthur Boyd, Australia's Chagall, must be seen: they are a shot in the arm."[21]

At one stage in London Boyd was asked to remove some of the pubic hair from his figures on the backcloths so as not to offend the Queen who was to be present at a performance and he did as he was asked,[22] but for the Australian production no observable change was made to his final London set. In fact Helpmann wrote to Boyd expressing his delight that the set was given intact to the Australian Ballet: "I am delighted," he wrote, "that Covent

Garden has given us the set as it was beautifully painted."[23]

However, Boyd's ideas for some costumes were changed, both before they even reached the London stage, and again, dramatically, for the Australian production. Boyd's original plan for Klytemnestra, for example, was to dress her in a costume decorated with a swirling snake with head and jaws located at the groin so that the jaws appeared to open with the dancer's leg movements. The visual effect Boyd was seeking from the costume was clearly meant to be erotic and the serpent refers to a dream Klytemnestra had in which she dreamt she was suckling a snake and it drew blood from her breast. Ultimately, in London, Klytemnestra was dressed in yellow body tights with a "tail" of yellow fabric at the back. The costume was painted with a black swirling snake whose head was positioned, less graphically than was the original intention, to the right of the groin about half-way down the thigh.

Boyd's plans for the costumes for the eight Furies were also altered to be less startling, although the costumes that were finally worn in London were still sensational and controversial – purple body tights incorporating a large yellow patch on the front with a face with large eyes at breast level, and hoods with faces painted on them with eyes on the side at ear level.[24] The multiple eyes were a disorienting device, as there were many moments in the ballet when the Furies appeared to be looking in one direction and their "side eyes" in another. Boyd, according to Bungey, was not impressed with the changes he was asked to make. She quotes him as saying of his original designs: "They were terrific, a bit erotic [...] [Helpmann] couldn't fit the choreography into the costumes [...] he chopped it all out and ruined my costumes."[25] While Boyd's set was generally admired, the same cannot be said for his costumes. Peter Williams was particularly scornful of his costumes for Orestes and Aegisthus who, he said, "wore nothing but wigs, metallic jock-straps and body brown". "Their appearance made me think," Williams continued, "that in a moment the Bluebell girls would come on."[26]

However, the British costumes, even in their watered-down form, were never seen in Australia and what resulted there appears to be an effort to make them appear less outrageous. Helpmann wrote to Boyd suggesting that the costumes for the Furies, for example, needed revision:

> I would very much like to have a talk to you regarding the costumes. I have felt [...] we made a mistake putting the Furies in purple and feel they should be in black and white as though they were part of the décor.[27]

In Australia the Furies wore white body-tights covered with black lines, curves and swirls, which were, as Helpmann had suggested, visually closer to Boyd's finely drawn backcloth. The hoods with painted eyes disappeared and were replaced by black wigs with sharp spikes of hair crossing the middle part of the wig. (See plates 69 and 72) In addition, each dancer created an individualistic make-up design consisting of black lines that swirled up from the neck and over the face. The make-up continued the style of the patterns on the body-tights and drew the viewer's eye upwards to the fine black lines on Boyd's backcloths and screens. (See plate 70) Klytemnestra was also dressed very differently: instead of body-tights with snaking patterns, she wore a gold leotard with an over-tunic made in gold lurex fabric. As for Elektra, the "black rags" described by one reviewer in London were replaced in Australia by white body tights over which was worn a ragged tunic in sheer, black fabric decorated with solid black, grey and white areas scattered unevenly across the tunic.[28]

The Australian reviews of *Elektra* were less caustic than in Britain, although they focused on similar issues and were far from positive. H.A. Standish, writing for *The Herald* in Melbourne, commented: "The whole mood of the ballet is violent and gymnastic, with erotic references like struggles in dreams."[29] And also from Melbourne, an unnamed critic looked at the work from a wider perspective:

> The trouble is that Helpmann can be too uninhibited. The classic Greek tragedy of murder and revenge is horrible enough but when it is translated into a choreographic form that is a moving incarnation of Gustave Doré at his weirdest, with more than a suggestion of impassioned physical sex, the impact is brutal.[30]

Others wrote just a paragraph or two recognising their need to comment on the other works that appeared alongside *Elektra* – *Illyria* by Garth Welch and John Cranko's *Lady and the Fool*. Some made an effort to be positive; Helpmann was after all an Australian by birth. Geoffrey Hutton, for example, wrote: "It is also full of erotic symbolism, which I find acceptable because it is expressed in formalised balletic language."[31] *Elektra* toured briefly to various Australian cities but van Praagh reported at the end of 1966 that, while it had had a very strong impact on audiences, it did not prove to be as big a box-office draw as the classical works in the Company's repertoire.[32] Unlike *The Display*, which was brought back in 1983 and again in 2012, *Elektra* has never been revived.

Despite the outrage it generated in many dance circles, and despite the fact that it was short-lived in both Britain and Australia, *Elektra* is not unusual in Helpmann's choreographic output, at least when compared with the first few works that he staged for the fledgling Australian Ballet. Both *Yugen* and *The Display* relied on a flamboyant sense of theatre and a lack of inhibition when it came to choosing themes and addressing subjects that might be thought of as taboo for the time. *The Display*, for example, was a comment on the social and sexual behaviour of the Australian male. Violence and the suggestion of rape hovered over the work. With *Yugen*, at a time when art and society beyond Britain, the mother country, were scarcely acknowledged in Australia, Helpmann threw caution to the wind, studied briefly at a school for geisha girls in Tokyo ("to learn something about the very complicated fan techniques"), and created a ballet based on a Noh play, Zeami's *Hagoromo*. In his programme notes Helpmann wrote: "I have choreographed this work for The Australian Ballet in the belief that this Company should draw on the legends, music and cultures that are their neighbours, just as the English Ballet has drawn on the countries of Europe."[33]

That Helpmann was theatrical, with "greasepaint in his veins" as Alexander Bland put it,[34] and was uninhibited in his choices, has really become something of a cliché. Helpmann's "theatricality" extended to all walks of life, to his clothing, to his speech, and even to the way he signed letters. Often in his letters to Geoffrey Ingram at the Australian Ballet he would sign as "The Lyrebird" or "The Moon Goddess," characters in *The Display* and *Yugen* respectively. But there are other distinguishing features, common attitudes and approaches in his practice, that need to be considered in order to understand the man and his work.

Helpmann was skilled at concealing certain matters connected with his ballets, in particular collaborative endeavours or ideas that did not come to fruition. As Zoë Anderson has pointed out, Francis Bacon was the first choice as designer for *Elektra* and it appears that the commission had got to a stage where Bacon had submitted designs. But, as Anderson notes, the Covent Garden Board found the Bacon designs "had a certain distinction", but rejected them as being too large and not a practical proposition.[35] So Helpmann approached Boyd. The situation recalls that of the choice of designer for *Yugen*. *Yugen* was ultimately designed by Desmond Heeley but his commission came only after designs by South Australian artist Lawrence Daws had been prepared, submitted, and finally rejected (Daws was politely paid out for his work). In a similar vein, a libretto for *The Display* was commissioned from Australian writer Patrick White, but it too was rejected; and Peggy van Praagh reported to the Australian Ballet Foundation, diplomatically, that while White had submitted a scenario, "it was decided to use Helpmann's own version as being more suitable to the medium of ballet".[36] White eventually saw *The Display* and it was perhaps not surprising that he wrote unfavourably of it, remarking that parts of it reminded him of *West Side Story*.[37]

Helpmann seems never to have made mention of Bacon, Daws or White, and neither have his biographers, despite the prominence of these discarded collaborators in their respective fields. But then Helpmann was good at ignoring what he didn't wish to talk about and the information is in various unpublished forms and hidden in archival repositories, not easily found. It is also perhaps an embarrassment to some who may wish to promote a sanitised version of ballet history. But Helpmann's frequent discarding of the work by the creatives on his team, and finding replacements for them, for whatever reason, was a recurring feature of his working procedures.

Perhaps of most interest, and certainly worthy of further investigation, is Helpmann's choreographic practices. His manner of leaving much of the choreography to the dancers, as described by Janet Karin for *Elektra*, was not unusual. It was also Helpmann's practice during the creative period for *The Display*. Bryan Lawrence, who danced the role of the Leader in *The Display*, a ballet that was superficially about an Australian picnic but that in large part dealt with male sexuality, group hostility and its effects, and even immigration trends in Australia, recalls that he was asked to create much of the choreography for his character:

> It was interesting working for Bobby. I did, I think, most of the choreography for my bits myself. Bobby was inclined to do that. He worked out, obviously, the general story, but I can remember him saying before lunch one day, "Well, think about something to do there", and I just worked something out myself and it was accepted. Of course it included a whole lot of big jumps and turns and things, but it was accepted. All done with a beer can in my hand.[38]

Janet Karin has also spoken of Helpmann's approach in *Yugen*. She notes that Helpmann issued general instructions such as "throw the fans in a circle", when choreographing certain sections of the ballet in which the dancers, dressed kimono-style, manipulated Japanese fans. She suggests that Helpmann "showed us the symbols, but did not develop the art form."[39]

Helpmann's most lasting, popular contribution to the world of Australian dance does not lie in his original choreographies, where he deliberately set out to shock with his lack of inhibition in his thematic and choreographic material, and where he frequently relied on others to create the work. It resides much more with one work that he brought into production during his artistic directorship of the Australian Ballet – *The Merry Widow*, choreographed by Ronald Hynd and premièred in 1975. This work has become something of a signature work for the Australian Ballet, having been constantly revived over the years, most recently in 2011. It has been a box-office hit every time. (See Appendix V, pp. 248-249) Helpmann's contribution also lies with his own, very powerful stage appearances with the Australian Ballet as, for example, the Don in Rudolf Nureyev's production of *Don Quixote* and the

Red King in Ninette de Valois' *Checkmate*.

"Robert Helpmann was above all else a star and a prince of the theatre," remarked William Akers in a eulogy for Helpmann following his death in 1986.[40] But Akers has also succinctly commented elsewhere on Helpmann's "wonderful ability to make spectacular things happen without necessarily creating great choreography".[41]

Endnotes

1 "'Elektra' magnificent but brutal", *The Advocate* (Melbourne), 21 April 1966. Papers of Robert Helpmann, National Library of Australia, MS 7161/19. (The National Library of Australia's Helpmann papers – MS 7161 – consist largely but not exclusively of clipping books covering the period 1933 to 1986.)

2 Craig Dodd, "Helpmann's Elektra", *The Bulletin* (Sydney), 13 April 1963. MS 7161/17.

3 To avoid confusion the editors have regularised the spelling as Klytemnestra, not Clytemnestra, since this appears to be Helpmann's own preference.

4 D.F.B., "Nerina's lurid Elektra", *The Stage* (London), 26 March 1963.

5 Clive Barnes, "Elektra: Staging", *Dance and Dancers*, May 1963, p. 14.

6 Alexander Bland, "Helpmann aims too low", *The Observer Weekend Review*, 31 March 1963. MS 7161/17.

7 Richard Buckle, "Helpmann in a Blaze", *The Sunday Times* (London), 31 March 1963, p. 40. For full text of the review, see Appendix IV.

8 K.S.W., "'Elektra' is in top class", *The Daily Telegraph* (London), 26 March 1963. MS 7161/17. See also Sorley Walker's comments on *Elektra* in her biography, *Robert Helpmann. A Rare Sense of the Theatre* (Alton: Dance Books, 2009), pp. 122–123.

9 Oleg Kerensky, "Ballet", *Daily Mail*, 27 March 1963. MS 7161/17.

10 Minutes of the meeting of the Board of the Australian Ballet Foundation, 15 February 1966. Records of the Australian Ballet, National Library of Australia, MS 7559/75/Australian Ballet Foundation 1966. (These minutes record that a letter of thanks was to be sent to Sir David Webster, which was duly dispatched on 14 April 1966, after the opening of *Elektra*. The gift may well have been arranged while the Australian Ballet was in London in the latter part of 1965.)

11 Memo, undated, from Geoffrey Ingram to Peggy van Praagh, Stefan Haag and John McCallum. Papers of Geoffrey Ingram, National Library of Australia, MS 7336/11/61.

12 The appointment of Helpmann as joint artistic director of the Australian Ballet is discussed in detail in my article "Robert Helpmann: Behind the Scenes with the Australian Ballet, 1962-1965", *Dance Research*, 34:1 (Summer 2016), pp. 47-62.

13 "Memorandum for Mr Haag", dated 3 May 1963. Records of the Australian Elizabethan Theatre Trust, National Library of Australia, MS 5908/63/15, box 35.

14 Letters dated 12 May, 14 May and 15 June 1965. MS 7336/11/62. Deborah Hart also records that Helpmann was in discussion with Boyd in January 1965 regarding changes to costumes. Deborah Hart, *Arthur Boyd: Agony and Ecstasy* (Canberra: National Gallery of Australia, 2014), pp. 81; 85.

15 Email, dated 15 September 2015, from Janet Karin to Michelle Potter.

16 Gilmour Coleman, "Sweat, Tears for Ballet", *The Advertiser* (Adelaide), 3 March 1966. MS 7161/19.

17   Janet Karin interviewed by Bill Stephens, 10-12 March 1996. National Library of Australia, Oral History and Folklore Collection, TRC 3428.

18   Ibid. I am grateful to Janet Karin for permission to quote from her interview.

19   Darleen Bungey, *Arthur Boyd. A Life* (Crows Nest, NSW: Allen & Unwin, 2007), p. 345.

20   Bland, "Helpmann aims too low".

21   Buckle, "Helpmann in a Blaze".

22   *Arthur Boyd: Agony and Ecstasy*, p. 80.

23   Ibid. p. 85. (Letter, dated 25 January 1965, from Robert Helpmann to Arthur Boyd)

24   The costumes were reproduced in colour in "That needs an X," *Today*, 8 June 1963. MS 7161/17.

25   Bungey, p. 346. A number of Boyd's sketches with ideas for his costumes, including those for Klytemnestra, are preserved in the National Gallery of Australia. Some are reproduced in Hart, pp. 82−84.

26   Peter Williams, "Elektra: Decor", *Dance and Dancers*, May 1963, p. 16.

27   Letter, dated 25 January 1965 from Robert Helpmann to Arthur Boyd, quoted in Hart, p. 81.

28   D.F.B, "Nerina's lurid Elektra" and *Ballet Dancer. Australian Colour Diary No. 27*, Commonwealth Film Unit, National Film Board, News and Information Bureau [1968], National Film and Sound Archive, Title no: 12682-7. (The film *Ballet Dancer* is a short documentary about Kathleen Geldard, who replaced Kathleen Gorham as Elektra when Gorham retired in 1966, and contains brief footage in which Elektra's costume is clearly visible.)

29   . H.A. Standish, "Contrast in dancing at Festival", *The Herald* (Melbourne), 16 March 1966. MS 7161/19.

30   "'Elektra' magnificent but brutal".

31   Geoffrey Hutton, "Ballet attains new planes in lyric drama", *The Age* (Melbourne), 16 March 1966. MS 7161/19.

32   "Artistic Directors' Report", dated 30 November 1966. MS 7559/75/ Australian Ballet Foundation 1966.

33   Robert Helpmann, programme notes for *Yugen*. MS 7336/10/59. For details of Helpmann's studying geisha movement, see Elizabeth Salter, *Helpmann, the Official Biography* (Brighton and Sydney: Angus & Robertson, 1978), p.223. He also studied Noh dancing with Koishito Nishikawa in Honolulu in 1964.

34   Bland, "Helpmann aims too low".

35   Zoë Anderson, *The Royal Ballet. 75 Years* (London: Faber and Faber, 2006), p. 155.

36   "Report of Artistic Director, 9 December 1963." MS 5908/63/15, box 35.

37   Detailed discussion of the commissions to White and Daws for *Display* and *Yugen* respectively are contained in my article "Robert Helpmann: Behind the Scenes with the Australian Ballet, 1962-1965", *Dance Research*, 34:1 (Summer 2016), pp.47-62.

38   Bryan Lawrence interviewed by Bill Stephens, 29 October & 12 November 1986. National Library of Australia, Oral History and Folklore Collection, TRC

2118.

39   Janet Karin quoted in Cheryl Stock, "Robert Helpmann. Master showman", *Brolga: an Australian journal about dance*, 5 (December 1996), p. 41.

40   Eulogy for Robert Helpmann delivered by William Akers. National Library of Australia, Oral History and Folklore Collection, TRC 4844.

41   William (Bill) Akers interviewed by Michelle Potter, February 2002. National Library of Australia, Oral History and Folklore Collection, TRC 4839. Online at http://nla.gov.au/nla.oh-vn1565943.

Postscript
Recollections of Robert Helpmann: colleague, choreographer and interpretive performer

Dame Monica Mason in discussion with Rupert Christiansen[1]

Rupert Christiansen (RC): [Your] association with Helpmann: when did that begin?

Monica Mason (MM): I think really very close to the beginning of starting with The Royal Ballet. I was a teenager, I was about seventeen I suppose, when I first saw Bobby and Fred [Ashton] rehearsing Ugly Sisters for *Cinderella* [ch. Ashton, 1948; revised 1965]; but even earlier than actually [being with him] in a rehearsal room, one was aware of Bobby. First of all he was known as "Bobby", which sort of astonished me.

RC: By everybody?

MM: Yes, by absolutely everybody and that amazed me when I first joined the Company. Fred was called "Fred" – and "Sir Fred" – and Bobby was "Bobby", Margot [Fonteyn] was "Margot". But Madam [Ninette de Valois] was "Madam"! But I remember very clearly, Madam being in a rehearsal room; I don't remember what it was, but Madam was taking the rehearsal and the atmosphere was very tense, as it always was when she was around. She was always slightly impatient and slightly on edge – she was always in such a hurry. And Bobby came in and knelt by the side of her chair and whispered something in her ear, whereupon she absolutely burst out laughing! And I remember thinking, "How amazing! What could he possibly have said to make her laugh like that?" And of course one saw it repeated, frequently, because she adored him and he was often around.

And you could sense the slight rivalry between Bobby and Fred, when they were rehearsing Ugly Sisters. And of course, they also never gave anything away to each other. If Bobby had got a new idea for a moment, he certainly wasn't going to show Fred what it was in the rehearsal studio. So when the performances came, it was constant improvisation really, I think, on their part, and they were absolutely "with it". We all used to just stand in the wings, *crowded* in the wings because that first opening scene in *Cinderella* is almost impossible to see from the wings, because of the nature of the room [the onstage setting], but somehow, you know, we used to be on top of one another to watch them – and, I mean, they were both absolutely outrageous!

I never saw Bobby do Carabosse [the evil Fairy in *The Sleeping Beauty*] – I saw Fred do Carabosse – but Bobby was just the most wonderful, for me warm [person]. I found him incredibly kind, because he was so conscious when people were totally "green". And he just took such a delight in teaching you something. And he'd take you to the side of a studio and just remind you that when you were going to be wearing a heel as a Court Lady, how differently that would make you walk, and how differently you needed to feel about yourself. He couldn't help but keep informing you, in the most generous way.

RC: I was very struck in the South Bank Film[2] that obviously he was very good with children; [one] felt he was one of those people who had a magic touch with children.

MM: Well, you know he was so charismatic, and so irresistible that it was like a moth to a flame. First of all – I always say this – I'd come from Johannesburg, which had so little theatre available in the 'fifties, and I landed here in London and, you know, to find myself in a room where there were Ashton and de Valois and Margot and Bobby all in a room together – having only ever seen their photographs in those wonderful *Baron at the Ballet* books[3]; and having read about the Sadler's Wells Ballet – and then there were all these people! But what was so wonderful about Bobby was that he was never intimidating. He was so welcoming and warm that you couldn't wait to ask him questions. And he would always take time to answer you.

RC: You are far too young ever to have seen him as a *danseur noble*, but probably you saw him in *[The]Red Shoes* when you were young?

MM: No, no I never saw the film.

RC: I was going to ask you whether you agreed with Beryl Grey's assessment of him as a dancer? [See DVD, Track 1] Have you had any sense of what his technical strengths and shortcoming were?

MM: By the time I knew him and saw him as an Ugly Sister I could never really believe he'd been a *danseur noble*. Because, by then of course, it was twenty years on. And by this time he was acting a lot. What amazed me was that this was somebody who seemed to fly around between theatre and ballet and travel the world!

One of my last memories of him was actually when I was in Australia. I was headhunted like Maina [Gielgud] was, for the job of Director of The Australian Ballet. Maina and I were there together. We had known each other because we'd danced together and, really, I think the final choice was down to Maina or me. (I say this here!) I decided in the end not to go for it; I wanted to come back to The Royal Ballet. But I bumped into Bobby – I was just leaving the Opera House as he was going in one day. And he was so *warm,* and I remember giving him such a hug – I almost felt I gave him too much of a hug, because I could feel him slightly think, "Oh my God, this woman!" And I think it was because I hadn't seen him in years, and he so belonged in that place, and yet of course I'd known him in *this* country. And he said, "I just want to wish you good luck with whatever your decision is"; and I think that was the last time I spoke to him.

RC: But, of course, you worked quite closely with him on the creation of *Elektra* didn't you, in 1963? You played Klytemnestra; [Nadia] Nerina was Elektra. What was he like in the rehearsal room? Was he one of those choreographers who knew exactly what he wanted, or was there room for you to contribute?

MM: Oh no, he very much worked on you – and, of course, he hadn't described the set very much before we saw it on the stage. He'd explained there was a long flight of stairs and there was a platform at the back, and that I would be with Derek Rencher, sort of "entwined". He said, "I want you to think of yourselves as two snakes, and I'm going to tie you into knots!" And he did – but it was all very erotic too. I think I had turned twenty-one, but I was very virginal, and he said to me, "Monica, you look a little confused from time to time". And I said, "Well, oh – I hoped that wasn't showing." He said, "Never mind about understanding, just do as I say. When you're in that costume and in the performance, you'll be fine! Is your mother coming?" And I said, "Oh yes, she comes to everything, but you don't have to worry, she just…understands!" So he always had such humour – but he was so generous.

Years later, I remember, we were performing in New York at the New Met[ropolitan Opera House], and he was sitting in the audience for a stage rehearsal – and this would probably have been in the 'seventies. And I went out front and he was at that time, I think, producing something on Broadway, and he was looking his usual elegant self. The thing I always remember: he would cross his legs and he had very, very pretty ankles, and he always wore black silk socks! I remember even there in the sort of semi-darkness, I looked down and he still had his silk socks on. But I actually said to him how lovely it was to see him, and he said, "Well I couldn't not come in and see the Company while you're here in New York, and how lovely to see you, and how are you?" And I said, "You know, I miss you because you always meant so much to me." I said, "I've always wanted to ask you this question and I'm so pleased I've got the chance now: 'How is it that you did so much?'" And he said, "I never said *No!* Whenever somebody asked me to do something I always said *Yes!*" I think it's quite a good lesson.

RC: *Elektra* of course, I think, was one of those ballets which audiences loved but critics hated. It died a sort of death, but was it any good?[4]

MM: Because I was in it, I never saw it...

RC: Did it feel good?

MM: It felt very sexy! I think it was a wonderful experience, because it was working with Bobby, and working with Bobby from square one, so that you watched him create this whole ballet. He was absolutely thrilled with the music that Malcolm Arnold [1921–2006] had written. [...] I was in Northampton last weekend because there was a festival for Malcolm Arnold. It was the eighth time they've done a Festival since he died, and I had been invited to come and open the Festival. And I was really very honoured to be there. Because although I felt I didn't know Malcolm Arnold, I knew he was around – and I knew he was around for *Elektra*. But I don't remember ever having a conversation with him. I might have been introduced, but everybody who worked with Malcolm Arnold loved the fact he was so amenable – and that, because he worked a lot in film, he was able to adapt music very easily. And so both Bobby and Fred, and Kenneth [MacMillan] in fact, too, always spoke about Malcolm Arnold as being somebody who so easily adapted their score. You know: "Malcolm can you please get rid of those last eight bars – I can't use that." And he just took the scissors, and chopped it; [he] went [straight] to the piano [and did this]. And he did *Homage to The Queen* [ch. Ashton, 1953] with Fred, and he was exactly the same when he did that. And of course he'd done *English Dances* for Kenneth [MacMillan, *Solitaire,* 1956]; and he also did *Sweeney Todd* for [John] Cranko [in 1959]. And Malcolm was this very, very amenable madcap who would chop music off and add a few bars, if that was what was required.

And so this again was, for Bobby, a very happy collaboration. The set for *Elektra* was shocking – because Arthur Boyd [1920–1999], an Australian painter and designer, had again drawn some very, very rude things on the wings! And I remember coming on stage for the very first time and seeing the set, and Bobby said to me, "Have you looked at the wing upstage there?" and I said, "Yes, I have." He said, "It's wonderful isn't it, so rude! What *will* Ninette [de Valois] say when she sees it?"

RC: Was it similar to *Hamlet* [ch. Helpmann, 1942], was it very compressed and intense and impressionistic?

MM: It was very intense – like *Hamlet* in the sense that it was again a very condensed version of the story.

RC: Twenty minutes or so?

MM: Yes, and of course Nadia Nerina was absolutely fearless. [She] had this wonderful [fearlessness]. I don't quite know *why* Elektra needed to be thrown from one end of the stage to the other, and from upstage to downstage – so much so, that I do remember in the audience in America during a performance, a woman out front let out the most incredible scream, and then we heard the most enormous bump as she passed out! They couldn't get anyone to understudy Nadia, because she was fearless; Annette Page was asked to be the cover, and Annette said, "I'm not going to be thrown around like that!" So there never was an understudy and, thankfully, Nadia was never off.

You know, you felt for Bobby. There was one wonderful moment where Klytemnestra had to enter from downstage, stage left. I put on this cloak, and then when I reached centre I had to spread the cloak so that it actually was its full size, and then he wanted me to crawl up the stairs, like a snake, with this cloak spread out behind me. Well, when I saw the size of the cloak I thought, "How am I ever going to manage that?" So of course the first time I did it, I came on from the side and I reached centre and I turned round and I raised it, and it went "plop" in a great lump. And Bobby said, "I think we need to try that again." So we did it a couple of times, and I said, "Show me how to do this." And he said, "Well..." So he took it off, and tied it round his neck, and then he came on and he turned round, and he did something completely magical – and the thing rose and fell completely perfectly. I don't think I ever achieved it, but he just did it *once*, and there was this little smile. And I said, "Trust you!" And he said, "I've done a few cloaks in my time!"

Endnotes

1   The conversation, transcribed by Nicola Katrak from a video recording, was held during The Royal Ballet School Symposium, *The Many Faces of Robert Helpmann*, 27 October 2013.

2   The reference is to the documentary, *Tales of Helpmann: A Profile of Sir Robert Helpmann* (dir. Don Featherstone; script Alan Sievewright; ed. Melvyn Bragg), a *South Bank Show* film produced by London Weekend Television for ITV, in association with the Australian Broadcasting Corporation (1990). (See Appendix V for an edited transcript)

3   *Baron at the Ballet* (London: Collins, 1950) and *Baron Encore* (London: Collins, 1952) were edited with commentaries by Arnold Haskell. Baron was the professional name of the photographer, Stirling Henry Nahum.

4   For a critical response, see Richard Buckle's review in Appendix IV.

Appendix I

Joan Littlefield (the British feature writer and film critic for Program), *"Review of Miracle in the Gorbals", The Military Man's Entertainment,* 4 November 1945, pp.1, 3. (From a scrapbook in the Cristelle Cleaver Collection, The Royal Ballet School Special Collections. Edited by Anna Meadmore)

Miracle in the Gorbals, music by Arthur Bliss, Choreography by Robert Helpmann, Décor by Edward Burra, was first performed by the Sadlers Wells [sic] Ballet Company at the Prince's Theatre, London, on October 26th, 1944. Based on a short story by Michael Benthall, it deals with the theme of Christ and Mary Magdalen (called here the Stranger and the Prostitute) and what would happen if Christ should come again.

The setting is modern Glasgow, where Michael Benthall has been serving as an anti-aircraft gunner, the Gorbals being a district where poor people live in a cramped existence, seeking their entertainment in the saloon and in the streets. Their aimless leisure is well conveyed by their restless crowded movements. Outside the saloon sits a beggar, ignored but observant; a street boy, avid for excitement, rushes hither and thither; two lovers snatch brief moments of happiness among the toughs and the talkative, inquisitive women; the local Pastor, called the Official, tries to fraternise with his indifferent flock; and the Prostitute, alluring in her scarlet dress, attracts many visitors to her tenement flat.

The Stranger Enters...

No one takes much notice of a girl in a black frock, distraught and lonely, who wanders hopelessly among them – until she drowns herself, and adds a moment of excitement to drab lives. The young men bring her in from the river and try to revive her, but the Official indicates that she is dead. And then the Stranger enters, hatless and wearing an open-necked shirt.

Up to this point the ballet is danced realistically. No conventional miming is used, but more of a film technique. That is to say, the dancers act their parts as in a silent movie, their movements springing naturally out of character and situation. The same rhythms are continued at different levels, as when the dancers climb the tenement stairs or emerge on the balconies of their apartments.

But with the entry of the Stranger, the rhythms change. They are based now on movements observed in El Greco's *Crucifixion*. The Official is the first to recognise the Stranger, and he is afraid. He symbolises the Church, which has failed in its task, or narrow Officialdom butting in and doing the wrong thing. Nevertheless he offers a timid friendship. When the Stranger, however, takes the dead girl in his arms and tenderly restores her to life, thus winning the praise and adoration of the crowd, who go off with him rejoicing, the Official, unwanted and alone, grows jealous, and in a frenzy at his own inadequacy, himself ascends the stairs to the Prostitute's apartment.

Mob Anger, Murder

When he comes away, ashamed of his weakness but jealous still, he sets the Street Boy on to lure the Stranger to the girl's apartment and then to show the crowd that their idol has feet of clay. Like all mobs, they are as quickly roused to anger as to hero-worship. Only the Suicide and the Beggar remain faithful, and when the Stranger descends the Prostitute's stairs the women stand aside, while the men do him to death with knives and razor blades. As they drag the body off-stage, a ship's siren sounds; and they drop their burden and return to work.

Edward Burra, noted for his paintings of Glasgow slums, contributes a drop curtain of a huge ship under construction, to emphasise the setting, as well as doing the decor for the ballet.

To convey all the implications of such a theme by means of dancing – avoiding crudity yet retaining the colour and movement essential to ballet – is no easy task, and that Robert Helpmann succeeds so well is partly due to Arthur Bliss's magnificent musical score, with its strong rhythms and subtle influence on the emotions. It adds terror and pity to the last dread scene, raising it from mere gangsterdom to the realm of tragedy. It lends poignancy to the scenes of the little Suicide, particularly when, as she comes to life again, she begins falteringly to dance the steps of a Scotch reel, which grows in strength and speed till the whole company is dancing. It adds excitement to the moments of climax, as when in their exultation at the revelation of the Stranger's powers, the crowd begin to jitter-bug, expressing their joy in the idiom best known to them, as negroes express theirs by singing Spirituals.

"Brutal" Realism, Say Critics

That last scene has been criticised for its somewhat brutal realism by those who think of ballet in terms only of *Les Sylphides*, *Swan Lake* and *[Le] Spectre de la Rose*.

Robert Helpmann thinks differently. Ballet must grow, he says, like any other art, and like the other arts it should be able to interpret anything, including the problems of the post-war world. It could, he believes, be used as a social force, as Shaw and Galsworthy used the theatre at the beginning of this century.

Being an actor as well as a dancer, Mr. Helpmann is interested, as a choreographer, in realistic rather than in abstract ballet; but ballet realism should not become drab and glamourless as modern plays and films tend to do.

Mr Helpmann is interested in the psychological ballet, and in the discreet use of speech and perhaps of singers. His *Hamlet*, in which all the action happens in Hamlet's mind in the moments between death and oblivion, is a psychological study, owing something to the theories of Freud, and completely successful on its own plane. In *Comus*, which sticks closely to Milton's text, he interpolates two speeches without in any way breaking up the rhythm of the ballet.

In his next production, based on the *Oedipus Rex* of Sophocles, Mr Helpmann hopes to use singing as well as speech, thus returning to the conventions of old Greek Tragedy, when dance was an integral part of theatre.

[Editors' note: this planned work did not materialise.]

Appendix II

Chiang Yee "What can I say about Ballet?" in Arnold L. Haskell (ed.), *The Ballet Annual, A Record and Year Book of the Ballet*, second issue (London: Adam & Charles Black, 1948), pp.113-114. (Edited by Anna Meadmore)

I cannot dance and I know very little about Western music, for neither art came into my Confucian upbringing. Nevertheless I became interested in ballet as soon as I made the first contact with it. Its combination of three arts – dance, music and painting – appealed to me. Being a painter myself I see the pictorial art in the ballet playing a genuine part of its own and at least sharing the attention, if not equally, with the other two arts, of the audience. My interest was stimulated by the suggestion made by Mr Constant Lambert that I should do the décor for Mr Robert Helpmann's ballet, *The Birds*. This was an unusual request for, from my little experience, a Chinese artist's work is not found on the Western stage even if the play or ballet has a Chinese setting. Mr Lambert foresaw that a Chinese rendering of a pictorial backcloth might be suitable for this particular ballet. He was not playing a game of curiosity or "Chinoiserie". I had already been thinking that our type of painting would go well with some ballet, because it is suggestive, imaginative and poetic. Dancing uses the movements of limbs to suggest emotion and mood in order to bring out imagination. Music uses sounds and melodies to produce the same effect. Why should not the pictorial design on the backcloth do the same if it is playing a genuine part in the formation of the ballet?

I had a talk with the choreographer about the dances and found out as well something about the music by Respighi before beginning to form any ideas for the décor and costumes. At first, I thought *The Birds* admirably suited to go with a flower painting or a landscape by one of our Sung masters, very simple and full of imaginative intuition. I actually tried to make use of a Sung masterpiece – "Two cranes playing by a spring", by Hsia Kuei – as a base. However, after further consideration of the dancing I felt that such a backcloth would be too simple, so I painted instead a rather detailed, leafy wood. (See plates 29 and 30) The result called forth many interesting remarks; one critic said the backcloth "looked like an illustration in a book", and another that it "overpowered the dancing and obscured the dancers". It is all a matter of opinion [...] The question remains whether the pictorial design of a backcloth should have an equal share in the importance of a ballet with music and dancing or how much more importance it should have. [...]

I must admit that I did not give much consideration to the effect of modern stage lighting in my design, which became rather too bright when lit up and may have distracted the audience.

Modern stage lighting is an improvement for a realistic, dramatic presentation of a play. Yet I am not sure if it is to the advantage of some kinds of ballets. One knows that a classical ballet has its original, established décor and that it is much safer to use this when the ballet is to be performed, for the audience cannot forget the already accepted convention. But modern stage lighting may be a disadvantage to the original design. If a new décor is tried, the designer must consider, I think, how to turn the minds of the audience from the already accepted convention. This is difficult. His design should not give too much prominence to his own character, yet must indicate what he thinks suits the dancing and music. There is a danger that he may either branch off from the ballet by emphasising himself or bow to the spell of convention and claim no share in importance with the dance and music.

Appendix III

Michael Benthall, "The Dance-Drama" in Arnold L. Haskell (ed.) *Hamlet and Miracle in the Gorbals*, Sadler's Wells Ballet Books, No. 3 (London: Bodley Head, 1949), pp. 7–12. (Edited by Richard Cave)

In order to maintain its hold on an ever-increasing public, ballet is continually seeking a new form of expression. The scope is not large. Ballet has been described by the eminent editor of this volume as "a form of theatrical entertainment that tells a story, develops a theme or suggests an atmosphere through the orchestration of a group of costumed dancers trained according to strict rules and guided in tempo and spirit by the music, against a decorative background; music, movement and decoration being parallel in thought". This bald, but apt, definition covers a multitude of combinations; music from Purcell to Britten, movement from *fouettés* to boogie-woogie, decoration from Fedorovitch to Beaton, but if Mr Haskell had added somewhere in his formula "without the spoken word", the problem of the ballet creator would be seen to be much more difficult.

The purely abstract work, if it is to be successful, is bound to be a sympathetic interpretation by the choreographer and designer of the music. This has recently been done supremely well by Frederick Ashton with his *Symphonic Variations*, using an economy of dramatic effect and a maximum of technique which no choreographer has ever dared before on so large a stage as Covent Garden. This type of ballet and those akin to it, Massine's Symphonic ballets, Fokine's *Les Sylphides*, Ashton's own *Dante Sonata* and *Les Patineurs* rely for their impression on the audience on their ability to create a mood parallel to the music while employing a minimum of theme. It is true that some of the *divertissement* ballets profess to tell a story – but a story so slight that it only serves as a peg on which to hang a series of dances.

The dance-drama, on the other hand, makes its dramatic effect by its ability to tell a story clearly, using the dance as its means of expression. The problem of he whom I suppose one must call the "dance-dramatist" is to tell his tale without the use of a single spoken or written word; a complete work of art should be intelligible without verbal explanation. For the great classical ballets, whose stories are undeniably complicated, a mime convention was devised which was understood by every *balletomane* of the period, and indeed by most Russian *balletomanes* today. The dances were linked by mime scenes, often long and elaborate, as important to the texture of the ballet as the dances themselves. How many members of the present-day "Lunatic Fringe" can say truthfully that they understand what the Swan Princess is saying to the Prince in Act II of *Lac des Cygnes?* How many realise that the Lake on which Odette swims was formed by the tears of her mother when her daughter was transformed into a swan? And yet it is all in the "dialogue"! It is doubtful whether this loss of detail is very destructive to these classical works, whose music and choreography have made them immortal rather than their stories, but it is significant that a very lengthy exposition is needed in the programme.

The word "mime" should be put in a class by itself, stamped as the conventional sign language which has puzzled the uninitiated in *Giselle* and all subsequent classical ballets. How often have people been heard to say that they do not approve of the modern dance-dramas, like *Petrouchka, The Rake's Progress, Hamlet, Miracle in the Gorbals* and the rest, because there is too much mime and *not enough dancing;* but has it ever occurred to them that there is more mime in *The Sleeping Princess* than all those four ballets put together.

Quite recently at Covent Garden, a voice was heard saying "I never think it's dancing unless they wear white frocks"; so it seems that this old-fashioned idea of ballet dies hard. A dancer should be expressive from finger-tips to toes. Every movement he makes, if it is expressing correctly the choreographer's intentions, is dancing. The lift of an eyebrow can often create a mood more effectively than an intricate step.

How, then, is the modern choreographer to overcome this dialogue difficulty when he is creating an entertainment for a generation which is not inclined to prepare its mind when going to the theatre by learning a mime language? His theme, of course, must be simple. He cannot, for example, make the Ghost in *Hamlet* express without words that his brother murdered him, while sleeping in his orchard one afternoon, by pouring poison in his ear, in order to gain his crown and his Queen. Nor has he solved the problem by putting all this in a programme note; an audience dislikes having to memorise a long explanation before a work becomes intelligible.

In the last forty years a new dance-convention has grown up, a combination of mime and movement which will tell a story without allowing the ballet to degenerate into mimed dramas to music. It has sometimes been called, rather obviously, "mimetic movement". This convention was developed over a period of years, reaching an apex in that father of dance-dramas, Fokine's *Petrouchka.* Since then it has been exploited until it has become probably the most popular form of ballet. Not because it has produced the greatest works, but because it is a form which appeals more readily to the emotions than any other; just as the latest Hitchcock film-thriller can stir the blood more quickly than a calculating scenario by Bernard Shaw.

The Sadler's Wells Company first made its mark in the dance-drama with de Valois' *The Rake's Progress*. Too well-known for detailed dissection, this work holds its own with any of the great character ballets. The story, told in a series of pictures after Hogarth, fails only to maintain the interest in the lyrical sequences before the front cloth, which are too long and indeterminate to serve as a link between the strong dramatic scenes. The ballet has a programme note, but its strength lies in the fact that it would be comprehensible without one. *The Rake's Progress* was the foundation stone for a tradition in modern English dancing. It seems that English dancers excel in this type of character-work and it is on their essentially English ballets, rather than their performances of the Russian classics or reliance on Continental composers, designers or technique, that the Sadler's Wells Company will make an international reputation.

These dance-dramas, however, require a great deal of acting which cannot be covered up by good dancing and it is a curious anomaly that, although the general histrionic ability reaches a competent level, the company can boast of few who can sustain an important character role. With the exception of Fonteyn, Brae, Helpmann and Paltenghi and, in supporting roles, Julia Farron and Leslie Edwards, there are no members whose talent in this direction has been developed. It is possible that this important item has been overlooked in their training. All dancers require to be actors, for presence on the stage and what is called "personality" are largely a matter of self-expression. The choreographer of dance-drama has to be a master at drawing out the best possible performances from his cast, and both de Valois and Helpmann excel at this. De Valois' *Rake's Progress* and *Checkmate* and Helpmann's *Hamlet* and *Miracle in the Gorbals* abound in rich character-studies which should be welcome to any actor-dancer, and all of which contribute to the theme and atmosphere of the ballets' stories. This question of acting and production is one which is all too often neglected by some companies. The big scenes in the great classical ballets are frequently reduced to a mere technical exhibition by an inexpertly grouped *corps de ballet* of onlooking Ladies and Gentlemen of the Court or Village, whose vacant expressions betray the fact that their minds are full of anything but the events taking place on the stage; such murderous lack of production in important works is a cardinal offence. That exciting work *Giselle* particularly suffers from lack of magic in modern presentations.

In *Hamlet,* Helpmann first tried to abolish the programme note, relying on an explanatory couplet and the supposition that the audience would have an elementary knowledge of the play, in order to supplement the mime. This is not wholly successful because there is no doubt that most of the audience do not know the play, and being moved only by the dramatic impact which is inherent in the choreography, in Tchaikovsky's music and in Hurry's décor, they are missing all the fascinating psychological comment that Helpmann has made on Shakespeare's work. In *Miracle in the Gorbals,* he eliminated the programme note altogether by telling a simple dramatic story in a straightforward way and this is fairly successful, although there is no doubt that much of the social comment is lost by those who do not realise that the character of "The Official" represents the "organised Church" and not just "petty officialdom". In his latest work, *Adam Zero,* the general theme is clear, and yet packed with as much symbolism as its audience cares to read into it. This is a ballet which has been planned on a grand scale to be played only in large opera houses, requiring a big company and two leading dancers of exceptional acting ability, and for these, if for no other reasons, is not likely to stand the test of time. A universal theme with an existentialist flavour has been tackled and it is an attempt to introduce philosophy as well as symbolism and psychology into the dance. As a new avenue for the dance-drama this can only lead to a dead end, for these -ologies and -isms are matters for verbal discussion and not for mime.

"So where" will *balletomanes* ask "do we go from here?" De Valois and Helpmann have skated down a well-worn track and made it seem fresh, but it would seem that no further advance can be made in the dance-drama without the introduction of the spoken (or sung) word. Several attempts have been made to combine ballet with opera, the dancers miming the action while the singers sing the words, but never with success, for music written for the voice is rarely suitable for dancing. If this combination is to be successful a new art-form for the theatre will have to be evolved and a new school of *artistes* will have to be trained. This may yet be possible and perhaps one day we shall see an *artiste* with the histrionic ability of Bernhardt, the ballet technique of Pavlova and the voice of Melba!

The future of the art cannot be prophesied, but to whatever direction dance-dramatists may turn, let them conceive their ballets as complete, full-blooded and tautly-drawn works for the theatre, whether to enchant, to thrill or to amuse.

Appendix IV

"Helpmann in a Blaze", review of Elektra by Richard Buckle, *Sunday Times* **31 March 1963, reprinted in** *Buckle at the Ballet,* **selected criticism by Richard Buckle (London: Dance Books, 1980), pp.189-190.**

The applause after Robert Helpmann's *Elektra* at Covent Garden on Tuesday seemed to last longer than the ballet. It was quite invigorating to hear such a demonstration – particularly as Helpmann took his calls with a smiling reticence which was the height of good style: and I wondered if the ovation was entirely due to the fact that people liked the ballet or to its being the first one Helpmann had staged since 1946, or to pleasure at seeing Nerina and Blair in a new work, or relief at not seeing Fonteyn and Nureyev, or to the house being full of Australians (I saw Coral Browne enthroned above).

Elektra is not only very short (it seemed like ten minutes) but also very sensational. It opens with drums and brass in a bursting boiling rage. Scarlet floorcloth and a flight of scarlet steps set off Arthur Boyd's huge images of love and death drawn in black and white. Nerina, made-up witchlike with streaming vermilion hair, gloating over her avenging axe, is Elektra. Blair, naked and redheaded, is Orestes.

There are eight male purple Erinyes or Spirits of Vengeance who fling Elektra through the air in a variety of breathtaking dives. Monica Mason and Derek Rencher as Klytemnestra and Aegisthus are the only other characters, and we see them having mad sex while the children gloat and suffer.

Later Klytemnestra becomes a loathsome thing and drags herself on by her hands, a long gold train worming behind her. This train reversed becomes a red blood-bath-mat. The Queen is axed and her husband runs to greet the weapon of retribution.

Aeschylus and Athene absolved Orestes. Helpmann doesn't. After the double-murder it takes the Erinyes just thirty seconds to crucify Orestes upstage, and we are left breathless.

Elektra is tremendously effective. It may be vulgar, but it isn't genteel. Helpmann has not lost his blazing sense of theatre; and his new work, though less profound, is the nearest thing to Martha Graham's *Phaedra* on this side of the drink.

Malcolm Arnold's railway music is clearly composed as film music would be – or, in fact, as Graham's scores are – as an atmospheric accompaniment to the drama. There are strange noises in it, including a weird whoohooing sound, which I am told is the brass doing glissandos.

The sets of Arthur Boyd, Australia's Chagall, must be seen: they are a shot in the arm. And the ballet is the more welcome for revealing to us the volcanic passions hitherto concealed beneath Nadia Nerina's pretty placid countenance.

Appendix V

A transcript of excerpts from the documentary film, *Tales of Helpmann: A Profile of Sir Robert Helpmann*, directed by Don Featherstone (1990). (As broadcast on London Weekend Television's *The South Bank Show*, 24 June 1990. Selected and edited by Anna Meadmore)

PART ONE
Introduction by Melvyn Bragg:
[...]. In the course of his long and versatile career [Robert Helpmann] was a ballet dancer, a choreographer, a Shakespearean actor, a theatre director, and an opera producer – and he made many memorable film appearances. Tonight's *South Bank Show*, directed by fellow Australian, Don Featherstone, enjoys the extraordinary life and times of Sir Robert Helpmann.

Margaret Rawlings, actress:
Oh, women fell in love with him, and he, I think, fell in love with *them* – he managed to make them *think* he was, which is very important, he was so... oh dear! He was so *attractive*...a magnet. I could find no fault with him at all.

Stewart Granger, actor:
[...] immediately when I think of Bobby I smile, because he was such a naughty little creature! He was brilliant, but so *funny*, so wicked too – so outrageous! All the terrible things he did...

Elspeth March, actress:
I can remember that he and Sir Frederick Ashton dressed up as nuns at some junket, and when they turned round [...] they had no *backs* to their habits [...] [she chuckles delightedly] which was fairly naughty!

Alan Sievewright, friend and biographer:
He could stand up to anybody, he wasn't frightened of anybody, and he could have looked into the face of the Devil himself and laughed.

Margaret Rawlings [speaking with reference to a return to England with her husband, Gabriel Toyne, in December 1932, following a tour of Australia where the young Helpmann had joined their company]:
I thought he [Helpmann] was beautiful – not everybody would, because there was such odd character in the face – but he was *beautiful*, and magnetic; you couldn't take your eyes off him. When the time came for us to go back, his father at last give his permission because he thought, oh well, they're a

married couple, they're respectable – which was far from the truth – and so he came with us! And I wrote off to Ninette de Valois, whom I knew quite well, and said: "I've got a discovery for you!"

Ninette de Valois:
Well it was strange – I still see him standing in the doorway leading into our rehearsal room. Not a very good-looking young man, but I remember saying, "I could do something with that face". It didn't seem to be at all an ordinary one, and there was a lot behind those great big eyes he had, of course. I was very fascinated by him.

Margot Fonteyn:
I was about fifteen when I [...] started working with him and I didn't realise what an extraordinary opportunity it was. And *he* was the star, for a long time [...], frankly, I mean trying to get some attention from the audience when he was on the stage was pretty hard, because everybody looked at him. It gave me the opportunity to develop, to *absorb* so much from him. In the ballet he could draw tears from the public, or he could make them just roll about in their seats with laughter. I think that he was one of those people who could go out on the stage, make the public cry tears of emotion at his acting, and at the same time he could be knowing *exactly* if he was in the spotlight or not.

Keith Michel, actor:
He used to tell the most extraordinary stories; he told one about when he was a dancer with Margot Fonteyn and – I'm sure it's not true – but he said, you know, he got rather tight one night and he got off the stage, and he was standing in the wings, and he had to run on and catch her, and he [...] said he saw *two* Margot Fonteyns coming at him and he didn't know which one to catch – well, I mean it's a lovely picture, but I'm not quite sure if it was true – but it made me laugh a lot.

Alan Sievewright [on Michael Benthall's life partnership with Helpmann]:
I think the chemistry of those two men gave a lot to the British theatre – and also internationally.

Robert Helpmann [on appearing as Hamlet in Shakespeare's play in 1944, having earlier created the title role in his own ballet, *Hamlet*, in 1942]:
And then I did indeed play the play. I must admit I planned it rather carefully, so people said, "Oh what a wonderful Hamlet you would make!" Well, they didn't know that I was already going to play Hamlet. And of course the

critics [...] said: "A ballet dancer playing Hamlet?" But I had been training my voice for, then, nearly ten years, and I played Hamlet for a twelve week season of eight performances a week, and never lost my voice.

Stewart Granger:

I went there [the Old Vic Theatre] when we were being bombed when he [Helpmann] played Hamlet, and there were doodle-bombs coming, and [...] it probably wasn't the greatest Hamlet ever, but it was the most *beautiful* Hamlet you've ever seen. You've never seen *anybody* move like Bobby when he was playing Hamlet. Larry [Olivier] was terribly jealous because he... [Granger chuckles] he packed the theatre, Bobby Helpmann, *packed* the theatre, and sometimes there were some empty seats at Larry's [...] Hamlet.

Robert Helpmann [on the hugely successful Sadler's Wells Ballet tour to the USA and Canada in 1949]:

[...] Fonteyn wasn't considered the great ballerina, I wasn't considered all that important to [...] the highbrows in England, until we had conquered New York; *then* we became great; *then* we became "the Royal Ballet"; *then* she became Dame Margot.

Margot Fonteyn [on she and Helpmann dancing the leading roles in *The Sleeping Beauty* on the opening night at Metropolitan Opera House, New York in 1949]:

I can remember *starting* my first entrance – and there was tremendous applause and I couldn't hear the music for a few minutes – and I can remember *ending* the last act, with Bobby, and it had the most *extraordinary* reception.

Alan Sievewright:

Helpmann, I always think, was a man with blazing theatrical ambition. He was not like some people today, I think, who are just artistically greedy – he was genuinely a man of theatrical ambition, and one field was never quite enough. And that is why when he got his teeth into playing Shakespeare he went for the "biggy" – he went to Stratford, and in one season he played King John; [...and] another *Hamlet*, known as "the Victorian *Hamlet*", where he shared on alternate nights the role with Paul Scofield; then he did his Shylock again [...]; and at the same time he was going up and down from Stratford and dancing at Covent Garden with Margot Fonteyn! Such a feat has never happened, I mean, it never *would* happen again.

Ninette de Valois:

He had such a talent he got away with whatever he was trying to do, even if it wasn't his major talent at that time. So I can understand, in a way, this rather *loose* way he behaved about his career – he was always dashing off to do a film or play somewhere.

Moira Shearer [on working with Helpmann during 1947-48 on the film, *The Red Shoes*]:

I found him a little alarming, a little disconcerting as a partner – actually, I thought he was going to push me over most of the time [she chuckles]. He didn't, in fact, but it was a near thing sometimes.

Margaret Rawlings: [On Ashton's ballet *Cinderella*, premièred in 1948, and revived in 1965, with Ashton and Helpmann reprising their original roles]:

When he danced the Ugly Sisters, Sir Frederick Ashton chose to be the pretty one, the "nimeny-pimeny" one, *trying* to be pretty. Bobby, on the other hand, just made her as ugly as he could, on the model of Miss Rawlings: the bombé forehead [she indicates the high round shape of her own forehead], the slipped wig – hair going back *black* – very black eyebrows, and "rocking horse" nostrils [she pushes up the end of her own nose], which he exaggerated with this blob on the end of the nose, which I've always had, and was always being caricatured...

Ninette de Valois:

I think it was a free fight on both sides [she gives a hearty laugh]... [to] see who won [she laughs again]. They got on extremely well; quarrelled a good bit at the same time, and they were really pals, of course, and I think they – after a good bit of shouting – they each listened to the other.

Jeremy Brett, actor [talking over footage of the BBC TV broadcast of Strindberg's play, *The Ghost Sonata* (16 March 1962), with Helpmann as The Old Man, who is wheelchair-bound, and Jeremy Brett as The Student]:

When we actually came to work together it was in that extraordinary, deranged play by Strindberg, called *The Ghost Sonata*, and I had him where I wanted him for the first time, because I had him in a wheelchair! And he said: "You've got me entirely at your mercy", because I [...] could push him wherever I wanted. [...] What was so amazing about Robert Helpmann was that, after this *immense* career as a dancer – I mean, there's no one else who's done it – what Robert did was to step into the classical theatre, which was absolutely unheard of, with the change in the breathing, the work on the voice, and he became a stage star, as well as a television star.

Alan Sievewright:
Robert Helpmann became as famous on the other side of the Atlantic as he was in Britain. He was fortunate in having had a film career – that takes you everywhere. But in America he [...] hit the big time on Broadway with his debut opposite Katharine Hepburn in a comedy by Bernard Shaw, *The Millionairess.* That production they also brought to London, where it was a huge success, with a screaming, ranting Miss Hepburn on the stage – he was devoted to her from thereon. [...]He fell under her spell, and the two of them together went on to have other triumphs in the theatre. They were such *fun* characters [...] as he always said, "Kate [is] the one woman I could [...have been] married to and I'd never have been bored".

Robert Helpmann [on Katharine Hepburn]:
I admire her because she has no... [he pauses to consider]; in the world of the theatre, where people are slightly inclined to be two-faced, or four-faced, or *six*-faced [he gives a wry smile], Kate's directness, and her absolute, 100% honesty, first attracted me to her.

PART TWO

Katharine Hepburn [on venturing with Helpmann, on a rainy day in 1955, into the Sherbrooke Forest in the Dandenong Mountains, near Melbourne, Australia, in order to see lyrebirds in the wild]:
We saw the lyrebird, we saw that *one* lyrebird, we saw *sixteen* lyrebirds that day. I said to Bobby, "I would not have come at all today, what made you come?", and he said, "I had a dream, and there you were lying stark naked on a throne, surrounded by lyrebirds that would bow to you" [she laughs] [...] and he was so fascinated by that, *that's* what made him go out to the Sherbrooke Forest.

Malcolm Williamson, Australian composer of Helpmann's ballet, *The Display* (1964):
If you look at [...] *The Display*, where as well as worshipping the grandeur of savage Australian nature, he [Helpmann] satirises society [and] invites [comparisons with] himself as an exceptional, eccentric "reject" from the Australian "norm". His scenes were all serious, and it's because he had a sense of what's serious that he had a sense of what's comic as well; he turned the serious inside-out, but he knew when to do it.

Unidentified Australian interviewer [c. 1968]:
Have you ever speculated about what life would have been like for you if you had married, if you had had children?
Robert Helpmann:
Oh yes, I have indeed, and […] in fact […] I was in love three times, but two of them were married, and one of them didn't like me [he laughs], so that was that.
Interviewer [pressing the point]:
You don't feel you've missed something in life by not having a family? [Helpmann slowly shakes his head]
Robert Helpmann:
No, no, no…I don't really. I'm not *that* fond of myself that I would like to think I was reproducing myself [he smiles disarmingly at the interviewer].

Alan Sievewright:
Once when we were talking in the garden at Eaton Square [on screen the entrance to No. 72 Eaton Square is seen] he looked at me and he said, "You know, an artist can't function without emotion, and for me", he said, "I find emotion in my relationships far more important than sex. It's the emotion of what I feel, and the stimulus I get from other people, that helps me go forward." And when you think about him you can see that *that* makes total sense, and it's very honest – that as a very young man he really did fall tremendously under the beauty and stimulation of meeting and getting to know Vivien Leigh. I mean, I think he had a great crush on her. Also earlier, he had come under the magnetism of Margaret Rawlings, and much later, in his more mature years, he became fascinated and close to Katharine Hepburn – who wouldn't be? She's a wonderful woman. But at the same time, you can understand his relationship with Michael Benthall, who was a very handsome, very British, very clever man, who stimulated his mind, and the two men went on to great heights together. And *that's* their emotional relationship, that I think is so important to their creativity, and what they were able to give to the British theatre.

Margot Fonteyn [on Ronald Hynd's ballet *The Merry Widow*, made for the Australian Ballet in 1976, during Helpmann's eighteen month tenure as the sole Director of the Company):

Right towards the end of my career he [Helpmann] gave me what was the most wonderful present. He had long-time wanted to do a ballet on *The Merry Widow* […] he didn't choreograph it, Ronald Hynd did the choreography, but Bobby had the whole concept of the ballet, chose the scene designer – again, it [the design] was wonderful – and made this ballet for the Australian Ballet Company [...] and it was the most delightful role I could possibly have had [...] it was like a farewell present from Bobby, and it brought to a full circle this wonderful relationship which I had had as an artist with him all my life [on screen we see the first night curtain call with Helpmann and Fonteyn, who then embrace warmly onstage].

Unidentified Australian interviewer [c. 1979]:
You've had a very long and fairly acrimonious reputation with boards in this country, haven't you?
Robert Helpmann:
Well I can't *bear* amateurs, you know, and it irritates me. I mean I don't go into a bank or a shipping firm and tell the directors there how to run [their business...]. I'm seventy years old and I've been on the stage for fifty-six years, and [he laughs drily] if I don't know it [my business] now, I *ought* to.

Maina Gielgud [interviewed about Helpmann, while she was Director of the Australian Ballet, c. 1989]:
He was obviously a prime example of what I call the enormously "gutsy" Australian, who had the courage to go elsewhere and show what he was made of, and then come back with that behind him [...] particularly, at that time, that took even more courage than it would have nowadays.

Keith Michel, actor [recalling a conversation with Helpmann in Australia]:
He said, "I suppose they're... getting on in London without me – I can never imagine anyone getting on without me!" [Michel chuckles] and, of course, he was right, in a funny sort of way...

Katharine Hepburn [speaking sometime after Helpmann's death in 1986]:
[...] very sweet and very tender and very nice, and very thoughtful, Bobby was – *very*!

Robert Helpmann [speaking straight to camera and recalling his eighteen-year-old self appearing as a dancer in a touring production of Franz Lehar's 1922 operetta *Frasquita*, which opened in Wellington, New Zealand on 27 December 1927. Minnie Everett, to whom he refers, was a choreographer for the show's production company, J.C. Williamson Ltd.; she ran a musical theatre school with her associate, Minnie Hooper, where Helpmann was a student]:

I remember after the first performance of *Frasquita* in New Zealand, Miss

Everett – "Minnie" – shouted from the stalls [he imitates a strident voice with a strong New Zealand twang]: "'Scuse me! Has your father got any money?" And I said [in a piping voice]: "I think so, Miss Everett." And she said: "Well he'd better buy you a flower shop, 'cos you're never gonna make good in the theatre!" [He smiles broadly].

Full credits:
Directed by Don Featherstone
Based on a concept and script by Alan Sievewright
Helpmann archive interview provided by The Australia Council
Produced with the assistance of the Australian Broadcasting Corporation
Produced by Primetime Television in association with Don Featherstone productions for London Weekend Television (LWT)
Executive Producer Nigel Wattis
Edited and Presented by Melvyn Bragg
© LWT MCMXC (1990)
An LWT production for ITV

Robert Helpmann: Sound and Screen

Olwen Terris

This selective list covers all Helpmann's feature films and key appearances on television and radio in Australia and the UK. Non-broadcast film footage and sound recordings are also included. Where a print/broadcast is known to be held in the National Film & Sound Archive, Australia, the BFI National Archive, the BBC Archive or the British Library Sound Archive (feature films excluded) this is noted; see notes at the end for guidance on access.

Abbreviations: chor. Choreographer /dir. Director /p.c. Production Company /prod. Producer

FILMS AND TV MOVIES (Helpmann's character name in parenthesis)

"...*One of our Aircraft Is Missing*" (De Jong), The Archers Film Company, dir. Michael Powell and Emeric Pressburger, 24 April 1942.
[The adventures of a British bomber crew forced to bale out over Holland after a raid on Germany, and who are assisted on their return home by the Dutch resistance.]

Henry V (Bishop of Ely), Two Cities Film, dir. Laurence Olivier, 23 November 1944.
[Filmed adaptation of Shakespeare's play.]

Caravan (Wycroft), Gainsborough Films, dir. Arthur Crabtree, 12 April 1946.
[Period romance: Richard Darrell, son of a country doctor, and Francis who is rich, are rivals for the hand of Oriana. Starring Stewart Granger, Dennis Price and Anne Crawford.]

The Red Shoes (Ivan Boleslawsky), The Archers Film Company, dir. Michael Powell & Emeric Pressburger, chor. Helpmann and Massine, 22 July 1948.
[Fantasy of a young girl who achieves fame in a ballet company dancing in the story of Hans Christian Andersen's "Red Shoes". Torn between love for a composer, and artistic devotion to the ballet master, she dances herself to death. Starring Moira Shearer, Léonide Massine and Helpmann.]

The Tales of Hoffmann (Lindorf, Dr. Coppélius, Dapertutto, Dr. Miracle), The Archers Film Company, dir. Michael Powell & Emeric Pressburger., chor.

Ashton, 1 April 1951.
[Version of the opera by Offenbach, chiefly mimed by dancers to the sung score.]

The Big Money (The Reverend or The Bogus Clergyman), Rank, dir. John Paddy Carstairs, 1956, but first screened 30 May 1958.
[Comedy crime drama: a crook steals a bag of £1 notes only to find they are forged. He desperately tries to spend them but ends up in jail. Starring Ian Carmichael and Kathleen Harrison.]

The Iron Petticoat (Ivan Kropotkin), Remus, dir. Ralph Thomas, 9 August 1956.
[Comedy about the love between a U.S. officer and a Soviet woman pilot. Starring Bob Hope and Katharine Hepburn.]

55 Days in Peking (Prince Tuan), Charles Bronston Productions, dir. Nicholas Ray, 1963. [Drama about the Boxer Rebellion in 1900. Starring Charlton Heston, Ava Gardner, David Niven and Flora Robson.]

The Soldier's Tale (The Devil), Ipsilon Films, dir. Michael Birkett, chor. Helpmann, 12 October 1964.
[Film version of Stravinsky's opera "L'Histoire du Soldat", modelled on the stage production mounted for Glyndebourne Opera Company by Gunther Rennert. With Helpmann, Brian Phelan plays the Soldier and Svetlana Beriosova the Princess.]

The Quiller Memorandum (Weng). Rank, dir. Michael Anderson, 10 November 1966.
[Spy thriller, set in Berlin, concerning attempts to uncover neo-Nazism. Based on the novel *The Quiller Memorandum* by "Adam Hall" (Elleston Trevor) with a screenplay by Harold Pinter. Starring George Segal, Alec Guinness, Max von Sydow and Senta Berger.]

Chitty Chitty Bang Bang (Child Catcher), Warfield Productions for United Artists, dir. Ken Hughes, 16 December 1968.
[Unsuccessful inventor, Potts, restores an old car and names it 'Chitty Chitty Bang Bang'; it has the power to become magically airborne. Based on a collection of short stories, *The Magical Car*, by Ian Fleming. Starring Dick Van Dyke, Sally Ann Howes and Lionel Jeffries.]
Alice's Adventures in Wonderland (The Mad Hatter), Shaftel Productions for Fox-Rank, dir. William Sterling, Winter 1972 (USA) – 1973 (U.K.).

[Musical version of Lewis Carroll's story. Starring Fiona Fullerton as Alice.]

Don Quixote (Don Quixote), International Arts with AIFC and the Australian Ballet Foundation, dir. Rudolf Nureyev/Robert Helpmann, 19 July, 1973.
[Filmed adaptation of Marius Petipa's ballet as staged in 1970 for Australian Ballet by Nureyev and Helpmann. Starring Nureyev, Helpmann and Lucette Aldous. Remastered for general circulation, 1999.]

Barney (uncredited cast member), Columbia Pictures, dir. David S. Waddington, 16 December 1976.
[Set in the 1880s, the story of a twelve-year-old , questing to find his father. Travelling on a ship from Sydney to Melbourne, he is shipwrecked with an Irish convict, who helps him find his way to Ballarat.]

The Mango Tree (Professor), Pisces Productions, dir. Kevin James Dobson, 13 December 1977.
[Story of the life of a boy growing up in a Queensland town in the early 1900s.]

Patrick (Doctor Roget), Australian International Film Corporation,. dir. Richard Franklin. 1 October 1978.
[Horror film about psychokinesis. Note: Helpmann seriously injured his back trying to lift the actor, Robert Thompson (Patrick).]

Puzzle (Buckminster Shepherd), Transatlantic Enterprises, dir. Gordon Hessler, Television Series created in December 1978, but first broadcast in England on BBC1, 25 October 1983.
[Drama: a faded tennis ace is approached by his former wife to help find two million dollars of missing gold. Starring James Franciscus and Wendy Hughes.]

Second Time Lucky (The Devil), Edenrock, dir. Michael Anderson, 1984.
[Comedy drama: for a bet, God (Robert Morley) and the Devil (Helpmann) plunge a contemporary couple, Adam and Eve, into the Garden of Eden, Ancient Rome, World War One and the Roaring Twenties.]

DOCUMENTARIES

Steps of the Ballet (Narrator), Crown Film Unit, dir. Muir Matheson. p. Alexander Shaw. chor. Andrée Howard, 30 September 1947. 24 mins. Available for streaming and download at http://film.britishcouncil.org/ steps-of-the-ballet, accessed 10/2013.
[Helpmann discusses the basic positions and movements in ballet; the first half of the film demonstrates various ballet steps and the process of staging a show; the second half is a short new ballet showcasing these techniques with dancers of the Covent Garden and Sadler's Wells Ballet Companies.]

The British – Are They Artistic? p.c. This Modern Age, prod. Sergei Nolbandov, (1948). 21 mins. Note: presumably the NFTVA cataloguer has not been able to identify the ballet/s. Located in the BFI National Archive.
[A survey of the popularity of the arts in Britain before and after the Second World War, calling for a rise in the general level of appreciation throughout the country. Includes an item on the Arts Council and how it made possible a performance of Benjamin Britten's opera *Albert Herring* at Glyndebourne, and also supported the Covent Garden Ballet. Robert Helpmann can be seen in some of the ballet footage.]

TELEVISION

Job, BBC (11/11/1936). 25 mins.
[Televised mounting of 1931 ballet by Ninette de Valois, based on William Blake's vision of the Book of Job with Helpmann in the role of Satan.]

Demonstration Film BBC (1937). 48 mins. BFI National Archive.
[A film promoting BBC television output in 1937, which includes a 2 min. sequence of Helpmann in the Tarantella from *Façade* (Mountaineer), chor. Frederick Ashton.]

Le Lac des Cygnes, BBC (13/12/1937). 40 mins.
[Act II of Petipa's ballet, performed by the Vic-Wells Ballet Company. Margot Fonteyn is Odette, the Swan Queen and Helpmann, Prince Siegfried.]

Arleccino (Arleccino). prod. Steven Thomas. BBC (12/02/1939). 60 mins.
[A theatrical capriccio in one act. Words and music by Ferruccio Busoni. Helpmann's role as Arleccino comprised entirely spoken dialogue in what was otherwise a sung libretto. Costumes designed by Hugh Stephenson.]

Box for One (Wednesday Theatre). (The Caller). dir. Tony Richardson. BBC (18/02/1953). 30 mins.

[A suspense play by Peter Brook, requiring a virtuoso performance by a single actor. The 'box for one' is a lonely outdoor telephone booth. A young gangster enters the booth, rings a number and asks if there are any messages for him. As he leaves, the booth the telephone rings. A new production with Helpmann again playing The Caller was broadcast by ABV 2 TV, Melbourne on 17 August 1958.]

HEPBURN-HELPMANN: Stars here for the Old Vic Season. p.c. Fox Movietone (12/051955). 1 min. National Screen & Sound Archive, Australia.
[Movietone newsreel. Arrival in Sydney of Katharine Hepburn and Robert Helpmann, actors with Old Vic Theatre Company. Soon to open in an Australian Shakespeare season. Hepburn and Helpmann disembark from the aircraft and walk towards the airport terminal where they make a short speech.]

Coppélia. dir. Margaret Dale, chor. Arthur Saint-Léon. BBC (27/10/1957). 50 mins. BFI National Archive. Note: this footage is part of a DVD compilation of classic performances released by ICA Classics. www.icaartists.co.uk.
[Live studio performance of the ballet. Helpmann is Doctor Coppélius and Nadia Nerina is Swanhilda.]

Interview with Robert Helpmann, ITV (3/3/1958). 1.5 mins. The clip is streamed at www.itnsource.com.
[News footage showing Helpmann practising with Julia Farron at Covent Garden. He is interviewed by Lynne Reid-Banks about his return to The Royal Ballet as guest artist. Note: The footage is mute.]

Nude with Violin (Sebastien), dir. Lionel Harris. (Play of the Week) ITV (21/07/1959). 89 mins.
[Play by Noël Coward satirising modern art, criticism, artistic pretension and the value placed on art. Helpmann had played the role, originally created for John Gielgud, at the Globe Theatre London from 25 November 1957 until the production closed in February 1958; he subsequently directed and starred in a production for a three-month tour of Australia and New Zealand in the summer of 1958.]

The Ghost Sonata (Old Man), dir. Stuart Burge. BBC (16/03/1962).70 mins. BFI National Archive.
[Strindberg's play with Helpmann, Beatrix Lehmann as the Mummy and Jeremy Brett as the Student].

An Evening with Robert Helpmann, BBC (1963).
[No further details known.]

Checkmate, dir. Margaret Dale. BBC (31/07/1963). 40 mins. BBC Archive.
[A studio performance with The Royal Ballet in Ninette de Valois' 1937 dance-drama, to music and a scenario by Arthur Bliss. Helpmann appears as the White [sic] King. The red players were altered to white as the performance was transmitted in black & white.]

Sing, Sing, Sing, ATN 7, Sydney (31/01/1964) Helpmann segment 2 mins. National Film & Screen Archive, Australia.
[Australian television variety show hosted by Johnny O'Keefe. Guests include Helpmann who performs 'Surfer Doll' in the studio. Note: the footage of Helpmann is posted to YouTube (accessed 11/2013).]

Behind the Scenes: Australia's Biggest Opera – Ballet Season (CINESOUND REVIEW. No. 1715). (10/09/1964). Duration unknown. National Film & Sound Archive, Australia.
[Newsfilm. The Australian Ballet and Australian Opera are seen rehearsing at the Australian Elizabethan Theatre Trust studios in Sydney. Shots of the ballet class and opera chorus rehearsing. Peggy van Praagh and Robert Helpmann discuss *The Display* choreographed by Helpmann. Brief footage of the ballet in performance includes shots of Barry Kitcher dancing in the Lyrebird costume designed by Sidney Nolan; Kathleen Gorham dancing the role of the Female; and brief shots of the *corps de ballet*.]

Palace Investiture, ITV (17/11/1964). 30 secs.
[News footage. Helpmann in morning dress accompanied by his sister. He looks at his medal, the CBE, and then speaks to an unseen interviewer. Note: The footage is mute. The clip is streamed at <www.itnsource.com.>]

BBC News (23/12/1965). c. 30 secs.
[Item which shows Helpmann and Frederick Ashton making up as the Stepsisters in Ashton's *Cinderella* (1948); Helpmann is seen applying lipstick and putting on his wig.]

"In For A Penny" (episode in TV series, *Contrabandits*), dir. Brian Faull. prod. Eric Taylor. Australian Broadcasting Corporation (22/09/1967). Note: The Australian National Film & Sound Archive holds stills of Helpmann in this episode but not the footage.
[Australian television series about the fight against crime by the Australian

Customs Department operating on Sydney Harbour. Helpmann, wearing his own clothes and jewellery, plays the lead guest role of the sinister Donald Steele.]

Cinderella, chor. Frederick Ashton. BBC2 (25/12/1970). 104 mins. BBC Archive.
[Helpmann and Ashton dance the Stepsisters; Antoinette Sibley and Anthony Dowell are Cinderella and the Prince. Recorded at the Royal Opera House.]

Review, BBC2 (28/01/1972). 15 mins. BBC Archive.
[The Sadler's Wells Theatre is threatened with closure and the administrator Douglas Craig, Ninette de Valois and Hugh Willat discuss its difficulties. Includes excerpts from Ashton's *A Wedding Bouquet* danced by the Vic-Wells Ballet with Margot Fonteyn as Julia and Helpmann as The Groom. Note: Robert Penman's *A Catalogue of Ballet and Contemporary Dance in the BBC Television and Videotape Library 1937-1984* notes that the extract from the rehearsal of *A Wedding Bouquet* is from a film owned by the Vic-Wells Association, which was shot at the Sadler's Wells theatre in the 1930s.]

Parkinson, BBC1 (10/02/1973). 69 mins.
[Helpmann is Michael Parkinson's guest on his chat show along with Claire Bloom and Eartha Kitt.]

Helpmann (OMNIBUS). dir. Julia Matheson, p. Margaret Dale. BBC1 (30/09/73). 53 mins. BBC Archive.
[Documentary profile: Ronald Eyre talks to Helpmann about his childhood in Australia and his career in dance, drama and the cinema. Includes excerpts from *The Soldier's Tale, The Tales of Hoffmann, Quiller Memorandum, 55 Days in Peking* and *Don Quixote*.]

Sir Robert Helpmann. dir/prod. Keith Salvat, cinematographer David Gribble, p.c. Keisal Films (1975). 52 mins. National Film & Sound Archive, Australia.
[Documentary: Helpmann talks about his lifelong involvement in theatre and ballet. He speaks of those who inspired him including Anna Pavlova and Margot Fonteyn; of his vision for the development of dance in Australia; and of his ballet *The Display*, entirely Australian in production and content. Note: the film was shot at the Princess Theatre in Melbourne where Helpmann is seated on the stage with the empty theatre behind him.]
Sir Robert Helpmann: This Is Your Life (Australian Version). dir. Ron Way, presenter Mike Willesee. Seven Network (19/09/1975). 60 mins. National

Film & Sound Archive, Australia.
[Michael Powell is one of the guests.]

Thank You, Madam (DANCE MONTH), BBC2 (04/06/1978). 65 mins.
[The story of The Royal Ballet, an eightieth birthday tribute to Dame Ninette de Valois, including a repeat of *Checkmate*, originally transmitted 31/7/63 with Helpmann as the Red King.]

"Save The Last Dance For Me" (two-instalment episode in *Country Practice*). dir. Peter Maxwell. (30/04/1985). 30 mins.
[Australian soap opera, set around a veterinary practice in Wandlin Valley. Helpmann plays Sir Adrian Dormin; the cast also included his sister, Sheila. Transmitted in Britain on ITV in the 1990s.]

Tales of Helpmann: A Profile of Sir Robert Helpmann (*THE SOUTH BANK SHOW*). dir. Don Featherstone. p.c. Australian Film Finance Corporation/ Don Featherstone Productions/Primetime Television, ITV (24/06/90). 60 mins. BFI National Archive.
[A profile with contributions from people who worked with him including Ninette de Valois, Margot Fonteyn, Alicia Markova, Malcolm Williamson and Margaret Rawlings. Note: The programme uses several clips from the Australian documentary, *Sir Robert Helpmann* (1975).]

Robert Helpmann Remembered, Performance (21/09/2001). 90 mins.
[A profile including interviews with, and contributions from, Rudolf Nureyev, Margot Fonteyn and Keith Michell.]

RADIO

Ballet First Night, prod. Stephen Potter. BBC Home Service (23/06/1941). 40 mins. British Library Sound Archive.
[A reconstruction of the production of Gluck's *Orfeo ed Euridice* from its first conception, through the stages of discussion and rehearsal, ending with the opening bars of the overture. Includes contributions from Constant Lambert, Ninette de Valois and Robert Helpmann.]

A Midsummer Night's Dream, prod. Val Gielgud. BBC Home Service (23/04/1944). 165 mins. including interval for the News.
[Shakespeare's play adapted by Cynthia Pugh with Helpmann as Oberon, Doris Lytton as Titania and Max Adrian as Puck.]

FROM THE LONDON THEATRE: Caesar and Cleopatra (1951). British Library Sound Archive.
[BBC radio broadcast with extracts from current stage plays. This edition covers Shaw's *Caesar and Cleopatra* and Shakespeare's *Antony and Cleopatra*. Includes Helpmann as Apollodorus in the former and as Octavius Caesar in Michael Benthall's production of the latter. A Festival of Britain production from the St James's Theatre, London.]

Desert Island Discs, BBC Home Service (19/06/1953).
[Helpmann is Roy Plomley's guest. This edition is not available for listening on the Desert Island Discs website, but the musical choices are listed. See: http://www.bbc.co.uk/radio4/features/desert-island-discs.]

A Midsummer Night's Dream (1954). British Library Sound Archive.
[Sound recording of Michael Benthall's 1954 production with Helpmann as Oberon, Moira Shearer as Titania and Stanley Holloway as Bottom.]

Surf Dance: Let-A-Go Your Heart (c1964). HMV EA-4665. National Film & Sound Archive, Australia. Preservation material only.
[Sound recording. Songs written by Eaton Magoon Jnr. "Let-a-Go Your Heart", is from the Broadway musical *13 Daughters*. Helpmann recorded this disc of surfing songs in 1963 in a studio in Honolulu on his way to Sydney. Note: This single is extremely rare and a collector's item; as is the sheet music which features Helpmann on a surfboard wearing a peroxide blonde wig.]

"Shakespeare in Ballet" (*TALKING OF THEATRE*), BBC Network Three (19/04/1964). 30 mins.
[BBC radio documentary introduced by Carl Wildman. Robert Helpmann talks to Gordon Gow about the new production of his ballet, *Hamlet*, first created and performed in 1942 and now with Rudolf Nureyev in the title role. Nureyev talks about his characterisation of Hamlet, his acquaintance with Shakespeare, and working with British choreographers.]

"Interview with Robert Helpmann" (*SPEAKING OF DANCE*), WNYC, New York (11/10/1973). 25 mins. New York Public Library, Jerome Robbins Dance Division.
[Lee Edward Steen interviews Helpmann, who talks about the problems of filming *Don Quixote*, Rudolf Nureyev, the Australian Ballet Company, its audience and his background.]

Interviews with Robert Helpmann, WRVR, New York (October 1973). 30 mins. New York Public Library, Jerome Robbins Dance Division.
[Part 1: Daniel Mack interviews Helpmann, who discusses his belief in the importance of dramatic training for actors dancing the role of Hamlet in his ballet and his philosophy of art as entertainment. Part 2: Ponchitta Pierce interviews Helpmann, who talks about how he and Rudolf Nureyev adapted *Don Quixote* for film. Note: The Ponchitta Pierce interview was broadcast by television station WNBC, New York on October 28 1973.]

Desert Island Discs, BBC Radio 4 (23/12/1978). 40 mins.
[Helpmann is Roy Plomley's guest, his second appearance on the programme. Favourite disc: Victoria de los Angeles singing *Bailero*. Available for listening on the Desert Island Discs website: http://www.bbc.co.uk/radio4/features/desert-island-discs.]

Start The Week, BBC Radio 4 (02/06/1980). 11 mins.
[Helpmann is interviewed by Richard Baker on his life and work.]

"Sir Robert Helpmann Goes Surfing" (*OFF THE WALL*), Raven Records (c. 1982). Preservation material only. National Film & Sound Archive, Australia.
[Sound recording. Helpmann sings "Surf Doll", "Surf Dance", "I Still Could Care", "Let-a-Go Your Heart".]

NON-BROADCAST MATERIAL

Aurora Pas de Deux – Margot Fonteyn (1936). 2.5 mins. BFI National Archive.
[A performance by Margot Fonteyn (and probably Robert Helpmann, her partner at the Sadler's Wells Ballet in 1936) of the *pas de deux* 'Aurora', depicting the wedding of Princess Aurora and Prince Désiré, a piece extrapolated from the ballet *The Sleeping Beauty*. The couple had performed the *pas de deux* as part of a divertissement at the Royal Opera House on 24 February 1936.]

Les Masques (1945). 1 min. BFI National Archive.
[Robert Helpmann, Sally Gilmour and Marie Rambert at rehearsals for the ballet *Les Masques*, choreographed by Ashton.]

LORD WAKEHURST BALLET FILMS: REEL 1 (1957). Colour. Silent. c. 2mins. BFI National Archive.
[Helpmann and Annette Page dancing in *Miracle in the Gorbals*. Episodes

include: The Suicide solo; Helpmann talking to dancers; street scene; Suicide solo (again); The Official with the dead body of the Suicide Girl and crowd behind, he puts the black cloth over her face; the Stranger brings the Suicide Girl back to life; crowd scene; the killing of the Stranger.]

LORD WAKEHURST BALLET FILMS: REEL 14 (1962). Colour. Silent. c. 2 mins. BFI National Archive.
[Helpmann rehearses *Elektra* with Nadia Nerina. The first part shows rehearsals with Helpmann and Nadia Nerina; Monica Mason can be seen at the beginning. The second part is the performance featuring Nadia Nerina, including the notoriously risky 'double throw' movement.]

The Royal Ballet, prod. John de Vere Loder (1964). Colour. 45 mins.
[The history, work, personalities and productions of The Royal Ballet. Includes footage of Helpmann dancing in the 1958 revival of *Miracle in the Gorbals* (duration of segment unknown).]

The Royal Ballet in Rehearsal: Hamlet (1964). dir. Edmée Wood. 17 mins. BFI National Archive.
[The Royal Ballet is filmed in dress rehearsal on stage at the Royal Ballet, Covent Garden with Nureyev as Hamlet and Monica Mason as Gertrude. Piano accompaniment by Anthony Twiner.]

The Royal Ballet in Rehearsal: Cinderella (1965). Duration unknown. BFI National Archive.
[Royal Ballet dress rehearsal of revised production (including newly-designed sets and costumes) of Ashton's *Cinderella*. Filmed by available light. Visibility of the opening of Act III is reduced by a stage gauze. Helpmann and Ashton are the Stepsisters with Margot Fonteyn as Cinderella.]

Travelling With Terpsichore, IIIB. prod. John de Vere Loder. (1965). Duration unknown. BFI National Archive.
[Includes footage of Australian Ballet's dress rehearsals at Covent Garden of Helpmann's *The Display* with Kathleen Gorham, Bryan Lawrence and Garth Welch and also Helpmann's *Yugen*.]

Robert Helpmann, CBE (21/08/1967). p.c. Cinesound. 3 mins. Note: This footage was unissued/unused. It is streamed on the British Pathe website: http://www.britishpathe.com/video/robert-helpmann/query/film.
[Newsreel item. Sydney, Australia. Shots in the dressing room of prima ballerina Marylyn Jones at a costume fitting for Ashton's *La Fille mal gardée*.

Helpmann is in the dressing room and speaks of the success of the recent world tour of The Australian Ballet. He talks of his role in the forthcoming film, *Chitty Chitty Bang Bang*.]

"Mixed Performance: *Façade*" (*THE MAGIC OF DANCE*), BBC, prod. Patricia Foy. (1979). 25 mins. BBC Archive.
[Two sets of camera rushes from the performance at the Royal Opera House marking Margot Fonteyn's 60th birthday. She and Helpmann dance the Tango and the Tarantella from Ashton's *Façade* with the rest of the cast.]

Lyrebird (Tales of Helpmann). 1999. No commercial release or archive holding known.
[Trailer for Tyler Coppin's one man show staged at the 1999 Edinburgh Festival. Posted on YouTube [accessed 5/2/13].]

ACCESS TO AUDIO-VISUAL ARCHIVES

Access to titles held at the BFI National Archive and the BBC Archive will depend on whether a screening print is held (as opposed to master preservation material). The contacts for booking material (including BBC broadcasts) and general discussion at the BFI National Archive are Fleur Buckley or Kathleen Dickson http://www.bfi.org.uk/about-bfi/help-faq/film-bookings or fleur.buckley@bfi.org.uk/kathleen.dickson@bfi.org.uk.

To arrange to listen to material at the British Library Sound Archive visit http://www.bl.uk/reshelp/inrrooms/stp/sound/listening.html.

To make enquiries of the National Film & Sound Archive, Australia visit http://www.nfsa.gov.au/about/contact.

To make enquiries of the New York Public Library, Jerome Robbins Dance Division visit http://www.nypl.org/ask-nypl.

Bibliography

Books and Articles

Ackland, Joss, Letter to *The Times*, 10 September 1974.

Aldred, Nanette, "Hein Heckroth and The Archers", in Ian Christie and Andrew Moor (eds.), *The Cinema of Michael Powell: International Perspectives on an English Film-Maker* (London: BFI, 2005).

Ambler, Dail, "'Where do we go from here?' An analysis of a career", *Ballet Carnaval*, No 6, June-July 1947, pp. 142-144.

Anderson, Zoë, *The Royal Ballet 75 Years* (London: Faber, 2006).

Andrews, Richard and Rex Gibson (eds.), *Hamlet Cambridge School Shakespeare* (Cambridge: Cambridge University Press, 2005).

Anonymous, "*Checkmate*: A New Ballet by Arthur Bliss", *Musical Times*, 78, 1937, pp. 522-523.

Anonymous, "Caravan (1946)", *Monthly Film Bulletin*, Vol 13, No 148, April 1946, p. 44.

Anonymous, "Robert Helpmann: A Portrait", *Dancing Times* (June 1953), p.539.

Anthony, Gordon, *Camera Studies, The Vic-Wells Ballet* (London: Geoffrey Bles, 1938).

Anthony, Gordon, *The Sleeping Princess* (London: George Routledge & Sons, 1940).

Anthony, Gordon, *Studies of Robert Helpmann*, (London: Home & Van Thal, 1946).

Barton, James, *James Barton on BRB and rehearsing with a legend...* (Birmingham: Birmingham Hippodrome, 2014), https://birminghamhippodrome. wordpress.com/2014/09/16/james-barton-on-brb-and-rehearsing-with-a-legend

Bartram, George, "Robert Helpmann – Human Dynamo", *Picturegoer*, 3 July 1948.

Bausch, Pina, *Speech* (Published by courtesy of the Inamori Foundation), http://www.pinabausch.org/en/pina/what-moves-me

Bemrose, Anna, *Robert Helpmann: A Servant of Art* (St Lucia, Queensland: University of Queensland Press, 2008).

Beauman, Sally, *The Royal Shakespeare Company: a History of Ten Decades* (Oxford: Oxford University Press, 1982).

Beaumont, Cyril W., *Complete Book of Ballets* (London: Putnam, 1937).

Beaumont, Cyril W., *The Sadler's Wells Ballet: A Detailed Account of Works in the Permanent Repertory with Critical Notes* (London: Wyman and Sons, 1946).

Benthall, Michael, "The Dance-Drama" in Arnold L. Haskell (ed.), *Sadler's Wells Ballet Books No. 3:* Hamlet *and* Miracle in the Gorbals (London: Bodley Head, 1949), pp. 7-12.

Berson, Jessia, "Old Dogs, New Tricks" in Valerie Barnes Lipscomb and Leni Marshall (eds.), *Staging Age: The Performance of Age in Theatre, Dance, and Film* (New York: Palgrave Macmillan, 2010).

Bland, Alexander, *Fonteyn and Nureyev: the Story of a Partnership* (London: Orbis, 1979).

Bland, Alexander, *The Royal Ballet: The First 50 Years* (London: Threshold Books, 1981).

Bliss, Arthur, *As I Remember* (London: Faber and Faber, 1970).

Bliss, Arthur, "Grace Notes on Ballet" in Gregory Roscow (ed.), *Bliss on Music: Selected Writings of Arthur Bliss, 1920-1975* (Oxford: Oxford University Press, 1991), pp. 187-188.

Bradshaw, Peter, "*The Tales of Hoffmann* – Powell and Pressburger's other magic ballet film", online review, 26 February 2015 at http://www.theguardian.com/film/2015/feb/26/tales-of-hoffmann-r 2015

Brahms, Caryl, *Robert Helpmann: Choreographer*, with photographs by Russell Sedgwick (London: Batsford, 1943).

Brahms, Caryl, "British Choreographers" in Peter Noble (ed.). *British Ballet* (London: Skelton Robinson, 1949).

Brahms, Caryl, *A Seat at the Ballet* (Bristol: Evans Brothers, 1951).

Brannigan, Erin, *Dancefilm: Choreography and the Moving Image* (Oxford: Oxford University Press, 2011).

Bratton, Jacky, *New Readings in Theatre History* (Cambridge: Cambridge University Press, 2003.

Brinson, Peter, and Peggy van Praagh, *The Choreographic Art* (London: Adam & Charles Black, 1963).

Brissenden, Alan, and Keith Glennon, *Australia Dances. Creating Australian Dance, 1945–1965* (Kent Town, South Australia: Wakefield Press, 2010).

Britton, Andrew, *Katharine Hepburn: Star as Feminist* (London: Studio Vista, 1995).

Bungey, Darleen. *Arthur Boyd. A Life* (Crows Nest, NSW: Allen & Unwin, 2007).

Christie, Ian, *Arrows of Desire* (London and Boston: Faber and Faber, 1994).

Clarke, Mary, *The Sadler's Wells Ballet: A History and an Appreciation* (London: Adam and Charles Black, 1955).

Clarke, Mary, *Shakespeare at the Old Vic: Fourth Season* (London: Hamish Hamilton, 1957).

Clarke, Mary, "Ballet in Wartime IV", *The Dancing Times*, June 1990.

Cole, Hugo and Andrew Burn, "Bliss, Sir Arthur" in Stanley Sadie and John

Tyrrell (eds.), *The New Grove Dictionary of Music and Musicians*, 2nd ed. (London: Macmillan, 2001), Vol. 3, pp. 699-702.

Denby, Edwin, *Dance Writings* (London: Dance Books, 1986).

De Valois, Ninette, "Robert Helpmann, His Place in the Theatre", in Gordon Anthony, *Studies of Robert Helpmann* (London: Home & Van Thal, 1946).

De Valois, Ninette, *Come Dance with Me* (London: Hamish Hamilton, 1957; Second Revised Edition, Dance Books, 1981).

De Valois, Ninette, "Helpmann: a rare sense of the theatre", *The Daily Telegraph*, 29 September, 1986.

Dickson, Barbara, "Age and the Dance Artist" in Valerie Barnes Lipscomb and Leni Marshall (eds.), *Staging Age: The Performance of Age in Theatre, Dance, and Film* (New York: Palgrave Macmillan, 2010).

Dowler, Gerald, "From Page to Stage", *Dancing Times*, October 2016, Vol. 107, Issue 1274, pp. 40-43.

Durgnant, Raymond, "Durgnant on Powell and Pressburger", in Ian Christie (ed.), *Powell, Pressburger and Others*, (London: BFI, 1978), pp. 65-78.

Edwards, Leslie, *In Good Company, Sixty Years with The Royal Ballet* (Alton: Dance Books, 2003).

Farjeon, Herbert, *The Shakespearean Scene. Dramatic Criticisms* (London: Hutchinson, 1948).

Fisher, Hugh, *The Sadler's Wells Theatre Ballet* (London: Adam and Charles Black, 1956).

Fonteyn, Margot, *The Magic of Dance* (New York: Alfred A. Knopf, 1979).

Garcia-Márquez, Vicente, *Massine: A Biography* (London: Nick Hern Books, 1996).

Goodwin, Noël, "Bliss at the Ballet", *Dance and Dancers*, August 1991, pp. 19-21.

Gourlay, J. Logan (ed.) *Robert Helpmann: Album* (Glasgow: Stage and Screen Press, Ltd., 1948).

Greenfield, Amy, "The Kinesthetics of Avant-Garde Dance Film: Deren and Harris", Judy Mitoma (ed.), *Envisioning Dance on Film and Video* (New York: Mcpherson and Company, 2005), p. 21-26.

Guthrie, Tyrone, *A Life in the Theatre* (London: Hamish Hamilton, 1960).

Hart, Deborah. *Arthur Boyd. Agony and Ecstasy* (Canberra: National Gallery of Australia, 2014.

Haskell, Arnold L., *Ballet, A Complete Guide to Appreciation*, Revised Edition (Harmondsworth: Penguin Books, 1945).

Haskell, Arnold L., *Miracle in the Gorbals: A Study* (Edinburgh: Albyn Press, 1946).

Haskell, Arnold L., "Outstanding Events of the Year" in Arnold L. Haskell (ed.), *The Ballet Annual: A Record and Year Book of the Ballet*, Issue 1

(London: Adam and Charles Black, 1947), pp. 7-38.

Haskell, Arnold L. (ed.) *Sadler's Wells Ballet Books No. 3:* Hamlet *and* Miracle in the Gorbals (London: Bodley Head, 1949).

Haskell, Arnold L. (ed.), *Baron at the Ballet* (London: Collins, 1950).

Haskell, Arnold L. (ed.), *Baron Encore* (London: Collins, 1952).

Haskell, Arnold L., "*The Tales of Hoffman* (sic): Carlton Cinema", in Arnold L. Haskell (ed.), *The Ballet Annual: A Record and Year Book of the Ballet*, Issue 6 (London: Adam and Charles Black, 1952), pp. 26-27.

Helpman, Mary, *The Helpman Family Story: 1796–1964* (Adelaide: Rigby, 1967).

Helpmann, Robert, "Learning to be a Good Dancer", *The Old Vic and Sadlers Wells Magazine*, April, 1934.

Helpmann, Robert, "Shakespeare and the Ballet", *The Old Vic and Sadlers Wells Magazine*, January, 1938.

Helpmann, Robert, "The Function of Ballet: A Reply to Some Critics", *Dancing Times*, 9, 1942, pp. 584-586.

Helpmann, Robert, "Dance and the Drama: Ballet Can Take Anything in Life and Art as Its Dramatic Theme", *Band Wagon*, July 1945, pp. 40-41.

Helpmann, Robert, "A Choreographer Speaks", *New Theatre*, March-April 1947, pp. 12-13.

Helpmann, Robert, "British Choreography and its Critics" in Peter Noble, (ed.), *British Ballet* (London: Skelton Robinson, 1949).

Helpmann, Robert, "The public has the final say. To become a cultural power Australia must train its own dancers and actors – and they'll have to be good", [Australian] *Woman*, 20 June 1955, p.155.

Hepburn, Katharine, *Me: Stories of My Life* (London: Random House, 1991).

Hodgdon, Barbara, "Photography, Theater, Mnemonics; or, Thirteen Ways of looking at a Still" in W.B. Worthen with Peter Holland (eds.), *Theorizing Practice: Redefining Theatre History* (Basingstoke & New York: Palgrave Macmillan, 2003).

Homans, Jennifer, *New Republic*, www.newrepublic.com/article/114707/crisis-contemporary-ballet-essay-jennifer-homans (2013).

Hopkins, Antony, "The Ballet Music of Arthur Bliss" in Arnold L. Haskell (ed.), *The Ballet Annual: A Record and Year Book of the Ballet*, Issue 1 (London: Adam and Charles Black, 1947), pp. 102-107; reprinted in Arnold L. Haskell (ed.), *Ballet Decade* (London: Adam and Charles Black, 1956), pp. 101-104.

Ingram, Raymond, *The Stage Designs of Leslie Hurry*, Theatre in Focus Series (Cambridge: Chadwyck-Healey, 1990).

Jackson, Buss, *Perfection*, (London: Went The Day Well, 2010), http://www.wentthedaywell.co.uk/wtdw_articles.html

Kavanagh, Julie, *Secret Muses: The Life of Frederick Ashton* (London: Faber and Faber, 1996).

Kemp, Thomas C. and J.C. Trewin, *The Stratford Festival* (Birmingham: Cornish Brothers, 1953).

Ladell, Daniel (ed.), *Leslie Hurry: A Painter for the Stage* (Stratford, Ontario: Stratford Festival and Gallery, 1984).

Lambert, John, Letter to *The Times*, 10 September 1974.

Lawson, Joan, "The Helpmann Revivals", *The Dancing Times*, May 1958, pp.371-372.

Lawson, Joan, *The Story of Ballet* (London: Ward Lock, 1976).

Lawson, Valerie, *Helpmann's Last Move on the Chessboard* (Sydney: Dancelines, 2011), http://dancelines.com.au/helpmanns-last-move-on-the-chessboard/

Le Coq, Jacques, in collaboration with Jean-Gabriel Carasso and Jean-Claude Lallias, *The Moving Body (Le Corps poétique) Teaching Creative Theatre* (London: Methuen 2000).

Lipscomb, Valerie Barnes, and Leni Marshall (eds.), *Staging Age: The Performance of Age in Theatre, Dance, and Film* (New York: Palgrave Macmillan, 2010).

Manchester, P.W., *Vic-Wells Ballet: A Ballet Progress* (London: Victor Gollancz, 1947).

Manchester, P. W., "The Royal Ballet at Fifty", *Dance Chronicle*, 5, 1982, pp. 107-112.

Mackrell, Judith, *Keep Dancing: The Ballet Stars Leaping Through The Age Barrier* (London: The Guardian, 2015), http://www.theguardian.com/stage/2015/jul/05/ballet-dance-age-barrier-wendy-whelan-alessandro-ferri-interview

Mcpherson, Bruce R. (ed.), *Essential Deren: Collected Writings on Film* (New York: McPherson and Company, 2005).

Mangan, Michael, *Staging Ageing: Theatre, Performance and the Narrative of Decline* (Bristol: Intellect, 2013).

Meinertz, Alexander, *Vera Volkova, a Biography* translated by Alexander Meinertz and Paula Hostrup-Jessen (Alton: Dance Books, 2007).

Miller, Tatlock, "Helpmann, Chameleon of the Theatre", *Dance and Dancers*, Vol.1, No. 5, May 1950.

Mitoma, Judy (ed.), *Envisioning Dance on Film and Video* (New York: Mcpherson and Company, 2005).

Noble, Peter (ed.), *British Ballet* (London: Skelton Robinson, 1949).

O'Connor, Garry, *Paul Scofield: The Biography* (London: Sidgwick & Jackson, 2002).

Parry, Jann, *Different Drummer: The Life of Kenneth MacMillan* (London:

Faber&Faber, 2009).

Partriege, Elizabeth and Ian M. Storey, "Robert Helpmann, A Study", *Dancing Times*, new series no. 362, November 1940, pp.63-65.

Potter, Michelle, "Robert Helpmann's Ballet *The Display*", http://michellepotter.org/articles/robert-helpmanns-ballet-the-display

Potter, Michelle, "'A burst of boiling rage': Arthur Boyd and the theatre". Talk given at the National Gallery of Australia, Canberra, 9 September 2014. Online, http://michellepotter.org/papers/arthur-boyd-in-the-theatre

Potter, Michelle, "Robert Helpmann: Behind the Scenes with the Australian Ballet, 1962-1965", *Dance Research*, 34:1 (Summer 2016), pp.47-62.

Powell, Michael, *A Life in Movies* (London: Mandarin, 1986).

Powell, Michael, "Robert Helpmann", *Spectator*, 4 October 1986, pp. 16 – 17.

Rylands, George, "Festival Shakespeare in the West End" in Allardyce Nicoll (ed.), *Shakespeare Survey 6* (Cambridge: Cambridge University Press, 1953).

Salter, Elizabeth, *Helpmann: The Authorised Biography of Sir Robert Helpmann, CBE* (Brighton: Angus and Robertson, 1978).

Schafer, Elizabeth (ed.), *The Taming of the Shrew: Shakespeare in Production*, (Cambridge: Cambridge University Press, 2002).

Schwaiger, Elisabeth, *Ageing, Gender, Embodiment and Dance: Finding a Balance* (Basingstoke: Palgrave Macmillan, 2012).

Scorsese, Martin, "The movie that plays in my heart", *The Independent*: 15 May 2009. See, http://www.independent.co.uk/arts-entertainment/films/features/martin-scorsese-the-movie-that-plays-in-my-heart-1685003.html

Severn, Merlyn, *Ballet in Action* (London: John Lane at the Bodley Head, 1938).

Severn, Merlyn, *Sadler's Wells Ballet at Covent Garden* (London: John Lane at the Bodley Head, 1947).

Sexton, Christopher, *Peggy van Praagh: A Life of Dance* (Melbourne: Macmillan, 1985).

Sorley Walker, Kathrine, *Brief for Ballet* (London: Pitfield, 1947).

Sorley Walker, Kathrine, *Robert Helpmann, Theatre World Monograph No. 9* (London: Rockcliff, 1957).

Sorley Walker, Kathrine, *Ninette de Valois, Idealist Without Illusions* (London: Hamish Hamilton, 1987).

Sorley Walker, Kathrine, *Robert Helpmann: A Rare Sense of the Theatre* (Alton: Dance Books, 2009).

Stevenson, Jane, *Edward Burra: Twentieth-Century Eye* (London: Pimlico, 2007).

Stock, Cheryl. "Robert Helpmann. Master Showman", *Brolga: an Australian journal about dance*, 5 (December 1996).

Thomas, Helen *The Body, Dance and Cultural Theory* (Basingstoke: Palgrave Macmillan, 2003).

Tynan, Kenneth, *A View of the English Stage* (London: Davis-Poynter, 1975), p.78.

Vaughan, David, *Frederick Ashton and His Ballets* (New York: Alfred A. Knopf, 1977).

Watts, Graham, *Review: Birmingham Royal Ballet - Shadows of War - Sadler's Wells* (London: Londondance.com, 2014), http://londondance.com/articles/reviews/birmingham-royal-ballet-shadows-of-war-sadlers-wel/

Williamson, Audrey, "Future of Ballet" in *Theatre World: Guide to the Sadler's Wells Ballet* (London: Practical Press, 1944).

Williamson, Audrey, *Contemporary Ballet* (London: Rockliff, 1946).

Williamson, Audrey, *Old Vic Drama* (London: Rockliff, 1948).

Williamson, Audrey, "Some Dancers" in Peter Noble (ed.), *British Ballet* (London: Skelton Robinson, 1949).

Wilson, Cecil, "Helpmann Turns Producer", *Daily Mail*, 28 March 1953, n.p.

Wu, Paul, *Ballet in the Blitz: How World War Two Made British Ballet* (film for BBC Four, 2014), https://www.youtube.com/watch?v=tHOpqjgOKJk

Yee, Chiang, "What can I say about Ballet", *The Ballet Annual: A Record and Year Book of the Ballet*, Issue 2 (London: Black, 1948).

Zinovieff, Sofka, *The Mad Boy, Lord Berners, My Grandmother and Me* (London: Jonathan Cape, 2014).

Zipes, Jack, *Breaking the Magic Spell: Radical Theories of Folk and Fairy Tales* (London: Heinemann, 1979).

Television and Video

Tales of Helpmann: A Profile of Sir Robert Helpmann (dir. Don Featherstone; script Alan Sievewright; ed. Melvyn Bragg), a *South Bank Show* film produced by London Weekend Television for ITV, in association with the Australian Broadcasting Corporation (1990).

Hamlet, ch. Robert Helpmann, Royal Ballet in rehearsal, dir. Edmée Wood, Royal Ballet Archive (1964).

Sea of Troubles, dir. and ch. Kenneth MacMillan, *Folio*, Documentary for Anglia Television (1989).

Hamlet, ch. Robert Helpmann, Royal Ballet in rehearsal, Royal Ballet Archive (1981).

Alphabetical List of Contributors

MICHAEL BYRNE is a postgraduate student at the University of Cambridge exploring creativity and ageing in the dance-dramas of Robert Helpmann. Using *Miracle in the Gorbals* and *Adam Zero* as central case studies, his research analyses the embodied histories of senior dancers and the intergenerational transmission of knowledge during (re)performance. He regularly performs as an actor within many of The Royal Ballet's narrative works.

RICHARD ALLEN CAVE is Professor Emeritus in Drama and Theatre Arts at Royal Holloway, University of London. His publications extend from Renaissance to modern theatre, dance and movement studies. His recent monograph, *Collaborations: Ninette de Valois and William Butler Yeats*, and the volume, *Ninette de Valois: Adventurous Traditionalist*, co-edited with Libby Worth, draw on the range of his scholarly, directorial, cultural and historical interests.

JENNIFER JACKSON is Artistic Director of Images Ballet Company at London Studio Centre. A former soloist with The Royal Ballet, her choreography includes commissioned work for ballet companies and vocational students. She combined roles as Lecturer at the University of Surrey and Choreography Teacher at The Royal Ballet School for 16 years, and has written book chapters and contributed articles to *Dancing Times* and *Research in Dance Education*.

ANNA MEADMORE is a graduate of The Royal Ballet School Teachers' Training Course. She has been the Archivist of The Royal Ballet School since 1997, and was also Head of Academic Dance Studies (2005-15). As Curator of White Lodge Museum she organised the 2011 conference, *Ninette de Valois: Adventurous Traditionalist*, and the 2013 symposium *The Many Faces of Robert Helpmann*. Anna is currently engaged in doctoral research at Royal Holloway, University of London, investigating the early career of Ninette de Valois.

GERALDINE MORRIS is a Reader in Dance Studies at the University of Roehampton. Her book, *Frederick Ashton's Ballets: Style, Performance, Choreography*, was published in 2012 and, together with Larraine Nicholas, she is editing a new version of *Rethinking Dance History: A Reader*. She also publishes in Dance Journals on history, analysis and contemporary issues and began her career in dance as a member of The Royal Ballet Company.

JANN PARRY was formerly dance critic of *The Observer* (1983 – 2004), and is the author of a major biography, *Different Drummer: the Life of Kenneth MacMillan* (2009). She currently reviews performances and writes feature articles for *Dance Tabs online* and regularly contributes to Royal Ballet and Birmingham Royal Ballet programmes about MacMillan's ballets.

MICHELLE POTTER is an independent dance writer, historian and curator with a doctorate in art history and dance history from the Australian National University, Canberra. She was inaugural Curator of Dance, National Library of Australia (2002 – 2006); and Curator, Jerome Robbins Dance Division, New York Public Library for the Performing Arts (2006 – 2008).

JANE PRITCHARD MBE is Curator of Dance for the Victoria and Albert Museum, London, for which she curated *Diaghilev and the Golden Age of the Ballets Russes, 1909–1929*. Other exhibitions include *Les Ballets 1933* (which toured Britain and the USA); *Rambert Dance Company at 75*; *A Flash of Light: The Dance Photography of Chris Nash* and *Hand in Glove*, a performed exhibition. She contributes to the *Oxford Dictionary of National Biography*, the *Annual Register, Dance Chronicle, Dance Research*, and the *Dancing Times*.

ELIZABETH SCHAFER is Professor of Drama and Theatre Studies at Royal Holloway, University of London. Her publications include performance histories of *The Taming of the Shrew* and *Twelfth Night*; *Lilian Baylis: A Biography* (2006); and *MsDirecting Shakespeare*. She is currently writing a performance history of *The Merry Wives of Windsor*.

OLWEN TERRIS was Chief Cataloguer at the British Film Institute, National Film and Television Archive (1991-2004). She is currently working as Senior Researcher at Learning on Screen (formerly the British Universities Film & Video Council) with responsibility for the development of An International Database of Shakespeare on Film, Television and Radio.

LIBBY WORTH, Senior Lecturer in Theatre Practice at Royal Holloway, University of London, is a movement practitioner trained in the Feldenkrais Method and in dance with Anna Halprin. She co-edited *Ninette de Valois: Adventurous Traditionalist* with Richard Cave; has published on Mabel Todd, Caryl Churchill, and Moshe Feldenkrais; co-authored a book on Anna Halprin and another on the work of Jasmin Vardimon. She co-edits the *Theatre, Dance and Performance Training* journal.

Index